M000189267

GENIUS
IN
BONDAGE

GENIUS

IN

BONDAGE

*Literature
of the
Early Black Atlantic*

Edited by
VINCENT CARRETTA
and
PHILIP GOULD

THE UNIVERSITY PRESS OF KENTUCKY

Publication of this volume was made possible in part
by a grant from the National Endowment for the Humanities.

Editorial and Sales Offices: The University Press of Kentucky
663 South Limestone Street, Lexington, Kentucky 40508–4008

05 04 03 02 01   5 4 3 2 1

Library of Congress Cataloging-in-Publication Data

Genius in bondage : literature of the early Black Atlantic / edited by Vincent
Carretta and Philip Gould.
        p. cm.
Includes bibliographical references.
    ISBN 0-9131-2203-1 (acid-free paper)
    1. African literature (English)—Foreign countries—History and criticism.
2. Equiano, Olaudah, b. 1745. Interesting narrative of the life of Olaudah
Equiano. 3. Hammon, Briton. Narrative of the uncommon sufferings, and
surprising deliverance of Briton Hammon, a Negro man. 4. Wheatley, Phillis,
1753-1784—Criticism and interpretation. 5. Sancho, Ignatius, 1729-1780—
Criticism and interpretation. 6. English literature—Black authors—History and
criticism. 7. English literature—18th century—History and criticism. 8. Slaves'
writings, English—History and criticism. 9. Africans—Foreign countries—
Historiography. 10. Slavery in literature. 11. Blacks in literature. I. Carretta,
Vincent. II. Gould, Philip, 1960-
PR9341.G46 2001
820.9'96—dc21   2001002581

This book is printed on acid-free recycled paper meeting
the requirements of the American National Standard
for Permanence in Paper for Printed Library Materials.

Manufactured in the United States of America.

CONTENTS

FIGURES

INTRODUCTION

Vincent Carretta and Philip Gould

In June 1780, Ignatius Sancho wrote a letter to one of his many white correspondents describing the Gordon riots that had just erupted on the streets of London. More surprising than Sancho's disdain for the anti-Catholic mob is his description of "the worse than Negro barbarity of the populace."[1] If his association of blackness with savagery disrupts our assumptions about the collective identity of black writing, it also opens up rhetorical possibilities for him. In describing in detail the "burnings and devastations" by the city's "poor, miserable, ragged rabble," Sancho actually dramatizes a savvy reversal of the racial terms for "barbarity." Violence, it would appear, implicitly derives from social condition. Exploiting the cultural distinction between liberty and licentiousness in English culture during this era ("This—this—is liberty! genuine British liberty!"), the letter denounces the excesses of those who conflate freedom and irresponsibility. In doing so, it implicitly highlights the absence of English "liberty"—freedom responsibly exercised—for most Britons, white and black. At a time when fewer than one in six adult males was qualified to vote in Britain, as the only known black voter Sancho was uniquely positioned to comment on the abuse of "liberty." By the letter's postscript, then, Sancho ironically manipulates the persona of the responsible English citizen to, of all things, invert his initial characterization of the urban mob: "I am not sorry I was born in Afric.—I shall tire you, I fear."[2] Sancho's own reaction to the rioters, the vast majority of whom were white, refutes the belief in "Negro barbarity" he ironically invokes.

This moment in *Letters of the Late Ignatius Sancho, an African* (1782) is representative of the complex identities and languages of eighteenth-century black writing. Simultaneously British and African, Sancho's identity resists easy national and racial identifications; assuming deferential humility, he soon parlays the persona into cultural critique. The black writing that appeared during the eighteenth and early nineteenth centuries—which included the genres of spiritual autobiography, captivity narrative, travel narrative, public epistle, sea adventure, and economic success story—is a literature of diasporic movement and cultural encounter. Born to enslaved African parents on a ship in the Middle Passage bearing its human cargo from Africa to the Americas and then brought to England, Sancho might serve as an emblem of most of the writers discussed in *Genius in Bondage*. Crossing the Atlantic meant that, while some were born with identities, and some had identities thrust upon them, by the very act of authoring their texts they all achieved identities they had played some significant role in fashioning.

As an emblematic figure, Sancho fittingly gives us the title for this collection of essays, the first devoted exclusively to transatlantic black writing between 1760, when religion first gave English-speaking black writers a voice, and 1833, when Britain ended slavery in its remaining colonies in the Americas. Not knowing that Phillis Wheatley had been manumitted shortly after her return to America in 1773 after a six-week visit to London, in 1778 Sancho wrote a letter of thanks to a Quaker correspondent in Philadelphia who had sent him a copy of Wheatley's *Poems*. With his comments on Wheatley, Sancho became the first Anglophone critic of a fellow black writer and one of the earliest black critics of the institution of slavery:

> Phyllis' poems do credit to nature—and put art—merely as art—to
> the blush.—It reflects nothing either to the glory or generosity of
> her master—if she is still his slave—except he glories in the *low
> vanity* of having in his wanton power a mind animated by Heaven—
> a genius superior to himself—the list of splendid—titled—learned
> names, in confirmation of her being the real authoress.—alas! Shews
> how very poor the acquisition of wealth and knowledge are—
> without generosity—feeling—and humanity. —These good great
> folks—all know—and perhaps admired—nay, praised Genius in
> bondage—and then, like the Priests and the Levites in sacred writ,
> passed by—not one good Samaritan amongst them.

The appearance of *Genius in Bondage* continues recent critical interests in the field of eighteenth-century black writing. Until fairly recently, critical studies and anthologies of African American literature generally began with the 1830s and 1840s, as American abolitionism gained strength and the African American slave narrative proliferated largely in support of this movement.[3] Prior to 1965, the idea that an early black-British tradition existed, or that any Anglophone black writer could (or perhaps should) be seen as having worked in any tradition other than American, was apparently unthinkable. During the past thirty years, however, several influential critical works of and on African-American, African-British, and transatlantic black literature have extended the historical and conceptual frames for the field into the eighteenth century.

During the 1960s, Paul Edwards led the way in the recovery of eighteenth-century transatlantic literature by people of African descent writing in English. With his magisterial introductions, Edwards's facsimile reprints of the works of Ignatius Sancho, Olaudah Equiano, and Quobna Ottabah Cugoano established the editorial, critical, and scholarly standards against which all subsequent workers in the field are measured.[4] Although criticism of these writers greatly diminished during the next decade, and Edwards's editions went out of print, the 1980s marked a renaissance of interest in early transatlantic black writers. For example, William Robertson, John Shields, and Julian Mason produced authoritative and deeply researched editions of the works of Phillis Wheatley; Henry Louis Gates Jr. developed the rhetorical and ideological implications of the trope of the talking book repeatedly used by early black writers on both sides of the Atlantic, a trope first identified by Edwards; Houston Baker produced an influential Marxist discussion of Equiano as *homo economicus*; William Andrews located the early writers in the literary history of the African-American slave narrative; and Angelo Costanzo and Keith Sandiford published studies of the literary and political contexts of the eighteenth-century authors. The last decade of the century opened with Paul Gilroy's revision of the transatlantic context in which the early texts may be seen. Adam Potkay and Sandra Burr's anthology of black Atlantic writers revived concern with the theological and intellectual influence of religion on early authors. As the decade closed, Vincent Carretta produced the fullest editions to date of the works of Equiano, Sancho, Cugoano, and other eighteenth-century black authors.[5]

This influential body of scholarship and criticism raises important questions about the nature of race and authorship in early black writing. As scholars such as Andrews and Gates emphasize, much of early black autobiography was spoken—rather than written—and transcribed by white editors who inevitably exerted a good deal of textual control. As Andrews has commented, "[F]rom the outset of black autobiography in America the presupposition reigns that a black narrator needs a white reader to complete his text, to build a hierarchy of abstract significance on the mere matter of his facts, to supply a presence where was only 'Negro,' only a dark absence."[6] Accordingly, John Sekora has figured this problem of black literary expression as a matter of the "black message" that resides within the formal and ideological prison of the "white envelope."[7] (For eighteenth-century black writers, this metaphoric envelope would include such powerful cultural institutions and influences as English Methodism—particularly figures like George Whitefield and the Countess of Huntingdon—as well as Anglo-American antislavery and prominent literary publishing houses in places like London and Philadelphia.) It is important to see that African Americanist scholarship did not invent this interrogation of the authenticity of black writing; rather, it derives in part from early postcolonial theory. As Franz Fanon, for example, argued long ago, every colonial society "finds itself face to face with the language of the civilizing nation": "The Antilles Negro who wants to be white will be the whiter as he gains greater mastery of the cultural tool that language is."[8]

How, then, do we account for "voice" and "authorship" in a rhetorical process comprising black storytellers and white editors? Perhaps recent thinking about identity politics in cultural studies and post-colonial studies provides a more flexible response to this critical dilemma. Gilroy's influential critical model of the "black Atlantic" questions the "overintegrated sense of cultural and ethnic particularity" in racial studies today and its accompanying "language of ethnic absolutism."[9] Imagining instead a diasporic model of racial identity—and one that is, by the way, suited for the itinerant movements of these black writers, whose travels encompassed West Africa, England, the West Indies, and North America—Gilroy envisions the Atlantic "as one, single, complex unit of analysis" for "an explicitly transnational and intercultural perspective."[10] Such a critical perspective is in keeping with the de-centering of ethnic identity that the postcolonial theorist Homi K. Bhabha claims in the concept of "hybridity": "The language of critique is effective . . . to the extent to which it overcomes the given grounds of opposition and opens up a space of translation: a place of hybridity, figuratively speaking, where the construction of a political object that is new, neither the one nor the other, properly alienates our political expectations, and changes . . . the very forms of our recognition of the moment of politics."[11]

Such critical declarations of the fluidity of identity suggest rhetorical possibilities for the creative engagement between black and white languages in the eighteenth century. They enable us, in other words, to reconsider the trope of the black message imprisoned in the white envelope. As Rafia Zafar recently has remarked, critics must identify in black writing "instances of appropriation from and accommodation to the European-American mainstream as trials and experiments in the development of an African American literary consciousness."[12] This certainly is in keeping with Karen Weyler's sense (in her essay below) that the autobiographies of Briton Hammon and John Marrant possessed sufficient "cultural capital" to "have value in the literary marketplace." Does such value imply fully *conscious* appropriation of white languages? Or do early black writers simply imbibe dominant ideological beliefs? These questions go right to the heart of the nature of what W.E.B. Du Bois (and Ralph Ellison after him) theorized was the crucial trope of the black "mask." Critics today have employed this trope to argue for black writing's ability to cultivate careful personae that ingeniously mimic—and subvert—dominant discourses. Consider, for example, a passage from the slave Belinda's petition to the Massachusetts legislature for her freedom. In describing her capture in Africa as a young girl, the narrative proclaims, "Could the tears, the sighs, the supplications, bursting from tortured parental affection, have blunted the keen edge of avarice, she might have been rescued from agony, which many of her country's children have felt, but which none ever described. In vain she lifted her supplicating voice to an insulted father, and her guiltless hands to a dishonored deity! She was ravished from the bosom of her country, from the arms of her friends."[13] For American readers of the English seduction novel (Benjamin Franklin, for example, printed much of Samuel Richardson's work), the plight of the young girl swept up violently in a world of greed and deception could not but resonate as a tale of seduction. Indeed, the effectiveness of black writing would appear to derive from its ability to re-deploy the language and tropes of the seduction novel in order to conflate the discourses of sentiment and politics that are associated with private and public life. Belinda conflates these discourses by sentimentally dramatizing the dismembered family and the "ravished" woman (both staples of late–eighteenth-century antislavery literature) in order to claim her public—her political—identity. But does her handling of seduction challenge racial stereotypes by incorporating black women—African women—into the world of western sympathy? Does it reproduce these stereotypes by merely victimizing them as objects of sympathetic identification? Or does it do both?

Recent conceptual models of diasporic and hybrid identities are congruent with the very instability of the meaning of "race" in the eighteenth century. Certainly, the period's rising debates over slavery engendered new theories of racial difference. As David Brion Davis has put it, "Insofar as the Enlightenment divorced anthropology and comparative anatomy from theological assumptions, it opened the way for theories of racial inferiority."[14] Traditionally, Anglo-Americans generally believed in the account of humanity founded upon biblical authority, specifically the account of Adam and Eve as told in the book of Genesis. Even increasingly "scientific" accounts of human classification, which derived from eighteenth-century natural philosophers such as Linnaeus, Buffon, and Blumenbach, did not challenge the idea that all human beings constituted a single species. However, during the eighteenth century self-consciously "enlightened" thinkers—David Hume, Lord Kames, and Thomas Jefferson among them—contested biblical authority as a form of ignorant superstition. They argued instead for the polygenist position that theorized the division of humanity into different species. It is important to recognize that both monogenist and polygenist theories situated Africans (whether by environment or nature) on an inferior place within a hierarchical order of civilization. "The Speech of Moses Bon Saam" (1735), for example, mocks the denigration of racial blackness by claiming, "What Preference, in the Name of that *mysterious God*, whom these Insulters of our *Colour* pretend to worship; what wild imaginary Superiority of Dignity has their pale sickly *Whiteness* to boast of, when compar'd with our *Majestick Glossiness!*"[15] The concept of race, moreover, was further complicated by the ambiguous potential of the Bible to "argue" for or against slavery. If antislavery advocates relied upon Genesis's account of creation, as well as New Testament principles of Christian charity (e.g., Acts 17.26), pro-slavery employed Genesis 9 to theorize that blacks were the descendants of the Hamites who (through the so-called "curse of Canaan") were destined for slavery.[16] Slave owners understandably feared that conversion to Christianity, with its theology of spiritual equality, might bring with it a conversion to an ideology of social, political, and economic equality, especially in the wake of the Great Awakening and the American Revolution, when the rhetoric of enslavement to sin and political enslavement already rendered whites and blacks equals in language if not reality.

The very subject of racial difference was complicated by semantic change during this era. Nicholas Hudson has argued that during the eighteenth century the meaning of "race" gradually changed from its original signification of "nation," "family," or a group of people defined geographically to one denoting skin color, appearance, and intellectual and moral qualities.[17] Consider, for example, the comment made by John Atkins in a narrative of a voyage made to Africa and the West Indies during the 1730s: "When the Nakedness, Poverty and Ignorance of these Species of men are considered; it would incline one think it a bettering their Condition, to transport them to the worst of Christian Slavery; but as we find them little mended in those respects at the West-Indies, their Patrons respecting them only as Beasts of Burden; there is rather Inhumanity in removing them from their Countries and Families."[18] To our ears such a denunciation of West Indian planters belies ethnocentric bias against African culture. In its historical context, however, the passage demonstrates how the category of *culture* mediates the very issue of *racial* difference. That is, Christianity theoretically retained the capacity to transform "savagery" into "civilization." Eighteenth-century black writing thus emerged during an era in which the relations between *race* and *culture* were highly unstable yet significantly contiguous. An example: one may recognize the thematic importance of literacy to black humanity as a motif allowing us to articulate a literary "tradition" that runs from Equiano to Frederick Douglass and beyond. But one must recognize that Equiano—unlike Douglass—thematized black humanity in a historical period in which quasi-scientific theories of "race" had not yet fully evolved.[19]

Early writers of the black Atlantic became the evidentiary material for proving or disputing black humanity—a topic that was of course central to the eighteenth-century debates over slavery. As Gates has argued, in the wake of Cartesian and Lockean philosophy, the subject of black writing was used as an argument for the intellectual enslavement of contemporary blacks. Writers like Phillis Wheatley and Ignatius Sancho became test cases for antislavery and pro-slavery movements as well as monogenist and polygenist racial positions. In *Letters on Slavery* (1789), for example, the English abolitionist and former resident of Barbados, William Dickson, praised Francis Williams's Latin ode, "the beautiful poetical pieces of Phillis Wheatley, and the letters of Ignatius Sancho" as admirable "specimens of *African literature.*"[20] Dickson and many other antislavery advocates were obviously responding at such moments to the infamous example of David Hume's "Of National Characters" (1753), which debunked Francis Williams as a representative case of black inferiority: "In Jamaica, indeed they talk of one negroe as a man of parts and learning; but 'tis likely he is admired for very slender accomplishments, like a parrot who speaks a few words plainly."[21] While Thomas Jefferson's disparaging remarks on Phillis Wheatley's artistic creativity echoed such a claim, the English antislavery writer Thomas Clarkson's *Essay on the Slavery and Commerce of the Human Species* (1786) refuted it by defending Wheatley's work.

The black claim to humanity rhetorically capitalized upon the simultaneously political and religious meanings of "liberty." Wielding Christ's words in John 8 ("Every one that committeth sin is the bondservant of sin") in their own unique ways, writers such as John Marrant, Briton Hammon, and Wheatley assailed the slavery of sin often to call attention to its shadowed double—the sin of chattel slavery. In both England and the American colonies, enslaved blacks understood baptism to confer physical as well as spiritual liberty (at least until judicial and political authorities acted against such assumptions). As Adam Potkay has observed, "Some whites indeed feared that the spiritual enfranchisement of blacks might translate all too easily into expectations of political power."[22] This historical situation lends significant complexity to the rhetorical and racial power of religious "conversion" in these narratives, and asks us as readers to consider the possible multivalence of religious discourse, particularly its transgressive possibilities.

Part One, "'Race' and 'Gender' in the Early Black Atlantic," examines eighteenth-century black writings in the context of evolving and unstable cultural assumptions about the nature of both race and gender. In "'Betrayed by Some of My Own Complexion': Cugoano, Abolition, and the Contemporary Language of Racialism," Roxann Wheeler reads Ottabah Cugoano's *Thoughts and Sentiments on the Evil and Wicked Traffic of the Slavery and Commerce of the Human Species* (1787) as a creative meditation on the nature of "race." Showing how this concept was informed by the uneasy relations among its constitutive discourses of civility, Christianity, and complexion, Wheeler situates Cugoano's famous antislavery treatise (whose title signifies upon Thomas Clarkson's seminal *Essay on the Slavery and Commerce of the Human Species*) in the context of complex cultural change marked by the new prominence of skin color, controversy over the environmentalist argument (which antislavery writers used to combat the Negro's "natural inferiority"), and the rise of comparative anatomy as a "scientific" discourse articulating human difference. "As Cugoano's text repeatedly demonstrates, skin color occupied a volatile place in contemporary discourse—ranging from the superficial and inconsequential to the very fabric of identity."

Whereas Wheeler emphasizes the advantages that biblical authority about universal humanity offered Cugoano, Karen Weyler considers the larger trope of Christianity as the touchstone for the mutability of "racial" difference. Examining the spiritual narratives of Briton Hammon or John Marrant, Weyler argues that early black writers refrain from "the marking of racial difference," and dramatize instead, through the narrative conventions of Protestant conversion, their equivalent humanity. Thematically prominent in *Narrative of the Uncommon Sufferings, and Surprizing Deliverance of Briton Hammon, a Negro Man* (1760) and *A Narrative of the Lord's Wonderful Dealings with John Marrant, a Black* (1785) are the self-representations of true Christians exhibiting virtuous character. In this way, the languages of liberty and slavery signify on dual levels simultaneously: these writers dramatize bodily and spiritual forms of "slavery." Rhetorically, then, their works avoid the sensational qualities of much of eighteenth-century captivity writing, thereby implicitly challenging contemporary stereotypes associating blackness with unregulated passions.

Felicity Nussbaum's "Being a Man: Olaudah Equiano and Ignatius Sancho" goes one step further in considering how these two writers engaged—and revised—prevailing gendered stereotypes of male blackness. Like Wheeler and Weyler, Nussbaum similarly argues that "public consensus concerning the actual nature of African men had not jelled and instead vacillated erratically from pro-slavery racism through benevolent amelioration bolstered by Enlightenment humanism to abolitionist sentiments." Yet Nussbaum shows how black men are written out British codes of masculinity, and, subsequently, how Equiano and Sancho write themselves back into the national narrative of masculinity. In doing so, they debunk these prevailing stereotypes by placing English "manners" within the reach of black men.

In "Volatile Subjects: *The History of Mary Prince*," Gillian Whitlock employs theories of feminism, narratology, colonial discourse, and reception to discuss the ways in which Prince's as-told-to *History* is carefully framed for its original British audience to appear to be far more about race than sex. The marked body that probably would have been foregrounded in a contemporaneous African-American autobiography becomes carefully contained in the commentary surrounding the text of the life itself. Concerned as much with the editorial marginalia in the texts of both the original 1831 edition and the late twentieth-century editions, Whitlock argues that the *History* represents Prince's identity through her contiguity—her relationships with others—rather than essence—the reconstruction of Prince's authentic self.

Part Two, "Market Culture and Racial Authority," explores how such identities were cultivated during a period characterized by the rise of commercial capitalism. Paul E. Lovejoy and David Richardson's "Letters of the Old Calabar Slave Trade, 1760–1789" examines the epistolary correspondence between British and Biafran merchants. Their historical analysis of this correspondence argues that literacy in English for the commercial elite took the form of a newly "creolized" language. Rather than see this linguistic development as simply the symptom of cultural hegemony enacted by the slave trade, Lovejoy and Richardson theorize it instead as the rhetorical product of cultural exchange, where both European and African traders exchanged more than captive Africans and market commodities. This involved as well the translation of Efik language into writing, which produced "a pictograph method of writing" that helped govern the world of international trade.

How identities are constructed in black autobiographies mediated by white editors is the subject of Philip Gould's "'Remarkable Liberty': Reading the Lives of the Early Black Atlantic." Gould investigates the deployment of liberal rights discourse and its relation to commodification in the as-told-to narratives of John Marrant and Venture Smith. Gould sees Marrant and Smith exploiting the polyvocality of such key terms during this era as "liberty," "property," "mastery" and "slavery." Rather than see the relationship between the black subject and white editor as one of erasure of the former, we might, Gould argues, see it instead as an "act of literary collaboration." While Marrant's captivity narrative inverts the tradition in which the white Christian is taken away from civilization, Smith's tale reveals how one can be at liberty while enslaved and still commodified when free.

Commodification is also the subject of Vincent Carretta's "'Property of Author': Olaudah Equiano's Place in the History of the Book." Carretta considers Equiano as both writer and businessman, who made a very large profit on the production, distribution, and sale of his life. By choosing to retain the copyright to his autobiography and to register his book with the Stationers' Company as the "Property of author," Equiano kept most of the profits from the nine editions of his book between 1789 and 1794, rather than signing them away to wholesalers and retailers, as most authors did. His control of the book's production and distribution is manifested in many ways, including the subscription lists and the illustrations. Earning him the equivalent of at least $120,000, Equiano's successful gamble on self-publication made him the richest person of African descent in eighteenth-century Britain, and one of the very few wealthy enough to have left a will.

Part Three, "Language and the 'Other': The Question of Difference," reads early black literature as an ongoing process of cultural encounters with Anglo-American languages and ideologies. The essays in this section trace the rhetorical processes by which black writers shape (and are shaped by) Anglo-American discourses, and they pay particular attention to specific personal and literary relations between black and white writers in the late eighteenth century. As Robert Desrochers argues in "'Surprizing Deliverance': Slavery and Freedom, Language and Identity in the *Narrative* of Briton Hammon, 'A Negro Man,'" Hammon's autobiography testifies to "the possibilities and limits of language and freedom in late-colonial Massachusetts and in the Atlantic world." By placing the publication of Hammon's *Narrative* in the context of the precarious state of New England slavery, as well as white anxieties about slave violence, Desrochers argues that the text was "something of an anomaly": "It contradicted familiar roles of blacks in print as chattel to be sold, runaways to be apprehended, and rebels and malcontents to be alternately quashed." Its conservative reception, however, was countered by the image of the diasporic traveler cultivated by writers like Hammon and Equiano, a persona that "tested the limits of national, colonial, imperial, and racial boundaries."

Frank Shuffleton similarly considers the shifting nature of such boundaries for Phillis Wheatley. In "On Her Own Footing: Phillis Wheatley in Freedom," he articulates the increasingly complex position the coming of the American Revolution placed on Wheatley. Creatively eschewing both "conservative" and "radical" readings of Wheatley's poetry, Shuffleton argues that this political crisis in the British empire actually disrupted the alliances she had built in England during her stay there in the early 1770s. This forced Wheatley to create in her later work "a more complex, pluralistic sense of audience" than before. By deploying "enlightened and Christian tropes of universal freedom," Wheatley delicately challenged the codes of zealous patriotism, replacing it instead with an enlightened sense of "cosmopolitan friendship" that reflected her strained position in Revolutionary America.

Rosemary Fithian Guruswamy shows that Wheatley could function as the object (as well as the subject) of such larger negotiations of identity and power. "'Thou Hast the Holy Word': Jupiter Hammon's 'Regards' to Phillis Wheatley" argues that the bible served Hammon as a rich rhetorical repository for a particular kind of cultural revisionism. Placing Hammon's status as a slave exhorter within the context of African shamans, Guruswamy makes an argument for cultural syncresis, showing how the "reinterpretive use of the Bible would sometimes involve covert communication through the use of the double entendre familiar to African oral narratives." In Gatesean terms, Hammon's poetic practice "signifies" upon biblical language to exercise the "pursuit of freedom." In this way, Guruswamy reads the critically undervalued "An Address to Miss Phillis Wheatly [sic]" as a poetic act of "conjuring with Scripture," which connects divine and temporal authority as well as black slaves typologically to the Old Testament's enslaved Israelites.

For Markman Ellis the discourses of sentimentalism provide the crucial rhetorical materials for the sort of cultural revisionism that Guruswamy locates in scripture. Ellis premises "Ignatius Sancho's *Letters*: Sentimental Libertinism and the Politics of Form" on the critical problem of an interdisciplinarity that might readily (and dangerously) make Sancho the "parrot" of his famous correspondent, Lawrence Sterne. "Rather than a falling away from his own voice, imitation [of Sterne's "Shandyism"] is a kind of inspiration, the mask that allows Sancho's voice to be heard." By considering the political and rhetorical possibilities for the Shandean traits of excited feeling and libertine imagination, Ellis charts a racial appropriation of an already suspect cultural discourse in eighteenth-century England. As Sancho took the genre of the familiar letter—one that possessed both private and public qualities—he re-worked conventional (though, to some, barely acceptable) Shandean conventions of "spontaneity, sincerity, and naturalness" to argue autobiographically for the black capacity for enlightened manners. "The libertine turn in Sancho's letters," moreover, "thus rounds out, and subverts, the picture of Sancho as a conservative and patriotic Whig."

The abolition of slavery, William Andrews suggests in "Benjamin Banneker's Revision of Thomas Jefferson: Conscience vs. Science in the Early American Antislavery Debate," is the subject not quite directly engaged in the public correspondence between Banneker and Jefferson. Banneker's famous 1791 letter to Jefferson signifies upon the language of the *Declaration of Independence*, recovering old meanings of "liberty" and "equality," and re-deploying them anew to ask when the ideology of the American Revolution will be applied to blacks. Through a careful rhetorical analysis of Banneker's letter, Andrews shows how Jefferson's ambivalent stand in *Notes of the State of Virginia* (1785) on racial inferiority and eventual emancipation, as well as the most famous line in the *Declaration*, may have given Banneker reason to hope that he could enlist the Secretary of State in his abolitionist cause: "Jefferson, in effect, would be thrust into a dialogue with himself."

Combining biography and criticism, Robert Levine's "Fifth of July: Nathaniel Paul and the Construction of Black Nationalism" recovers a relatively little known international and transatlantic abolitionist, and argues for the literary value of his works. Levine notes that Paul anticipated Frederick Douglass in calling on his fellow African Americans to observe the Fifth of July as a way of reminding white citizens of the Fourth's unkept promises. Like Equiano before him and Douglass after, Paul's fund-raising travels in England during the 1830s on behalf of black nationalism in America was a transforming event in his personal and political life. He returned to America with an English wife and a transnational vision of the possibilities for interracial relations. Levine demonstrates that nineteenth-century racist reaction to Paul's marriage accounts for much of the misinformation about the last years of his life and the unfamiliarity of his writings, many of which compare favorably with those of his contemporaries.

We might conclude by emphasizing that this anthology aims to situate early black writing in its own historical terms. Much of the most important criticism, which initially gave this field new prominence, situated early black writing in a black literary "tradition." This approach maps out important relations among black writers over time (as in Gates' notion of signifying) as well as evolving literary conventions (as in Andrews' sense of the increasing importance the slave narrative invests in black control of literacy). Not only does the paradigm of the black Atlantic challenge the very notion of "African American" literature (Is Olaudah Equiano, for example, the "prophet, if not the father" of this tradition?[23]), but it highlights the unsettling critical ramifications of positioning early black writing within the larger, national "story" of African American literary history. As one critic in the field recently put it, "How, accordingly, to argue for [Phillis] Wheatley and her contemporaries as other than merely prologue? Or does the usual version still hold, Afro-America's first literary presences summoned only on grounds of cultural-historical piety?"[24] In other words, does the value we invest in such scenes as Frederick Douglass' victory over Mr. Covey, or Linda Brent's sentimental "confession" of her sexual affair with a white man, critically determine the aesthetic and cultural material we seek in eighteenth-century black writing? Literary traditions, in other words, create their own teleological distortions. As the essays in *Genius in Bondage* amply demonstrate, the value of the early black Atlantic writers is independent of the achievements of those who followed them.

NOTES

1. See *Letters of the Late Ignatius Sancho, an African*, ed. Vincent Carretta (New York: Penguin, 1998), 217.

2. Ed Carretta, 219.

3. The critical literature in this field is of course extremely large, but representative work with this kind of historical frame includes Stephen Butterfield, *Black Autobiography in America* (Amherst: University of Massachusetts Press, 1974) and Robert Stepto, *From Behind the Veil* (New Haven: Yale University Press, 1979).

4. *Sancho's Letters, with Memoirs of His Life by Joseph Jekyll Esqr. M.P.* (London, 1803; Reprinted London: Dawsons of Pall Mall, 1968), ed. Paul Edwards; *The Interesting Narrative of the Life of Olaudah Equiano, or Gustavas Vassa, the African. Written by Himself* (London, 1789; Reprinted London: Dawsons of Pall Mall, 1969), ed. Paul Edwards; *Thoughts and Sentiments on the Evil of the Wicked Traffic of the Slavery and Commerce of the Human Species* (London, 1787; Reprinted London: Dawsons of Pall Mall, 1969), ed. Paul Edwards.

5. William H. Robinson, ed., *Phillis Wheatley and Her Writings* (New York and London: Garland Publishing, Inc.: 1984); John Shields, ed., *The Collected Works of Phillis Wheatley* (New York: Oxford University Press, 1988); Julian D. Mason, Jr., ed., *The Poems of Phillis Wheatley* (Chapel Hill and London: University of North Carolina Press, 1989); Henry Louis Gates, Jr., *The Signifying Monkey: A Theory of Afro-American Literary Criticism* (New York: Oxford University Press, 1988); Houston Baker, *Blues, Ideology and Afro-American Literature: A Vernacular Theory* (Chicago: University of Chicago Press, 1984); William Andrews,

To Tell a Free Story: The First Century of Afro-American Autobiography, 1760–1865 (Urbana and Chicago: University of Illinois Press, 1986); Angelo Costanzo, *Surprizing Narrative: Olaudah Equiano and the Beginnings of Black Autobiography* (New York: Greenwood Press, 1987); Keith Sandiford, *Measuring the Moment: Strategies of Protest in Eighteenth-Century Afro-English Writing* (London: Associated University Presses, 1988); Paul Gilroy, *The Black Atlantic: Modernity and Double Consciousness* (Cambridge, MA.: Harvard University Press, 1993); Adam Potkay and Sandra Burr, eds., *Black Atlantic Writers of the Eighteenth Century: Living the New Exodus in England and the Americas* (New York: St. Martin's Press, 1995); Olaudah Equiano, *The Interesting Narrative and Other Writings*, ed. Vincent Carretta (New York: Penguin Putnam, Inc., 1995); *Letters of the Late Ignatius Sancho, an African,* ed. Vincent Carretta (New York: Penguin Putnam, Inc., 1998); Quobna Ottobah Cugoano, *Thoughts and Sentiments on the Evil of Slavery and Other Writings*, ed. Vincent Carretta (New York: Penguin Putnam, Inc., 1999); Vincent Carretta, ed., *Unchained Voices: An Anthology of Black Authors in the English-Speaking World of the Eighteenth Century* (Lexington: University Press of Kentucky, 1996).

6. Andrews, *To Tell a Free Story*, 32–3.

7. John Sekora, "Black Message/White Envelope: Genre, Authenticity, and Authority in the Antebellum Slave Narrative," *Callalloo* 10 (1987), 482–515.

8. *Black Skin, White Masks* (New York: Grove Press, 1967), 18, 38.

9. Paul Gilroy, *The Black Atlantic: Modernity and Double Consciousness* (Cambridge, MA.: Harvard University Press, 1993), 31.

10. Gilroy, 15,

11. Homi K. Bhabha, *The Location of Culture* (London: Routledge, 1994), 25.

12. Rafia Zafar, *"We Wear the Mask:" African Americans Write American Literature, 1760–1870* (New York: Columbia University Press, 1997), 3.

13. "Petition of an African slave, to the legislature of Massachusetts," in *Unchained Voices: An Anthology of Black Authors in the English-Speaking World of the 18th Century*, ed. Vincent Carretta (Lexington: University of Kentucky Press, 1997), 142.

14. David Brion Davis, *The Problem of Slavery in Western Culture* (Ithaca: Cornell University Press, 1966), 446.

15. "The Speech of Moses Bon Saam, a Free Negro, to the revolted Slaves in one of the most considerable Colonies of the West Indies." In *Caribbeana: Anthology of English Literature of the West Indies, 1657–1777*, ed. Thomas Krise (Chicago: University of Chicago Press, 1999), 103. As Krise notes, however, "Readers are divided over the question of whether this speech is a fabrication by a British abolitionist or a genuine representation of an actual maroon leader" (101).

16. Benjamin Braude, "The Sons of Noah and the Construction of Ethnic and Geographical Identities in the Medieval and Early Modern Periods," *William and Mary Quarterly*, 3rd series, 54 (January 1997), 102–142.

17. Nicholas Hudson, "From 'Nation' to 'Race': The Origins of Racial Classification in Eighteenth-Century Thought," *Eighteenth-Century Studies* 29 (1996), 247–64.

18. John Atkins, *A Voyage to Guinea, Brasil, and the West-Indies; in His Majesty's Ships the Swallow and Weymouth* (London: Ward and Chandler, 1737).

19. Some critics have objected to recent critical trends in problematizing the concepts of "nation" and "race." Reviewing the recent anthologies of eighteenth-century black writing, Wilfred Samuels has argued that, "The globalization of the Black Atlantic experience obscures the subtle ways in which their marginalization—due directly to race and despite membership in the Church of England, political platforms from which they spoke, and varying degrees of economic success—forced the writers to adopt veiled or duplicitous

voices to manipulate and revise prevailing paradigms…." See "Enlightened Black Voices: Witnesses and Participants." *Eighteenth-Century Studies* 31 (1997–98), 244.

20. William Dickson, *Letters on Slavery* (London: J. Phillips, 1789), 76–77.

21. Hume added these lines to the 1753 and later editions of his essay, debunking Francis Williams as an extraordinary case of black literary achievement.

22. Adam Potkay and Sandra Burr, eds., *Black Atlantic Writers of the Eighteenth Century: Living the New Exodus in England and the Americas* (New York: St. Martin's, 1995), 8.

23. See Andrews, 60.

24. A. Robert Lee, "Selves Subscribed: Early Afro-America and the Signifying of Phillis Wheatley, Jupiter Hammon, Olaudah Equiano, and David Walker," in *Making America, Making American Literature: Franklin to Cooper*, eds. Lee and W.M. Verhoeven (Amsterdam: Rodolpi, 1996), 278. Curiously, however, Lee's argument then goes on to problematically cite the *Narrative of Frederick Douglass* "as a kind of template or grid for the fuller reading of the prior 'self-subscriptions' of Wheatley, Hammon, Equiano/Vassa and Walker."

PART ONE

"Race" and "Gender" in the Early Black Atlantic

"BETRAYED BY SOME OF MY OWN COMPLEXION"

Cugoano, Abolition, and the Contemporary Language of Racialism

Roxann Wheeler

Riddled with contradictions raised by the languages of abolition and racial differ-ence, Ottobah Cugoano's *Thoughts and Sentiments on the Evil and Wicked Traffic of the Slavery and Commerce of the Human Species* (1787) illustrates the logical con-tortions that these two discursive registers elicited. Focusing more on contempo-rary political, economic, and religious issues than on his experiences as a slave, Cugoano's text engages typical religious and secular arguments marshaled to jus-tify slavery and examines some of the major institutions of his day in terms of their alleviating or worsening the situation of slaves. In this respect, his *Thoughts and Sentiments* resembles James Ramsay's *An Essay on the Treatment and Conver-sion of African Slaves in the British Sugar Colonies* (1784) and Thomas Clarkson's *An Essay on the Slavery and Commerce of the Human Species* (1785), two of the more influential anti-slave trade texts.

Even though the arguments of the former slave's jeremiad may be compared to other abolitionist writers, some of whom also struggled with the constraints posed by the conservatism of contemporary aims to abolish the slave trade, Cugoano's text differs in its sustained focus on religion, its condemnation of Brit-ish beliefs and practices, its exhortation to change, as well as its call for restitution to slaves.[1] In this way, according to Vincent Carretta, "Cugoano raised the most overt and extended challenge to slavery ever made by a person of African descent" in the eighteenth century.[2] Cugoano's text is further distinguished from most other contemporary documents in its radical proposal that "a total abolition of slavery should be made and proclaimed; and that universal emancipation of slaves should begin from the date thereof" (98). Much of the ground that he lays for an end to slavery concerns the nature of Africans, particularly their receptiveness to Chris-tianity and commerce (100-101, 107-8). In Cugoano's attempts to refute contem-

porary speculations about Negro inferiority and to use the prevailing ideology of human variety to argue against slavery, we may discern the boundaries of British beliefs about race and social hierarchy when they are forced to figure in slavery. For instance, the widely accepted difference between the upper and lower ranks and between men and women were based on the conviction that bodily strength and intellectual acumen created different abilities, abilities which naturalized the political hierarchy. Although slavery was an extreme case, it lent itself to articulation in these terms.[3]

As is true of most other contemporary writers, Cugoano explains the differences among people through a hodgepodge of references to climate and humoral theory, natural history, Christianity, and four-stages theory, or the distinction between civil and savage societies. Climate and humoral theory, natural history, and four-stages theory all looked to the environment, especially temperature and terrain, to explain human variation in manners, body, and society, respectively. Even the biblical explanation of the common descent from Adam and Eve relied on climatic change to explain differences in human appearance in the contemporary world. Similar to other abolitionists, Cugoano uses the more egalitarian impulses of these theories of human variety in *Thoughts and Sentiments*.[4] Yet these very same discourses prove difficult to manuever since they also had a strong Eurocentric impulse. Indeed, the same theories were used by slavery advocates and by people who believed that, although they should not be enslaved, Africans were possibly inferior to Europeans. Writers against the slave trade and writers in support of it often agreed, for example, about the striking nature of black color and about the negligible state of African civilization.[5] This common ground made it extremely difficult for abolitionists to refer to the state of civil society or black skin neutrally or to use them as arguments against African slavery or inferiority.

Abolitionist texts, including Cugoano's, show that the dominant contemporary assumption about shared humanity also encompassed a conviction of African cultural inferiority and a concern about the meaning of dark skin color. Writers of African descent responded quite similarly to their European counterparts to issues of power, religion, complexion, and civil society in regard to slavery. This fact is hardly surprising given the workings of ideology and the fact that abolitionists were in close contact with each other during the efforts to campaign in Parliament and marshal public opinion. Through their critique of the opposition's assumptions, most abolitionists tried, with varying degrees of success, to treat the issue of skin color in a neutral way at this historical moment, although this relativism did not usually extend to Africa's civilizational attainments.

In addition to the proximity of the anti-slave and pro-slave positions on some important issues, Cugoano's task, and that of other abolitionist writers, was made more difficult because resistance to abolition took the form of economic injury to Britons and political injury to the empire.[6] In fact, *justice* and *reason* were concepts invoked by both sides. On the one hand, writers invoked these concepts in regard to the rights of British slaveowners, merchants, and laborers to secure their property and profits. On the other hand, other writers, including Cugoano, called on these concepts in reference to what Christian teaching dictated and what the British nation should adhere to by abolishing the slave trade. As David Brion Davis contends about these competing claims embodied in the same terms, "The Enlightenment disseminated ideas that could serve the defender of slavery as well as the abolitionist."[7] Cugoano's *Thoughts and Sentiments* was further complicated by the abstract nature of most abolitionist arguments to date. Historian C. Duncan Rice reminds us that the secular critique of slavery, at least in Scotland, "carried with it neither the expectation not the demand that involvement in the slave system should be abandoned."[8] It was only with the emergence of the evangelicals working on behalf of abolition in the 1780s that "the secular critique of the enlightenment was translated into a genuine attack on slavery and the slave trade" (136). A multifaceted, politically coordinated attack on the slave trade was just underway when Cugoano published *Thoughts and Sentiments*, and Cugoano's text is a key document bridging the previous, more abstract approach and the new offensive, which viewed Britain's present course as misguided and the future as imperiled.[9] In Britain's urban centers especially, race and slavery were politicized and publicly debated as they never had been before.

In examining the constraints that shaped Cugoano's using theories of human society to argue against slavery, I analyze two orders of discourse for their internal logic as they appear in *Thoughts and Sentiments*: the distinction between civil and savage society and the meanings attached to complexion, with special reference to its place in Christian aesthetics. These discourses mutually reinforced each other and, occasionally, undermined each other in anti-slave documents. Overall, this essay situates Cugoano's analysis of human variety in regard to other British writers about slavery—writers whose primary interest was in halting the slave trade and in ameliorating the conditions that shaped slaves' lives, as well as writers who wished to promote slavery. None of these writers was interested in race per se. Interpreting the conjunction of slavery and racial ideology in contemporary discourse illustrates that legal and economic rationales for slavery were less likely than before mid-century to stand alone as justifications. Moreover, in studying the intersection of slavery and racial ideology, we discover that cultural criteria were more acceptable to Britons as a defense of slavery than physical differences. Before turning to Cugoano's text, I map late eighteenth-century British representation in regard to race, slavery, their connection and discontinuity. In doing so, I wish to illuminate the proximity of pro-slave and abolitionist assumptions about Africans as a primary constraint Cugoano faces. The shared assumptions mean that the gap between the two positions was narrower than is commonly believed.

At least three main trends are detectable in racial ideology in 1790s Britain as it bears on slavery. First, skin color was more prominent as a public issue than at any time earlier in the century, a phenomenon effected, in part, by natural historians and some philosphers settling on skin color as the predominant factor separating human groups.[10] Abolitionist writings also asserted color's prominence; skin color was fast becoming a shorthand for complex issues and a point of reference to register the extent of perceived differences among the globe's inhabitants. In public documents, many proslavery writers omitted mentioning black skin color and the more hostile meanings associated with it. In fact we know of its prominence chiefly by indirection—by the abolitionists' reference to it as a common rationale for enslavement, especially in the colonies.

A second trend in late-century racial ideology in regard to Africans was that while climatological explanations of manners and physical appearance still dominated all discussions of human variety, among some colonial writers and influential European moral philosophers there was an intensified questioning of climate's deterministic effect on national character. Some writers abandoned the dominant position that favored the theoretical changeability of a people's character and appearance according to changes in climate. Nevertheless, some philosophers—David Hume, Adam Ferguson, Henry Home (Lord Kames), to name a few—raised the possibility that Africans were subject to different laws of social and commercial development than other groups of people; other moral philosophers, such as John Millar and James Beattie strenuously refuted such speculations.[11] The same issue of exception that some Europeans had originally raised in regard to native Americans in the sixteenth century, their contemporary counterparts posed in regard to Africans. A large proportion of the writers who doubted the impact of climate on human social formation did not argue strenuously for an essential difference between Africans and Europeans but for the influence of other external factors on those societies. In fact, mode of government or the extent to which a society was commercialized were increasingly offered as the most important factors shaping societal development.[12]

A third trend in racial ideology as it bore on slavery concerned the physical body and the skeleton. The pursuit of natural history in the eighteenth century codified a new interest in the generic racial body as the primary mark of difference among the world's inhabitants. Natural history provided a rubric of difference usually arranged by geography and/or skin color to group populations. About the time that Cugoano writes, there was a budding European question whether any deeper meaning should be assigned to the outward variation of bodies. For instance, comparative anatomists looked to the skeleton, especially the skull, for indication of the moral or intellectual differences among the world's population. Although comparative anatomy was just gaining momentum in Germany and France in the 1780s, its influence in Britain was attenuated. Across Europe, however, there was a more entrenched conviction in some quarters that anatomical variation may be a sign of actual moral difference, an issue particularly debated in regard to European women.[13] Indeed, the value accorded difference of all kinds—appearance, gender, geography, religion—was under revision in European culture at large during the Enlightenment. In Britain, slavery was a prime occasion for debating the extent to which people differed from one another and how to value—and if to value—those distinctions.

In a letter to Josiah Wedgwood, the poet Anna Seward expresses a commonly held belief about the relationship between racial theory and slavery. Recording her change of heart in regard to slave trade, Seward reveals the way that private opinion incorporated conflicting desires. Before reading Wedgwood's letter and the tracts against the slave trade that he supplied, Seward testified to having a desire for universal justice but one that included an acceptance of slavery. This position records a bifurcated impulse in dominant ideology that Seymour Drescher analyzes in *Capitalism and Antislavery* (1986).[14] Claiming that her "heart always recoiled with horror from the miseries which I heard were inflicted on the negro slaves," Seward was, nevertheless, encouraged by family friends to perceive abolition as "fruitless and dangerous" (47).[15] In explaining Wedgwood's effect on her, Seward notes the previous influence her neighbor had wielded. This neighbor had made a large fortune in the West Indies, "where slavery pervades every opulent establishment. He constantly assured me, that the purchase, employment, and strict discipline of the negroes were absolutely necessary to maintain our empire, and our commerce, in the Indies" (46). She had worked from the premise that slavery resulted in economic benefits that were necessary to expand the empire. According to Drescher, the main rationale for eighteenth-century British slavery "was its apparent contribution to the collective wealth and power of the empire" (20). The nature of slave owners and slaves was invoked to further the primarily patriotic/economic justification: Seward records being assured that slaves' nature was "so sordid and insensible" that severe treatment was necessary to maintain order. The neighbor offered a common reassurance that even the most corrupt people, much less slave owners, abstained from vice when their financial interests were at stake (46). The story her neighbor told about slaves' nature was reiterated by a maimed survivor of a slave rebellion known to Seward. Until being moved by Wedgwood's appeal, Seward did not question these opinions based in other people's experience. Seward's observations suggest that the contemporary endorsement of slavery was more complicated that a personal dislike of black skin color or than an investment in the putative inferiority of Africans.

Seward's letter indicates that the reality of the empire required banishing sentiment and that reason eventually prevailed in her conversion to the anti-slave trade position. In *Thoughts and Sentiments,* Cugoano, like most of his contemporaries, treats color prejudice and slavery as issues rectified through reason and moral suasion. What many late-eighteenth-century colonial documents intimate, however, is that slavery and common disciplinary measures were not governed by rational decisions as much as by fear, strict discipline, and harsh punishment vital to the continuation of slave society. Referring to the ten-to-one ratio of slaves to owners, Samual Estwick declares that 100,000 Negroes were not to be held in obedience without operating on their fears.[16] This ominous statement avers that, while contemporary debates centered on economic rationale and logical argument, we might be better served in the present by focusing on the more nebulous emotions and inconsistencies in reasoning to elucidate contemporary ideology and practices of slavery.

Indeed, Britons liked to think of themselves as more enlightened than their colonial counterparts in regard to slavery and attitudes about racial difference.

The clergyman Andrew Burnaby and the traveler W. Winterbotham advised Englishmen to avoid the slaveholding southern regions of North America because of the uncomfortably hot climate and lack of general civility. Burnaby notes that slave owners in Virginia did not resemble polished Englishmen because of their absolute authority over their slaves. In warning his readers about these men, Burnaby paints a liberal portrait of Britons by implication: "Their ignorance of mankind and of learning, exposes them to many errors and prejudices, especially in regard to Indians and Negroes, whom they scarcely consider as of the human species.[17] Even more strongly, Winterbotham urges Englishmen wishing to settle in America to avoid the South altogether: "The Southern States of Georgia and North and South-carolina seem at present quite out of the question, at least they are not so convenient to an European, from the extreme heat of the climate, and the prevalence of the negroe slavery."[18] The experience of Anna Seward and others intimates that in Britain theories of racial difference and endorsement of slavery did not always reinforce each other. They intersected occasionally but were not co-dependent. Not all Britons automatically connected enslaved Africans to racial inferiority, especially in written documents. This fact is important to highlight since legally and customarily, racial slavery defined the late-eighteenth-century Caribbean. Additionally, by the late 1780s, when the British slave trade was reaching its peak, many Britons were variously benefitting from slavery in terms of profits, availability of credit and jobs, and, of course, affordable consumer items, such as printed cloth, ivory curios, sugar, and rum. An antislavery position was not solely an ethical issue for Cugoano and his contemporaries but an economic and political one shaped by profound respect for the social order and a concern about Britain's European hegemony.

The lack of clear cut moral issues connected to slavery and the empire made a jeremiad like Cugoano's even more anomalous because of its uncompromising stance. Cugoano and other abolitionists faced proslavery arguments that featured assumptions of fundamental difference between European and slave as well as arguments that admitted little real difference between the two. The latter were decidedly more difficult to combat. Indeed, some advocates of slavery and abolitionists agreed about the degree of African civilization, the shared humanity of Africans and Europeans, and the need to reform slavery. Bryan Edwards, one of the most complex writers about the Caribbean, penned the magisterial *The History, Civil and Commercial, of the British Colonies in the West Indies* (1791), which went into five editions by 1819 alone, and *An Historical Survey of the French Colony in the Island of St. Domingo* (1797).[19] Edwards's interaction with Edward Long's text on the West Indies reveals the disagreement about the nature of Africa and Africans even among supporters of slavery. In preparation for writing *History of the British Colonies*, an analysis of this crucial region, Edwards heavily annotated his mentor's influential *History of Jamaica* (1774). What emerges from his manuscript notes is an ongoing disagreement with Long about the nature of slaves. Edwards's publications offer the most common British explanation of African "degeneracy" based on the conditions of their enslavement, not their nature, a stance shared by most abolitionists.[20]

Edward Long, on the other hand, maintains that Africans in Africa fail to evince the same variety as other people, that they are the closest human group to the orang-outangs, and that they are probably incapable of the higher mechanical and intellectual arts by virtue of their birth in Africa. Objecting strenuously to such a negative depiction, Edwards contends that Long not only contradicts this stance in *The History of Jamaica* but that he himself had met several "Civilized" Senegal Negroes, in particular, who could read and write in Arabic (353, 1. 34). Moreover, Edwards finds it difficult to believe that Long was unaware of the popular cotton cloths imported from Akim. Edwards remarks about this evidence of a sophisticated material culture: "in manufacture [the cotton cloths] are equal and in Color far superior to those made at Manchester in Imitation of them" (355, 1. 6). Cultural factors were crucial to indicating intellectual proclivities, so much so that a sizable proportion of people who commented on the putative inferior understanding of African did so in terms couched in their cultural behavior. Rather than focusing on physical differences, these writers pronounced on Africans' allegedly inferior mental faculties by regretting that they had failed to emulate European consumerism and agricultural practices.[21] Edwards's mentioning the Akim textiles prompts him to refute the larger claim that Long tenders. Concluding that Long fails to prove that Africans are naturally inferior to Europeans, because he does not show that a white person of the meanest intellect is superior to a black person of the brightest parts, Edwards complains: "To say that Men differ from each other in point of intellect proves nothing" (372, 1. 34). As appealing as Edwards's observation about intellectual variation may be, however, he ignores a major contemporary resonance of it. The difference between reason and sentiment or between intellectual pursuits and manual labor was key to justifying many aspects of the social order, such as the superiority of men to women or the upper ranks to the lower stations. In all cases, the notion of intellectual or moral difference was crucial to justifying necessary subordination.

An apologist for slavery, Edwards argues that slavery made African genius impossible to know; moreover, the lack of extensive information about Africa allowed ample room for negative European pronouncements (303). As to the debate over Africans' skin color, Edwards concludes repeatedly that it is complexion, with few exceptions, that distinguishes freedom from slavery in the West Indies. Notably, he relies on a sociological interpretation of skin color when he observes that "Contempt and degradation will attach to the colour by which that condition [slavery] is generally recognized."[22] Edwards likens the colonial black man to the self-made European man who rises above humble beginnings. He maintains that differences in color and station are accidents of birth and not signs of natural inferiority or servitude (8). Many abolitionists featured these same points. In mentioning Bryan Edwards's comments on Edward Long's text, I wish to emphasize the competing images of African slaves within proslavery discourse: how much humanity to accord slaves was not merely debated between pro- and antislavery factions. Edwards's sense of Caribbean slave society's injustice to the reputation of Africans does not, however, militate against his own condemnation of African "superstition" and social habits under slavery.

Despite his fundamental disagreement with those who degrade Africans from similarity to Europeans, Edwards supports the continuation of slavery. Edwards's text reveals that by the 1790s the proslavery position was best served by humanizing slaves more than previously in order to rationalize slavery to the British populace. This was a significant change over Long's dehumanizing Africans by claiming limited improvements in Creole slaves because of their proximity to European society. In consulting contemporary British magazines and parliamentary debates, R.A. Austen and W.D. Smith conclude that by 1789, "it was no longer really possible for the slavery interest to defend the trade morally by asserting that the African was not human."[23] A striking example of the new prevailing strategy occurs in *History of the British Colonies* in which Edwards harps on slave ownership of property, their participation in local markets, and their lives independent of forced labor, as did his contemporaries John Gabriel Stedman, John Stewart, and Sir William Young, to name a few.[24] For instance, James Hakewill dedicated *A Picturesque Tour of the Island of Jamaica* (1825) to the planters whom he defends; he begins his book with the story of negro slaves bargaining with their masters for terms of labor and various "privileges."[25] He adds extensive remarks on the wealth accruing to Negroes who trade at the market (4-5). Highlighting these aspects of everyday life, aspects that show slaves as wage earners, enjoying leisure, and as having some power over the conditions of their existence, allowed supporters of slavery to argue that slavery was not as bad as detractors portrayed.

The proslavery strategy to humanize slaves worked well with the tendency to disparage African political and material culture. The combined force of this representation quelled some Britons' discomfort with the idea of slavery: the unfortunate institution of slavery was compensated for by introducing Africans to civil society; this was certainly Edward Long's position. The general proslavery emphasis on slaves as similar but inferior to the British laboring classes, on the one hand, and on African culture as barbarous, on the other hand, stemmed partially from what we now call four-stages theory. Discussions of slavery in the 1780s that did not dwell on the financial benefit of it focused on the trademark of four-stages theory that Edward Long employed: the way that Africans organized their society. The distinction between civil and savage societies that tended to hierarchize populations based on their mode of production was, arguably, the most significant rubric for understanding eighteenth-century racial arguments—and their convolutions— about Africans. The difference between hunting, shepherding, agricultural, and commercial societies ignored physical typology and emphasized the role of institutions as well as labor and social practices in creating variations among the world's population. Accounting for the factors that contributed to these global differences in ways of living, Scottish Enlightenment philosophers posited that the division of labor and the protection of private property were key aspects responsible for the various paces at which societies developed. By comparing socio-economic arrangements around the globe and throughout history, moral philosophers analyzed the causes and effects that seemed to operate in encouraging societies toward commercial expansion or retarding it.[26] Although not hierarchical in all of its formulations, four-stages theory tended to establish superiority based on the organization of what John Millar calls "the common arts of life."[27]

Britons put great faith in the felicitous effects of commercial society, especially the development of the arts and sciences, the wearing of layered clothing, and Christian religion as ways to distinguish themselves from others. The development of a coherent theory about the origin of the arts and sciences, their flourishing and decline did not occur until mid-century with the publication of David Hume's essays, Adam Ferguson's *An Essay on the History of Civil Society* (1796), John Millar's *The Origin of the Distinction of Ranks* (1771), and Adam Smith's *The Wealth of Nations* (1776). Notions of polished, barbaric, and savage societies were honed by these writers. Although these works tended to challenge the economic, legal, and moral arguments for slavery and often denounced its practice, they elucidated civil society as a key concept defining British eminence. Since antislavery sentiment and racialist thinking often shared this way of seeing societies, it made for a good deal of agreement about the nature of Africans.

Variations in four-stages theory allowed it to be used by both slavery advocates and abolitionists. Like natural historians, most Scottish Enlightenment writers assumed that human nature was uniform throughout time and responsive to environmental and institutional forces.[28] This argument was compatible with a range of proslavery positions, not to mention abolitionist claims. Undergirding one version of four-stages theory was a belief in the progress and the perfectibility of society; the premise of most versions was, however, that history was cyclical over the long term: empires rose and fell. In both versions, contemporary writers often looked to consumerism and trade as vital defining features of sophisticated societies. Responding to the pre-eminence accorded trade in defining Britain, commonplaces such as the one that appeared in *The Royal Magazine* of 1760 were ubiquitous, especially after the conclusion of the Seven Years' War: "every country must be luxurious before it can make any progress in human knowledge."[29] The intimate connection of consumerism and reason did not bode well for Africa, not least because much of Britain's consumer potential relied on slave labor and other exploitative labor and commercial relationships.

One of the most widely shared sentiments of late-century writers is what motivational speakers today call "retail therapy." Olaudah Equiano and, to a lesser extent, Cugoano, following the early Quaker abolitionist Anthony Benezet, adopt this view. Popular beliefs about human difference were often inextricable from the British experience of commercial society. In contemporary documents, consumption of English goods figures as a primary antidote to savagery and as the key to cultural assimilation with the British. Myriad texts about Caribbean Indians, Native Americans, and West Africans, as diverse as Aphra Behn's *Oroonoko* (1688), William Snelgrave's *A New Account of Some Parts of Guinea and the Slave-Trade* (1734), and Long's *History of Jamaica*, urge this view. It is no small paradox that commercial society held out contradictory possibilities. One potential was for it to retard the force of racial ideology based on assumptions about cultural difference through encouraging others to emulate English behavior and dress. The other potential was for British commercial society to depend on the perceived bodily differences of Africans economically and culturally.

As suggested by the disagreement between Long and Edwards and by the thrust of four-stages theory, for many Britons, consciously or not, fathoming the nature of African cultural life bore on the legitimacy of European involvement in the slave trade. The unpolished state of African society largely preoccupied most writers for or against the slave trade when they broached matters not solely connected to Britain's financial gain. Abolitionists mined the language of four-stages theory to persuade British readers to support the legal reform of slavery, including eliminating the slave trade. A twenty-year residence in St. Kitts converted the Anglican clergyman James Ramsay to abolition.[30] His influential *An Essay on the Treatment and Conversion of African Slaves* exhaustively attempts to rebut all of the contemporary objections to Africans on physical and mental grounds. He concludes that the accidental differences characteristic of Africans derive from the fact that they do not live in a polished society. Similarly, William Dickson, a former private secretary to the Governor of Barbados, who wrote *Letters on Slavery* (1789), used his insider's knowledge to argue that the main issue in the case of slavery was the state of African society.[31] Dickson, whose publication garnered the endorsement of the Sons of Africa, refers to his personal experience with slaves to substantiate his comments on African society: "I never did observe in them any mark of inferiority which might not very fairly be referred to those most powerful causes *the Savage state*, which suffers not the faculties to expand themselves" (61). Dickson counsels that converting slaves to Christianity would help civilize them and thus prepare them for freedom later, a position Cugoano shares. Even Richard Nisbet, a slave owner from Nevis, urges his contemporaries to abandon the fruitless discussion over Negro faculties. Desiring reform of slavery, not its abandonment, Nisbet finds ample ammunition for his position on slavery by referring to African's rude state of government.[32]

Abolitionists often found themselves obliged to comment on African cultural and political life in a way that militated against establishing African similarity to Europeans, an issue with which Cugoano repeatedly struggles. A case in point is the role Sons of Africa and other former slaves played in contemporary debates. Cugoano and Olaudah Equiano frequently signed letters as part of the London activist group known as the Sons of Africa. Dedicated to promoting abolition of the slave trade, the Sons of Africa also supported efforts to create a more tolerant British society. A letter from the Sons of Africa to fellow abolitionist Granville Sharp confirms the use of the truism about the comparative rudeness of African society in their own correspondence: "it is said that we are the factors of our own slavery, and sell one another at our own market for a price. No doubt but in our uncivilized state we commit much evil" (189). In *Thoughts and Sentiments*, Cugoano concedes that there is African "ignorance in somethings," but he emends this statement immediately by claiming that Africans are "not so learned, [but] are just as wise as Europeans" (28) In this way, Cugoano grants British book learning but denies any fundamental distinction in abilities between Europeans and Africans. This concession is compatible with the claims of Christianity, natural history, climate, and four-stages theory, but it is a stumbling block. As Enlightenment thinkers such as Samuel Johnson believed, the printed word allowed one culture to participate with others in the advancement of knowledge, but where there were no books there was no contribution. Indeed, elsewhere, Cugoano uses book learning and Christian religion to distinguish Britons positively from Africans, as does Equiano (17, 23).

Cugoano refers to another subset of four-stages theory when he comments on an argument that some Europeans used to justify African enslavement: because Africans are dispersed geographically and not concentrated in urban centers, they are therefore unsociable and, thus, acceptable candidates for forced labor (25). Conceding the widespread lack of civil society–that some Africans are poor, miserable, and capriciously governed–Cugoano's main counterargument is that these deficiencies are no reason for Europeans to enslave Africans (16, 19). In a similar vein, Cugoano, unlike most of his contemporaries, finds the Africans involved in the slave trade to be the most depraved because of their contact with Europeans (26). Cugoano's position harks back to anti-empire discourse that claimed that the lure of luxury topples nations, that pursuit of unregulated commerce is suspicious. Most versions of four-stages theory, the history of representation of contact between Britons and others, and British prejudice strongly favored the civilizing effects of trade. For example, in arguing for the reformation of slavery, not its abandonment, slave owner Richard Nisbet makes the long-standard claim that because of their conduct with Europeans and role in trade, coastal Africans are more civil and superior in intelligence to Africans in the interior regions. Because coastal Africans differ from their more isolated countrymen, Nisbet reasons, all Africans must be endowed with the capacity for improvement given the appropriate conditions (9). Cugoano's position on the corrupting influence of attractive foreign commodities tries to fend off the claims that the slave trade could civilize Africans, urging that sociable commerce (of non-human commodities), tempered by Christian convictions, is the only route to civil, commercial society in Africa. Non-slave commerce and , especially, Christian conversion, Cugoano declares, are preferable, longer-lasting remedies for Africa (99–101). Both of these solutions would bring Africans in contact with Europeans, thereby increasing their sociability but for worthy ends.

A common proslavery argument about the barbarism permeating Africa often blamed slavery on Africans by invoking categories from four-stages theory. In *An Essay on the Slave Trade* (1788), the author dismisses European demand as an issue fostering African slavery to focus on a popular myth about the cultural life of Gold Coast Inhabitants: "without a settled life employed in agriculture and arts, in science and manufactures, it is impossible for the inhabitants of the Gold coast to live free from those evils which introduce slavery."[33] This proslavery position is almost identical to the abolitionist argument that a leading Philadelphia Quaker makes. In *A Caution and A Warning to Great Britain* (1766), Anthony Benezet interprets the effects of enslavement on Africans in Africa with reference to it suppressing the development of civil society. Enslavement, he declares, "tends to suppress all improvements in arts and sciences; without which it is morally impossible that any nation should be happy or powerful."[34] Cugoano tackles the issue of slavery in Africa somewhat differently than these two contemporaries by arguing that African slavery differs positively from West Indian slavery, a position that Olaudah Equiano also espouses. Suggesting that Africans enslave rival Africans legitimately through the logical outcome of warfare and treat them well because they are incorporated into all aspects of society, Cugoano argues explicitly for the illegitimacy of Europeans taking Africans and for the dehumanizing way they practice slavery. While this is an argument of some force, it encouraged a focus on reform of slavery in the West Indies, not abandonment of it; moreover, it tended to confirm that Africans were culturally habituated to slavery.

Even though issues of economics and civility dominated exchanges about the slave trade, concerns about black skin color had a place in these texts. Natural history was the primary discipline that made physical appearance a central factor in distinguishing among the globe's inhabitants. The curious position that skin color occupies is most apparent in the way that abolitionists treated it. Cugoano, for one, engages with color at great length, especially with the value assigned it in biblical and natural history contexts. By examining his engagement with it, we may see a pertinent illustration of the logical conflict color raised in a society that had not quite decided on the value complexion should carry. Indeed, Cugoano's desire to tackle the interpretation of black complexion is even more understandable after considering the way fellow abolitionists treated it. In his *Elements of Moral Science* (1790), for example, the Scottish moral philosopher James Beattie condemns slavery in no uncertain terms, a discussion that takes place under the heading of "Economics."[35] Despite his desire to treat slavery as an economic issue, his preoccupation with other matters keeps surfacing. Within the space of thirty pages, Beattie returns to Africans' distinctive physical features, especially black color, no fewer than six times, either to confirm that some writers cite them as a reason to enslave Africans or to deny that dark color is a legitimate ground for enslavement (2:81-110). Skin color occupied a similarly symptomatic, if less obsessive, place in mid-century abolitionist documents by John Woolman and J. Philmore, who begin their works with the assertion that Africans and Europeans are the same kind of men. These documents regard dark color as a false rationale commonly offered for enslavement, usually listed after religious difference as reasons espoused by supporters of slavery in the colonies. The superficiality of complexion generally assumes the primary position in a list of reasons not to enslave Africans. Benjamin Rush, for instance, begins his tract with considerations of color before moving on to other issues.[36] When writers give more than a passing mention to black skin color or when they become entangled in detailed denials of its pertinence, we can detect a change in British racial ideology.

Afro-British writers, like their white British counterparts, demonstrate repeatedly that dark color raises certain ideological tangles that the discourse on
civility does not. Complexion first becomes a topic of narration in writings of
people of black African descent during the 1770s, a decade after their first known
writings appear in the Anglo-American world. In *A Narrative of the Most Remarkable Life* (1772), the young James Albert Ukawsaw Gronniosaw wonders if he is
despised by God because he is black. The adult Gronniosaw, however, records that
after he is baptized, he wished to marry an Englishwoman. He mentions the objections that their friends raise to the intended nuptials, which are based on her
poverty. Neither his color nor former slave status seem to stand in the way of
their union.[37] Gronniosaw's contemporaries Phillis Wheatley and Francis Williams explicitly mention the standard abolitionist claim of the similarity of blacks
and whites despite differences in complexion, but the writers of the 1780s—
Sancho, Cugoano, and Equiano—engage more thoroughly with blackness than
previous writers.[38]

In *Thoughts and Sentiments*, Cugoano invokes the full range of religious and
secular interpretations of skin color. He combats erroneous interpretations of Scripture and scientific speculation by claiming that color variations are natural rather
than God's curse or an unnatural degeneracy from white skin. His chief
counterargument is that a variety of skin colors should not signify anything other
than the wonder of creation. Cugoano calls on the biblical account of creation to
argue for the common heritage of all humans. His supporting evidence is that
humans originated from Adam and Eve, so that all humans are bound by one
nature, blood, and form (29). Explaining that today's people are descended from
Noah's family "and were then all of one complexion," Cugoano notes that "the
difference which we now find" occurred rapidly after they dispersed throughout
the globe (29). The changes after the Flood arose from climatic differences to which
the scattered people were exposed. Accounting for the similarity of all humans, he
provides an analogy between the family unit and the human race. This typical
abolitionist claim is that children in the same family often have hair and features
that differ from one another (29). In a related attempt, Cugoano invokes the brotherhood of Christians created through baptism and conversion to emphasize his
similarity to his readers. In these and other passages, Cugoano lobbies against the
status quo of slavery and the specious assumptions that support it. For instance, he
criticizes the standard proslavery claim that Moses sanctioned slavery, that slavery
had been integral to diverse nations for ages, and "that the Africans are peculiarly
marked out by some signal prediction in nature and complexion for that purpose"
(28). In his critique, he opines that it is easy (and intellectually shoddy) to pick and
choose tidbits from Scripture to support either a proslavery or anti-slave trade
position. The chief message of the Bible, he notes, is an overall moral lesson arrived at through revelation and reason: it is wrong to enslave another human being (28).

As Cugoano's lengthy engagement with the interpretation of *Genesis*, Mo-
saic law, and Hebrew practices of slavery suggests, the Bible was easier to use in

regard to an argument about shared human origins than in regard to the injustice of slavery. In fact, many proslavery writers of the late 1780s and 1790s were perfectly at ease with the sense of Africans' general humanity and their enslavement; this approach usually chastised the worst excesses of the slave trade and a few capricious slave owners whose punishments exceeded the general climate of cruelty and bodily pain tolerated in a variety of socio-economic realms.[40] As a goal, amelioration of slavery characterized the position held by advocates of the status quo and by abolitionists. Cugoano's sustained interaction with these arguments serves at once to display his thoughtful knowledge of the Bible and the extent to which biblical arguments—no matter how loosely devolved—still carried a good deal of cultural weight, especially for a former slave writing in 1780s Britain.

Even though large interpretive issues such as the immorality of slavery might be supported by an intimate knowledge of the Bible, other aspects of Christian teaching were not as easy to manipulate. One of the more inflexible concepts that Cugoano engages is the biblical language of color, especially images associated with dark and light, black and white. The problem he encounters is most noticeable when he invokes the association between blackness and sin at the same time that he claims that black skin color is only a superficial difference of Africans. In *Thoughts and Sentiments,* the discrepancy between the symbolic religious signification of blackness and its neutrally descriptive usage creates the main ideological tangle over skin color and value; this tension is most apparent in the passages where Cugoano uses both registers simultaneously. Alluding to the proverbial impossible task of washing an Ethiop white, Cugoano quotes Jeremiah when he asks his British readers: "Can the Ethiopian change his skin, or the leopard his spots? Then, may ye also do good that are accustomed to do evil" (39). In these references to permanent (though natural) conditions based loosely on the Christian tradition, Cugoano's rather strained analogy of complexion to human agency breaks down as soon as he introduces the figurative washing away of sin. Cugoano reasons that none "among the fallen" by himself can change his nature from "the blackness and guilt of the sable dye of sin and pollution" (39). The Christian exhortation that makes the standard association of black with sin and white with redemption follows; the inherent evil in every man can be removed only through the purifying blood of Jesus and submission to him. According to Cugoano, "all the stains and blackest dyes of sin and pollution can be washed away for ever, and the darkest sinner be made to shine as the brightest angel" (40). Although Cugoano refers to a metaphorical, or spiritual, brightness, he repeatedly juxtaposes the neutral fact of black skin with the interpretation of black color as sinful.

This repeated connection makes it difficult to keep various meanings of blackness separate. For example, when he animadverts against Europeans who believe that Africans are an inferior link in the chain of being, he asserts that "if such men can boast of greater degrees of knowledge, than any African is entitled to, I shall let them enjoy all the advantages of it unenvied, as I fear it consists only in greater share of infidelity, and that of a blacker kind than only skin deep" (12). In these references, Cugoano allows for all humans to be stained with the blackness of sin or covered with the brightness of redemption, regardless of their actual complexion. Nevertheless, the literal manifestation of black and white skin creates a disjunction with the biblical and aesthetic registers. Indeed, the natural historian's emphasis on the changeability of color is often sacrificed to the more basic insistence that black color is natural, not an aberration.

Color and agency are curiously connected in Cugoano's representation of sin and redemption. Cugoano argues that extreme difference in color, embodied in black men, was intended to teach the white man that there is a sinful blackness in his own nature, which he cannot change by himself. Nonetheless, Cugoano contends that actual black skin has nothing to do with God's displeasure, which prompts him to compare the colors of the rainbow to human complexion, intimating that both range naturally across a spectrum of color. As these textual examples indicate, fluid movement between metaphorical and neutral descriptive registers proves difficult when the black and white binary is invoked in Christian logic. Christian discourse generated contradictory traditions about the value of color. One logic, the metaphorical register, creates a hierarchy of aesthetics: black equals sin, white equals purity. The other biblical logic of value concerning people in the eyes of God disregards color difference and its embodiment by focusing on their common heritage and their possession of souls. Cugoano confronts the problem of these two contradictory registers in his claims about God and Nature: both love variety, which he concludes, means that diversity is good. In contemporary usage, however, diversity was not simply variety among equal entities but usually assumed inequality such as in the British social order of various ranks. In Cugoano's search for a representation of commensurability, we can detect the limitation of common religious and secular beliefs to this task.

The fact that the intimate connection between color, diversity, and inequality troubles Cugoano is evident because he returns to it several times in the space of a few pages to attack it from different angles. Finally, changing tactics once again in regard to the signification of color, Cugoano contends that the nature and quality of a man is constant "whether he wears a black or a white coat, whether he puts it on or strips it off, he is still the same man" (41). In addressing the periodically popular argument that Africans' color derived from God's curse, Cugoano engages in biblical exegesis and attempts to make the mark usually associated with complexion a metaphorical one only. Offering a common alternative reading of African ancestry, Cugoano reckons that black Africans descend from Noah through Cush and their color arises naturally from the effect of the sun and heat in the torrid zone (33).[41] Cugoano speculates slyly that if God's curse ever rested on people, then it was "upon those who committed the most outrageous acts of violence and oppression," not upon those with a particular complexion (33). In implicating slave owners, Cugoano reworks God's curse from visible blackness to an invisible condemnation. Rehearsing received stereotypes of blackness and whiteness at the same time that he tries to reject them, Cugoano's *Thoughts and Sentiments* moves with difficulty through the many registers of meaning in which black and white complexion signifies in a binary logic.

Cugoano encounters fewer ideological problems when he discusses differences in complexion in a purely secular context. Although he offers God's delight in variety as a primary explanation for differences among humans, he also provides the standard argument about human variety that derived from humoral and climate theory. This intellectual heritage imagined that bodies responded to the heat of the sun and other climatic factors by varying in height, color, and ability. Nature, too, delights in variety, he posits, "as the bodies of men are tempered with a different degree to enable them to endure the respective climates of their habitations, so their colours vary" (30). Compatible with his biblical approach to the superficiality of color, humoral theory suggested that color variation was natural and easily changed by climatic factors. Taking a page from Montesquieu and Millar, Cugoano claims about all people that, "Long custom and the different way of living . . . has [sic]a very great effect in distinguishing them by a difference of features and complexion" (30). Cugoano commonly mixes humoral, climatic, and divine explanations of human variety. He offers a psychosocial explanation about the predilection of Europeans who misread the Bible, particularly the Curse of Ham: "According, as we find that the difference of colour among men is only incidental, and equally natural to all, and agreeable to the place of their habitation; and that if nothing else be different or contrary among them, but that of features and complexion, because they are not black, whose ignorance and insolence leads them to think, that those who are black, were marked out in that manner by some signal interdiction of curse, as originally descending from their progenitors" (30). He contends that the problem lies with some Europeans who locate color and difference only in Africans as opposed to viewing all humans as varying from each other.

Although Cugoano's references to skin color often try to reconcile the apparently intractable differences embodied in the black/white binary, he also intimates that complexion should function as a visible reminder of shared origins, despite language and other cultural variations. As Cugoano, Ramsay, and other contemporary writers reveal, the concepts of complexion and country were occasionally linked. In fact, "country" and "complexion," although invoked as separate terms in contemporary documents, tend to signify identity and emotional cathexis among former residents of the colonies. One of the several ways that Cugoano's *Thoughts and Sentiments* shows complexion in a positive way is by conjuring up fellowship. He consistently refers to other Africans and Afro-Britons as men "of my own complexion" (12), as Equiano and other black Atlantic writers. In the many references that he makes to men of his own complexion, Cugoano suggests that skin color, in fact, carried communal meaning among Africans and was not simply a descriptive feature. He invokes repeatedly the phrase "countrymen in complexion" to establish a connection among all who suffer enslavement in the West Indies (60, 96). This phrase signals his sympathy with Africans' plight, even though he is no longer enslaved himself. This phrase also reproaches those who initially betrayed him into slavery, accusing them of unnatural behavior, of failing to demonstrate appropriate regard for one's countrymen. In these instances, Cugoano tries to invest complexion with a positive connotation, even though he usually wishes to treat it neutrally. In referring to black men who kidnapped and sold him, and in referring to the black woman on his slave ship who alerted her white lover to a slave rebellion, Cugoano hints at the way that politics and economics in the Atlantic slave system were not always or even naturally linked to shared complexion.

Black and white writers who had lived in the North American and West Indian colonies tended to accord complexion more conscious importance than their contemporaries who had never left Britain—both in their invocation of it as a significant feature of people and as a way to mark group allegiance. For example, it is clear from James Ramsay's comments in *An Essay on the Treatment and Conversion of African Slaves* that colonists believed that people with the same skin color had a natural affinity for each other.[42] Ramsay provides an excellent case in point of the abolitionists' dilemma in regard to the significance of physical appearance. Although Ramsay blames external forces for African cultural inferiority and the European lust for inordinate financial gain from slavery, he stumbles when it comes to the perceived physical differences of Africans: "It is true, there are marks, that appear now to be established, as if set by the hand of nature to distinguish them from the whites: their noses are flat, their chins prominent, their hair woolly, their skin black" (172–73). Like natural historians and other anti-slave trade proponents, however, Ramsay claims that the visible attributes of Negroes—while striking to European eyes—do not, in fact, set them apart from other humans in a significant way. He develops this line of thinking further when he meditates on the way that visible distinctions work in general: "And, let it be remarked, that the characteristics of negroes shew themselves chiefly about the face, where nature has fixed both the national attributes and the discriminating features of individuals, as if intended to distinguish them from other families, and bind them in the social tie with their brethren" (173). While couched in familial discourse, which intimates sibling affection and common parentage, Ramsay manages to convey the sense that because of their visible features, Negroes, like other groups, form a separate "family." It may be that Ramsay offers insight into issues such as national preference and prejudice, but his supposition about Negro appearance sits oddly with his efforts to deny that it bears on their enslavement. Ramsay is typical of former residents of the colonies, both black and white, in finding physical appearance a phenomenon requiring lengthy discussion.

Cugoano's usage and Ramsay's speculation on the beneficial social role of complexion extends Adam Smith's observations in *The Theory of Moral Sentiments* (1759) about the natural attachment individuals feel toward their own rank or society to the realm of vision.[44] This way of seeing fellowship suggests an important revision to Benedict Anderson's thesis in *Imagined Communities* (1983): print culture was not the only factor responsible for suturing Britons to a new sense of their identity in the eighteenth century. As the documents I have cited above intimate, visual compatibility among subjects seems to have played a role. It would seem that complexion, as it was invoked in the slave trade debates and in natural history writings, helped constitute a conscious sense of group belonging quite early in the colonies and in Britain by this time as well. This undeveloped assumption in eighteenth-century writing should be factored into Seymour Drescher's argument that it was difficult to sustain an ideology of slavery based on racial inferiority and biblical sanction in 1780's Britain (20). Drescher's conclusion is an important corrective to ahistorical assertions of Britons' color-based racism, but by studying abolitionists' tortuous engagement with the meanings attached to black skin color, we discover its maverick nature at the time.

As Cugoano's text repeatedly demonstrates, skin color occupied a volatile place in contemporary discourse—ranging from the superficial and inconsequential to the very fabric of identity. Cugoano's changes to the 1791 version of *Thoughts and Sentiments* in regard to the language of racialism suggest that he continued to find the metaphorical register for blackness problematic in the context of abolition. This problem is evident because he reshaped and clarified many of the passages dealing with color, although he did not eliminate them. To remove the metaphorical resonance of blackness would have erased his best bet for questioning the way some Britons interpreted dark skin color; it would have also undermined the biblical authority for his position on which his text rests. One of the few additions Cugoano makes to the shortened 1791 version of *Thoughts and Sentiments* concerns the history of black skin color. Cugoano inserts a passage about Noah's complexion: "According to the researchers [*sic*] of the most learned, it is evidently that Noah was of an olive black in colour" (123).[45] The addition of the olive black Noah in 1791 indicates Cugoano's desire to make black complexion more ancient, natural, and divinely sanctioned than he conveyed in his original text.

Thoughts and Sentiments, like many other contemporary documents, demonstrates the necessary negotiation with the categories of four-stages theory in discussions of Africans, slavery, and Europeans. Cugoano's text also emphasizes the way that skin color was significant to some contemporary discussions of slavery but uncertainly configured in them. *Thoughts and Sentiments* is remarkable for its peculiar mix of a range of conservative and radical positions to persuade readers against slavery and the slave trade. For example, Cugoano's conservative view of the commercial stage of society means that he can condemn unregulated trade and highlight the widely perceived negative effects of commerce on some segments of the British population, including slaves. This traditional argument against luxury fits well with his Christian demand for more moral treatment of Africans and a more moderate approach to global expansion. But this conservative stance is less successful in justifying Cugoano's call for British intervention in Africa, even by invitation. In showing how fellowship and the golden rule are lacking in the contemporary trade networks, Cugoano imagines, instead, a friendly political, commercial, and religious alliance between Britain and Africa in which British learning would initiate a period in which the arts and sciences would flourish in Africa. In return for civil society, Africa would accord Britain a favored nation status in trade; instead of slaves, Britain would still benefit by African bodies, but these would be a lawful, willing labor force or an army for its colonial outposts (100-101). *Thoughts and Sentiments* registers an important transition in British engagement with the effects of its empire. Slavery had long been an economic and political phenomenon; in its newer phase as a public, moral issue, the contours of attack and support were, for the most part, involuted.

NOTES

1. On the conservatism of the early Abolitionist movement, see Christopher L. Brown, "Empire without Slaves: British Concepts of Emancipation in the Age of the American Revolution," *William and Mary Quarterly* 56 (April 1999): 273-306. Also consult Judith Jenning, "Joseph Woods, 'Merchant and Philosopher': The Making of the British Anti Slave Trade Ethic," *Slavery and Abolition* 14.3 (December 1993), 168 especially.

2. Quobna Ottobah Cugoano, *Thoughts and Sentiments on the Evil of Slavery,* ed. and intro. Vincent Carretta (New York: Penguin Books 1999): xx. Carretta treats the jeremiad on xxii.

3. Many of the radical writers of the 1790s grappled with these ubiquitous assumptions even as they envisioned a more equitable political and social system; I am thinking especially of Mary Wollstonecraft in *A Vindication of the Rights of Woman* (1792) and William Godwin in *Enquiry Concerning Political Justice* (1793). Accepting the desirability of hierarchy within Britain was even further complicated by imagining a ranking of global proportions. Showing how similarity of nature as well as difference were minutely factored into slavery discussions, Gordon Turnbull, an apologist for slavery, went so far as to concede that all men possessed the same potential at birth, but he went on to contend that they did not develop equally as individuals or as societies. Arguing that a minute observation of African character and disposition indicates "that they are not at all fitted to fill the superior stations, or more elevated ranks in civil society" (34), Turnbull made a judgment compatible with a strain of four-stages theory and expressed a claim with which most Britons could agree in principle. See Gordon Turnbull, *An Apology for Negro Slavery: Or the West-India Planters Vindicated from the Charge of Inhumanity,* 2d ed. (London: J. Stevenson. 1786).

4. On the racist and anti-racist impulses of Enlightenment discourse, see Henry Louis Gates, Jr., "Critical Remarks," *Anatomy of Racism,* ed. David Theo Goldberg (Minneapolis: University of Minnesota Press, 1990): 323, 319-29.

5. Richard M. Kain, "The Problem of Civilization in English Abolition Literature, 1772-1808," *Philological Quarterly* 50.2 (April 1936), 115, makes a similar point. "With the pro-slavery writers they [progressive abolitionists] admitted the stupidity, dishonesty, treachery, and brutality of the negro, but they went on to point out that the negro was still in a state of nature, and that his slow emergence from that state was due to the climate, or to the inaccessibility of Africa, or to the inroads of slave trading." Common ground between opponents could extend from large issues to small. For instance, both the proslavery James Tobin and an antislavery Dissenting preacher agreed that it was the philosophers who were to blame for degrading Africans by insinuating that there were distinct races of men essentially different from one another. See James Tobin, *Cursory Remarks upon the Reverend Mr. Ramsays's Essay on the Treatment and Conversion of the African Slaves in the Sugar Colonies* (London: G. and T. Wilkie, 1785) 140-1 and John Beatson, *A Sermon, Occasioned by that Branch of British Commerce which Extends to the Human Species* (Hull: G. Prince, 1789), 11.

6. See James Rawley, "London's Defense of the Slave Trade, 1787-1807," *Slavery and Abolition* 14.2 (August 1993), 48-69, 51-53.

7. David Brion Davis, *The Problem of Slavery in Western Culture* (1966; New York: Oxford University Press, 1988), 438.

8. C. Duncan Rice, "Archibald Dalzel, the Scottish Intelligentsia, and the Problem of Slavery," *The Scottish Historical Review* 62.2 (October 1983): 121-36, 129.

9. In 1787, for instance, twelve London abolitionists organized the Committee for the Abolition of the Slave Trade, composed mostly of Quakers (and three Anglicans). For the full range of lobbying activities during 1787, see Judith Jennings, *The Business of Abolishing the British Slave Trade, 1783-1807* (London: Frank Cass and Co., 1997), chapter 3.

10. For a contemporary sampling of the new emphasis on color as the primary characteristic distinguishing among human groups, see Johann Friedrich Blumenbach, "On the Natural Variety of Mankind," in *The Anthropological Treatises of Johann Friedrich Blumenbach,* trans./ed. Thomas Bendyshe (1775; London: Longman et al, 1865), Oliver Goldsmith, *An History of the Earth and Animated Nature,* 8 vols. (London: J. Nourse, 1774) on humans in volume 2, and Samuel Stanhope Smith, *An Essay on the Causes of the Variety of Complexion and Figure in the Human Species* (Philadelphia: Robert Aitken, 1787).

11. In "Archibald Dalzel," Rice suggests that the Scottish critique—despite the economic involvement of Scots in slavery and the slave trade—circulated very widely because it appeared in the form of lecture notes to generations of students. A significant proportion of these notes were finally published and transmitted to an even wider readership (127).

12. When writers fully or partially abandon climate as an explanation for human appearance and national character, their writing becomes confused and even contradictory. For example, in William Robertson's *History of America,* 2 vols. (London: W. Stachan, 1777), he argues on the one hand that "Moral and political causes, as I have formerly observed, affect the disposition and character of individuals as well as nations, still more powerfully than the influence of climate" (1:417). On the other hand, he claims that "Even the law of climate, more universal than any that affects the human species, cannot be applied, in judging of their conduct, without many exceptions" (418).

13. See Londa Schiebinger, "The Anatomy of Difference: Race and Sex in Eighteenth Century Science," *Eighteenth Century Studies* 23.4 (1990): 387-405 and Thomas Laqueur, *Making Sex: Body and Gender from the Greeks to Foucault* (Cambridge: Harvard University Press, 1990).

14. See Seymour Drescher, *Capitalism and Antislavery: British Mobilization in Comparative Perspective* (New York: Oxford University Press, 1986), 19 and Jennings, "Joseph Woods, 'Merchant and Philosopher,'" 166-67.

15. Jennifer Breen, *Women Romantics, 1785-1832: Writing in Prose* (London: J.M. Dent, 1996), 46.

16. For proslavery commentary on fear as a significant force in the treatment of slaves, see Samuel Estwick, *Considerations on the Negroe Cause Commonly So Called* (London: J. Dodsley, 1772), 28 and Bryan Edwards, *An Historical Survey of the French Colony in the Island of St. Domingo* (London: John Stockdale, 1797), 11.

17. Andrew Burnaby, *Travels through the Middle Settlements in North America in the Years 1759 and 1760,* 3d ed. (London: T. Payne, 1798), 25.

18. W. Winterbotham, *An Historical, Geographical, Commercial, and Philosophical View of the American United States,* 4 vols. (London: J. Ridgway et al, 1795), 3:312.

19. David Brion Davis, *The Problem of Slavery in the Age of Revolution, 1770-1823* (Ithaca: Cornell University Press, 1975), 189-95 fully treats Bryan Edwards' writings.

20. Bryan Edwards' manuscript notes are at The John Carter Brown Library, Providence, RI. The manuscript notes refer to Edward Long, *History of Jamaica,* 3 vols. (London: R. Lowndes, 1774) by volume, page number, and line number. All citations refer to volume 2. Bryan Edwards also addressed the representation of slaves, black skin color, and Africans in Africa in his *St. Domingo,* 6-8.

21. See, for example, Long, *History of Jamaica,* 2:353-55.

22. Edwards, *St. Domingo,* 6-7. John Stewart, *An Account of Jamaica,* (Kingston, Jamica, c. 1809) argues similarly that the disposition to cunning and falsehood that he observed in

many Negoes is of "a superadded nature, nurtured in slavery, rather than one originally implanted in them; perhaps the European would be equally debased by this condition" (97).

23. R.A. Austen and W.D. Smith, "Images of Africa and British Slave Trade Abolition: The Transition to an Imperialist Ideology, 1787-1807, *African Historical Studies* 2.1 (1969), 76.

24. See John Gabriel Stedman, *The Narrative of Five Years Expedition Against the Revolted Negroes of Surinam*, ed. Richard Price and Sally Price (1796: Baltimore: John Hopkins University Press, 1988) and Sir William Young, *A Tour through the Several Islands of Barbados, St. Vincent, Antigua, Tobago, and Grenada, in the Years 1791-1792*, in Bryan Edwards, *The History, Civil and Commercial, of the British West Indies*, 5th ed., 5 vols. (London: T. Miller, 1819), 3: 244-54.

25. James Hakewill, *A Picturesque Tour of the Island of Jamaica* (London: Hurst and Robinson, 1825), 3.

26. Ronald Meek's *Social Science and the Ignoble Savage* (Cambridge: Cambridge University Press, 1976) traces the rise, development, and uses of four-stages theory in the eighteenth century, especially the way that native Americans were used as exemplary savages in philosophic discourse.

27. John Millar, *The Origin of the Disctinction of Ranks*, 3d ed., in *John Millar of Glasgow 1735-1801: His Life and Thought and his Contributions to Sociological Analysis*, ed. William Lehmann (1781; Cambridge: The University Press, 1960), 228.

28. Anand C. Chitnis, *The Scottish Enlightenment: A Social History* (London: Croom Helm, 1976), 95.

29. *The Royal Magazine: or Gentleman's Monthly Companion*, vol. 2 (June 1760), 341. This anonymous author, believed to be Goldsmith, provides an "intellectual map" of the world. Because of the extreme temperatures at either end of the globe, the people "are capable of being reduced into society, or any degree of politeness" (341). The severe climate precludes leisure for advancement and the conditions to produce luxuries. In contrast, the English crown Europe; their excellence derives from their mode of government: "They are distinguished from the rest of Europe by their superior accuracy in reasoning . . . [which] is only the consequence of their freedom." On England, see *The Royal Magazine* (September 1760), 140.

30. Brown, "Empire without Slaves," 298-301, for the salient omissions from Ramsay's original manuscript that turned his published document into an anti-slave trade text rather than one providing for the gradual emancipation of slaves.

31. William Dickson, *Letters on Slavery* (London: James Phillips, 1789), 61.

32. Richard Nisbet, *The Capacity of Negoes for Religions and Moral Improvement* (London: James Phillips, 1789), 8-9

33. [Professor Thorkelin?], *An Essay on the Slave Trade* (London: G. Nicol, 1788), 28.

34. Anthony Benezet, *A Caution and a Warning to Great Britain and Her Colonies* (Philadelphia: H. Miller, 1766), 25.

35. James Beattie, *Elements of Moral Science*, 2 vols. (Edinburgh: T. Cadell, 1790), 2:81.

36. J. Philmore, *Two Dialogues on the Man Trade* (London, 1760), 37-8; John Woolman, *Some Considerations on the Keeping of Negroes* (Philadelphia; James Chattin, 1754), 2; Benjamin Rush (a Pennsylvanian), *An Address to the Inhabitants of the British Settlements on the Slavery of Negroes in America* (Philadelphia: John Dunlap, 1773), 1.

37. James Albert Ukawsaw Gronniosaw, *A Narrative of the Most Remarkable Particulars in the Life . . .* (1772) in *Unchained Voices: An Anthology of Black Authors in the English-Speaking World of the Eighteenth Century*, ed. Vincent Carretta (Lexington: The University Press of Kentucky), 38, 49.

38. At the same time, these Anglo-African writers provide evidence that Britons treated Blacks often in the same way that they did Catholics, Jews, Scots, and the French, despite the fact that some Africans in Britain were unpaid laborers. On the treatment of the Scots in London public places, see James Boswell, *London Journal, 1762-1763,* ed. Frederick Pottle, New York: McGraw Hill Book Company, Inc., 1950; on Catholics, see Chris Haydon, *Anti-Catholicism in Eighteenth Century England* (Manchester: Manchester University Press, 1993); on the treatment of the French, see Paul Langford, *A Polite and Commercial People: England 1727-1783* (Oxford: Clarendon Press, 1989).

39. Many supporters of slavery believed that they had found scriptural support for slavery and for the Africans' plight in general. As decades of annual sermons preached before the Society for the Propagation of the Gospel in Foreign Parts attest, representatives of the Church of England routinely helped in this endeavor. Indeed, the proslavery writer James Tobin reminds his readers that the Society for the Propagation of the Gospel owns slaves on a sugar plantation in Barbados (and profits from them); thus, according to the practice of the Church of England, there was no contradiction between Christianity and slavery. See Tobin, *A Short Rejoinder,* 81. See Davis, *The Problem of Slavery in Western Culture,* 219-22, for an analysis of the Codrington bequest to the Society for the Propagation of the Gospel in Foreign Parts.

40. John Gabriel Stedman's *Narrative of a Five Years Expedition Asgainst the Revolted Negroes of Surinam* (1796) is a typical embodiment of the wild contradictions of this position.

41. On the checkered history of the Curse of Ham in Europe as an explanation for black skin and as a justification for slavery, see Winthrop Jordan, *White over Black: American Attitudes toward the Negros, 1550-1812* (1968; New York: W.W. Norton & Co., 1977), 17-20, 35-37, 54-56; Robin Blackburn, "The Old World Background to European Colonial Slavery," *William and Mary Quarterly* 54.1 (January 1997), 91, 94-95 and, in the same volume, Benjamin Braude, "The Sons of Noah and the Construction of Ethnic and Geographical Identities in the Medieval and Early Modern Periods," 104, 134-5. Davis, *The Problem of Slavery in the Age of Revolution,* chapter 11, especially 538, provides a useful summary of the role of the Bible in slavery debates.

42. Ramsay, *Treatment and Conversion,* 200.

43. Ibid., 172-3. Also see Stewart, *An Account of Jamaica,* who observes that Negroes are attached to Jamaica (but not to their masters) by their passions and affections, and they are also attached in the same way "to their colour, their fellow bondsmen" (52). In fact, Stewart believed the attachment so strong that he proposed importing East Indian sepoys and exporting slaves to reduce the political threat that arose from the bond uniting those in a similar condition.

44. Adam Smith, *The Theory of Moral Sentiments,* ed. D.D. Raphael and A.L. Macfie (Oxford: Clarendon Press, 1976), 376.

45. The comparable passage in the 1787 version occurs on 34. Thomas Clarkson, *An Essay on the Slavery and Commerce of the Human Species* worries over the original color of humans. Most of his contemporaries believed white was the original color; he decides that it must be dark olive, a medium color between black and white (120). He reasons that the descendants of Noah who now live in the region are of that complexion. See 120-132 for his extended meditation about the origin and meanings of skin color.

RACE, REDEMPTION, AND CAPTIVITY IN

A Narrative of the Lord's Wonderful Dealings with John Marrant, a Black

AND

Narrative of the Uncommon Sufferings and Surprizing Deliverance of Briton Hammon, a Negro Man

Karen A. Weyler

In *Heroic Women of the West* (1854), John Frost relates a lengthy anecdote about an episode of Indian attack and captivity that reveals the intermingled lives of blacks, whites, and Indians during the late eighteenth century. While moving westward in 1788 into Tennessee, the Brown party was attacked by Cherokee and Creek Indians, who killed several members of the family (including the father, James Brown), stole their livestock, and took captive the mother (Jane Brown), several children, and the family's slaves. The white members of the Brown household later escaped or were ransomed, but the slaves remained in captivity. Twenty-five years later, Colonel Joseph Brown, who had been a child when taken captive, served under General Andrew Jackson during the 1812–13 Creek War. During this time, he came across Cutty-a-toy, the Tuskeegee chief who had led the attack on his family. General Jackson supported Brown's subsequent claim against Cutty-a-toy for damages—damages not for the deaths of Brown's father and brothers, but rather for the value of the black slaves that had been stolen from his family. Cutty-a-toy disputed Brown's losses and his own role in these losses; but the physical evidence of the stolen slaves still living with Cutty-a-toy's tribe belied, in the eyes of a commission of American officers and Cherokee military allies, his denials. The case was ultimately resolved to the satisfaction of Brown and Cutty-a-toy when Brown allowed him to keep a young black man but reclaimed two black women and their children as slaves for his family. Brown's narrative ceases there. But what of the female slaves? What were their feelings upon being held in captivity alternately by whites, then by Indians, and then once again by whites? The female slaves' stories remain untold, likely because they were illiterate, but even more likely because the stories that they, as African Americans and slaves, might tell—of their personal losses, of the shock of cultural dislocation—simply were not important to Frost in comparison to the losses suffered by the Brown family. The black women and their children represent, at least in Frost's rendering of these events, little more than pieces of legal evidence for the Brown family and the military commission. Writing nearly 70 years after these events took place, Frost does not conceive of these black women as numbering among his "Heroic Women of the West." He cannot even conceive that these women might have stories of their own to tell, especially since he is framing this narrative in terms of property and capital lost, and these women did not even own themselves.[1] But what if the terms of value for this narrative emphasized cultural capital, rather than real property? What kind of cultural capital would a black captive in the eighteenth century need to manifest in order for his or her story to have value in the literary marketplace?

That blacks, as well as whites, were often either killed or taken captive during Indian attacks is well-documented, for many local histories and Indian captivity narratives, especially those from the eighteenth century and set in the southeastern part of what would later become the United States, note in passing the fate of slaves or black servants. Much less well-documented are the *experiences* of those blacks held captive among the Indians, with two early exceptions, Briton Hammon and John Marrant.[2] Both *Narrative of the Uncommon Sufferings, and Surprizing Deliverance of Briton Hammon, a Negro Man* and *A Narrative of the Lord's Wonderful Dealings with John Marrant, a Black* are hybrid texts, appealing to the large audience for captivity narratives but also drawing heavily upon the conventions of both the conversion narrative and the sea adventure story. What perhaps is most interesting about these narratives, however, is the way in which Hammon and Marrant are textually embodied—one might say disembodied—in order to give their narratives value in a literary market dominated by sentimental, dramatized captivity narratives. Hammon's and Marrant's status as devout Christians of good character lent credence and value to their experiences, which are in turn enhanced by narratives eschewing the secular, sentimental style of narratives produced by their contemporaries and instead returning to the piety of the first generation of captivity narratives, exemplified by a work such as *A True History of the Captivity and Restoration of Mrs. Mary Rowlandson* (1682). Hammon's and Marrant's narratives thus share a common religious underpinning, and both use Christianity to claim for their subjects portable identities as Christian Englishmen in the fluid transatlantic world of the late eighteenth century.[3] Their juxtaposition against their respective Spanish and Indian captors helps stabilize, for the purposes of the narrative, their English status. In Hammon's narrative, Christianity functions as a further means of access to an English identity, which serves to minimize his racial difference from his white readers. Marrant, although a free black, invokes the language of chattel slavery to explore the nature of sin. In his narrative, the Christian faith liberates believers from the bonds of sin and likewise is capable of uniting individuals of different races in Christian fellowship; at the same time, he uses Christianity to scourge slave owners who would deny their slaves this spiritual communion.

Vexed questions of authorship and authority surround Hammon's and Marrant's narratives, for the extent to which they exercised control over their respective narratives is unclear. While John Sekora has persuasively noted similarities between the style and language of Thomas Brown's and Hammon's narratives, it is unclear whether Hammon independently authored his own tale according to the house style of his printers or whether he had the assistance of an amanuensis-editor, as was commonly the case with captivity narratives.[4] By way of contrast, the title page of the 1785 first edition of Marrant's narrative describes it as a text "Taken down from his own relation, Arranged, Corrected, and Published By the Rev. Mr. ALDRIDGE." Aldridge's preface further explains that "I have always preserved Mr. Marrant's ideas, tho' I could not his language; no more alterations, however, have been made, than were thought necessary."[5] Despite these narrative interventions by his amanuensis-editor, Marrant was obviously a much more sophisticated participant in print culture than Hammon, whose text went into only one edition.[6] Marrant oversaw the publication of an expanded version of his narrative, the title page of which reads: "The Fourth Edition, Enlarged by Mr. MARRANT, and Printed (with Permission) for his Sole Benefit, WITH NOTES EXPLANATORY."[7] The degree to which Hammon's and Marrant's narratives represent the individual voice of their respective subjects is thus debatable, and they figure in a larger debate about the role of editors and amanuenses in the tradition of African and African-American autobiography. As William L. Andrews has argued about such texts, "From a literary standpoint . . . it is not the moral integrity of these editors that is at issue but the linguistic, structural, and tonal integrity of the narratives they produced." "It is the editor," he concludes, "who contextualizes the essential facts of the narrator's dictation and thus has much to do with how they will be received as institutional facts by their white readers."[8]

Further complicating any question of authentic voice is the issue of generic convention, for the well-established genre of the captivity narrative itself likely gave shape to the experiences of Hammon and Marrant. As Christopher Castiglia explains in *Bound and Determined*, captivity narratives frequently "blur the line between what a captive witnessed and what she added or invented for the sake of narrative convention or the projected prurience of her audience."[9] Both texts thus need to be situated within the field of captivity literature, a field in which the borrowing of tropes and images is widespread, and in which experiences tend to be fitted into common frameworks. The complicated circumstances surrounding the publication of these texts have thus understandably given rise to questions about the degree to which authentic, individual black voices emerge from them. It is important to note that these questions of authority are not reserved for the narratives of Marrant and Hammon. Similar considerations surround many captivity narratives, including those of near contemporaries of Hammon and Marrant such as Mary Kinnan and Frances Scott, although the authenticity of captivity texts detailing the experiences of women or non-whites are more frequently subject to such questioning than texts purporting to be authored by white men.

Regardless of who actually wrote the narratives that appeared under the names of Hammon and Marrant, they were presented and received as the narratives of black men, with probably little regard paid by readers to the exact mode of transmission. Given this circumstance, it seems useful to consider how the narratives of Hammon and Marrant were received as literary artifacts within the particular context of captivity literature. Most critics who discuss the narratives of Marrant and Hammon acknowledge their position in the history of Indian captivity narratives, as well as their debt to the conversion narrative and spiritual autobiography, and then move quickly either to establish the singularity of these particular narrators as "inaugurat[ing] the black tradition of English literature," as Henry Louis Gates, Jr. suggests of John Marrant,[10] or to establish these particular narratives as forerunners to the genre of the slave narrative, as John Sekora does of Briton Hammon (even though it is not unequivocally clear that Hammon was a slave).[11] Certainly these *are* singular narratives, narratives which helped establish a tradition of black writing in English as well as suggest how the slave narrative might have evolved from both the spiritual autobiography and the captivity narrative, as Sekora, Andrews, and Rafia Zafar, among others, have discussed.[12] In this essay, however, I wish to emphasize Hammon's and Marrant's position within the genre of eighteenth-century Anglophone captivity literature, the generic context in which they were likely read and understood at the time of their initial publication.

Although the literature of captivity continually evolved from the seventeenth century through the nineteenth century (and even into the late twentieth century, as Castiglia has argued),[13] most captivity narratives appearing in the second half of the eighteenth century share certain basic features. Virtually all captivity narratives emphasize the mental suffering brought about by loss of and separation from parents, spouses, and children, as well as the physical hardships of enduring strange food, temperature extremes, and lengthy marches. Although most captivity narratives do not regard Native Americans with outright sympathy—the point of most narratives being to expose cultures in conflict—only the most blatantly propagandistic narratives paint Native Americans as lacking any redeeming qualities.[14] Most narrators record occasional instances of kindness or generosity on the part of their captors, especially with regard to the sharing of limited provisions. In these respects, Hammon's and Marrant's narratives are typical of the genre.[15]

Despite these similarities in experiences, Hammon's and Marrant's narratives differ in interesting ways from other contemporaneous narratives. Neither tale relies upon the tone that dominates the narratives of the last half of the eighteenth century, a tone which might best be described as manifesting a sort of sensational sensibility, a trait which is most marked among female-authored captivity narratives, but which also appears in male-authored texts.[16] Popular narratives displaying this tone of sensational sensibility include those of Peter Williamson (1757), Frances Scott (1786), and Mary Kinnan (1795). In these texts, sensibility appears as a marker to distinguish the civilized nature of the white captives from the barbarity of their captors, a barbarity wrought not merely by cultural differences, but also by the darker skins of their Indian captors. Narrating their captivity experience seems to have been a cathartic experience that allowed them to assert their whiteness (especially important if they were to be adopted into the tribe of their captors). *A True Narrative of the Sufferings of Mary Kinnan*, for example, melodramatically evokes pathos; the narrative begins by asking readers: "Whilst the tear of sensibility so often flows at the unreal tale of woe, which glows under the pen of the poet and the novelists, shall our heart refuse to be melted with sorrow at the unaffected and unvarnished tale of a female, who has surmounted difficulties and dangers, which on a review appear romantic, even to herself."[17] Throughout this tale, Kinnan repeatedly emphasizes the effects of captivity on her body, which becomes not merely the site of intense physical suffering, but also the seat of sensibility: Her heaving bosom and glistening eyes illustrate her civilized sensibility, which is juxtaposed against the savage cruelty of the Indian squaws, who revel in the torment of their captives. Similar expressions of sensibility in other late–eighteenth-century captivity narratives largely supplant the religious sentiments of earlier texts more closely modeled after Rowlandson's, with this sensibility re-affirming the white writers' racial difference from their captors and refuting the possibility of transculturation.

Marrant's and Hammon's narratives, however, for the most part avoid both expressions of sensibility and the marking of racial difference. Indeed, as several critics have noted, the only real marker of race in Hammon's text appears in his title, which reads: "NARRATIVE of the UNCOMMON SUFFERINGS AND Surprizing DELIVERANCE OF BRITON HAMMON, A Negro Man."[18] Hammon likely had no control over this title, and the word "Negro" in the title may well have been used by the printers in order to market the narrative as an exotic curiosity. Rather than racial differences, the narratives of Hammon and Marrant instead mark their subjects' cultural difference from their captors, a difference rooted in their Christian faith and good character, as well as their presumed affinity with their similarly pious white readers. While Marrant acculturates to a certain degree by learning the language of his Cherokee captors and adopting their dress, he likewise transforms his captors by successfully proselytizing among them, a feat seldom accomplished by Protestant captives. In hearkening back to an earlier, more religiously-oriented model of captivity narrative, Hammon's and Marrant's narratives create for their subjects identities marked not by race, but by piety. This piety granted them narrative legitimacy as Englishmen and devout sojourners in the North American wilderness, a legitimacy apparently not granted to the female slaves in Frost's anecdote, for whom race and sex serve as the determining factors of their existence.

Narrative of the Uncommon Sufferings and Surprizing Deliverance of Briton Hammon, a Negro Man was first published in Boston in 1760. Hammon relates that with the permission of General Winslow, his "master," he left Marshfield for Jamaica, shipping out from Plymouth, Massachusetts in December 1747 (20). In

June of 1748, after several voyages, the ship ran afoul on a reef off the coast of Florida, which at that time was under the control of the Spanish and various Native American groups. Unwilling to discard any of his cargo of logwood, the Captain ordered some of his hands to go ashore in a small boat. During this journey, they saw several canoes, one of which bore an English flag. The appearance of this flag was revealed to be treachery, for sixty Indians aboard twenty canoes soon captured their boat and overpowered the men left on the sloop, killing all aboard. When the smaller boat returned to the sloop, the Indians then turned upon those men and shot them. Hammon jumped overboard, "chusing," as he says, "rather to be drowned, than to be kill'd by those barbarous and inhuman Savages" (21). The Indians eventually recaptured and beat Hammon, holding him for five weeks until he escaped from their captivity into a second captivity by the Spanish in Cuba.

Hammon generically labels his first set of captors "Indians," never distinguishing them by tribe. Indeed, in this narrative, "Indians," "Savages," and "Devils" are interchangeable terms, for "Indian" is a category marked not so much by race and skin color as by the absence of Christian faith. Descriptions of skin color, often used in captivity narratives in a derogatory fashion (e.g. in racial epithets such as "tawny devils" to describe Native Americans) are absent from his narrative. In this respect, Hammon's narrative reflects contemporary theories of racial differences, which were in flux in the transatlantic world throughout the eighteenth century. Thomas Jefferson's infamous comments in *Notes on the State of Virginia* (1785) on the racial inferiority of Africans notwithstanding, these race theories generally propagated a less rigid sense of racial differences than would operate in the nineteenth-century United States under the system of slavery, often emphasizing the cultural differences between people resulting from differing environments, climates, levels of civilization, and so forth.[19] Thus, Hammon's Indians are "barbarous" and "inhuman," yet these labels are stripped of specific racial characteristics. It is not that skin color means nothing to Hammon. Indeed, he is sensitive to distinctions in national origin, rank, and color, carefully identifying his fellow sailors in the following fashion: "*Reuben Young* of *Cape-Cod*, Mate; *Joseph Little* and *Lemuel Doty* of *Plymouth*," and "*Moses Newmock*, Molatto" (21). We may reasonably assume that the first three sailors are white, since he notes race only in the case of "*Moses Newmock*, Molatto." Yet in discussing the Indians, Hammon evacuates racial content from his construction of difference for obvious reasons: to mark the Indians as essentially different because of race, rather than culture, would be to expose Hammon's own racial difference from his presumed audience of white English colonials. Instead, Hammon's narrative constructs him as a Christian Englishman, albeit black, who owes his "preservation" and his return to his friends to "the kind Providence of a good GOD" (20). As Ira Berlin notes in *Many Thousands Gone: The First Two Centuries of Slavery in North America*, professing Christianity was one means for creolized slaves, as well as for free blacks, to incorporate themselves into the English-speaking community and to demonstrate their belonging to the larger Atlantic world.[20] Christianity thus erases, or at least minimizes, racial difference between Hammon and his readers, as his narrative shrewdly negotiates racial issues: The title allows it to be marketed as a curiosity, the story of a black man, and at the same time the body of the narrative glosses over the element of Hammon's racial difference from his white audience and establishes his authority based on his faith.

Hammon's escape from the Indians and decade-long stay among the Spanish in Cuba further highlight his identity as a Christian Englishman. After five weeks in captivity among the Indians, Hammon escaped to Cuba with the aid of another ship's captain. Despite the demands of Hammon's captors, the Governor of Cuba refused to return him to captivity, paying a ten dollar ransom for Hammon and providing accommodations for him. One might assume that was the end of Hammon's tale, but his narrative of captivity gains an added dimension when the Spanish in turn hold him captive after a Spanish press gang impressed him. Patriotically refusing to serve on a Spanish ship, Hammon was jailed for four years and seven months. An American ship's captain aided Hammon, and he once again went to live with the Governor, who would not allow him to leave Havana, although Hammon was able to negotiate employment for himself. Hammon unsuccessfully attempted escape from Havana several times aboard British ships; finally an English ship captain took him up along with several others who were trying to escape. When accosted by the Spanish military, this captain refused to surrender Hammon and the others, claiming that he would never give up any "*Englishman* under *English* Colours" (23). Although Hammon humbly describes himself as "low" in his "capacities and condition," the English visitors to Havana recognize Hammon as one of their own—an Anglo-American Christian in the transatlantic world (20).

After a number of other voyages, which included voluntary service on British navy ships, Hammon found himself on the same ship as General Winslow, whom he calls "*my good Master*" (24). After their joyful reunion following a separation of nearly thirteen years, both sailed for New England, where Hammon's remarkable story was published, a testament, he explains, to the "Divine Goodness" at work in his own life (24). His is not the conventional eighteenth-century tale of captivity, encompassing as it does multiple captivities among both the Indians and Spanish, with the added spice of sea adventure. Yet even though only a small portion of his narrative discusses his Indian captivity, that is the genre in which his experiences were cast. For as Sekora explains, in the eighteenth century, "If the story of a black man or woman was to be told at all, that story would necessarily be shaped into a popular form. No form was more popular than the captivity [narrative], and no figure loomed larger in the colonial imagination than the Native American."[21] By virtue of his juxtaposition against both the un-Christian Indians and the despotic Spanish empire, Hammon's tale of captivity creates a literary identity that grants him the efficacy of the Christian Englishman, an identity that would overshadow his racial identity and make his story one that could be told in that time.

Although only one edition of Briton Hammon's narrative appeared prior to the twentieth century, John Marrant's tale was extraordinarily popular, appearing in at least 44 printings (some appear to be multiple printings of the same edition) between 1785 and 1850, in England, Ireland, Wales, Nova Scotia, and Connecticut.[22] Originally published in London, Marrant's narrative was guaranteed a broader circulation than was Hammon's, particularly given its connection to the Reverend William Aldridge, a Methodist clergyman closely linked to the Countess of Huntingdon, who became Marrant's nominal patron. Marrant's text also appealed to audiences in three important ways. First, it includes considerable information about his experiences as a captive among the Cherokee, which likely would have appealed to readers of other captivity narratives. Moreover, the fourth edition (and subsequent editions based on it) provides insight into black/white relationships in the southern part of the United States, particularly important given the on-going early abolition work in Britain at that time. Finally, whereas Hammon's text operates under the prima facie claim of his faith, Marrant's text powerfully details his conversion experience. His own marveling at the workings of God's providence in each of these arenas would have made his narrative enormously appealing for an evangelical audience. The multiple uses, then, to which Marrant's narrative could be put likely increased its popularity.

While Hammon's narrative alternatively capitalizes on his status as a black man (in the title) and then minimizes his race (in the body of the narrative), Marrant's text more consistently invokes race and images of slavery. Even though Marrant was a free man, he invokes the powerful language of chattel slavery to depict his early relationship to sin. The first part of Marrant's narrative describes his early life and conversion experience. Born free in New York in 1755, Marrant grew up in Florida, Georgia, and South Carolina with no particular religious calling. Apprenticed to a music master by his own request, Marrant soon learned to play the violin and the French horn. By the age of thirteen, his skill enabled him to support himself by playing at balls and dances. His freedom and economic success led to his moral downfall, making him a "slave" to sin. He describes himself as "devoted to pleasure, and drinking in iniquity like water; a slave to every vice suited to my nature and years" (112).

Marrant's conversion to evangelical Christianity is sudden and dramatic. Dared by a mischief-making friend, Marrant prepares to blow the French horn in order to disrupt a church service led by George Whitefield, the British Methodist evangelist. Instead, Marrant feels himself struck to the ground, where he "lay both speechless and senseless near half an hour" (113). Whitefield's words, "PREPARE TO MEET THY GOD, O ISRAEL" (113) seem to have been spoken directly to Marrant; later Whitefield tells him that "JESUS CHRIST HAS GOT THEE AT LAST" (113). Unable to walk, Marrant is carried to his sister's house, where he lay in distress for three days, drinking only a little water. Only after a minister, directed by Whitefield, visits Marrant does he begin to recover, and only then after three sessions of prayer, prayer which according to Marrant "set my soul at perfect liberty," freeing him from slavery to sin (114). Although a free man, Marrant deliberately invokes the language of slavery as familiar to his readers. Chattel slavery might constrain the body, but sin damns one to eternal slavery; conversely, prayer and piety free his soul for eternal liberty.

Liberty from sin, however, turns out to be a more complicated endeavor than Marrant first suspects, for his friends and family members revile and ridicule his evangelical faith. Marrant eventually leaves his family at the age of fourteen to wander in the South Carolina wilderness, armed only with a Bible and one of Isaac Watts's hymnbooks. Marrant spends considerable time detailing his physical travail: The presence of wolves and bears drives him to sleep in trees, and he has only the word of God and "deer-grass" (115) to nourish him and water muddied by wild pigs to drink (116). Sorely tested, Marrant makes clear analogies between his rather incredible sojourn in the wilderness and those of John the Baptist and Jesus. Marrant explains that he remains unscathed during his wandering, offering "God thanks for my escape, who had tamed the wild beasts of the forest and made them friendly to me" (116). When a Cherokee hunter known to his family finds him fifty-five miles into the wilderness, Marrant weeps, fearing neither captivity nor death, but rather the threat of being taken home to his family and once again falling captive to sin. The hunter refuses to leave Marrant to wander alone, so Marrant agrees to hunt with him for several months.

At the end of hunting season, the Indian hunter takes Marrant to a large Cherokee town. Only then, separated from his companion, is Marrant taken into physical captivity and ordered put to death for trespassing on Cherokee lands. Rather than being frightened by the prospect of death, Marrant welcomes it, for he sees it as an end to his bodily and spiritual travails and as the beginning of his true union with Christ. Marrant's praying and constant references to Jesus perplex his Cherokee captors, for they cannot conceive why he speaks to someone whom he insists is present but whom they themselves cannot see. Marrant's passionate prayers, which at one point he feels divinely inspired to deliver in the Cherokee language, bring about the conversion of his would-be executioner, who refuses to put him to death until he has met with the Cherokee King.

Marrant's subsequent interactions with the King and his daughter highlight his cultural differences from the Indians and allow him to emphasize to his white readers the power of his Christian faith. Upon meeting with the King and his daughter, Marrant sees that the King's daughter is powerfully moved by his faith, repeatedly taking up his Bible and kissing it. She explains, however, "with much sorrow, [that] the book would not speak to her" (119).[23] The Bible in this episode functions both as a symbol of cultural power—the power of the English Protestant God, whom only Marrant has the skill to understand—as well as a sign of colonial difference between Marrant and his captors.[24] This colonial difference and the power inherent in it matter far more than racial difference in this portion of Marrant's narrative. Subsequently, Marrant claims, his prayers awaken the King's daughter to a sense of her sin, inducing a physical collapse. Threatened with imminent death if he can not make the King's daughter well again, he explains, "I was not afraid, but the Lord tried my faith sharply" (120). Like Mary Rowlandson, Marrant interprets his survival as a test of his faith. Only after his prayers bring about the King's daughter's rejuvenation and spiritual conversion, as well as that of her father, is Marrant's life spared and is he free to proselytize among the Cherokee and neigh-

boring tribes. Throughout his witnessing among the Cherokee, Marrant continues to use the language of captivity and slavery to describe the state of the sinner.
Conversion to Christian faith "set[s] at liberty" (120) even those who do not recognize their own enthrallment, with the newfound spiritual liberty of the King
and his daughter bringing about the physical liberty of Marrant from Indian captivity. Marrant never attributes the conversion of the Cherokee to his own actions;
rather, as he carefully points out, it is God, working through him, who converts the
Cherokee, just as it is God, working through the Cherokee, who saves Marrant.

One of the most interesting aspects of Marrant's text is his willingness to
acculturate to the Cherokee way of life. The typical eighteenth-century captivity
narrative emphasizes its white subject's resistance to acculturation—eating Indian
food only when faced with starvation and adopting Indian dress only when his or
her own clothes are no longer wearable. Further, most captives remain focused on
the ultimate goal of redemption to white society. Marrant, not white and alienated
from his family, has no such longings for earthly redemption. Indeed, he is already
redeemed in the sense of the word that matters most, for he is sure not only of his
own salvation but also that of some of his Cherokee captors. After being freed by
the Cherokee king, Marrant chooses to live among them for several months, learning their language "in the highest stile" and adopting "the habit of the country"
(120). Marrant later describes his dress in this manner: "My dress was purely in
the Indian stile; the skins of wild beasts composed my garments; my head was set
out in the savage manner, with a long pendant down my back, a sash round my
middle, without breeches, and a tomohawk by my side" (121). Marrant is able to
live contentedly among the Cherokee because he sees them not as a racial other,
but rather as a community of potential converts. As Michelle Burnham explains,
"Marrant's narrative never demonizes the Indians; in fact, the Cherokee's conversion
unites them with their captive-turned-minister in a Christian community where
violence becomes unthinkable and utterly obviates the imagination of escape."[25]

When Marrant feels moved to return to his family and country after being
absent for nearly two years, his friends and family (with the exception of his youngest
sister) fail to recognize him, for he has undergone a dramatic testing, both physically and spiritually.[26] While he claims to have greatly affected the Cherokee among
whom he lived, they also powerfully affected him, for crossing "over the fence,"
the image he creates for us of the dividing line between civilization and wilderness,
enables him to explore the power of his faith (115). He can truly speak of himself
as being re-born when he returns to his family, for his spiritual rebirth has enabled
him to effect conversions among those he meets. While Marrant relies on biblical
typology to reinforce his reader's understanding of his spiritual rebirth, his use of
the New Testament language of resurrection differentiates his text from Mary
Rowlandson's, as Benilde Montgomery has noted, a difference which reflects
Marrant's historical position in eighteenth-century evangelical culture.[27] Only after his youngest sister recognizes him does he admit his identity to his grieving
family, which has long assumed him dead. Marrant concludes, "Thus the dead was
brought to life again; thus the lost was found" (122). While Marrant is here allud-

ing both to Lazarus and the parables of the lost sheep and the prodigal son, he himself was only truly lost when he lived among his family. By leaving them, he found himself and gained the spiritual confidence to withstand their disbelief.

Although Marrant initially found his Native American captors to be cruel and feared the torture they threatened, his narrative demonstrates no sense of racial difference between himself and the Cherokee. Once converted, they become his brothers and sisters in Christ, for true Christianity, according to his narrative, supersedes race, rendering it unimportant. Only after Marrant returns to his family does race truly draw his attention. While working with his brother as a carpenter on a plantation seventy miles from Charleston, Marrant begins to pray with the slaves on the plantation, an act which prompts the slaves' owners to beat them. Marrant describes the scene this way: "Men, women, and children were strip'd naked and tied, their feet to a stake, their hands to the arm of a tree, and so savagely flogg'd that the blood ran from their backs and sides to the floor" (123). Whereas Hammon freely labeled his Indian captors "savages," Marrant reserves derivations of the word "savage" to describe the white, ostensibly Christian slave owners, who fear that conversion to Christianity will ruin their slaves as workers. Although one slave owner eventually becomes more amenable to allowing his slaves to worship, even attending their services at times, Marrant represents the Indians not only as less savage than the white slave owners, but indeed as more amenable to the word of God.

Marrant's narrative concludes with a short relation of his life as a sailor in the Royal Navy, an interlude which eventually took him to London, where the publication of his narrative was set into motion. Preparing to return to North America to preach as an ordained minister, Marrant offers a prayer for his continued ministry:

> I have now only to intreat the earnest prayers of all my kind Christian friends, that I may be carried safe there; kept humble, made faithful, and successful; that strangers may hear of and run to Christ; that Indian tribes may stretch out their hands to God; that the black nations may be made white in the blood of the Lamb; that vast multitudes, of hard tongues, and of a strange speech, may learn the language of Canaan, and sing the song of Moses, and of the Lamb; and, anticipating the glorious prospect, may we all with fervent hearts, and willing tongues, sing Hallelujah; the kingdoms of the world are become the kingdoms of our God, and of his Christ. Amen and Amen.

Marrant's prayer invokes not a color- or race-free world, but a world where Christianity will render race a null category.

The narratives of both Hammon and Marrant leave readers with indelible impressions of their mobility and of the sense of displacement which likely both ensued from and brought about this mobility. Both perpetual wanderers, with Hammon sailing among New England, Florida, Cuba, and England, and Marrant moving from colony to colony as a child, sailing in the Atlantic as a young man, and making multiple moves among England, Nova Scotia, and Boston as an adult. Their perpetual wandering suggests their cultural displacement, their sense of never quite belonging to one place or another, much as the female slaves of Frost's narrative must have felt. In this context, Hammon's joy at reuniting with General Winslow makes more sense; after years living first as a Christian among Indians and then as a Protestant Englishman among Spanish Catholics, Hammon was returning to his "own Native Land," the place which seemed most like home, regardless of the nature of his subsequent servitude (24). Neither Hammon nor Marrant seems to have possessed much in the way of material goods, but what they did possess was cultural capital in the guise of their identities as pious Christians, a kind of capital eminently portable and suitable to their peripatetic lifestyles. Their self-chosen Protestant English identities, communicated via the popular captivity genre, helped open up a space for them to enter into print culture in the late eighteenth century, while their narratives allowed readers to witness their faith and their profound belief in the workings of Providence in their lives.

NOTES

1. John Frost, "Captivity of Jane Brown and Her Family," in *Heroic Women of the West: Comprising Thrilling Examples of Courage, Fortitude, Devotedness, and Self-Sacrifice Among the Pioneer Mothers of the Western Country* (Philadelphia: A. Hart, 1854), 122–63.

2. Here I want to distinguish between those blacks who fled to freedom among Indian tribes and those taken captive. Further, Patrick Riordan points out that slavery even within Indian tribes differed from the Anglo-American hereditary chattel slavery; among the Cherokees, for instance, captives or slaves "might become free by adoption, marriage, ransom, or exchange" (33). There is a wealth of information about blacks living free among Indian tribes, especially the Seminoles; see, for example: Kenneth W. Porter, *The Black Seminoles: History of a Freedom-Seeking People* (Rev. and ed. Alcione M. Amos and Thomas P. Senter. Gainesville: Univ. of Florida Press, 1996); Kevin Mulroy, *Freedom on the Border: The Seminole Maroons in Florida, the Indian Territory, Coahuila, and Texas* (Lubbock: Texas Tech Univ. Press, 1993); and Riordan, "Finding Freedom in Florida: Native Peoples, African Americans, and Colonists, 1670–1816," *Florida Historical Quarterly* 75.1 (1996): 24–43.

3. By "fluid transatlantic world," I mean to suggest the increasing presence, over the course of the eighteenth century, of social, economic, and geographic mobility, especially in British North America. Useful for discussion of this topic is James A. Henretta, *The Evolution of American Society, 1700–1815* (Lexington: Heath, 1973). This mobility was not limited to whites. Ira Berlin demonstrates that some Atlantic creoles, a term which he uses "to refer to those of African descent but connected to the larger Atlantic World" (381), at different times and places likewise shared in this social, economic, and geographic mobility. See Berlin, *Many Thousands Gone: The First Two Centuries of Slavery in North America* (Cambridge and London: The Belknap Press of Harvard Univ. Press, 1998), *passim*.

4. Sekora notes certain similarities between the typography and language of *A Plain Narrative of the Uncommon Sufferings and Remarkable Deliverance of Thomas Brown* (1760) and *Narrative of the Uncommon Sufferings and Surprizing Deliverance of Briton Hammon* (1760), commonalties which make sense given the cooperative relationship between their respective Boston printers, Fowle and Draper and Green and Russell. Sekora also explores the combination of events and situations that enabled the captivity of a black man to be-

come noteworthy, at a time in Boston during which able-bodied men and loyal servants were particularly important to the local economy. See Sekora, "Red, White, and Black: Indian Captivities, Colonial Printers, and the Early African-American Narrative," *A Mixed Race: Ethnicity in Early America* (Ed. Frank Shuffelton. New York: Oxford Univ. Press, 1993), 92–104.

For a discussion of the general problems of determining authorship with regard to captivity narratives, see Kathryn Zabelle Derounian-Stodola and James Arthur Levernier, *The Indian Captivity Narrative, 1550–1900* (New York: Twayne, 1993), 10–15.

5. Marrant, *A Narrative of the Lord's Wonderful Dealings with John Marrant, a Black.* 4th edition, enlarged (London: 1785. Rptd. in *Unchained Voices: An Anthology of Black Authors in the English-Speaking World of the Eighteenth Century.* Ed. Vincent Carretta. Lexington: Univ. of Kentucky Press, 1996), 111. All subsequent references are to this edition and will be cited parenthetically in the text.

6. Several other works are credited to Marrant: *A Sermon Preached on the 24th Day of June 1789, being the Festival of St. John the Baptist, at the Request of the Right Worshipful the Grand Master Prince Hall, and the Rest of the Brethren of the African Lodge of the Honorable Society of Free and Accepted Masons in Boston* (Boston, 1789) and *A Journal of the Rev. John Marrant, from August the 18th, 1785 to the 16th of March 1790. To which are Added, Two Sermons: One Preached on Ragged Island on Sabbath Day, the 27th Day of October 1787; the Other at Boston, in New England, on Thursday, the 24th of June, 1787* (London, 1790). While Marrant undeniably delivered *A Sermon Preached on the 24th Day of June 1789*, Adam Potkay and Sandra Burr question whether Marrant independently authored this text. They suggest that Prince Hall may, at the least, have edited this work. See Potkay and Burr, *Black Atlantic Writers of the Eighteenth Century: Living the New Exodus in England and the Americas* (New York: St. Martin's Press, 1995), 73.

7. This expanded text is the version most often cited by scholars. In addition to the Carretta edition, a version of this edition is reprinted in Potkay and Burr's *Black Atlantic Writers of the Eighteenth Century.*

8. William L. Andrews, *To Tell a Free Story: The First Century of Afro-American Autobiography, 1760–1865* (Urbana and Chicago: Univ. of Illinois Press, 1986), 20. For further discussion of the role of editors, see 19–22 and 33–37.

9. Christopher Castiglia, *Bound and Determined: Captivity, Culture-Crossing, and White Womanhood from Mary Rowlandson to Patty Hearst* (Chicago and London: Univ. of Chicago Press, 1996), 107. As Derounian-Stodola and Levernier have noted, most English-speaking persons of the eighteenth century who encountered Native Americans generally did so encumbered by preconceived notions of them, often propagated by captivity narratives; such stereotypes then inflect future narratives of captivity. See Derounian-Stodola and Levernier, 51–73.

10. Henry Louis Gates, Jr., *The Signifying Monkey: A Theory of Afro-American Literary Criticism* (New York: Oxford Univ. Press, 1988), 145.

11. Scholarly opinion is divided as to Hammon's status. Obviously he was a servant, but whether he was slave or free is not clear. The internal evidence through which to determine his status is slight. The title of Hammon's work identifies him as "A Negro Man,— Servant to GENERAL WINSLOW." At the beginning of the narrative, Hammon identifies Winslow as his "Master" and labels his own status as "low"; at its conclusion he once again calls Winslow "My good Master." John Sekora labels Hammon's text the earliest slave narrative. He is not alone in this assumption, for Marion Wilson Starling, William L. Andrews, and Michelle Burnham also discuss this text as a slave narrative. Frances Smith Foster also seems inclined to believe that Hammon was a slave, commenting that his emphasis on his freedom to negotiate his employment likely signals the unusual nature of these activities. She goes on to note, however, that "Marrant's and Hammon's narratives are stories of a

different sort of bondage and freedom from that dealt with in the genre identified as slave narratives. Nonetheless, they may be considered precursors to the slave narrative." Vincent Carretta, on the other hand, suggests that Hammon may have used "master" merely to mean employer, rather than owner, when in his title page he labels General John Winslow his master. John Marrant, who we know was a free man and not a slave, uses "master" in this fashion to designate the musician to whom he was bound as an apprentice (112) as well as a carpenter who employed him but to whom he was not bound (112). While Hammon's status cannot be proven conclusively one way or another based solely on the text, it does seem odd that Hammon, after thirteen years of independently managing his affairs, would express such joy and gratitude at being reunited with an owner. See Sekora, 92; Starling, "The Slave Narrative: Its Place in American Literary History." Ph.D. diss. New York University (1946), 70–71; Andrews, 40; Burnham, *Captivity and Sentiment: Cultural Exchange in American Literature, 1682–1861* (Hanover and London: Univ. Press of New England, 1997), 173; Foster, *Witnessing Slavery: The Development of Ante-bellum Slave Narratives* (1979. 2nd. ed. Madison: Univ. of Wisconsin Press, 1994), 40, 42; and, Carretta, 24.

12. See Sekora, especially 96–97 and 102–03. As Sekora argues, "Briton Hammon's presence as a subject for a captivity for a time expands the scope of the captivity tale, but at the same time it creates the terms of possibility for the slave narrative.... The earlier tale of Indian captivity is easily turned to the later story of southern bondage. One escape teaches another" (103). See also Andrews, 7–12 and Zafar, *We Wear the Mask: African Americans Write American Literature, 1760–1870* (New York: Columbia Univ. Press, 1997), 67–69.

13. See Castiglia, 87–105 and 190–93.

14. For examples of propaganda designed to stir up anti-Indian sentiment, see *Captivity and Sufferings of Mrs. Mason, with an Account of the Massacre of Her Youngest Child* (c. 1836) and *An Affecting Narrative of the Captivity of Mrs. Mary Smith* (Providence: L. Scott, 1815), both of which appear to be faked atrocity stories.

15. Both Rafia Zafar and Benilde Montgomery have noted the similarities in experience and language between John Marrant's narrative and that of Mary Rowlandson, which was published in 1682, more than a century before Marrant's text. See Zafar, 57–58 and Montgomery, "Recapturing John Marrant," *A Mixed Race: Ethnicity in Early America* (Ed. Frank Shuffelton. New York: Oxford Univ. Press, 1993), 106–12.

16. Montgomery notes the difference in tone between Marrant's narrative and that of Mary Kinnan, arguing that "Although published a hundred years after the Rowlandson narrative, Marrant's narrative more closely adheres to her spirit and design than it does to those of Kinnan, his contemporary." He explains this disparity in this way: "Mary Kinnan's self-proclaimed 'romantic' adventure claims no significance beyond the psychological.... Unlike Kinnan, Marrant does not understand himself as the victim of frivolous circumstance but rather as an active participant in the evolution of a providential design." See Montgomery, 106, 107.

17. Shepard Kollock, *A True Narrative of the Sufferings of Mary Kinnan* (1795. *Women's Indian Captivity Narratives*. Ed. Kathryn Zabelle Derounian-Stodola. New York: Penguin, 1998), 109.

18. Hammon, *Narrative of the Uncommon Sufferings, and Surprizing Deliverance of Briton Hammon, a Negro Man* (Boston: 1760. Rptd. in *Unchained Voices: An Anthology of Black Authors in the English-Speaking World of the Eighteenth Century*. Ed. Vincent Carretta. Lexington: Univ. of Kentucky Press, 1996), 20. All subsequent references are to this edition and will be cited parenthetically in the text.

19. For an overview of evolving theories of race in the seventeenth and eighteenth centuries, see Thomas F. Gossett, *Race: The History of an Idea in America* (1963. New York: Oxford, 1997), 3–53 and Nicholas Hudson, "From 'Nation' to 'Race': The Origin of Racial

Classification in Eighteenth-Century Thought," *Eighteenth-Century Studies* 29.3 (1996): 247–264. Hudson succinctly summarizes these evolving racial theories, arguing that, influenced by the slave trade and by imperialism, "Over the period of a century, 'race' gradually mutated from its original sense of a people or single nation, linked by origin, to its later sense of a biological subdivision of the human species. And 'tribe' was lifted from its originally specialized meaning in the Bible to replace 'nation' in the descriptions of 'savage' peoples. These changes … derived in part from the rise of a new science of human taxonomy" (258).

20. See Berlin, 42, 75–76, and 138–40.

21. Sekora, 94.

22. See Potkay and Burr, 70–73. Richard VanDerBeets also notes an 1820 Middletown, Connecticut, edition in *Held Captive by Indians: Selected Narratives 1642–1836* (Knoxville: Univ. of Tennessee Press, 1973), 177. See also Dorothy B. Porter, "Early American Negro Writings: A Bibliographical Study," *Papers of the Bibliographical Society of America* 39 (1945): 192–268.

23. Marrant's entire captivity experience illustrates the multiple genres in which his text operates. Henry Louis Gates, Jr. makes much of the episode of the talking book, for this trope also appears in the narratives of James Albert Ukawsaw Gronniosaw, Olaudah Equiano, Ottobah Cugoano, and John Jea. While Gates acknowledges the pull of Marrant's conversion tale, he argues that it is "his reworking of Gronniosaw's trope of the Talking Book" which lends Marrant's text its historical significance in the black literary tradition, "because he was the tradition's first revisionist. My idea of tradition, in part, turns upon this definition of texts read by an author and then Signified upon in some formal way, as an implicit commentary on grounding and on satisfactory modes of representation—in this instance, a mode of representation of the black pious pilgrim who descends into a chaotic wilderness of sin, is captured, suffers through several rather unbelievable trials of faith, then emerges whole and cleansed and devout" (145).

The captivity genre operates under a similar principle of repetition of structural principles, language, images, and tropes. Certainly Marrant's narrative, while playing a double role as a conversion narrative and a captivity narrative, participates in this circulation of tropes. The torture to which the Cherokees initially sentence him—having a basket of splinters soaked in turpentine driven into his body and then set alight—appears repeatedly in narratives published after Marrant's, among them: "Affecting History of the Dreadful Distresses of Frederic Manheim's Family," which purports to have occurred in 1779, but was not actually published until 1793, when it gave its name to the so-called "Manheim Anthology"; *An Affecting Narrative of Mrs. Mary Smith* (1815); and, Eunice Barber's *Narrative of the Tragical Death of Mr. Darius Barber and His Seven Children* (1818). Both "Distresses" and *An Affecting Narrative* are likely faked texts, as no one has ever verified even the existence of the Manheim family or Mrs. Mary Smith. Regardless of whether Marrant originated this trope, his text certainly helped to popularize and increase the circulation of this image of Indian torture of the Anglo-American.

24. Homi K. Bhabha discusses extensively the varied meanings of English books among colonialists. See Bhabha, *The Location of Culture* (London and New York: Routledge, 1994), 102–22.

25. Burnham, 125.

26. Before Marrant returns home, he proselytizes among other Indian nations, eventually visiting the Creek, Chickasaw, and Choctaw tribes, although he does not see that he has any "saving" effect upon them (120–21).

27. Montgomery, 108.

Being a Man

Olaudah Equiano and Ignatius Sancho

Felicity A. Nussbaum

I offer here the history of neither a saint, a hero, nor a tyrant.
—Olaudah Equiano

Aphra Behn's description of Oroonoko's partially classical, partially African features has become quite familiar to students of Restoration and eighteenth-century England. The royal slave's ideal physique, Roman nose, piercing eyes, and finely shaped mouth are reminiscent of the most elegant Greek and Roman statues, except for the blight of his color: "His face was not of that brown, rusty black which most of that nation are, but a perfect ebony, or polished jet.... The whole proportion and air of his face was so noble, and exactly formed, that, *bating his colour*, there could be nothing in nature more beautiful, agreeable and handsome."[1] In addition, Oroonoko's greatness of soul, his civility and refinement, suggest that his ability to be a wise ruler equaled that of any European prince. These elements of physical and mental perfection testify to his humanity and to his manliness, both of which are at issue in a century which drew frequent and facile parallels between Africans and pets such as parrots, monkeys, and lapdogs, and when the black male bodies most often known to Europeans were either commodities to own or showpieces to exhibit.

Another well-known fictional man of color in the early eighteenth century, Robinson Crusoe's Friday, similarly embodies perfect symmetry and conveys "something very manly in his Face." His savagery is mitigated by "the Sweetness and Softness of an *European* in his Countenance too, especially when he smil'd."[2] Like Oroonoko, his features are distinguished from most blacks or negroes since his color is nearly indescribable—"not quite black, but very tawny"—and his well-shaped nose is small above thin lips. Again the combination of civility and barbarism yokes a European gentleness with an ostensibly generic manliness that seems untethered to geography, and yet tenuously connected to a distinctive coloring. European manliness appears to be strangely incongruous when it derives from a black or tawny body. It is difficult to conceive of a coherent black masculinity in the face of these popular representations, as fractured as they are between the ugly and the perfectly formed, the savage and the princely, the soft and the manly. These fictional characters, and the real men who lived in their shadows, combine the highest status with the lowest rung on the chain of being, noble and slave, refined and fierce, tangled together in emblematic figurations which both replicate our understandings of British manhood in the period and threaten to expose the myths of a white masculinity uncertain of its nationalist moorings and seeking to justify its imperial violence.

It may seem somewhat odd to analyze issues of masculinity in Olaudah Equiano's *Interesting Narrative* (1789) and Ignatius Sancho's *Letters* (1782) before abolition. Both works were written, one might argue, when the question of the humanity of Africans superseded all other elements worthy of consideration, including gender and sexuality. Equiano (1745?-1797), Sancho (1729–1780), and the other thousands of black men living in London, Bristol, and Liverpool in the later eighteenth century struggled to establish their humanity regardless of social class against the overt and virulent racism of slavery's defenders such as Edward Long, author of *The History of Jamaica* (1774) and Philip Thicknesse in *A Year's Journey Through France, and Part of Spain* (1778) who did not believe that blacks are "in all respects human creatures" but are instead "men of a lower order."[3] Free blackmen in London and elsewhere faced a press teeming with racial hatreds in the midst of abolition debates. One treatise claimed that "the negro-race seems to be the farthest removed from the line of true cultivation of any of the human species; their defect of form and complexion being, I imagine, as strong an obstacle to their acquiring true taste (the product of mental cultivation) as any natural defect they may have in their intellectual faculties."[4] Unlike the fictional Oroonoko or the actual African princes who visited England, Equiano and Sancho could not easily claim a status sufficiently elevated to allow them to be treated deferentially in spite of their color and their geographical origins. A published review of Equiano's popular *Narrative* in *The Gentleman's Magazine* grudgingly acknowledges that he, unlike most men of his rank, deserved to be "on a par with the general mass of men in the *subordinate stations of civilized society,* and so prove[s] that there is no general rule without an exception."[5] Yet the poem on the title page of *The Royal African: Or, Memoirs of the Young Prince of Annamaboe* testifies to the equality of all mankind and invokes Othello, Oroonoko, and Juba as justification for the belief that the visiting dignitary of the title, the black prince, demonstrates the universal truth that "human Nature is the same in all Countries, and under all Complexions."[6] In short, public consensus concerning the nature of actual African men had not jelled and instead vacillated erratically from proslavery racism, through benevolent amelioration bolstered by Enlightenment humanism, to abolitionist sentiments. The few standard dramatic and narrative fictions that portrayed black men carried a cultural weight out of all proportion to the limited range of imagined masculinities that they offered.

The cultural construction of black male subjectivity rests, according to W.E.B. Du Bois' theory of "double consciousness," upon a simple if powerful bifurcation of possible identities, an oxymoronic opposition between being loyal to nation or to negritude: "It is a peculiar sensation, this color-consciousness, this sense of always looking at one's self through the eyes of others, of measuring one's soul by the tape of a world that looks on in amused contempt and pity. One ever feels his twoness. . . . The history of the American Negro is the history of the strife,—this longing to attain self-conscious manhood, to merge his double self into a better and truer self."[7] This influential theory is often invoked with reference to black manhood to characterize the impossibility of maintaining a coherent masculine subjectivity in the face of racism. The struggle to form a consistent identity as a black *man* in the later decades of the eighteenth century is less, I suggest, one of achieving an indigenous or national purity carved from the hybridity of being both African and Briton, but rather a more complex consciousness that is variously constituted across regions. Equiano and Sancho intermingle their British affiliations with African ones before marginal, hyphenated, or even national designations were available to them. As Hazel Carby and other critics have recently pointed out, "Identities, like cultures, are negotiated not hermetically and in isolation, but in relation to others . . . and . . . those identities shore up, respond to, and react against the cultures that the operating individuals identify with *and* against."[8] The presence of black men in England paradoxically threatened an emerging national masculinity steeped in racism and homophobia even as they helped to shape its increasingly colorbound parameters. Gender and sexuality have been among the most prominent quandaries in relation to black identity, integrally interwoven into questions of natural rights, and Equiano generically employs the masculine gender in a manner typical of the later eighteenth century in references to the rights of man, to the rights of freemen, and to his countrymen. The plight of black women would seem to be subsumed within those of black men within those political arguments. In *The Vindication of the Rights of Woman* (1792), published in response to Thomas Paine's *Rights of Man*, Mary Wollstonecraft radically challenged the inclusiveness of a similar linguistic usage, and thus the *idea* of being conscious of gender differentiation in regard to political rights was not unthinkable when Equiano published his *Narrative* a few years earlier in 1789. In short, black men were crucial to the formation of gender and sexual difference in England in that marginalized persons often provide the negative terms that help the dominant culture define itself.

Inevitably then, racialized expectations of masculinity in the period compete with black men's attempts to possess sufficient personal authority to shape their own destinies, which were often elusive even after gaining or purchasing manumission. To enact a recognizable notion of black masculinity inevitably reinscribed the racial fictions of popular culture even as black men resisted impersonating white men's versions of what a black man should be. I want to argue, then, that Equiano and Sancho generate original enactments of black manhood as newly free black subjects in spite of functioning under the pall of characters such as Othello and Friday, of visiting African princes and Oroonoko, and that both former slaves refuse to be limited to the incommensurable elements they are assumed to embody, or in particular, to allow virility, especially in relation to white women, to stand as the primary measure of their person. Both Equiano and Sancho are acutely aware that British culture interprets black masculinity as conveniently distinct from white masculinity in order to subject black men to unjust and inconsistent moral measures because of their complexion, and thus to maintain their inequality.

If national identity at the end of the eighteenth century was largely predicated on the assumptions of white metropolitan privileged men—what Kathleen Wilson has called "a critical, objective, manly, and hence white male subject"[9]—how then were former slaves like Equiano and Sancho to locate a masculinity and a British identity which did not simply replicate fictional stereotypes? How was a black man in England to shape a masculinity when male sociability rested on imperialism, commerce, and trade, the very trade to which he was subject and which made of him a commodity? In the early eighteenth century large numbers of blacks were kidnapped from Africa as boys and flaunted as prized young servants who were ornaments to their masters and especially to their mistresses, making the problem of how a black *man*hood was to be imagined and lived by a first generation of Africans who grew to maturity in England particularly vexing.[10] It is the black boy rather than the black man who prevails in English high culture of the period, a child who is converted to an *object d'art* and a status symbol who represents colonial wealth.[11] During the early portion of *The Interesting Narrative of the Life of Olaudah Equiano, or Gustavus Vassa, the African*, Equiano is, after all, narrating his childhood, and to expect a mature masculinity to issue from the person described in that portion of his autobiographical tale would be ludicrous.[12] Though the status of black male servants attending women surely must have changed rather abruptly after they had reached puberty, Equiano is baptized and becomes a favourite of the eldest Miss Guerin. In fact, much more than Sancho, Olaudah Equiano has been interpreted as exemplifying the entire gendered spectrum from a "mother's boy" (suspected of homosexual leanings) to a manly warrior.[13]

Forged in part in the image of God, Equiano's manliness in his own account exudes the dignity, courage, and discipline of the Old Testament prophets. Several recent critical assessments of Equiano imply that he is exemplary of a rugged African masculinity made in the image of such heroes. Folarin Shyllon, for example, found that Equiano "stood uncompromisingly for black manhood, dignity, and freedom."[14] Paul Edwards similarly thinks of the *Narrative* as depicting a universal epic quest for the lost father or mentor after Equiano was abducted from his family as a child,[15] since Equiano finds a master in Richard Baker and later is befriended by Daniel Queen who teaches him the Bible—and to dress hair. Closely attached to another father figure in Captain James Doran, Equiano occupies the somewhat anomalous posture of black man who wields power over others when he becomes

a "sable captain" who acts as a kind of "chieftain" (144) among the people for
whom he is responsible. His connections to these and other older white Englishmen suggest an intense male bonding which either ignores color or covets the adoption of male authority. Equiano also presents himself as possessing a kind of
muscular, sinewy masculinity which manifests itself in naval battles during the
Seven Years' War as well as in his ability to withstand the mistreatment of slave
owners and captains. Yet Equiano also adopts a modest posture on the first page of
his *Narrative* indicating that, though he counts himself among the most fortunate
of slaves, he is no better than the common man, "neither a saint, a hero, nor a
tyrant" (31).

    Neither Equiano or Sancho emphasizes his manliness as a gendered charac-
teristic, a fact worth remarking since England was increasingly constructing a manly
national identity after the Seven Years' War. National fears about the loss of territory during the military conflict seemed to fuel British anxieties about metaphorical emasculation in the later eighteenth century. The British empire "was now
represented as the antidote to aristocratic 'cultural treason' and effeteness, the bul-
wark and proving ground for the true national character and (middle class) potency and virtue."[16] Since a passion for liberty was synonymous with manliness,
citizenship was also a function of maleness; Equiano, both the subject and object
of empire, is a patriotic and active citizen who seeks to change national policy. He
reports growing comfortable with the English and that he "relished their society
and manners, wished to imbibe their spirit, and imitate their manners" (77), though
he also gives vent to considerable ambivalence toward England's imperial vision.
Well-versed in the doctrines of civic humanism, he shows a real cultural fluency in
these principles when, as Adam Potkay has argued, in Equiano's early sketch of
Eboe manners, he presents his native people not only as "the descendants of
Abraham, but also as the true heirs of Cincinnatus—small farmers and militia-
warriors, utterly unacquainted with the 'luxury' of modern Europe."[17] But he also
reveals his social class aspirations when, though thoroughly lacking the self-depre-
catory quality of Sancho, Equiano is embarrassed by poor horsemanship which
would disqualify him to participate in the gentlemanly sport. Equiano's quandary
is nothing less than the maddeningly puzzling conundrum of presenting in narrative a convincingly manly African who is *neither* noble or savage, prince or slave, in
spite of cultural expectations to the contrary, while at the same time demanding
that he be accepted as a full citizen when the proper color of a citizen was unques-
tionably white.

    Equiano clearly recognizes the economics of the British interest in Africa;
and just as Wollstonecraft will later claim that vindicating the rights of woman will
snap the chains that bind men, Equiano argues that freeing slaves will benefit the
British oppressors: "A commercial Intercourse with Africa opens an inexhaustible
Source of Wealth to the manufacturing interests of Great Britain."[18] Equiano believes that slavery is an investment in an inhuman system of commerce, but that
Africans would clearly benefit from the civilizing influences of British manufactures and culture, its "Fashions, Manners, Customs, &c.&c." (333). At times he even

seems to disassociate England from the evils of slavery as when he vilifies the West Indies as a site of horror and inequity as distinct from the British isles. Equiano demands "an humane and generous Treatment of *Negroes*, and indeed of all barbarous Nations in general, [and] that we must expect such Discoveries, as well as reap greater Advantages in Trade, than other nations." Abolition and its attention to slavery served partly as a distraction from other aspects of brutality on foreign shores as empire served to unify an English nationalism.[19]

While Equiano's heroic fighting in the Battle of Gibraltar (1759) and throughout the war offers him the opportunity to display his considerable fighting abilities—and he gains confidence when he knows that his ships will be entering the war (70)—the *Narrative* seems to give no hint of self-doubt in these matters of masculine prowess but only of the injustice with which he is treated.[20] The conventional rules of commerce do not apply to a man of Equiano's color since the money he earns can be withheld, his word refused to be accepted against a white man's, and by his own account he "suffered so many impositions in the commercial transactions in different parts of the world." Equiano's manliness is constantly compromised because his status as a freeman is not secure, though he never voices doubt that he is a rational and intelligent being. As a black man he is, of course, an object of exchange rather than the possessor of property, and the idea of the precariousness and unpredictability of exchange afforded to a black man is a regular refrain, "for, being a negro man, I could not oblige him to pay me" (128). A new, though illegal, slavery could be imposed at almost anytime, arbitrarily, no matter how high Equiano's own estimation of himself (220). The identity as a slave is, however, an assignation that Equiano never accepts as an accurate one, and he repeatedly and courageously asserts his humanity throughout the account of his life as he deals with the material reality of the status he refuses to accept.

In the ethnography which Equiano offers of his native Benin in the early pages of the *Narrative*, a portion heavily indebted to Benezet's travel accounts, he proudly presents his country's people as "warlike" (32). This is particularly pertinent to a discussion of manliness since during the later eighteenth century Britons measured manhood in part by the willingness to serve in the military.[21] To be a warrior is not, however, necessarily synonymous with masculinity for an Ibo since, according to his testimony, women too were warriors.[22] The manliness he describes as typical of his native people also incorporates endeavors in the arts since he testifies that both sexes were dancers, singers, poets, and musicians, though the women as well as the men participate in military action throughout the African nations that Equiano visits. The rites of manhood, *ichi* or painful ritual scarification, however, were quite distinct from the requirements for women, and he reports that women and slaves ate separately from the men.

Oyeronke Oyewumi in particular has questioned the applicability of Western notions of gender, construed as unequal relations of power based on sexual characteristics, to West African societies (though her research concentrates on the Yoruba rather than the Ibo).[23] In fact Equiano would seem to be remarkably sensitive to these matters when he remarks that Ibo women joined the men in fighting and in tilling the soil, though their more typical occupations involved basket weaving, dyeing, sewing, and making earthen vessels. He does observe, however, that African women cultivate the crops while men fish and make canoes (26). Clearly the "head of family" is masculine, and the pipesmoking Creator whom the Ibos worship is referred to with masculine pronouns, as are the priests and healers of the tribe. Equiano boasts that in his Ibo tribe, scarification gave evidence of his father's extraordinary manliness, though later Equiano rejoices that he himself had not been similarly marked or had his teeth filed to points since those disfiguring features would have distinguished him as an exotic other in the non-African world (69). Like most European travel narratives, which measure the level of civilization by the position of women, the *Narrative* seems eager to avoid accusations of Benin as primitive. At the same time, the typical division of labor between men and women, between public and the private spheres, generally characteristic of eighteenth-century Europe does not precisely correspond to the men and women of eighteenth-century Africa, at least as Equiano reports it.

Equiano further maintains that the qualities of cleanliness, strength, beauty, and intelligence are universally distributed among his people without regard to gender. A distinction is made, however, regarding modesty: "Our women too were, in my eyes at least, uncommonly graceful, alert, and modest to a degree of bashfulness; nor do I remember to have ever heard of an instance of incontinence amongst them before marriage." All African woman are not the same, he is quick to add, and he remarks in disgust upon the lack of modesty in another tribe in another part of the continent to which he was taken (54). Thus the chastity of women is to be guarded, especially against enslaving men, even among warrior women. Similarly, he associates femininity with modesty, or its absence, when regarding the remarkably slender white women of Falmouth who seem to command less respect than the African women he had known. Yet notably there is not a hint of misogyny or satire against women, white or black, in *The Interesting Narrative*, nor does Equiano's language reflect the common eighteenth-century associations of femininity with commerce and luxury. These are not the metaphors by which he lives or those by which he conceptualizes his life. His language is all politeness to "his kind patronesses, the Miss Guerins" (79), who recommend him as apprentice to a hairdresser, and to his former hostess in Guernsey and her daughter. Rather, Equiano's animus is reserved for the savage, brutal, and cannibalizing whites. Always aware of women and their fate from the screams of slave women in the ship's hold, to their strife even while pregnant in the fields, for him the worst aspects of slavery are typified in the injustices done to black women including a cook whose jaw is cruelly muzzled with irons.

Other aspects of mid-eighteenth-century British assumptions about black manhood are revealed unwittingly when the young Equiano confronts in close succession a white girl, white boys, and a black boy. Fearing being betrothed to a little white girl because such an obligation would take him away from his benevolent master, he reveals similar worries after a shipmate's daughter shows extraordinary attentiveness to him. In a wellworn phrase that echoes the trope of the Ethiop

washed white, he documents becoming "mortified at the difference in our complexions" (69) when a white female playmate's face is made rosy with washing.
The substitution he seems to desire is to possess for himself the red and white
female beauty that is conventionally British. When Equiano longs to change his
skin color, then, it is in relation to white womanhood, though he also wishes to
escape from the compromisingly romantic potential of white femininity into male
companionship.

Encounters with white femininity, even in children, create fears that he will
be coerced into marriage; meetings with white boys lead to combat; and bonding
with a black boy seems based on color in spite of his not recognizing its "naturalness," especially since he knows that there are differences among African nations.
Coerced by the ship's company into fighting as a spectacle for shipmates with a
white boy on board ship, Equiano gains a bloody nose, though he defines it as
"sport." On the Isle of Wight he famously encounters a black boy who is servant to
a gentleman: "This boy having observed me from his master's house, was trans-
ported at the sight of one of his own countrymen, and ran to meet me with the
utmost haste. I not knowing what he was about, turned a little out of his way at
first, but to no purpose; he soon came close to me, and caught hold of me in his
arms as if I had been his brother, though we had never seen each other before"
(85). At this point Equiano does not recognize that sameness of complexion is
supposed to be sufficient to bind boy to boy, man to man. Once he accepts the
cultural force of that brotherhood, their friendship subsequently blossoms. Thus
in the space of a few short pages, Equiano uncannily releases the culture's anxieties
about black men in these consecutive vignettes. These incidents acculturate him to
fabular ideas of Africanness, blackness, and black manliness while also reinforcing
his own determinedly strong sense of self.

In sum, Equiano exemplifies the way that blackness, and in particular black
maleness, artificially melts the incoherence of diverse African religions, customs,
and tribes into a false unity through a perceived similarity of complexion. This
fact becomes poignantly clear in Equiano's tale when others imagine that a young
African woman must be his lost sister, though he immediately recognizes that the
slave girl is from a different area of the Gold Coast. It is certainly undeniable that
he seems proud of choosing his own countrymen when purchasing slaves for Doc-
tor Charles Irving (205), again demonstrating that he is highly aware of the variations among African nations. It was, of course, useful for Equiano and Sancho to
employ inaccurate and inexact epithets such as "Aethiopianus" or "unlettered African" as generic terms in order to draw together Ibos, Guineans, and other blacks
in England who shared an interest in the abolition of slave trade. Equiano, for
example, described the African slaves thrown alive into the ocean from the slave
ship Zong as his countrymen; and as a leader in seeking justice, he talks of the
Black Poor as "my countrymen" on several occasions. Sancho calls himself "an
African" or a "Negur" (74) and refers to his "brother Moors" (75), yet when asked
to write in behalf of a fellow black who is seeking a position, Sancho notes that
sharing a similarity of color is not sufficient to merit a recommendation. His mock-

ing self-description runs the national gamut in claiming French, African, and English influences on a "merry—chirping—white tooth'd—clean—tight—and light
little fellow;—with a woolly pate—and face as dark as your humble;—and Guiney-
born, and French-bred—the sulky gloom of Africa dispelled by Gallic vivacity—
and that softened again with English sedateness" (60).[24] Though color may
constitute a politics, neither Sancho nor Equiano conveys that the shade of complexion alone composes a predictable and consistent identity. The emergent European categories for "race" in the later eighteenth century, more plastic and
permeable than contemporary categories, do not provide sufficient variety to match
the black men's understandings of difference.[25]

A growing empire meant encountering various and confusing gendered and
racial differences that had to be integrated into existing paradigms or new ones
had to be invented. Exotics and savages were invariably assigned epithets that reflected assumptions about their relations to each other and to European sexuality.
Stereotypic blackness is often associated with hypersexualized virility, a fact which
makes all the more curious Catherine Obianuju Acholonu's search for Equiano's
African origins to argue that the historical Equiano may have been sold because he
was insufficiently manly. The charge of "effeminacy" arises largely because, as the
youngest son of seven children, he has an unusually close relationship to his mother
in Benin who lovingly tutored him and from whom he remembers being insepa-
rable. His inordinate fondness for her kept him close by her side at the market,
when sleeping, and even during the forbidden period of menstruation. When describing the sublime pleasure of their visiting his grandmother's tomb together in
the gloom of night, he becomes nostalgically euphoric. Equiano ignores, I am arguing, the conventional European gender restrictions that might label such behaviors as womanish or perversely feminine. Especially intimate with his sister with
whom he was kidnapped, he laments that "the only comfort we had was in being
in one another's arms all that night, and bathing each other with our tears" (47),
encircled around the man who owned them. Seeking his sister throughout the
narrative, he worries in an apostrophe that her innocence and virtue might have
been trammeled. He also exhibits sentimental sympathy for the oppressed of which
he is a part, and he openly cries when Captain James Doran, his master, refuses to
take him to London. He reveals his intimacy with his mother and sister, his closeness with male friends on board ship, and other friends who were oblivious to
color or sex, seemingly without embarrassment or elaborate protestations of manliness. He notes in particular that violent acts are committed against "the poor,
wretched, and helpless females" (108), and he readily recognizes that European
culture does not judge a white woman to be equivalent to a black woman. Clearly
then, Equiano's autobiographical posture is often that of a public hero, an independent spirit and adventurer, who possesses a reassuringly secure masculinity
which, in its lack of brutal aggressiveness and apparent asexuality, does not arouse
white male anxieties or feminine libido.

It is difficult to ascertain the extent of Equiano's "effeminacy" as judged in
eighteenth-century terms, especially since the term was loaded with nationalist

prejudices and implications. When Acholonu queries Mazi Ambrose Osakwe, a native medicine man in contemporary Nigeria, as to whether a son's habit of following his mother so closely would have been considered excessively feminine, he confirms that both parents would have been displeased by this behavior. Acholonu postulates, with the agreement of those she questions, that it was in fact Equiano's close adherence to his mother that would have led his family to send him away.[26] She also provides strong hints of an impenetrable family secret that would explain Equiano's enslavement. Later she seems to reverse her conclusions, however, in indicating that though she "believed at first that Olaudah was singled out for sale because of his effeminate nature," she finally believes that Equiano was regarded fondly by his father and may have been sold by brothers or other relatives.

Effeminacy is a charge seldom lodged against black men, though Julius Soubise, a contemporary of Sancho who was born a slave in Saint Kitts, and who became the riding and fencing master to the Duchess of Queensberry is a famous counterexample. Soubise, I suggest, was most probably named by the Duchess of Queensberry after Charles de Rohan, Prince de Soubise (1715–1787), a hero of the Seven Years' War and later a fashionable French courtier in the court of Louis XV and Madame de Pompadour. Soubise's perfumed rooms, high fashion, and extravagant lifestyle were true to the French stereotypes associated with his name, and he allegedly boasted of his sexual conquests which gave rise to titillating stories of racy behavior. According to the sparse and somewhat suspect biographical information that is extant, Soubise (whom Sancho counseled to live a regular life, perhaps because Soubise's behavior led Sancho to remember his own sexual wanderings) lived for a time with "the sons of persons of rank" in quarters lavishly decorated with flowers and became "one of the most conspicuous fops of the town."[27] Styling himself the *Black Prince* and the son of African royalty, his pretensions to high social rank and habits of the rich sparked his caricature as Mungo Macaroni. African princes might have been expected to be linked by social class with aristocratic corruption and its attendant luxury, most frequently figured as a troubling contaminant to British masculinity entering from France, the Mediterranean, or the East; but effeminacy was seldom associated with African men, in part perhaps because few Africans in Britain rose above the laboring classes and the poor, and as African princes they were instead linked with being military leaders.

There is considerable evidence of increasing white apprehension about black male sexuality as greater numbers of freed slaves, largely male, enter Britain and develop some economic mobility, however limited it might be, in the later eighteenth century. Equiano and Sancho are of course fully aware that the two most influential representations of the black man were the noble Africans Othello and Oroonoko, each of whom was married to a white woman.[28] Equiano, like most African men in England in the eighteenth century, took a white English wife in spite of strong cultural objections to intermarriage and his own early association of whiteness with deformity (17).[29] In addition, as we have noted, Equiano negatively distinguishes white masculinity from black, in part by calling attention to the lack of morality of slaveowners in their raping of young slave girls and his inability to help them. Equiano is quick to recognize the double standard for black men who are tortured and castrated for sex with white women, even prostitutes, "as if it were no crime in the whites to rob an innocent African girl of her virtue; but most heinous in a black man only to gratify a passion of nature, where the temptation was offered by one of a different color, though that the most abandoned woman of her species" (104). Rather than alluding to the sexual characteristics of women slaves, he confines gender difference to their inequitable treatment to suggest that in the New World such issues rest on white men's perverse notions of their right to power rather than African men's respect for women's modesty. These arguments in behalf of a black male equality, and even their moral superiority to white men, are obviously intended to arouse abolitionist sentiments in Equiano's readers in claiming not only slavery's inhumanity, but that the color of virtue may be black.

The character of Othello carried enormous cultural valence for all black men in the eighteenth century whether or not they married white women—and the majority did exactly that because of the relative scarcity of black women in England.[30] In the fifth edition of his *Narrative* published in 1792, the year of his marriage, Equiano ventriloquizes Othello's words to justify his action. Like the Shakespearean hero, he claims that love is the only witchcraft he applied in wooing a Desdemona. He protests that his "round unvarnished tale" (13), like the witchcraft of love, is the only magic and conjuring he used to win her, and thus by analogy the autobiography becomes a narrative love letter to the white feminized reader. In short, Equiano "becomes" Othello in order to sell his text even as he emphasizes his distance from the superstition and seduction inherent in the analogy.

Sancho too encountered the white mentality which could not recognize the disparity between his person and that of the murderous dramatic character. When *The Gentleman's Magazine* (January 1776) reprints Sancho's letter to Sterne urging his support of abolition, he is figured as possessing a white heart under a black exterior: 'though black as Othello [he] has a heart as humanized as any of the fairest about St. James's.'"[31] Othello's words leap immediately to his consciousness as a tragic figure swayed by evil forces. When his friend John Meheux provides food and clothing in response to his petition, the weeping Sancho "quoted Othello, the fictional Moor whose life was wrecked by a planted handkerchief, and who, although 'unused to the melting mood,' wept at the sight of Desdemona's corpse. It is the shared experience of being black, socially buffeted and on the verge of ruination because of (a lack of) cloth that connects these two characters across the centuries" (59).[32] Yet Sancho's most characteristic mode of dealing with entrenched cultural inscriptions is a sharp satiric humor finely attuned to the race and social class of the accuser. On another occasion Sancho is confronted by a rude white man who, thinking only of Shakespeare's tragic hero when seeing a black man, calls out "Smoke Othello!" William Stevenson recounts that Sancho responded vehemently with "manly resentment" at being identified in such a manner: "'Aye,

Sir, such Othellos you meet with but once in a century,' clapping his hand upon his goodly round paunch. 'Such Iagos as you, we meet with in every dirty passage. Proceed, Sir!'"[33] In this exchange Sancho calls attention to the incongruity of imagining Othello with a paunch and reflects racism back onto the white man by identifying him as a malevolent Iago-like creature. He is self-mocking as well in telling Meheux that he should choose more wisely than picking a blackamoor as a friend since all such "from Othello to Sancho the big—we are either foolish—or mulish—all—all without a single exception" (180). Such satire may possibly coat Sancho's feelings of inadequacy, but more likely it engages the offender at his level while demonstrating his superior trickster mode and his improvisational abilities with mimicry.[34] When hailed as Othello, Sancho thinks of Iago's trickery and Equiano ponders cultural fears about miscegenation; each keeps Othello high in his consciousness, yet each resists too intimate an association with that identity.

Ignatius Sancho's letters date largely from the 1770s, a period of time when foppish effeminacy is tightly bound to foreign influences, and homophobia reigns. Sancho's friend Soubise was similarly haunted and taunted by the shadow of an Othello imagined to be a romance hero: "The duchess's maids [of the Duchess of Queensberry], who had little more to do than read novels, romances, and plays, lackadasically called him the young Othello."[35] Like Sancho, he was known as a womanizer, and after being charged with too much familiarity with the Duchess's maidservant, he was sent to India to teach the skills thought to be too elevated for a black in England who had boasted of being the son of an African prince: "Why, Mrs. GAD, I'll tell you who he is: it is not Omiah [the Tahitian visitor to England Omai]; no, nor the Prince of—of—Oroonoko, who was here some years ago:—he is a Prince of Ana—Anna—madboe, who is come here to make peace or war with the *Premier*, and the rest of the great folks, for not having properly protected his father's Forts and Settlements. Remember the story of *Zanga* [in Edward Young's *Revenge*], and we must tremble.'" Mrs. Gad worries about the "dark design" she associates with any blackman, especially the vengeful Zanga, and she wonders whether he might turn out to be a Prince of France (like the hero of the Seven Years' War, for whom he was most probably named): "The name of S—se is known all over the world. He was a little tanned in the wars in Flanders; but our present Prince here has, if we are not much ill-informed, somewhat tarnished his reputation, if not his complexion, in the wars of VENUS, even in this Metropolis." She goes on to repeat the gossip of his having frequented the "nunneries" or houses of prostitution in King's Place because his constitution was full as warm as his complexion. The whores, regardless of his complexion, allegedly admired him, as Desdemona admired Othello, for "his manly *parts* and *abilities*." Soubise's shenanigans are gleefully reported in order to confirm salacious expectations of black men and the attraction they hold for white women: "As to me, I acknowledge a Black man was always the favourite of my affections; and that I never yet saw either OROONOKO or OTHELLO without rapture." Thus Soubise, even as the plaything of gentlewomen's maids, is supposed to resemble the infinitely expandable well-known black characters simply because of a resemblance of complexion.

Unlike Equiano, Ignatius Sancho married a black woman, the West Indian Anne Osborne, apparently an unusual phenomenon in England in the eighteenth century, to curb his wildness and habituate himself to to a wife whom he characterizes as "pretty well, pretty round, and pretty tame!" (38). It also seems possible that Sancho may have had less access to potentially marriageable white women than Equiano because his lesser situation as a butler, grocer, and merchant would not have been commensurate with middling expectations. Sancho had no objection to miscegenation, though his utopian vision of a raceless society is confined to the afterlife: "We will mix, my boy, with all countries, colours, faiths—see the countless multitudes of the first world—the myriads descended from the Ark— the Patriarchs—Sages—Prophets—and Heroes! My head turns round at the vast idea! We will mingle with them and untwist the vast chain of blessed Providence— which puzzles and baffles human understanding"(86). In particular Sancho seems driven by class concerns since he barely scrapes by with his large family, and he exhibits a certain class-consciousness in suggesting that every wealthy person should willingly relinquish the family plate. There can be no pretence of African nobility here, and Sancho goes to the opposite extreme in condemning some of his race as "Blackamoor dunderheads" (182).

It is this appeal to sentimentality and its attendant social rank that most distinguishes Sancho from Equiano, a characteristic which has made him subject to critics who prefer to represent him as more manly.[36] His self-presentation as a man of sentiment is perhaps a kind of social reaching: "My soul melts at kindness—but the contrary—I own with shame—makes me almost a savage" (45). An admirer of Sir Charles Grandison, a man of sentiment and fashion, he also wants to separate himself from "the whole detail of eastern, effeminate foppery" (204) characteristic of the British aristocracy at mid-century, but he acknowledges his soft and malleable character: "My fortitude (which is wove of very flimsy materials) too oft gives way in the rough and unfriendly jostles of life." A review of the first edition of the *Letters of the Late Ignatius Sancho* claims that the collection "presents to us the naked effusions of a negroe's heart, and shews it glowing with the finest philanthropy and the purest affections."[37] While this is an obvious appeal to readers who wish to engage in sentimentality, it also echoes a slavery history in which slaves were regarded while stark naked and chosen for their physical strength. According to Sancho, a viable masculinity includes sensibility to the slaves' sufferings, a view he shares with Ottobah Cugoano: "Every man of any sensibility, whether he be a Christian or an heathen, if he has any discernment at all, must think that for any men, or any class of men, to deal with their fellowcreatures as with the beasts of the field . . . that those men, that are the procurers and holders of slaves, are the greatest villains in the world."[38] He jauntily reveals his libertine streak and passion for gambling, yet he also insists that he is a family man. Jekyll's biographical sketch commends his "domestic virtue," a phrase usually reserved for women (7).

Sancho signals in his frequent allusions to his color and to racial stereotypes his recognition that African authenticity is partially a performance doomed to predictable reviews even before its opening night.[39] He refers to himself as "a poor, thick-lipped son of Afric" (216) whose seven children, the Sanchonettes, were compared to little monkeys. At least one critic has argued that Sancho bore a "diseased psyche" twisted into believing he was the Caliban-like monster the society had assumed he was, [40] but alternatively we might regard Sancho as parodying himself or his children as dogs or monkeys precisely in order to insist on his humanity, and on his masculinity as well. Sancho's letters describing himself as "a coal-black, jolly African" (210) and a "Black-a-moor" (118) exhibit a playfulness and self-deprecating humor which is lacking in Equiano. These references from the accomplished author and musician, friend of Sterne, and spokesperson for abolition are often tinged with an ironic recognition that such designations are culturally imposed.

Though Sancho mocks himself as fat, jolly, and ugly, he never impersonates or parodies the highly sexualized barbarian. More culturally adept than Equiano in adopting conventional attitudes toward women and the relationship between the sexes ("our sex are cowards" [65] or "Time shrivels female faces"), he mockingly reserves his right to demean the sex (62). On women's equality, he is fawningly conventional and chivalrous: "Could I new-model Nature—your sex should rule supreme—there should be no other ambition but that of pleasing ladies." Sancho presents himself as erotically driven, guilty of an impossible relationship that leads to his ouster from the safe haven provided by three women and a self-confessed womanizer; on the other hand, Equiano does not hint of any such desires and does not talk about himself as a sexual being with one rare exception after he is freed and wishes to go to London: "Some of the sable females, who formerly stood aloof, now began to relax, and appear less coy, but my heart was still fixed on London, where I hoped to be ere long" (138). For him sexuality involves white slaveowners brutally preying upon and ravaging African slave women when they "commit violent depredations on the chastity of the female slaves" (104) who thus disgrace themselves as Christians and as men. He does, however, speak openly in response to James Tobin's racist writings in *The Public Advertiser,* 28 January 1788, about the irrationality of confining masculine desire to women of the same color and the hypocrisy of forced and furtive liaisons between French planters and their black slaves. Equiano publicly questions the open resistance to the union of black men with white women, while the brutalizing of black women by white plantation owners is ignored.

Sancho's early experience with white women, unlike Equiano's, was difficult since his mistresses treated him badly and considered forcing his return to the West Indian slave plantations. Instead he was taken into service as a butler by the Duchess of Montagu who left him a generous legacy in 1751. The ostensible reason for his dismissal was a sexual offense, a mark of his virility that proved threatening to his chaste mistresses. According to Jekyll's biography, "Indignation, and the dread of constant reproach arising from the detection of an amour, infinitely criminal in the eyes of three Maiden Ladies, finally determined him to abandon the family."[41] But Jekyll's account is itself racist, and it portrays Sancho—who documents his financial struggles—as luxuriating in the pleasures most often associated with aristocrats and nabobs. According to Jekyll, Sancho's passionate love of cards and women were inbred because of his geographical origins: "Freedom, riches, and leisure, naturally led a disposition of African texture into indulgences; and that which dissipated the mind of Ignatius completely drained the purse." Sancho positions himself clearly in opposition to "an effeminate gallimawfry" (48) and wants to participate in rescuing "this once manly and martial people from the silken slavery of foreign luxury and debauchery" (48). Here he firmly distances himself from the English, though elsewhere he identifies himself as a man of London rather than of the empire.

In sum, Sancho refuses to adopt an English masculinity based on commercial excess, or on foreign effeminacy, or even consistently as a man of feeling. When he speaks of the love for his country, he means England, though he signs a paper "Africanus"(114) and writes a set of dances called "Mungo's Delight," an obvious reference to the character in the popular operatic play by Charles Dibdin and Isaac Bickerstaffe, *The Padlock* (1768).[42] At a time when British manliness is most associated with economic man and imperial designs, Sancho wonders at the pursuit of commercial growth and trade. He is "more and more convinced of the futility of all our eagerness after worldly riches" (77), and "Trade is duller than every I knew it—and money scarcer—foppery runs higher—and vanity stronger;—extravagance is the adored idol of this sweet town." He cautions his friend Jack Wingrave to "despise poor paltry Europeans—titled—Nabobs" (129). The conquering British, he suggests, taught the natives of the East and West Indies bad behavior, not the opposite. He urges racial intermixture on Christian principles: "Blessed expiation of the Son of the most high God—who died for the sins of all—all—Jew, Turk, Infidel, Heretic;—fair—sallow—brown—tawney—black—and you—and I—and every son and daughter of Adam" (93), and he wants to knit the British empire together. Yet it was empire itself that demonstrated the limits of nationalist thinking, just as it was black masculinity that threatened to make British masculinity into a caricature of itself.

Defined in negative terms, black manhood meant *not* being a boy, *not* being a beast or monster, *not* being effeminate or a woman. Neither Sancho or Equiano found foppishness a way to negotiate a black manhood that would not simply replicate the racial fictions of the pervasive representations of Othello and Oroonoko on the one hand or of the imperial white mercantilist man on the other. By the end of the century negative attitudes toward miscegenation and the fetishization of the sexual potency of black men had begun to coalesce and prevail. Being a (black) man involved skewing, twisting, and violating expectations based on the small but massively influential sampling of characters such as Friday, Zanga, Othello, and Oroonoko. Equiano and Sancho are remarkable in circumventing the monstrous racial fictions that erroneously and egregiously mapped the domestic and imperial regions of black masculinity to forge themselves instead into viable subjects who offered compelling alternatives to reigning notions of white British manhood in the later eighteenth century. In a culture struggling to reconcile masculinity with sentiment while avoiding effeminacy, it was the very palpable presence of these real alternatives to national molds which made these black men at once both threatening and appealing to white women and white men alike.

Notes

Epigraph from *The Interesting Narrative of the Life of Olaudah Equiano, or Gustauvus Vassa the African. Written by Himself* (London 1789).

1. Aphra Behn, *Oroonoko, The Rover and Other Works*, ed. Janet Todd (London: Penguin Books, 1992), 80–81. I have added the italics.

2. Daniel Defoe, *The Life and Surprizing Adventures of Robinson Crusoe, of York, Mariner*, ed. J. Donald Crowley (Oxford: Oxford University Press, 1972), 205.

3. Edward Long, *The History of Jamaica* 3 vols. (London 1774), and Philip Thicknesse, *A Year's Journey Through France, and Part of Spain*, 2nd ed. with additions (London, 1778) 2: 102.

4. *An Enquiry Concerning the Principles of Taste, and of the Origin of our Ideas of Beauty* (London 1785), 26.

5. Review of Olaudah Equiano's *Narrative*, *Gentleman's Magazine*, June 1789, I: 539.

6. *The Royal African: Or, Memoirs of the Young Prince of Annamaboe* (London: c. 1749).

7. W.E.B. Du Bois, *The Souls of Black Folk* (1903; rpt. New York: New American Library, 1982). Susan M. Marren sees the limitations of binary models and finds Equiano's conflict arises "between his commitment to speaking as an African for his fellow Africans and the necessity of speaking as a white Englishman to make himself credible in eighteenth-century England," as both "the illiterate, suffering child-slave and as the articulate freedman and visionary who offers his narrative to readers" in "Between Slavery and Freedom: The Transgressive Self in Olaudah Equiano's Autobiography," *PMLA* 108 (1993), 104.

8. See Hazel Carby, "The Canon: Civil War and Reconstruction," *Michigan Quarterly Review* 28 (1989): 42–43 and *Race Men* (Cambridge: Harvard University Press, 1998), Charles W. Mills, *The Racial Contract* (Ithaca: Cornell University Press, 1997), and Nicholas Thomas, *In Oceania: Visions, Artifacts, Histories* (Durham: Duke University Press, 1997). Srinivas Aravamudan usefully coins the term "tropicopolitan" to describe the fictive colonized subject and the actual person who is both the "object of representation *and* agent of resistance," *Tropicopolitans: Colonialism and Agency, 1688–1804* (Durham and London: Duke University Press, 1999), 4.

9. Kathleen Wilson, "Citizenship, Empire, and Modernity in the English Provinces, c. 1720–1790," *Eighteenth-Century Studies* 29.1 (1995): 75.

10. See Gretchen Gerzina, *Black England: Life before Emancipation* (London: John Murray, 1995), 53.

11. David Dabydeen, *Hogarth's Blacks: Images of Blacks in Eighteenth Century English Art* (Dangaroo Press, 1985), 87, 88.

12. Valerie Smith, *Self-Discovery and Authority in Afro-American Narrative* (Cambridge: Harvard University Press, 1987) usefully interprets his slave narrative as a conflict between the "uninitiated, native" young African and the adult Christian convert.

13. Wilfred D. Samuels, "Disguised Voice in *The Interesting Narrative of Olaudah Equiano, or Gustavus Vassa, the African*," *Black American Literature Forum* 19 (1985): 64–69; and Catherine Obianuju Acholonu, *The Igbo Roots of Olaudah Equiano* (Owerri, Nigeria: AFA Publications, 1989).

14. Folarin Shyllon, "Olaudah Equiano: Nigerian Abolitionist and First National Leader of Africans in Britain," *Journal of African Studies* 4 (1977): 433–51, 451.

15. Paul Edwards, "'Master' and 'Father' in Equiano's Interesting Narrative," *Slavery and Abolition* 11 (1990): 216–226; and Valerie Smith, *Self-Discovery and Authority in Afro-American Narrative*.

16. Kathleen Wilson, "Citizenship, Empire, and Modernity," 85.

17. Adam Potkay, "Olaudah Equiano and the Art of Spiritual Autobiography," *Eighteenth-Century Studies* 27.4 (Summer 1994), 677–92.

18. "Letter from Gustavus Vassa, Late Commissary for the African Settlement, to the Right Honourable Lord Hawkesbury," in *Interesting Narrative*, p. 333.

19. Kathleen Wilson, "Citizenship, Empire, and Modernity," 69–96.

20. Wilfrid Samuels, "Disguised Voice," has argued that Equiano presents the Seven Years' War as "an avenue for regaining the power, valor, honor, and respect—in short, the humanity—of which he had been robbed by his abduction into slavery," though I am not convinced that Equiano ever accepts this demeaning cultural assessment as his own.

21. Linda Colley, *Britons: Forging the Nation 1707–1837* (New Haven and London: Yale University Press, 1992), 283–320.

22. Katalin Orban, "Dominant and Submerged Discourses in *The Life of Olaudah Equiano (or Gustavus Vassa)*," *African American Review* 27.4 (1993): 655–64, confronts the stereotyping inherent in the claim that Equiano's heroic performance in the war is typical of African men: "One might want to ask whether all the heroes of the Seven Years' War epitomize the traditional African man."

23. Oyeronke Oyewumi, *The Invention of Women: Making an African Sense of Western Gender Discourses* (Minneapolis: University of Minnesota Press, 1997). I would argue, however, that elements of uneven relations of power based on gender seem to persist in Equiano's account.

24. Ignatius Sancho, *Letters of the Late Ignatius Sancho, An African*, ed. Vincent Carretta (New York: Penguin, 1998). All subsequent quotations from this text will be cited parenthetically.

25. Felicity Nussbaum, "Women and Race: 'A Difference of Complexion,'" in *Women and Literature in Britain, 1700–1800*, ed. Vivien Jones (Cambridge: Cambridge University Press, 2000), 69–88.

26. Catherine Obianuju Acholonu, *The Igbo Roots of Olaudah Equiano*, 50, 90, 101.

27. Henry Charles William Angelo, *Reminiscences of Henry Angelo, with Memoirs of his late Father* (London 1828), I. 349.

28. Aphra Behn's Imoinda, Oroonoko's wife, was of course black, but in Thomas Southene's popular stage play frequently produced throughout the eighteenth century, Imoinda is a white woman.

29. Equiano and his wife, Susanna Cullen, were parents to two mixed-race daughters, Anna Maria and Johanna.

30. Vincent Carretta notes that marriages in which both parties were African were extremely uncommon in eighteenth-century England in Ignatius Sancho, *Letters of the Late Ignatius Sancho*, 250n14.

31. Cited in Vincent Carretta, ed. Introduction to Ignatius Sancho, *Letters of the Late Ignatius Sancho*, xv.

32. Introduction to *Ignatius Sancho: An African Man of Letters*, ed. Reyahn King (London: National Portrait Gallery, 1997), 9.

33. William Stevenson, 14 September, 1814, in John Nichols, *Literary Anecdotes of the Eighteenth Century* vol. 8 (London 1815).

34. Homi Bhabha, "Of Mimicry and Man: The Ambivalence of Colonial Discourse," *October 28* (1984): 125–133, is the classic text on the concept of mimicry as camouflage that "mimics the forms of authority at the point at which it deauthorizes them" (132).

35. Henry Charles William Angelo, *Reminiscences*, I. 347.

36. See Paul Edwards, "Introduction" in Ignatius Sancho, *Sancho's Letters, with Memoirs of his Life by Joseph Jekyll Esq. M.P.*, 5th ed. (London: William Sancho, 1803) fascimile edition, ed. Paul Edwards (London: Dawsons, 1968), 6–7, and Keith A. Sandiford, *Measuring the Moment: Strategies of Protest in Eighteenth-Century Afro-English Writing* (Selinsgrove: Susquehanna University Press, 1988), 75–76, cited in Markman Ellis, *The Politics of Sensibility: Race, Gender and Commerce in the Sentimental Novel* (Cambridge: Cambridge University Press, 1996), 83. For these critics, sentimentality would seem to compromise Sancho's masculinity and associate him with the aristocratic, the foreign, and the effete.

37. Caryl Phillips, foreword to *Ignatius Sancho: An African Man of Letters* (London: National Portrait Gallery, 1997).

38. Quobna Ottobah Cugoano, *Thoughts and Sentiments on the Evil of Slavery*, ed Vincent Carretta (New York: Penguin Books, 1999), 25.

39. Though [Joseph Jekyll], "The Life of Ignatius Sancho," in *Letters of the Late Ignatius Sancho* reports "it is during this period [after 1751] that he may briefly have taken up employment as an actor in Garrick's theatrical company," I am not aware of any other evidence to support this. See Edwards and Rewt, p. 2.

40. André Dommergues, "Ignatius Sancho (1729–180), the White-Masked African in *The History and Historiography of Commonwealth Literature*, ed. Dieter Riemenschneider (Tübuingen: Narr, 1983), 195.

41. See [Joseph Jekyll], "The Life of Ignatius Sancho," in *Letters of the Late Ignatius Sancho*, 6.

42. Jane Girdham, "Black Musicians in England: Ignatius Sancho and his Contemporaries," *Ignatius Sancho: An African Man of Letters*, ed. Reyahn King et al (London: National Portriat Gallery, 1997), 115–24.

Volatile Subjects

The History of Mary Prince

Gillian Whitlock

The Borderlands are physically present wherever two or more
cultures edge each other, where people of different races occupy the
same territory, where under, lower, middle and upper classes touch,
where the space between two individuals shrinks with intimacy.
—Gloria Anzaldua, *Borderlands La Frontera*

Slave narrators came forth to write stories on paper as vivid as the
ones engraved on their backs.
—Stephen Butterfield, *Black Autobiography in America*

This reading circles around the relations between the two women who came together in the production of *The History of Mary Prince*. This is the narrative of a
former slave born in Bermuda and was first published in 1831. The relationship
between Mary Prince and her amanuensis Susanna Strickland Moodie was played
out at the writing scene of Mary Prince's *History* and raises issues that are fundamental to how we read autobiographies, and what it might mean to read these
with colonialism and its aftermath in view. There is for some autobiographic subjects a kind of extreme, a crisis of authority and expression where, as a last resort,
in pursuit of the authority that autobiography can confer, body itself becomes
text. Gloria Anzaldua characterizes the self-representations of the most brutally
colonized subjects in visceral terms: "It's not on paper that you create but in your
innards, in the gut and out of living tissue—organic writing I call it."[1] This is the
edge that, when all else is said and done, Mary Prince must resort to in order to
convince her reader of her veracity and character. What can we make of the particular relations between these women, Prince and Moodie? Their intimacy is fundamental to this reading of the *History*, "intimacy" as understood by Anzaldua in

the epigraph to this chapter: the meeting of two very different subjects in border-lands of identity.

As these remarks suggest, I am interested in placing Moodie and Prince through their relationship each to the other, not just in terms of their literal conti-guity in a place and time, but also the way in which their identities can be under-stood to be implicated one in the other. Autobiographies by those subjected to the most brutal forms of colonial rule allow us to examine more carefully the connec-tions of women's texts with the production of truth and authority in autobiogra-phy and how they negotiate with existing conventions of biographic writing. The autobiographical text itself is engaged in an ongoing process of authorization to capture not its subject so much as its object: the reader. The importance of these elements—subject, reader, negotiation and authorization—become patently ob-vious in *The History of Mary Prince: A West Indian Slave, Related by Herself.* Mary Prince was the first British woman to escape from slavery and publish a record of her experiences; she is, then, by any reckoning an unlikely autobiographer. Her story foregrounds those visceral processes which determined who might speak, how, when, where and why, and how they might engage a "believing" reader. Prince's *History* becomes something of a limit case, from which we might read back to other, less violent passages in autobiographic writing.

The "History"

Mary Prince is, as far as we know, the first black British woman to escape from slavery. She was born in Bermuda around 1788: "My mother was a household slave; and my father, whose name was Prince, was a sawyer belonging to Mr Trimmingham, a ship-builder at Crow-Lane."[2] As Moira Ferguson reminds us in the introduction to her edition of the *History*, Bermuda was a self-governing Brit-ish colony at the time of Prince's birth. It was not a plantation colony, and Prince's father worked in one of the two major industries on the island: shipbuilding. The other, salting, would later occupy Mary Prince. At the time of Prince's birth about half the population of 10,000 were slaves. She was sold for the first time with her mother as an infant, purchased and given to a girl her own age, who regarded her as a "pet." Until she was twelve Prince lived with her mother and brothers and sisters in a household where the kindness of the mistress allowed the "piccaninnies" an illusion of freedom. Prince was twelve before she was again traded, hired out to another mistress when her owner could no longer maintain her. Around 1805, upon the death of their owner, Prince's mother prepared Mary and her sisters Hannah and Dinah for the slave market, where they were sold "like sheep or cattle"": "I was soon surrounded by strange men, who examined and handled me in the same manner that a butcher would a calf or lamb he was about to purchase, and who talked about my shape and size in like words—as if I could no more under-stand their meaning than the dumb beasts." (62). She fetched about £38, "a great sum for so young a slave" and became the property of Captain Ingram at Spanish Point.

This initiates a long sequence in which Prince is traded as private property, with each transaction leading to more abusive relations. This gradual descent into evil, and a deepening exploration of its immoralities, shape her *History*. There is both subjection and resistance in Prince's narrative. She is powerless to resist the bondage, the trade in slaves that reduces them to the status of cattle, and she submits to demands that cause her shame. And yet the narrative suggests some means of agency. So, for example, when she returns to Bermuda from Turk's Island allegedly she reminds her master that she cannot be treated "the same in Bermuda as he has done in Turk's Island" (67). Around 1815, despite being "pretty comfortable," Prince negotiates to leave her "indecent master" by asking to be sold into the service of John Wood. This is the fifth and final time she is traded, for about £65, and she is taken to Antigua as the property of the Woods. She was taken to London by the Woods family in 1828. After two or three months of abuse, Prince, who "knew that I was free in England, but did not know where to go, or how to get my living" (78), walked out in search of the Moravian mission house, renewing affiliations she had made in Antigua. Through them Prince took her case to the Anti-Slavery Society in November 1828 and her final campaign for freedom was played out before the British public, where it assumed symbolic importance in the abolition campaigns of 1830/1. Thomas Pringle, Secretary of the Society and the editor of the *History*, became her employer, and she entered service in his house at Claremont Square, London, where she dictated her *History* to the amanuensis Susanna Strickland "to let English people know the truth." Her narrative was subjected to intense and public scrutiny, republished several times in that first year of publication. Its legitimacy was challenged by the proslavery lobby while her character was defended by Pringle and the campaigners for emancipation. This struggle for authority and veracity was played out in the English courts in 1833, the same year the Emancipation Bill came into effect.

My interest here is the struggle to authorize Mary Prince as an autobiographic subject in the *History* itself, for this first autobiography by a British black woman is not only eloquent testimony to the inhumanity of slavery, it is also a record of how an unlikely autobiographer could gain access to the British public in 1831, and then again, to a contemporary cross-Atlantic constituency in 1987.

Marginalia

The reading I want to pursue here brings into the frame a narratee, Susanna Strickland. Mary Prince's amanuensis is the ear and the hand in Prince's text, and she went on to become author, in her own "write" as it were, of one of the most celebrated settler narratives, *Roughing It in the Bush, or Life in Canada*. There can be no simple equation between these two women's bodies, the prematurely aged black woman in exile in London and the young evangelist and abolitionist. A published poet who married John Dunbar Moodie shortly after transcribing the *History*, Susanna Strickland Moodie emigrated to Upper Canada with her husband and baby daughter the following year. However, their collaboration to produce the

History at Claremont Square in London late in 1830 and early in 1831 allows us to consider an autobiographical occasion where quite different ideologies and identifications intersect and dissect one another "in contradiction, consonance and adjacency."[3] Here is a place to examine adjacency, intimacy, the production of identities through relationship rather than authenticity, through intersubjectivity, and, furthermore, the reversals of attributes that attached to gender, race, and class positions at that time. This may seem perverse, given the obscurity of Mary Prince—who gains recognition for only a few years and then is lost from view. Why displace her into adjacency rather than pursue what would seem to be the more appropriate approach and recognize the sovereignty she fought so hard to establish?

In part the answer to this is the text itself. The edition now available to us was first reprinted in 1987 in Britain and the United States, a mark of the growing and cross-Atlantic interest in the history of black women. Of this edition less than a quarter is the "History Related By Herself." Mary's narrative is embedded in a series of prefaces, introductions, and appendices that proliferate with each edition. In these, Prince's solicitous editors, her contemporary Thomas Pringles and ours, Moira Ferguson, guide the reader's entry and exit with great care. In this Prince's *History* is not unusual, for slave narratives in the United States frequently were published with some authenticating documentation—a bill of sale, for example. However, in this *History* the process and strategy of authentication is unusually detailed. We have then an autobiographical text that is overwhelmed by marginalia, and rather than peeling this away to read the *History* as a core, I want to read it amid its supplementations. This will not lead to the retrieval of an authentic subject; rather what emerges is a subject constituted in and through differences as these were understood in two quite precise historical conjunctures: the antislavery campaigns of the early 1830s and the western neo-feminism of the late twentieth century. This writing scene is crowded, and my reading here will focus on the amanuensis Susanna Strickland and the text's first editor, Thomas Pringle.

By bringing the marginalia into the framework of the reading, rather than placing it as a distraction from the main game, I am drawing in part on Ross Chambers's understanding of a politics of oppositionality and the way that texts can make a form of resistance available to the relatively disempowered. There is, he suggests, between the possibility of disturbance in the system and the system's power to recuperate that disturbance, "room for maneuver," a space of play or leeway in the system where oppositionality arises and change can occur, "not radical, universal or immediate change; only changes local and scattered that might one day take collective shape and work socially significant transformations."[4] Prince's autobiography is a particularly complex instance of oppositionality at work in the text, for there is both the explicit agenda of the antislavery intelligentsia, her champion, which employs her text as an instrument in their campaign for reform; and beyond this there are the maneuverings of that narrator herself within the prescriptions and formulations of the slave narrative that authorize her to speak.

Mr Pringle

Thomas Pringle is a vital figure in the writing scene of Prince's *History*. It is Pringle who reads the text produced by Prince and Strickland. It is preceded and succeeded by Pringle's commentaries, which position the text precisely and which attempt to secure the reader's belief and allegiance by anticipating disbelief. This is tricky work, for he must both establish Prince's veracity and authority as a subject yet also offer other affirmations, other authorities, to buttress this speaker who is, after all, beyond the pale.

The marginalia of the first editions of the *History*, which went through three editions very quickly, begin with the editor. Pringle's Preface gives us the first glimpse of the writing scene at Claremont Square, stressing Mary Prince's agency in establishing the project:

> The idea of writing Mary Prince's history was first suggested by
> herself. She wished it to be done, she said, that the good people of
> England might hear from a slave what a slave had felt and suffered. . . .
> The narrative was taken down from Mary's lips by a lady who
> happened to be at the time residing in my family as a visitor. It was
> written out fully, with all the narrator's repetitions and prolixities,
> and afterwards pruned into its present shape; retaining, as far as was
> practicable, Mary's exact expressions and particular phraseology . . .
> It is essentially her own, without any material alteration farther than
> was requisite to exclude redundancies and gross grammatical errors,
> so as to render it clearly intelligible. (45)

This, and other marginalia and correspondence, allows us to place the autobiographical occasion in time and space: Claremont Square, London, 1830/1. Pringle remains on the borders of the page, a sotto voce presence throughout Mary Prince's first person narration, which follows Pringle's preface. This editorial presence translates West Indian phrases, assures that "the whole of this paragraph especially, is given as nearly as possible in Mary's precise words," points out that "she refers to a written certificate which will be inserted afterwards." Ironically, he assures us of the truth from Mary's lips—and the certification of this truth by others more authoritative. He assures us that Mary's account is characteristic, pointing out, for example, similarities between Prince's account of the slave market in Bermuda and an account of a vendue of slaves at the Cape of Good Hope: "slavery wherever it prevails produces similar effects" (53). As tempting as it is to regard Pringle's assurances as a diversion, we might more usefully keep them in view as a reminder of the crowded autobiographic occasion *through* which Prince's narration emerged, that writing scene where lips, ears, and hand on the page are not embodied in a single authorial presence. Pringle is ever-anxious to get this text down "cold," to prune the narrative, to control the reading. The *History* emerges as an extreme example of Leigh Gilmore's argument that whether and when autobiography emerges as an authoritative discourse of reality and identity has less to do with a text's presumed accuracy about what really happened than with its apprehended fit into culturally prevalent discourses of truth and identity.[5] As we have seen, Prince's *History* fits into an archetypal slave history in many respects, recording experiences which were thought to be typical, proving her suitable to speak for all slaves, both men and women. However, her ability to tell or tell true is always in question, and Prince is ultimately required to show and tell, to authenticate the story on paper with the marks on her body.

MISS STRICKLAND

If we read Mary Prince's *History* as a narrative in which "Mary" is the narrator and the amanuensis the narratee, we can amplify the politics of opposition at work. The presence of the amanuensis alerts us to intersubjectivity in two ways. Firstly, the possibilities and forms of collaboration between these two women can be seen to shape the emergence of the text. Secondly, making this relationship visible allows me to foreground contiguity, the making of identities through relationships rather than essence. The differences between Prince and Strickland enable the production of the text, the presentation of the autobiographic subject "Mary Prince," even though ultimately the text calls into question the nature of these differences and the means by which they are anchored in shifting social and cultural domains. Prince gains access to a British reading public at that moment and in that place in large part because of the politics of abolitionism. The *History* is precisely located in time and would not have found a patron and a public in Britain other than in that particular juncture in the antislavery campaign being waged by Thomas Pringle and the Anti-Slavery Society. Here is a particularly acute formulation of the textual politics that both enable and disable women writing as autobiographic subjects and which Strickland herself will later negotiate in very different ways as a settler subject, Mrs Moodie. As Prince's amanuensis, Strickland is the conduit through which the *History* is taken down and the beginning of that process by which the text is shaped for its political and polemical purpose. But, more than this, she is also in every sense Prince's foil: the white English woman who is able to embody the precepts of femininity, domestic respectability, and innocent womanhood, an Englishness that casts Prince as "the other woman." The writing scene of Prince's *History* is a hall of mirrors in which the image of each figure is secured by its reverse, the establishment of "identities through differences" that is germane to colonialist thinking. However, the life story that Strickland takes down also throws the nature of femininity and its place in the colonial order of things into question and disarray; the opposition between slave and spinster, between the colony and the metropolis that seem to anchor this writing scene are undermined by what Prince has to tell—and show.

In her collected correspondence we find that in January 1831 the "lady" visitor to Pringle's household, Susanna Strickland, gives a different glimpse of the writing scene of Prince's *History*. She writes to her friends James and Emma Bird:

"I have been writing Mr Pringle's black Mary's life from her own dictation and for her benefit adhering to her own simple story and language without deviating to the paths of flourish or romance. It is a pathetic little history and is now printing in the form of a pamphlet to be laid before the Houses of Parliament. Of course my name does not appear. Mr Pringle has added a very interesting appendix and I hope the work will do much good."[6]

There are a number of reasons that Strickland's name "of course does not appear." By convention an amanuensis remains unnamed, appropriately so in that the appearance of a proper name on the title page suggests authorship, the cohering of identity and style of narration. Traditionally the "proper" naming of the text has particular resonance in thinking about autobiographical writing. Phillipe Lejeune stresses the importance of the name of the author on the title page as the signature of the autobiographical pact. He suggests that it signifies the coherence of textual identity that autobiographical writing seems to guarantee and conveys the ownership of one's self as property. Lejeune's idea that the autobiographer asserts ownership of the self through naming has particular resonance here, for this is precisely what Mary Prince contests in her autobiographical history. As the supplementary materials prove, the ownership of Mary Prince remains in contention: her owner in Antigua will not relinquish his claim to her, and as a result she is unable to return to the colony to join her husband as a free woman. Her story is all about the ways in which her body was quite literally marketed, traded as currency by slavery. For these reasons, the use of Mary's paternal name of Prince on the title page of the *History* is a strategic part of a claim to the legitimacy and truth of what she has to say and part of a strategy to claim an identity beyond the economy of slavery. It is Mary Prince's name as a free woman in England and her patrilineal name. However, this name is unstable through the text; for her owners in Antigua and Bermuda she has been Mary, Princess of Wales, or Molly Wood, a woman of dubious moral character. For others she is Mary James, wife of Daniel James. In supplements to the *History* she is Mary Prince, the woman able to speak for all slaves, "a woman remarkable for decency and propriety of conduct" and delicacy in Pringle's testimony from Claremont Square. On the other hand she is also "the woman Molly," depraved and base, in the letter from her Master in Antigua. The struggle to hold that name of Mary Prince in the title is part, then, of her claim to truth and veracity as a speaking subject of an autobiography. The slippage around the name Mary Prince alerts us to ways that those claiming marginalized identities negotiate round and about the autobiographical "I" with great difficulty. Ironically, Strickland's letter offers us yet another owner of Mary Prince: "Mr Pringle's black Mary."

I suggested earlier that there are two oppositional agendas at work here. The first is the most obvious: the editor, Pringle, who wishes to put before the public a slave narrative that will have the marks of authenticity but not the signs of what would be construed as depravity. The other is the concerns of the narrator, Mary Prince, who desires that the good people of England hear from a slave what a slave felt and suffered. These two agendas may overlap, but they are not of course coextensive. There is an obvious tension between the need to authenticate and the desire not to alienate or appall the reader. Given these constraints, where does Prince find room to maneuver in the text? How does she find ways of inhabiting this space defined by the other? One example is in Prince's own reference to the narrator/amanuensis relationship at the very end of her story: "I will say the truth to English people who may read the history that my good friend, Miss S——, is now writing down for me" (84). Here, as in Strickland's description of their relationship, the scribe works to and for Prince; the allusion to friendship here stresses the sense of equality and alliance in their relationship.

The amanuensis embodies at the scene of writing the epitome of English womanhood as it was understood in terms of the cult of domesticity. As a young, unmarried woman recently converted to Methodism, Strickland is an innocent scribe. On the other hand, Prince has to tell a story of degradation and punishment, a history about things of which she herself has been "too ashamed to speak" on occasion. How is decency preserved here? Patterns of exposure and concealment that occur in the text suggest some answers. There are aspects of her life that need to be spoken of, but not by Prince in the narrator/amanuensis framework. For example, it is in Pringle's supplementary materials that the issue of Prince's relationship with a white man in Antigua is discussed and rationalized. It is there that Wood's allegations of depravity and licentiousness are presented, edited given that they are "too indecent to appear in a publication likely to be perused by females." These sections of the text are not copied by the amanuensis. The section Prince and Strickland do produce together is strictly-policed, first-person narration, with no sexually compromising material. We see here what is "acceptable." As I suggested earlier, this history of a slave is marked by race not gender. Beyond this, it is the life cycle of a slave, quite archetypal and staged: the coming to knowledge of the power that "white people's law" has over her body that ends the innocence of childhood; the sale in the market "exposed to view" "surrounded by strange men," and severed from family in adolescence; the cruel hands that "strip me naked" and "lay my flesh open," the smart of the rope on her naked body. The descent into bestiality in the hands of the "Buckra people" is ended only after a process of conversion, marriage, and escape from her master and mistress in London, where she enters Pringle's employ as a servant and becomes a champion for the abolitionist movement. One of the marks of vernacular that recurs in the *History* is Mary's refrain that the "thread of my story" is hard to maintain. This must be so, for there are threads that must be excised from the fabric entirely given that the abuse is "too, too bad to speak in England" (58). There is much that the "good people of England" cannot hear, and Prince infers the gap between what she might say and what will be heard in England. The constraints of what might be said and heard were figured right there in the intimacy of the narrator/amanuensis relationship.

In this way the *History* tells us a good deal about the cultural construction of truth and authenticity in autobiography. Prince's amanuensis and editor do not set out to record her experience, and for this woman to tell her life story is not to tell all. The occasion requires truth, not experience. Rarely does an autobiography demonstrate so well how these are not coextensive. The "truthful" subject position that Prince is required to embody is a particular ensemble of race, gender, and sexual characteristics that allow her to speak to the good people of England in the abolitionist cause in 1831. A public presentation of self as virtuous, docile, and domesticated is mandatory for her to speak with cultural authority then and there. But the conditions Mary Prince describes in her *History* are hardly conducive to purity and domesticity; the gap between "experience" and "telling the truth" in this case is considerable. "Truth" here allows descriptions of brutal and repeated violence, but there is only the slightest hint of the sexual abuse that more than likely accompanied these beatings, of which she cannot speak "for shame." There were of course ways that gender and race intersected to mark the bodies of slave women particularly; however, these are not recorded here. The relationship between the amanuensis and narrator, ear and voice, must be carefully managed, for the distinctions between permissable entrance into the ear and invasive impropriety are subtle. As Deborah Garfield points out, the challenge for the black female abolitionist was to be an agent without appearing to be one. Her aim was to attract public attention through a "living" word that provoked sensation, yet without provoking lecherous interest or anti-feminist disgust in her sympathetic auditor. The woman had to tell and not tell, to speak of degradation and violence yet sustain the apparent innocence of the auditor and reader, and her own vocal propriety.[7]

The problem here is not the narrator but the reader. The *History* invited disbelief on two levels: first, the narrator must describe behaviors that question the civility of white colonists, the English abroad, quite fundamentally. Second, as a black woman, Prince's emergence as an autobiographer, where her life is invested with particular and individual meaning, is unlikely, and letters from her owner that label her base and depraved offer a quite different story, perhaps even a more feasible one. The *History* courts dismissal, and the proliferation of marginalia and the silences reflect the struggle to counter and contain these disturbances created by the text. Only a former slave might speak with authority of the atrocities of slavery, but, of course, black women were not authoritative speakers. Thus "truth" is dependent on black and white collaborations to authorize a text that, to achieve its objectives, must not only generate readers but also believers for a cause.

The hybrid quality of the texts, the proliferation of marginalia, means that the challenge to the narrator's authority is re-enacted in every reading. As Shari Benstock remarks, marginalia of all kinds (prefaces, appendixes, footnotes, afterwords, and the like) reflect on the text, engage in dialogue with it, perform an interpretive and critical act on it, and break down the semblance of a carefully controlled textual voice: "they reflect, I think, genuine ambivalence—toward the text, toward the speaker in the text, and toward the audience."[8] In the slave narrative this struggle for authority encodes a racial divide in the text and each reading of it. The supporting documentation promotes acceptance of the text as historical evidence, however, ironically, it leaves these texts open in literary terms to readings that stress the corrosive interplay of narrator, editor, correspondents, and the like—in short, the narrator's character, authority, veracity are called into account on every reading as the first-person narration is surrounded by, bound along with, prefatory and supplementary material in which collaborators and critics debate the truth.

AUTHORIZATION

The writing scene at Claremont Square I have been discussing here is succeeded by a quite different episode in a testimonial that was appended to the third edition of the *History*. This, the final marginal text, has the last word about Mary Prince. It was added following inquiries "from various quarters respecting the existence of marks of severe punishment on Mary Prince's body" (119). So Mary Pringle, the editor's wife, writes to Mrs. Townsend, one of the secretaries of the Birmingham Ladies' Society for the Relief of Negro Slaves, from Claremont Square on March 28, 1831:

> My husband having read to me the passage in your last letter to him, expressing a desire to be furnished with some description of the marks of former ill-usage on Mary Prince's person,—I beg in reply to state that the whole back part of her body is distinctly scarred, and, as it were, *chequered,* with the vestiges of severe floggings. Besides this, there are many large scars on other parts of her person, exhibiting an appearance as if the flesh had been deeply cut, or lacerated with *gashes,* by some instrument wielded by most unmerciful hands. . . .
>
> In order to put you in possession of such full and authentic evidence, respecting the marks on Mary Prince's person, as may serve your benevolent purpose in making the enquiry, I beg to add my own testimony to that of Miss Strickland (the lady who wrote down in this house the narratives of Mary Prince and Ashton Warner), together with the testimonies of my sister Susan and my friend Miss Martha Browne—all of whom were present and assisted me this day in a second inspection of Mary's body. (120)

Here, as is so often the case, the body is seen to represent truth. Although what is taken from Mary's lips remains suspect, her scars on her back, her flesh, cannot lie. This final piece of authentication is as managed as the other certifications and suggests how carefully the various layers of the text were generated to show proof and to anticipate and contain the skeptical reading. In this testimony that completes Prince's *History*, the amanuensis, the auditor, becomes the spectator and speaks under her own name. Here is a final grasp to assert truth on Prince's behalf through a white reading of her body, through recourse to the marks of her history on her back. So the relationship between Prince and Strickland, their adjacency, takes a different form. Ultimately the inscriptions of flogging on the body of the Caribbean woman, a body made grotesque and painful by abuse, are what speaks authentically to the good people of England. These marks are not spoken of by Mary herself, but by the amanuensis.

There are a number of disturbing features in this viewing, this last case for truth in the *History*. First, although benevolence has replaced brutality, the viewing recorded in this appendix hearkens back to those parts elsewhere in Prince's narration where she was exposed, open to view. This occurs at the market, where she is sold, and the floggings, where she is stripped, hanged, and her flesh is laid open. These brutalities haunt the viewing at Claremont Square and bring the good people of England into a different relationship to the "buckra people" of the West Indies, supposedly a quite different moral and ethical sphere. Second, this haunting of earlier scenes is more evident when we go back to those descriptions of flogging and note that in fact Prince was a victim of a savage mistress as well as brutal masters. The pitiless fingers, the licking and flogging of her naked body, the knowledge of corporal punishment is at the hands of a mistress. The brutalization of women in slavery goes both ways. This is stressed in Pringle's remarks in the supplement: slavery is a curse of the oppressor and the oppressed, and its natural tendency is to brutalize both. He includes a description from his friend Dr. Walsh to compare with Mary's narrative: "I saw in the back yard of the house, a black girl of about fourteen years old; before her stood her mistress, a white woman, with a large stick in her hand. She was undressed except her petticoat and chemise, which had fallen down and left her shoulders and bosom bare. Her hair was streaming behind, and every fierce and malevolent passion was depicted on her face. She too, like my hostess at Governo [another striking illustration of the *dehumanizing* effects of slavery] was the very representation of a fury."

A reversal has taken place here: it is the body of the white woman that is unveiled, grotesque and passionate. The presentation of slavery as a disease of the social body, a debauchery that is written on the bodies of all who are involved, was a common feature of abolitionist rhetoric. This calls into question those constructions of blackness and whiteness that shaped racial identifications and opens white subjects to moral and political scrutiny. The disembodied white reader, like the amanuensis, is drawn into the text, named. The associations of white domesticity and continence, and black depravity are called into question; the stereotypical qualities attributed to race and gender, to white women in domesticity and to black slaves who are their property, are confused.

Rhetorically, this disturbance is often met by assertions of the separation between England and its colonies, much as the journey north is a progress to freedom in antebellum slave narratives in the United States. However, this separation is not sustained in Mary Prince's *History*. To be sure she remarks that she suffers abuse "too, too bad to speak in England" at the hands of "the Buckra people," the white colonists and owners. However, in the final pages she openly questions this separation: "I have often wondered how English people can go into the West Indies and act in such a beastly manner. But when they go to the West Indies, they forget

God and all feeling of shame" (83). This calls into question the character of the English and dismantles that seemingly fixed opposition between black and white, that anchor of not only racial but also ethnic, class, and gendered identities. In the *History* we find monstrous white women and a slave woman who has all the attributes of English middle-class domestic gentility: "she is remarkable for her decency and propriety of conduct—and her delicacy, even in trifling minutiae, has been a trait of special remark by the females of my family," says Pringle (105). These are the kind of uncertainties and reversals that the unauthorized narrator can induce, even with little room to maneuver.

These complications suggest that although skin fixed identities, the opposition of black and white needs to be carefully examined in particular discursive formations. Prince's claim to truth ultimately rests not on reason or speech but on evidence that outweighs rhetoric: "Thus, according to Aristotle's logic, representative or not, the slave's truth is the master's truth; it is in the body of the slave that the master's truth lies, and it is in torture that his truth is revealed. . . . The master can conceal the truth, since he possesses reason and can choose between truth and lie, can choose the penalty associated with false testimony. His own point of vulnerability is the body of his slave."[9]

VOLATILE BODIES

As we have seen, no simple equation can be made between Mary Prince and Susanna Strickland on the basis of gender alone. Nor can we establish a relationship between them by recourse to terms of doubled, tripled colonizations of women. Race, gender, class, and nation have imprinted their bodies in very different ways. Their differences alert us to the appropriateness of Denise Riley's description of women as a "volatile collectivity." Females, she says, "can be very differently positioned so that the apparent continuity of the subject 'women' isn't to be relied on; 'women' is both synchronically and diachronically erratic as a collectivity . . . for the individual 'being a woman' is also inconstant."[10] Riley's idea of the volatile collectivity of women alerts us to instability and change not only across the range of women's experiences but also within the life of the individual. Characterizations of women vary historically and socially between women and within the life history of one woman. Mary Prince and her amanuensis are forceful examples of how women are positioned very differently, synchronically, and how carefully they must negotiate access to the public at any one time. They also remind us, as critics of autobiography, that women's access to the status of autobiographer is negotiated through a passage from which subjectivity emerges bearing the imprints of experience and culture, self and society. The body is always embedded in history. However, the imprints, the readings can shift, and *The History of Mary Prince* suggests to us some ways that the identities of women could become implicated in unpredictable ways and disturbed in oppositional texts.

The relationship between Prince and Strickland alerts us to the radically different positionings of women synchronically and also to the variations of gender and sexuality experienced in a single life. Susanna Strickland, no less than Mary Prince, will go on to be situated as a colonial subject. Silent as she was in Prince's *History,* she nevertheless became acutely aware of her own voice during the stay at Claremont Square. We know this from another piece of correspondence. Within a week of the inspection of Mary Prince's body and the testimony, the relationship between Strickland and Prince took a new turn. Here Mary Prince becomes the spectator, and the amanuensis is the autobiographical subject. A letter written by Strickland on April 9, 1831, reads: "I was on the 4th instant at St Pancras Church made the happiest girl on earth, in being united to the beloved being in whom I have long centred all my affections. Mr Pringle 'gave me' away, and Black Mary, who had treated herself with a complete new suit upon the occasion, went on the coach box, to see her dear Missie and Biographer wed."[11]

The glimpse of Mary Prince as "Black Mary," resplendent in a new suit and perched on the coach box of the bridal carriage, is almost the last report we have of her. It is of note that in the bridal letter Strickland appears as Prince's "dear Missie and Biographer." This confirms our sense of a close relationship and mutual affection between the women; however, it is also worth remarking that the title "Missie" appears in Prince's *History* when Mary refers to Miss Betsey, the little girl for whom Mary Prince was purchased "as a pet": "She used to lead me about by the hand, and call me her little nigger. This was the happiest period in my life; for I was too young to understand rightly my condition as a slave" (47). Even in a very different time and place, the title "Missie" causes seepage, carries connotations of possession, as does the title "Mr Pringle's black Mary." This also appears to be the only occasion in which Strickland claims the title of biographer for *The History of Mary Prince.*

As Elizabeth Fox-Genovese suggests, to categorize autobiographies according to the race and gender of those who write them is to acknowledge some relation, however problematical, between the text and its author and, more, between the text and its author's experience.[12] However, is it useful to transpose terms like self and author, or authenticity and experience, into the *History?* These terms belong to a register that is alien to the negotiations that took place around this hybrid text. They also seem to foreclose on the ongoing and open-ended process of reading and judgment that the *History* produces. An alternative strategy may be to suggest that what we have bound together before us now, the complex and sometimes tortuous series of oppositional maneuvers by Prince, by her amanuensis and editor, by abolitionist and proslavery interests, and—as I have suggested elsewhere— by the most recent editor, may well be a highly appropriate artifact and record of that "relation, however problematical, between the text and its author and, more, between the text and its author's experience" which Fox-Genovese requires. There is no retrieving the *History* from its genesis in an autobiographical occasion marked by "contradiction, consonance and adjacency" into the singularity and comfort of a single personality and a heroine. The *History* suggests that gender and race are highly volatile components of a life story, played out in different, unpredictable ways in the life of the individual subject and in the lives of women in general.

To return to Prince, then, I would suggest that we can best understand that body in time and place by reading it alongside and with that very differently gendered subject, Susanna Strickland, a woman who was herself in the process of change. Their identities emerge in relational terms. This is to some extent a "black" and "white" issue. Race was an organizing grammar of the imperial order, where policing of the body and the body politic both began and ended with "blood" and "skin." It is after all skin that determines Mary Prince's status and her authority to speak as an autobiographic subject; it is the skin on her back that verifies her speech. We can equally understand Strickland's bourgeois civility as a function of race, and a particular expression of racially gendered identity, a politics of whiteness. However, for all that we set out to understand how the modern, bourgeois self, was fashioned against the grotesque undisciplined bodies of "other women," [13] it is also evident that identities might come adrift, that as a West Indian slave might become a decent, even delicate, member of an English household, so too the femininity, self-discipline, and restraint of white women and men might come undone out of England. These are the confusions, "the ground between," where the makings of the black and the white are unraveled. And so, as she looks at her mistress, Mary Prince assures us, "I saw her change color" (76).

NOTES

Epigraphs from Gloria Anzaldua, preface of *Borderlands La Frontera: The New Mestiza* (San Francisco: Aunt Lute Books, 1987) and Stephen Butterfield, *Black Autobiography in America*, p. 12.

1. Gloria Anzaldua, "Speaking in Tongues: A Letter to 3rd World Women Writers," in Cherrie Moraga and Gloria Anzaldua, eds., *This Bridge Called My Back: Writing by Radical Women of Colour*, 2nd ed. (New York: Kitchen Table Women of Color, 1983), p. 172.

2. Moira Ferguson, ed., *The History of Mary Prince. A West Indian Slave, Related by Herself* (London; Pandora, 1987), 47. Further references to this edition in text.

3. Sidonie Smith & Julia Watson, eds., *De/Colonizing the Subject. The Politics of Gender in Women's Autobiography* (Minneapolis: University of Minnesota Press, 1992), p. xix

4. Ross Chambers, *Room for Maneuver. Reading Oppositional Narrative* (Chicago: The University of Chicago Press, 1991), p. ix. Further references in text.

5. Leigh Gilmore, *Autobiographics: A Feminist Theory of Women's Self-Representation* (Ithaca: Cornell University Press, 1994), p. ix.

6. Carl Ballstadt, et.al., *Susanna Moodie: Letters of a Lifetime* (Toronto: University of Toronto Press, 1985). p. 57.

7. Deborah Garfield, "Earwitness: Female Abolitionism, Sexuality, and Incidents in the Life of a Slave Girl," in Deborah M. Garfield amd Rafia Zafar, eds., *Harriet Jacobs and Incidents in the Life of a Slave Girl* (New York: Cambridge University Press, 1996), p. 106

8. Shari Benstock, "At the Margin of Discourse: Footnotes in the Fictional Text," *PMLA* 98 (March 1983), pp. 204–25.

9. Page du Bois, *Torture and Truth* (New York: Routledge, 1991), p. 66.

10. Denise Riley. *"Am I That Name?" Feminism and the Category of "Women" in History* (Minneapolis: University if Minnesota Press, 1988), p. 2

11. Ballstadt, *Moodie*, p. 61.

12. Elizabeth Fox Genovese, "To Write My Self: The Autobiographies of Afro-Ameri-

can Women," in Shari Benstock, ed., *Feminist Issues in Literary Scholarship* (Bloomington: Indiana University Press, 1987), p. 161.

13. See Anita Levy, *Other Women: The Writing of Class, Race, and Gender, 1832–1898* (New Jersey: Princeton University Press, 1991).

PART TWO

Market Culture
and
Racial Authority

LETTERS OF THE OLD CALABAR SLAVE TRADE 1760–1789

Paul E. Lovejoy and David Richardson

In this paper, we draw attention to the correspondence of the slave trade of Old Calabar in 1760–89.[1] Fourteen letters are included here, twelve by Old Calabar merchants and two by Liverpool merchants that provide evidence of correspondence as early as July 1760 and the arrangements for education in Britain in the late 1760s (see appendix). The individuals mentioned in the letters include many of the most important slave merchants in Old Calabar, Liverpool and Bristol, as well as captains of slave ships. Although the surviving correspondence is meager, the letters demonstrate that some of the merchants at Old Calabar were literate, with considerable command of English, confirming that a creole form of English was common on the coast. Together with the better known diary of Ntiero Edem Efiom of Duke Town, more commonly known by his anglicized name, Antera Duke,[2] the letters reveal a degree of friendship and personal acquaintance between British and Biafran merchants that suggests long-standing relationships. We are presented with the voices of slave traders, not slaves, but African voices nonetheless.[3]

The letters are commercial in nature, and perhaps of little literary value, but linguistically important as evidence that English was spoken in a creole form at Old Calabar, and that this cultural interaction for purposes of trade happened in the context of the slave trade. The earliest letter [Letter 1] is from William Earle to Duke Abashi on 10 February 1761, but this letter refers to two earlier letters, one dating to the previous July and the second to sometime between July and February. Duke Abashi was a leading merchant of Duke Town ward, whose merchants had been heavily involved in the expansion of trade in the 1740s and 1750s. It is important to note that Earle had been to Old Calabar on three voyages in 1748–51 when he presumably met Duke Abashi. The letter is written with a degree of famil-

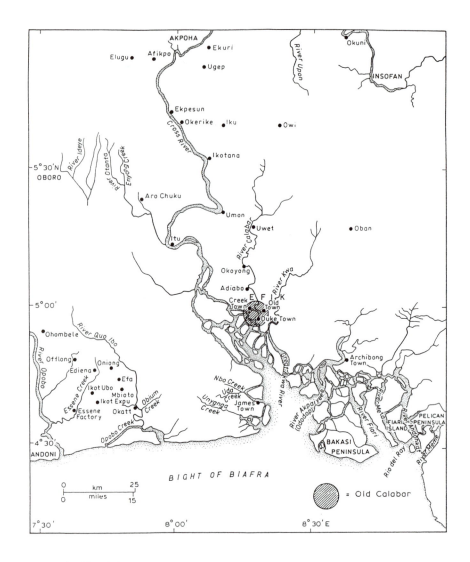

Map of Old Calabar, circa 1780s

iarity that suggests long acquaintance. Duke Abashi had apparently written to Earle in July 1760 requesting or demanding the return of "Cobham Abashy" and his "two Boys" from Virginia, where they had been wrongfully taken, as Earle admitted in recognizing that "they are all Freemen & No Slaves." The reference in the letter to São Thomé suggests that the ship, under the command of Captain Hindle, had proceeded from Old Calabar to São Thomé before heading for Virginia, under Earle's instructions. Earle refers to an earlier letter to Duke Abashi, but this has apparently not survived.

The degree of familiarity is revealed in the greetings from his wife ("my Wife is well & sends you her Love") and reference to his own three boys, Thomas, Ralph and William, and daughter Mary. By implication, Duke Abashi had asked after Earle's wife and children in his July letter, but the reply suggests that Duke Abashi probably did not know the details of Earle's family, indicating that contact was probably not that extensive. Whether or not Duke Abashi had ever met Earle's wife is not clear, but it seems likely, which meant that at some point, Duke Abashi must have been in Liverpool. Mrs. Earle most certainly did not go to Old Calabar.

Some of the surviving letters reproduced and discussed here have been previously published—one in a contemporary newspaper[4] and several by Gomer Williams in 1897.[5] In addition there are letters in the Earle and Rogers Papers and letters arising from a legal case in London involving the sons of an Old Calabar trader taken from the Bight of Biafra in 1767.[6] Other letters are known to have existed, as for example those reported in Ntiero Duke's diary, as well as tax or "coomey" books.[7] The selected letters overlap in time with the surviving excerpts of Ntiero's diary (1785–88) and thereby help to put the better known diary into perspective.

Perhaps it is not surprising that the commercial elite of Old Calabar spoke a creole English, especially in light of the information given to the Committee of the Privy Council in 1788 and the Parliamentary Enquiry into the Slave Trade in 1789. Earle's letter of 1761 suggests that a creolized form of English already existed at Old Calabar by then, and further indicates that those who went to Britain to study were already fluent in creole, before they learned to read and write in Britain. As several letters to the Bristol merchant, Thomas Jones [Letters 3–5], suggest, Liverpool and Bristol merchants, too, had to know creole. Indeed it is likely that Earle probably learned the creole that is revealed in his 1761 letter when he was at Old Calabar in 1748–51.

Elsewhere along the western African coast, merchants and officials travelled to Europe and sent their children there and to Bahia for educational purposes. As a result, a literate elite had emerged in most of the places where European and American slave ships operated.[8] The Old Calabar case is thus one among many. Moreover, Muslim merchants who operated in the interior of much of West Africa as well as in many of the coastal ports of the Atlantic, although not Old Calabar, were also literate, but in Arabic.[9] The presence of literate merchants in western Africa in the eighteenth century was not unusual, but that letters have survived that describe the problems of trade is unusual.[10]

At the time the letters were written, Old Calabar was one of the largest ports of embarkation for enslaved Africans sent to the Americas, ranking only behind Ouidah (Whydah), Luanda, Bonny, Benguela and Cabinda.[11] Old Calabar and neighboring Bonny dominated the trade of the Bight of Biafra, accounting for perhaps 90 percent of all slaves leaving the region. The trade from the Bight was relatively small until the 1740s, amounting to about 3,000 slaves per year. Most were sent out at this time through the Niger delta ports of Elem Kalabari (sometimes called New Calabar, although bearing no relation to Old Calabar) and Bonny, as well as Old Calabar on the Cross River. The volume of deported slaves then grew rapidly, increasing fourfold between the 1730s and 1760s, or from about 3,400 slaves per year in 1731–40 to over 15,000 per year in 1761–70. The number being exported peaked in the 1780s, averaging about 17,500 enslaved people annually. Thereafter there was a slow decline until British abolition in 1807, whereupon the trade temporarily collapsed before rebounding in a final surge from the late 1810s through the early 1830s. Almost 900,000 slaves left the Bight of Biafra in the period from the 1740s to 1807, very largely through Old Calabar and Bonny, with Elem Kalabari, Gabon, and Cameroons being of lesser importance in general, though of some importance in certain years.[12] Old Calabar alone probably accounted for 250,000 to 300,000 slaves in this period.

The trade from the Bight of Biafra, whether at Old Calabar or at neighboring Bonny, was almost entirely in the hands of British merchants before 1807. Most were from Liverpool and Bristol, with some ships also coming from London. British shipping accounted for about 86 percent of all slaves shipped from the Bight of Biafra before 1807, while French ships accounted for most of the rest. Indeed the rise of Bristol and Liverpool as major ports was directly related to the expansion of trade in the Bight of Biafra in the eighteenth century. A sample of over 640,000 slaves from the Bight of Biafra suggests that Liverpool ships took about half of all slaves leaving Old Calabar, while another quarter left on Bristol ships. London ships took another 6.6 per cent while French ships accounted for 13.8 percent.[13]

Although the surviving letters are not numerous, the range of topics covered in the extant correspondence reveals a lot about Old Calabar society in the period from the 1760s to the 1780s. The letters deal principally with matters of trade, including the assessment and collection of taxes ("coomey"), the ordering of goods, the issuing of credit, the provision for human pawns who were being held as collateral, and the local politics that affected trade. We see a society trying to maintain traditions that in fact were being altered rapidly under the pressures, opportunities, and benefits of the external slave trade. The letters contain important historical information about the 1767 massacre at Old Calabar, when Duke Ward emerged supreme as a result of subterfuge and the massacre of an estimated 300 of their rivals in Old Town, and the enslavement of others, including the boys referred to in Letters 3–5.[14] Thus the letters flesh out the history of Old Calabar in the period when Duke Town emerged as the dominant ward at Old Calabar.

As these letters of trade and friendship reveal, credit arrangements were based on personal relationships of long standing. Specifically, efforts were made to reduce the incidence of arbitrary actions in a slaving atmosphere that was often violent through personal ties between the key families at Old Calabar and the ship captains and owners of major Bristol and Liverpool slaving firms. Like inscribed ivory disks and bells that have also survived from this period, the letters are testimony to ongoing linkages and "trust" in this credit system.[15]

Despite the importance of personal relationships, the risks of doing business remained so serious that Old Calabar merchants resorted to the pawning of relatives and dependents as a means of underpinning credit arrangements.[16] Neither literacy nor personal relationships could prevent a conspiracy like the one in 1767, and hence people were held as commercial hostages. For example, on 27 June 1785, Ntiero Duke instructed Abasi Cameroon Backsider and "one of his boys to take pawns to the ship, and I went on board the Cooper [i.e., the ship of Capt. Cooper] to give pawns and I gave him some goods and we drank all day."[17]

Pawns were held on board ship at Old Calabar in lieu of the delivery of slaves to clear the debts arising from the provision of goods on credit. Hence when slaves were delivered to the ships, the pawns were released, but should the slaves not be delivered in time, ships could set sail with the pawns as slaves. Often ships traded pawns against slaves among themselves to avoid departing with supposedly "free" people and incurring the potential risks to the maintenance of ongoing, friendly commercial relations with the local merchants. As a result there were considerable efforts to secure the release of pawns.[18] As discussed elsewhere, human pawning for purposes of securing the slave trade was not unique to Old Calabar but was common in other parts of Atlantic Africa, though not apparently at nearby Bonny.[19] In coastal societies and in the interior pawns seem often to have been girls or women,[20] but in the maritime trade, pawns seem largely to have been males.

At Old Calabar, the *ekpe* (leopard) society regulated commercial relations, including the settlement of debts, and otherwise intervened in the treatment of individuals being held as pawns. *Ekpe* was a graded, titled society of males that was found in many communities in the region of the Cross River, extending into Igbo country, where *ekpe* was sometimes called *okonko*.[21] The society was common in the Cross River basin when Old Calabar emerged as an Atlantic port in the middle of the seventeenth century, and was certainly well established by the middle of the eighteenth century, not only at Old Calabar but also along the Aro commercial network into the interior.

The society was theoretically "secret" in that the decisions of the *ekpe* council were enforced collectively, thereby absolving individuals of responsibility for its policies and decrees. The secrecy was reinforced through masquerades and the use of elaborate costumes, as well as the use of coded hand body gestures and an elaborate pictograph system, of unknown antiquity, that effectively reduced Efik, Ibibio, Igbo and other languages to writing.[22] The secrecy in meaning that underlay the hundreds of pictographs in use allowed communication language frontiers, but only to those who had been initiated, and thereby was adopted along the trade routes into the interior. Moreover, initiation into each of the seven grades involved mastering specific rituals, dances, and signs that allowed initiates to communicate with each other in secret.[23]

Because of initiation fees for the various grades of the society, *ekpe* was dominated by the leading merchants of the different wards, regulated trade, settled disputes, protected pawns, and enforced debt repayment. Through the collective decisions of the senior *ekpe* council, whose members were the leading merchants themselves, individuals could be forced to comply or suffer the consequences. As Ntiero Duke recorded in his diary on 18 January 1785, "we got all the Ekpe men to go to the Ekpe Bush to make bob [i.e., reach a settlement] about the Egbo Young and Little Otto palaver."[24] Although the cause of the dispute between the two men is not mentioned, a settlement was reached and the two men forced to pay a fine: "Egbo Young paid one goat and 4 rods and Little Otto paid 4 rods." Virtually all men in Old Calabar had to belong to one of the grades of the society and pay its fees, which in turn were shared among the members of the highest grade of the society, that is the principal merchants. Ntiero Duke refers to these payments in his diary.[25]

Ekpe also sought to regulate European shipping, serving as a collective means of imposing sanctions, boycotting specific ships, and protecting pawns held on board from being taken to the Americas and sold as slaves.[26] As noted by Ntiero Duke, *ekpe* would isolate a ship, even if this adversely affected the interests of other merchants. According to the entry in his diary for 26 October 1786:

> so I hear Egbo [*ekpe*] Run and I com to know I walk up to Egbo
> Young so wee see Egbo [i.e., the masquerade] com Down & the Egbo
> men he say Sam Ambo and Georg Cobham brow [blow, i.e. "blow
> *ekpe*"] for Captain Fairwether so all us family Dam angary about
> brow [blow] that and wee send to call Captin Fairwether to com
> ashor and after 3 clock noon wee see Eyo & Ebetim com Down and
> Eshen Ambo so the want to Sam & Georg Cobham for mak the settle
> with Captin Fairwether.[27]

As the diary makes clear, Antera Duke was upset that other merchants (Sam Ambo and George Cobham) had imposed *ekpe* on Captain Fairweather's ship, thereby stopping trade, which could only resume once a settlement had been reached.[28]

As is clear from several of the letters, the reliance on personal contact supplemented the pawning system, guaranteeing a method of recourse through written appeal to known business partners in two of the key ports of the British trade. The letters and Ntiero Duke's diary suggest that the leading merchants at Old Calabar were fluent in English and often literate as well. As noted above, the earliest letter reproduced here [Letter 1] dates to 1761 and was written in response to yet earlier correspondence from Duke Abashi in July 1760. There is every reason to believe that there were earlier letters still. We have suggested that Duke Abashi may have been to Liverpool and there met William Earle's wife. While it is uncertain when the first person from Old Calabar was educated in Britain, at least one person was being taught in Liverpool in 1767, as noted in Ambrose Lace's letter to Thomas Jones (Letter 9). By the 1780s, there were others who had been educated there.

Thomas Clarkson reported in the 1788 edition of his famous Cambridge thesis, *An Essay on the Slavery and Commerce of the Human Species, & particularly the African*:

> I must not forget here, that several of the African traders or great men, are not unacquainted with letters. This is particularly the case at Bonny and [Old] Calabar, where they not only speak the English language with fluency, but *write* it. These traders send letters repeatedly to the merchants here, stating the situation of the markets, the goods which they would wish to be sent out to them the next voyage, the number of slaves which they expect to receive by that time, and such other particulars, as might be expected from one merchant to another. These letters are always legible, void of ambiguity, and easy to be understood. They contain, of course, sufficient arguments to shew, that they are as capable of conducting trade, and possess as good an understanding as those to whom they write.[29]

According to John Adams, who traded at Old Calabar in the 1790s, "many of the natives write English, an art first acquired by some of the traders' sons, who had visited England, and which they have had the sagacity to retain up to the present period."[30] Adams reported that the merchants of Old Calabar "have established schools and schoolmasters, for the purpose of instructing in this art the youths belonging to the families of consequence,"[31] although it is unclear from the context if the schools were already established in the 1790s or later, several years after British abolition in 1807, when he was writing his account.[32] In any event, if Adams is correct, there were schools in Old Calabar for decades before the first missionaries arrived in the 1840s.

Written English was in evidence in other forms, too. British slaving firms gave large bells that were inscribed in English to specific Old Calabar merchants, as the one to King Effiwatt in 1799.[33] At Bonny, at least, there were also ivory disks that were inscribed in a manner that suggests that they were being used as references as part of the trust-building regime.[34] The close commercial connection with Bristol and Liverpool tied Old Calabar, like Bonny, to the British sphere of trade and determined that English would be its commercial tongue.

The close association between mercantile connections and education in England is clear, as noted in the correspondence. In 1788, John Matthews, James Penny, and Robert Norris, representing the merchants of Liverpool, told the Committee of the Privy Council, "respecting the Natives of Africa, who have been sent from thence to England to be educated": "It has always been the Practice of Merchants and Commanders of Ships trading to Africa, to encourage the Natives to send their Children to England, as it not only conciliates their Friendship and softens their Manners, but adds greatly to the Security of the Trader, which answers the Purposes both of Interest and Humanity."[35] What "always" means in this context is unclear, but it suggests that West Africans had been educated in Britain for at least a generation or two, with the result that their command of English must have improved but even more important with the result that commercial connections were consolidated.

How many children and youths from Old Calabar were educated in England during the second half of the eighteenth century is difficult to judge, although it seems likely that quite a few were. According to Matthews, Penny and Norris, "There are at present [1787] about Fifty Mulatto and Negro Children, Natives of Africa, in this Town [Liverpool] and its Vicinity, who have been sent here by their Parents to receive the Advantage of an European Education. During the Time of Peace, there is generally that Number here, and sometimes a few more, but we do not know that they are more than Seventy at any one Time, nor are we able to say, what Number are sent to London or Bristol, but we believe there are some at both Places."[36] From his experience on the coast in the 1780s and 1790s, the slave trader and former governor of the English fort at Ouidah, Archibald Dalzell, reported "that at Bonny and Callabar there are many negroes who speak English; and that there is rarely a period that there are not at Liverpool, Callabar negroes sent there expressly to learn English."[37]

In his letter of 11 November 1773 (Letter 9), Ambrose Lace reveals that he took Robin John Otto Ephraim to Liverpool in 1767 "and had him at School near two years." Robin John Otto Ephraim was a member of the family of Grandy King George (Robin John Ephraim) of Old Town, and also the author of two letters here [letters 6 and 8].[38] In 1769, once "Little Ephraim" had finished his education, Lace "then sent him out" to Old Calabar, where the young man became Lace's agent. While Lace gives no details of the boy's curriculum, the schooling cost him £60.[39] In the 1780s, according to Matthews, Penny and Norris, "the Education of these Children here [Liverpool] is confined to Reading, Writing, and a little Arithmetic, with as much of Religion as Persons of their Age and situation usually receive from their School Masters."[40] Other evidence suggests that not much, if any, of the religion was transferred. Christianity had no presence at Old Calabar before the 1840s.

Why were merchants prepared to invest in the education of West African children in Britain, and what does this mean in terms of trust (the term used to describe the credit system whereby goods were advanced to Old Calabar merchants)? Perhaps to some extent the bonds of trust between traders on both sides are revealed again in the comments of Matthews, Penny, and Norris in 1788: "Exclusive of those who are sent here for Education, many Adults visit this Country from Motives of Curiosity, and some Parents send their Children occasionally from almost all Parts of that Coast, to receive some Advantage and Improvement, by observing the Manners and Customs of civilized society, (or as they phrase it, 'To Learn Sense and get a good Head'). These make but a short Stay here, and usually return with the favourite Captain to whose Care they have been entrusted."[41] At the very least, some Africans were prepared to trust Europeans whom they knew with the welfare of their children, and British merchants saw in this sponsorship the basis of commercial clientage.

In his letter of 11 November 1773 (Letter 9), Lace makes it clear that the education of Otto Robin Ephraim was an investment in future business relations;

the son being seen as the eventual replacement for a difficult father. Perhaps also, if proof were necessary, the protection of children being educated in Britain demonstrates the capacity of British merchants to distinguish between free and enslaved individuals, as well as those in pawn. These crucial distinctions are referred to in Ntiero Duke's diary and echoed, for example, in Duke Ephraim's letter to James Rogers (Letter 14). Clearly merchants trading at Old Calabar understood the complexities of social relationships there. The correspondence also brings out the importance of family and kinship at Old Calabar in defining insiders (i.e., those who could not be enslaved, even if they could be pawned) and outsiders (i.e., both slaves and those who could be pawned and it was permissible to sell). Pawns were clearly in an ambiguous position. Moreover, the inquiries about the well-being of wives and children suggest that there was some attempt to equate the kinship ties in West Africa with customs of family in middle class Britain.

Knowledge of English spread at Old Calabar without a resident European or mulatto population. Hence interaction with native English speakers had to occur in the context of trade. Europeans, almost entirely British, visited the Bight of Biafra and stayed on board their ships for months while trading, but they almost never stayed longer.[42] One consequence of this situation was that there appear to have been few liaisons between Europeans and the women of Old Calabar, and thus few, if any mulatto offspring, suggesting even sexual relations were minimal.[43] Instead, boys and young men at Old Calabar learned English because they spent a considerable amount of time on board ships, often being held as pawns and therefore serving as collateral for goods advanced on credit, as discussed earlier. Sometimes the sons of Old Calabar merchants served as cabin boys or otherwise worked on a ship, learning English in the course. Studying in England was an extension of this system of trade and trust.

The spread of literacy in English at Old Calabar may have been related to the development of the indigenous *nsibidi* script. Each grade of *ekpe* had its unique signs and written symbols that were known only by initiates. Hand and body signs that were secret were essential mechanisms of identification, especially in matters of trade with distant towns, while *nsibidi* texts and symbols played an important role in the transmission of decrees. The written script was used in contexts other than *ekpe*, but an essential feature of the system was its restricted use in society, and this inevitably affected *ekpe*.[44]

Like literacy and fluency in English, knowledge of *nsibidi* required formal training and initiation. In effect, written English was useful in matters of trade with Europeans and therefore was inaccessible except to the elite with specialized training. It seems unlikely that the development of *nsibidi* was inspired by the use of written English in matters of trade, although this has been suggested. In fact, there is no demonstrable connection between *nsibidi* and English. There is at least circumstantial evidence that members of the highest grade of *ekpe*, the commercial elite, may have manipulated literacy in English as another "set" of *nsibidi* symbols and representations. The adaptation of written English was effectively an "extension" of an indigenous method of communication.

Literacy at Old Calabar developed and was maintained despite the absence of literate Muslims, a resident European population, or the presence of mulattoes. The spread of English was directly related to the dominance of British trade, yet no foreign English speakers appear to have resided at Old Calabar for longer than a few months, at least not before the Presbyterian Mission established a station in the 1840s.[45] The adoption of English, therefore, appears to have been a conscious decision of the Old Calabar merchant families. Knowledge of English was partially a protective measure as well, sometimes preventing the enslavement of pawns or securing the return of relatives from the Americas.

The merchants and their extended families who facilitated the deportation of the enslaved were not immune to enslavement, as the letters reveal, most especially the letter from Duke Ephraim to Richard Rogers in 1789 (Letter 14). There were various ways that members of the literate elite might end up in slavery. For example, people were sometimes simply "panyarred" for some debt or abuse that was being dealt with in a collective fashion. What constituted "panyarring" was open to debate, since *ekpe* could seize people or force the payment of debts through the arbitrary sale of relatives of the debtor, as Ntiero's diary makes clear. Moreover, the letters make it clear that pawns were occasionally exported, giving rise to appeals for their return. The massacre of Old Town residents in 1767 also resulted in the seizure and sale into foreign slavery of many of the survivors, although again there is evidence that several people who were taken in 1767 were considered to be pawns and were subsequently released and returned to Old Calabar.[46]

These cases demonstrate that some people who were fluent in creole English and even literate were sent to the Americas as slaves. The voices of these individuals who might have ended up as slaves and pawns were representative of people from Old Calabar, but not from the interior of the Bight of Biafra. That some of these people, although held as slaves in the Americas, also returned to Africa reveals the thin line between pawnship and commercial hostage taking. The presence of a few literate individuals from Old Calabar in the diaspora has to be taken into consideration in discussions of literacy and its spread wherever people identified as Igbo or Moko (Ibibio and other Cross River peoples) were to be found. Whether these letters represent the voices of slavers or not, their existence and the social relationships they uncover raise questions about what people knew about the diaspora and slavery in the Americas along the slave routes, and where exactly the enslaved learned what they gradually found out about their future.

The letters reveal a strong cultural divide that the correspondence itself helped to bridge. The pidginized language shows that both British and Biafran merchants crossed cultural boundaries to trade, with selective borrowing and censuring of information that remained culturally specific, such as the pawning of family members, human sacrifices at funerals, and the use of poison ordeals to reveal guilt. Although British merchants had access to the goods of trade and monopolized shipping, their effectiveness in trade depended upon some accommodation with local practices. Each side had specialist knowledge of the other, including what was socially acceptable and what was not: hence the reference to wives and other family members in business letters. Such protocol was not unique to Old Calabar, but that is surely the point: there is much that is commonplace as well as different in this correspondence. This specialized knowledge was crucial in creating conditions that favored insiders, reinforcing their position and making it difficult for newcomers to enter the trade.

APPENDIX

LETTER NO. 1

Liverpool, 10 February 1761

Willm Earle to Duke Abashy

Sr, I Re'ced your obliging Letter by Captn. Lewis of the 28 July last this day. I wou'd have you Look at what I wrote you by Captn. Jasper[?]. Captn. Hindle got my order at St Thomas to proceed to Virginia with his Negroes, which he did & had Cobham Abashy & your two Boys from St Thos aboard. we have not yet heard of the Schooner being Brought into frenchmans port[.] as I told you Before[,] I make no doubt of getting your Boys and Cobham Back from french man[,] for they are all Freemen & No Slaves. Now if you have a mind to have your Coppers for Cobham[,] I gave an order for him to pay Captn. Farrar that man which he may [owe?] you & you may show Captn. Farrar This Letter & he will give you up the order. You know very well I Love all Calabar, I do not want to wrong. Nor I never did Wrong any man one Copper & if your two Boys from St Thoms. be Living I will get them for you & send them to you. So do not make Portuguese Ship Suffer, because 1 Portuguese man has not Paid you, that Grandy Portuguese man here make them at St Thomas Pay you for Shallop & Teeth & I will get your 2 Boys back again. I have 3 Boys[,] Thomas[,] Ralph & William & one girl Mary. my Wife is well & sends you her Love[.] & tho' I do not Come to Callabar[,] I send ship there. I only Rec'd one of your Letters[,] that by Captn. Holland. I am glad to hear Tom Henshaw first man give my Service to him & All the Dukes Family, to King Egbo & all his family[,] To R John & Divet[?] Tom Robin & Every body you know that Knows me & I Remains Duke Abashys Friend
 Wm Earle

Source: Letter book of William Earle, 1760–1, Earle papers, Merseyside Maritime Museum, Albert Dock, Liverpool. We are grateful to the Museum for permission to reproduce this letter.

LETTER No. 2

Old Calabar, August 22, 1776 [1767]

This is to certify whom it doth or may concern that the within is a True List of Debts owing by the Natives of Old Town to Captain Lace of Liverpoole, and that the Boy named Assogua was not stoped by Captain Lace has as been Reported, but was put on board by Orrock Robin John unto whom he belonged, and that Captain Lace carried him of [off] for the within debts, because we made no application for him nor did we even offer to Redeem him whilst the ship staid in the River, as Witness our hands

Witness	his
John Richards	King X George
James Hargreaves	mark
	his
	Jno. X Robin John
	mark
	Otto Ephraim
	his
	Orrock Robin X John
	Mark
	[another signature, undecipherable]

12 August 1767

An Acct. of Goods and Slaves Owing to the ship *Edgar* from the Traders of Old Town as under:

Archibong Robin John five slaves

Goods		Dr	
	Co[ppers]		
20 Iron 5 Nicconees 5 Brawels	155		
4 Romales 3 Cushtaes 2 Photaes	106		
8 B. Pipes 5 Flagons 50 Rods	102		
3 Basons 4 Guinea stuffs	25	Recd Nothing	
3 Blunderbus's 8 Kegs	<u>112</u>		
[Total]	500		

24th July 1767 Goods for 5 slaves.

Received a further trust 10 rods 1 Nicconee 20 [coppers]

Orrock Robin John   Dr

                                                Co[ppers]
23rd July 1767   To 1 Keg of Powder   8
                   By a boy left on board
                   name Asuqu not stoped
                   by me as Orrok says
                   nor was Orrock's son

Ambo Robin John   Dr

August 7. 1767   To Goods for two men slaves
                                                Co[ppers]
2 Blunderbss 3 Kegs 8 Iron 1 Nicconee   98
2 Brawels 1 Cushtae 2 Romales   44
1 Photae 2 Flagons 2 basons 3 Pipe bds   44   Recd Nothing
10 Rods 8 Chints   <u>18</u>

[Total]   204

Ephraim Robin John   Dr
                                                Co[ppers]
July 23rd 1767   To 20 Rods 1 Romale
                   4 Basons 4 L Meneles   48
1 Neganepaut 1 Blunderbus 20 Rods   Recd Nothing
                   1 Baft, 12 Knives   <u>74</u>

[Total]   122

24th To Goods for 2 men slaves as under
                                                Co[ppers]
4 Kegs 8 Iron 2 Nicconees 2 Brawels
                   1 Cushtae   104
1 Romale 1 Photae 16 Chello
                   4 Bs Pipe bds   60   Recd Nothing
2 bs Red 2 G. Stuffs 1 Flagon 14 rods   <u>36</u>

[Total]   200

John Robin John   Dr
                                                Co[ppers]
July 7th 1767 To 10 rods 1 Nicconee
              6 Romale   26

Augt 2 To 8 Chello 1 hatt 1 Jug		Recd Nothing	
brandy	16		
	42		

			Dr	
Augt 1, 1767 Otto Rob. John		Co[ppers]		
	To 5 Rods	5	Recd Nothing	
do	Tom Andrew Honesty, do	5	do	do

July 30th Robin John 6 L Meneles 1 Rom	18	do	do

Augt 1st Rob. Rob. Jno. 1 Keg 2 Cups			
1 Shenda[?] 1 Br[awl?]	20	do	do

All Coppers makes. 240 and 9 slaves makes 11 slaves and 20 Copers Tom Robin makes near 12 slaves

Source: Williams, *Liverpool Privateers*, 539–41

LETTER No. 3

To Marchant [Thomas] Jones, [Bristol]

[undated, 1769?]

Sir

My humble servant to you[.] I have Done good for your Snow Venus and well the Cato was her[.] I was a Boy and Now I be Man for had a first ship that Come for the Water[.] I hop you will Send me a Letter[,] one fine morng. Gown and one Silver Cane to my Named and one Lettle Crew tore[.] and one D[ozen] h[ats?] Cap Red trime send me[.] I Desire you will send to my son is Named Aswaroa and Young Ephraim to Liverpool att Capt Lace and Send to Look for it them[.] If you will get him I will give it you three Slaves and I Lett you no that again one Archebong Robin John son is Named Otto to[.] we him because he ben Cary two Slave on board Indian Qaueen so then Capt Lewis teake him hom of Bristol & I we father son Lettle Ephraim & Ancone[.] Capt Bevens & all men Swer for Book that we will not hurt no man belong to them[.] Don't you Lett any Canow Come for Ship sid that belonging to new town[.] Pl[ea]s[e] send me one larg Bole to make Chop for my war canow & I har on the say Capt A[mbrose] Lace ben Cary him for the Antiguas Country[.] You may look to me[.] Yours [deleted] I am Yours friend Humble Servantt

Orrock Robin John
and this is hand Young Archebong Robin John

Source: Public Record Office KB 1/19, Mich 1773

LETTER NO. 4

Old Callabar, June 16the 1769

[Grandee Ephraim Robin John] to Marchant [Thomas] Jones in Bristol

Marchant Jones Sir[,] I should be Very Much obliged to You and I Lett you know what I do no more then good tread on board snow Venus[.] well the Cato was her[.] I was a Boy & now I be Man for had I Desire you to send me an answer by the first ship Come in this river and one fine Morning Gown and one silver Caim to put my Named and one Lettle Crew tove to god two Boxes & one Dossen Do: h: Capps Red trim[.] & I Desire your will send to Look for my son is Named Asworea and Young Ephraim in to Liverpooll att Capt Alace and send to goin Look for it him and If your will get him in you House[.]

Source: Public Record Office KB 1/19, Mich 1773

LETTER NO. 5

[undated, 1769?] to Marchant [Thomas] Jones in Bristol

My friend

Sr.[,] I take this opertunity of writing to you[.] My old Acquaintances & I let you know what Capt Lewis ben due me 20 Slave & I ben sell[.] all My first Treade Don & he no Pay Me Coomey & he take all My [unclear] free Men a Way for I now owes him nothing & I hop you send ships for My oun Water[.] I will slaves you ship & Desire all Marchant in Bristol to them[.] Wee son[Wilson?][,] biven & Lewis ben cary a Way his[,] 1 name Lettle Ephraim & Ancone and am Tom & Archibong tom Robin & young Robin Robin Jno & Archibong Robin Jno son & My Boys he Name abash & I hop all you will Lete Me have them again[,]
     Yours friend King George

Source: Public Record Office KB 1/19, Mich 1773

LETTER No. 6

Mr. Ambrose Lace and Companey, Marchents in Liverpool

Ould Town, Ould Callabar, January 13, 1773

Marchent Lace, S^r,

    I take this opertunety of Wrighting to you and to acquaint you of the behaveor of Sum ships Lately in my water[.] there was Capt Bishop of Bristol and Capt. Jackson of Liverpool laying in the river when Capt Sharp arived and wanted to purchese his cargo as I supose he ought to do[.] but this Bishop and Jackson cunsoulted not to let him slave with out he payed the same Coomey that they did[.] thy sent him out of the River[,] so he went to the Camoroons and was awy two munths[.] then he arived in my water again and thy still isisted upon his paying the Coomey[.] acordingly he did a Nuff to Blind them[.] so I gave him slaves to his content and so did all my people, till he was full and is now ready to sail[,] only weats for to have a fue afairs sattled and this sall be don before he sails to his sattisfection, and now he may very well Laffe at them that was so much his Enemeys before, for that same day thy sent him out of the River this Jackson and Bishop and a brig that was to Jackson at night began to fire at my town without the least provecation and continued it for twenty-four hours for which I gave then two cows[.] but it seemed as after words Jackson confirmed that Bishop and him was to cary away all our pawns[.] as it was lickely true for Jackson did cary of his but more than that[,] before he sailed[,] he tould me that if I went on bord of Bishop I shuld be stoped by him and my hed cut of and sent to the Duke at Nuetown, but I put that out of his power for to cut of my hed or cary of the pawns by stoping his boats and sum of his peeple[.] and so I would Jackson had I known his entent when he informed me of Bishop, but he took care not to divulge his own secrets which he was much to bleam if he did[.] so my friend marchant Lace[,] if you Send ship to my water again[,] Send good man all same your Self or same marchant black. No Send ould man or man to be grandy man, if he want to be grandy man let he stand home for marchant one time, no let him com heare or all Same Capt Sharp he very good man, but I no tell before that time Capt. Sharp go to Camoroons he left his mate till he came back again, so they say I do bad for them but I will leave you to Jude that[.] for if any ship fire at my town I will fire for ship again[.] Marchant Lace Sr[,] there is Mr Canes Capt. Sharp and second mate a young man and a very good man[.] he is very much Liked by me and all my peeple of Callabar, so if you plase to sand him he will make as quick a dispatch as any man you can send and I believe as much to your advantage for I want a good many ship to cum, for the more ships the more treade wee have for them[.] for the New town peeple and has blowed abuncko for no ship to go from my water to them nor any to cum from them to me[.] tho Bishop is now lying in Cross River but thy only lat him stay till this pelaver is satteled for I have ofered him 10 slaves to Readeem the Pawns and let him have his white people, but he will not[.] for I dount want to do any bad thing to him or any ship that cums to my water but there is 4 of my sons gone allredy with Jackson and I dont want any more of them caried of by any other vausell[.] the coomy in all my water now is 24 thousand coprs besidges hats[,] case and ship gun, Marchant Lace[,] I did as you bob me for Lettrs[.] when this tendr com[,] I no chop for all man[,] for you bob me No Chop t[w]o times[.] for bionbi I back to much Cop[ppers] for Coomy so I do all same you bob me who make my father grandy no more white man[.] so now[,] marchant Lace[,] send good ship and make me grandy again for war take two much copr from me[,] who man trade like me that it be peace or break book like me[.] so Marchent Lace[,] if you Send ship now and good cargo[,] I will be bound shee no stand long before shee full for go away.

[signed]
Grandy King George King of Old Town Tribe

Source: Williams, *Liverpool Privateers*, 543–45

Letter No. 7

Parrot Island, July 19th 1773

Sir [Ambrose Lace],
    I take this opportunity to write to you[.] I send Joshua 1 Little Boy by Captain Cooper[.] I have send you one Boy by Captain faireweather[.] I ask Captain Cooper wether Captain faireweather give you that Boy or not[;] he told me Captain faireweather sold the Boy in the West India and give you the money[.] I desire you will Let me know wether faireeweather give you money or not[.] my mother Send your wife one Teeth By Captain Sharp[.] I done very well for Captain Cooper and my father too[.] I am going to give a Town of my own I dar say you knows that place I am going to Live[.] Bashey Dukey there once[.] send Gun Enough for Trad. I want 2 Gun for every Slave I sell[.] Send me 2 or 3 fine chint for my self and handkerchief[.] any thing you want from Callabar Send me Letter[.] I think I come to see next voyage[.] Send me some writing paper and Books[.] my Coomey his 1600 Copper[.] Send me 2 sheep a Life[.] Sir I am your Best friend Otto Ephraim
    S.P. I will Sell Captain Doyle slave because he told me you have part for his ship[.] I expect Captain Sharp here in 4 months time[.] Remember me to your Wife and Mr. Chiffies [Chaffers].

Source: Williams, *Liverpool Privateers*, 547

LETTER No. 8

Undated [1773?]

[To Ambrose Lace]

And now war be don Wee have all the Trade true the Cuntry so that wee want nothing but ships to Incorige us and back us to cary it on[.] so I hope you and marchant Black wount Lat ous want for that In Curigement Or the other marchants of that Pleasce thut has a mind for to send their ships[.] thy shall be used with Nothing but Sivellety and fare trade[.] other Captns may say what they Please about my doing them any bad thing[,] for what I did was their own faults[.] for you may think[,] Sr[,] that it was vary vaxing to have my sons caried of by Captn Jackson and Robbin sons and the King of Qua son[;] thier names is Otto Imbass Egshiom Enick Ogen Acandom Ebetham Ephiyoung Aset[.] and to vex ous more[,] the time that wee ware fireing at each other thy hisseted on[e] of our sons to the yard arm of Bishop and another to Jacksons yard arm[,] and then would cary all of them away and cut of my hed if it had not been Prevented in time[.] and yet thy say I do them bad only stoping Sum of thier peeple till I get my Pawns from them[.] Marchant Lace[,] when you Send a ship[,] send drinking horns for Coomey and sum fine white mugs and sum glass tanckards with Leds to them[.] Send Pleanty of ships guns[,] the same as Sharp had[.] I dount care if there was 2 or 3 on a Slave[.] Send one Chints for me of a hundrerd yard[,] 1 Neckonees of one hundrd yards[,] 1 photar of a hundrd y's[,] 1 Reamall 1 Hund. yards[,] one Cushita of a hundred yds[,] one well baft of the same[.] Send sum Leaced hats for trade and Vicor Bottles and cases to much[,] for all gon for war[.] Send sum Lucking glasses at 2 Coprs and 4 Coprs for trade and Coomey to[.] and send Planty of hack and Bally for Trade and Comey and Small Bells[.] Let them be good ones[.] and send sum Lango[,] Sum Large and sum small and sum Curl beads[.] Send me one Lucking glass six foot long and six foot wide[.] Let it have a strong woden freme[.] Send two small Scrustones that their Leds may Lift up[.] send Plenty of Cutlashs for Coomey of 2 Coprs price[.] Let your Indgey goods be Right good and your ship no stand long[.] send me one table and six Chears for my house and one two arm Schere for my Salf to sat in and 12 Puter plates and 4 dishes 12 Nifes and 12 forcks and 2 Large table spoons and a trowen and one Pear of ballonses 2 brass Juggs with thier Cisers to lift the same as a tanckard and two Copr ones[,] the same two brass falagons of two gallons each Pleanty for trade[.] of puter ones[,] Send Plenty of Puter Jugs for trade[.] send me two Large brass beasons and puter ones for trade[.] Send me one close stool and Send me one Large Red[ ][.] Send me one gun for my own shuting[,] 5 foot barill and two pueter piss pots[.] Send one good Case of Rezars for my Saveing[.] Send me sum Vavey brade Iron bars of 16 foot long[.] Send 100 of them[.] Send Large caps of 2 Coprs for Coomey &c[.]. Please to show this to Marchant black and shend sum Large Locks for trade[,] Sum chanes for my Salf[,] two brass kittles and two scacepang[,] a fue brass

Kittles[,] 12 or fifteen Coprs each[.] Send Pleanty of canes for Coomey and one long cane for my self[,] gould mounted[,] and small Neals for Coomey[.] you may pay your Coomey Very Reasonable[.] Saws or aney tools[.] No Send Small Iron moulds for to cast mustcats and sum small 3 pounders[.] Send me sum banue canvess to make sails for my cannows and sum large Leg monelones with hendges to thim to lock with a Screw and two large iron wans for two sarve in the Room of irons[.] and Send me one ship shaw and one cross cut shaw[.] Send red[,] green and white hats for trade[.] Send me one red and one blue coat with gould Lace for to fit a Large man[.] Send buttr and Suger for to trade[.] Send sum green[,] sum red[,] sum blue Velvet caps with small Leace[.] and Send Sum files for trade, So no more at Preasant from your best friend.

GRANDY KING GEORGE

give my Complements to the gentlemen owners of the brigg Swift Mr Devenport Marchant Black and Captⁿ Black and as allso Mr Erll.

Please to have my name put on Everything that you send for me.

Source: Williams, *Liverpool Privateers*, 545–46

LETTER No. 9

Liverpool, 11 November 1773

Sir [Thomas Jones, Bristol],
      Yours of the 7th I received wherein you disire I will send an Affidavit concerning the two black men you mention, Little Epm. and Ancoy, and in what manner the ware taken off the coast, and that I know them to be Brothers to Grandy Epm. Robin John; as to Little Epm. I remember him very well, as to Ancoy Rob. Rob. John I cant recolect I ever saw him. I knew old Robin John the Father of Grandy Epm. and I think all the family, but I never found that little Epm. was one of Old Robins sons, and as to Rob. Rob. John he was not Old Rob. Johns son. Old Robin took Rob. Rob. Jno. mother for a wife when Robin Rob. Jno. was a boy of 6 or eight years old, and as to Rob. Rob. Jno. hen ever [he never] had a son that I heard of. You know very well the custom of that place whatever Man or Woman gos to live in any family they take the Name of the first man in the family and call him Father, how little Epm. came into the family I cant tell, and as to what ship they came off the coast in I know no more than you, therefore cant make Affadavit Eather to their being Brothers to Grandy Epm. or the manner he was brought off the Coast, as to Grandy Epm. you know very well has been Guilty of many bad Act[i]ons, no man can say anything in his

favour, a History of his life would exceed any of our Pirates, the whole sett at Old Town you know as well as me. I brought young Epm. home, and had him at School near two years, then sent him out, he cost me above sixty pounds and when his Fathers gone I hope the son will be a good man. As to Mr. Floyd he says more then I ever knew or heard of hes in many Errors, even in the Name of the vessell I was in hes wrong, there was no such a ship as the hector while I was at Callebarr, a man should be carefull when on Oath, how he knows the two men to be brothers to Epm. I cant tell, I have several times had the pedigree of all the familys from Abashey[.] the foregoing acct. of Rob. Rob. was from him, but to prove the two men to be Epms. brothers I dont know how you will do it, I assure you I dont think they are, if you think to send a vessell to Old Town it might ansr for you to purchas the two men[.] I once bogt [bought] one at Jamaica a man of no consiquance in family but it ansrd the Expence.

I am Sir your hbl. Servt.

[Ambrose Lace]

Source: Williams, *Liverpool Privateers*, 541–42

LETTER No. 10

Old Town Callabar, December 24th 1775

To Captain Ambrose Lace merchant in Liverpool

Captain Lace I take this opportunity to write to you by Captain Jolly[.] that letter you Send me by Sharp you did not put your name[.] as for Captain Sharp[,] I will do anything hys in my power to obliged you[.] when Captain Cooper comes Let him [bring] Guns enough[.] I want 2 Gun for every Slave I sell and father we Don't want Iron[,] only 2 for one slave[.] so no more at present from your friend

Ephraim Robin John

S.P. Remember me to your wife.

Source: Williams, *Liverpool Privateer*, 547–48

LETTER NO. 11

Old Town Old Callabar August 23the 1776

Mr. Lace,

    Sir, - I take this opportunity to write to you[.] I received by Captain Cooper one painted cloth[,] one book in the box[,] one gown[,] one ink cake and some wafers[.] I was in the country when Orrock send that letter to you[.] now I put my hand and my that is enough what Orrock can do[.] he can do anything without my father[.] and I please I pay Egbo men yesterday[.] I have done now for Egbo[.] I received by Captain Sharp one lace hat[.] I make monkey[.] Captain Loan pay me for that cap[.] I got one hundred Copper for it[.] I put him in the iron 5 days in Quabacke sea[.] he told me that Captain Barley give the Willy Honesty but I make him pay for all that[.] I was on board Barley myself[.] he never mention it to me that you Send me a cap by him[.] I have sent you by Cooper one teeth 50 weight

Your most obedent Humble Servant

Otto Ephraim

Source: Williams, *Liverpool Privateer*, 548.

LETTER NO. 12

Old Callabar, June 24the 1780

Gentlemen

Sir We Lett your know whate newse We have hear[.] as we was war again with one part our country now we make peace again[;] one King for all Callabar and trad one places[.] We Belive no war tell [till?] Longtime now[.] we Cant tell what Reason[.] no more We think it be war make you Send Ship Sam[e] as Befor. We we no been See 24 moonth no more Captain Beggs Come for tooth that we erever See befor[.] but we all go for Country and no Been Keep him longtime[.] and we think as soon as you have way for Sell Slaves that your will send Ship for Slaves and tooth Tooth[.] togetter that will be better for us - now We [are] fewer[.] no whitemen shall be stop onshor any more long as we be Callabar and we make Great Law about whitemen not hurt[.] and Suppose one family Stop any whiteman[,] We Will Brock that family because all Country Stand by that Law this time[.] We have Slaves Same a[s] Bonny or other place[.] is Slaves full our Country[.] we beg you Dont Lett we go without Ship Every Year[.] Suppose you Doese[,] We Spoill Directly for we have nothing to Live but Ship [slaves?][.] Genttement[,] we Desire your Would not Look upon this Letter to be word of

one man or one family but to be senss of Old Callabar Country Country[.]
togetter your Know very well we Cant Do without Some Coomy but we do [
missing   ] Would Send us Ship Soon as you Cant and give Captain Copy
this Letter for we have one hear to shew Captain first Day he Come too. We Shall
Sewer to observe Every thing We promised in this Letter for Do good for Every
Ship Come hear[,] all Same as Captain Beggs will tell you we Do for he

We are Gentlemen
Your most obedt humble
Servant Witness Our hands

KING HENSHAW
DUKE EPHRAIM
WILLY HONESTY

Source: *Liverpool General Advertiser*, 21 February 1788

LETTER 13

Old Town Old Callabarr March 20th 1783

Mr. Ambrose Lace
Merchant in Liverpool
Sent by ship *Jenny*

Mr Lace,
    Sir,
        I take this oportunity by Captain Faireweather[.] we have no News here
only Tom King John come Down to live with my father[.] is here now with us[.]
Orrock Robin John is Dead May 24th 1782[?][.] we give all his coppers to his
both son George Orrock and Ephraim Orrock[.] Send me some Writing papers
and 1 Bureaus to Buy

Your Humble Servant
Otto Ephraim

P.S. Remember me to your Wife and your son Joshua[,] Ambrose[,] William and
Polly

Source: Williams, *Liverpool Privateer*, 548–49

LETTER 14

Old Callabar   October 16th 1789

Messrs Rogers & Lroach

Gentlemam
       Sir   I Lett your Know This newese for Ship Jupeter[.] I been very good
freend for that Ship and I have settle all my Debt & Family – I go far [for?]
Porrott Island with Ship And Come Back for freend – So two my Canow Man go
onboard hime to Sold Som Yames – he Carry of for nothing and Supose Sold my
people – I will make Bristal Ship pay[,] for them two my People free man[.] but
if him Send Them Back by Aney Other Ship or him Self I thank – I Lett your
know people Names – one Abashey and other Antegra – I Done very well with
Capt Leroach and he tok my people of[.]
I am your Freend

Duke Ephraim

Source: Public Record Office, C 107/12. There are three copies of this letter, the first marked
Old Callabar November 17th 1789, the second November 25th 1789 and the third October
16th, reproduced here. There are minor variations in spelling and the odd word inserted or
left out, but the names of those seized and shipped overseas are spelled as in the above.

NOTES

       1. We thank Silke Strickrodt and Caroline Sorensen-Gilmour for their assistance in
tracking down documents; Ruth Paley for reference to the King's Bench letters, Public Record
Office; Stephen Behrendt for drawing our attention to the letter published in the *Liverpool
General Advertiser*; and Robin Law, Colleen Kriger, Ivor Miller, and David Trotman for their
comments and suggestons. We also wish to acknowledge the support of the Social Sciences
and Humanities Research Council of Canada, York University and the University of Hull
Research Support Fund. This paper was presented at the Forum on European Expansion
and Global Interaction, St. Augustine, Florida, February 17–19, 2000.
       2. A fragment of the diary, for the years 1785–88, survived the bombing of World
War II and was published as "The Diary of Antera Duke, an Efik Slave-Trading Chief of the
Eighteenth Century," in Daryll Forde, ed., *Efik Traders of Old Calabar* (London, 1956), 79–
115, with modern English translation on pp. 27–65, and notes by D. Simmons, who indicates that "Duke" is the anglicized form of "Orok." Also see Ukorebi U. Asuoquo,"The
Diary of Antera Duke of Old Calabar (1785–1788)," *Calabar Historical Journal*, 2 (1978),
36–38; D. Simmons, "Notes on the Diary of Antera Duke," in Forde, *Efik Traders*, 66; Ekei
Essien Oku, *The Kings and Chiefs of Old Calabar (1785–1925)* (Calabar, 1989); and P.E.H.
Hair, "Antera Duke of Old Calabar – A Little More about an African Entrepreneur," *History in Africa*, 17 (1990), 363. For the history of the manuscript, see Stephen Behrendt, "The
Diary of Antera Duke and the Eighteenth-Century Old Calabar Slave Trade to the Americas" unpublished paper, W.E.B. Du Bois Institute, Harvard University, 1998. It should be
noted that John Latham and Stephen Behrendt are preparing a new edition of the diary.

3. Paul E. Lovejoy and David Richardson, "Trust, Pawnship, and Atlantic History: The Institutional Foundations of the Old Calabar Slave Trade," *American Historical Review*, 104:2 (1999), 333–55.

4. *Liverpool General Advertiser*, 21 February 1788, p. 3.

5. Gomer Williams, *History of the Liverpool Privateers and Letters of Marque, with an Account of the Liverpool Slave Trade* (London, 1897).

6. Letter Book of William Earle, 1760–61, Earle Papers, Merseyside Maritime Museum, Albert Dock, Liverpool; Rogers Papers, C 107/12, Public Record Office (PRO); King's Bench (KB) 1/19 Mich 1773 (PRO). For a discussion of the Somerset case, see Ruth Paley, "After Somerset: Mansfield, Slavery and the Law in England 1772–1830," in Norma Landau and Donna Andrews (eds.), *Crime, Law and Society* (Cambridge, 2000).

7. Ntiero Duke notes the use of letters in a number of contexts, and also mentions various "coomey books"; see entry for 12 March 1785, reporting a meeting in Palaver House with Duke, Esin, and Willy Honesty to discuss the arrival of a new ship, "So we write to ask him [the captain] to come ashore" ("Diary," 29).

8. For information on the extent of literacy along the coast in the eighteenth century, see the eighteenth-century accounts in Philip D. Curtin (ed.), *Africa Remembered: Narratives of Africans from the Era of the Slave Trade* (Madison, 1967); John Matthews, James Penney, and Robert Norris, "Letter from the Delegates from Liverpool, in answer to the Enquiry made the Committee respecting the Natives of Africa who have been sent to England for Education, addressed to John Tarleton Esquire, Liverpool, 16 April 1788," in Sheila Lambert (ed.), *House of Commons Sessional Papers of the Eighteenth Century* (Wilmington, 1975), vol. 69, 83–84. Also see the list of 15 individuals in John Matthews, "Further Account relative to the preceding Subject, containing Observations on the Conduct of the Mulatto or Black Children who had been educated in England, on their Return to their Native Country," Ibid., 85–86. This material is also to be found in BT 6/7 (Public Record Office). Also see Robin Law and Kristin Mann, "West Africa in the Atlantic Community: The Case of the Slave Coast," *William and Mary Quarterly*, 55:2 (1999), 318–28; Pierre Verger, *Trade Relations between the Bight of Benin and Bahia 17th – 19th Century* (Ibadan, 1968), 186–88; and Alberto da Costa e Silva, "Portraits of African Royalty in Brazil," in Paul E. Lovejoy (ed.), *Identity in the Shadow of Slavery* (London, 2000).

9. Sylvanie Diouf, *Servants of Allah: African Muslims Enslaved in the Americas* (New York, 1998); and Melvyn Hiskett, *The Course of Islam in Africa* (Edinburgh, 1994), 177–83.

10. David Henderson, testifying before the House of Commons for the Report of the Lords of Trade on the Slave Trade in 1789, claimed that he had sailed from New York to Gabon in 1770, and that on board was "the Son of one of the Kings of a District on that River. This young Man had been Twelve Months at New York for Education, and was then returning home"; see Evidence of Mr. David Henderson, in Lambert, *Sessional Papers*, vol. 69, Part l, 55. Also see, for example, Curtin, "Forward to Part I," in Curtin, *Africa Remembered*, 15.

11. David Eltis, Paul E. Lovejoy and David Richardson, "Slave Trading Ports: Towards an Atlantic-Wide Perspective, 1676–1832," in Robin Law (ed.), *Ports of the Bights of Benin and Biafra* (Stirling, 1999). For a history of Old Calabar, see A.J.H. Latham, *Old Calabar 1600–1891* (London, 1973); Monday Efiong Noah, *Old Calabar: The City States and the Europeans, 1800–1885* (Uyo, Nigeria, 1980); E.U. Aye, *Old Calabar through the Ages* (Calabar, 1967); E.O. Akak, *The Palestine Origin of the Efiks* (Calabar, 1986), 3 vols.

12. Lovejoy and Richardson, "Trust, Pawnship, and Atlantic History," 337.

13. Ibid., 338.

14. The massacre has been documented by abolitionist Thomas Clarkson, in *An Essay on the Slavery and Commerce of the Human Species & particularly the African* (London,

2nd ed., 1788). The first edition was presented in 1785 at Cambridge in Latin, while the second edition, in English, included information on the massacre that Clarkson gathered in Liverpool and Bristol in 1788. Further testimony on the massacre was recorded in the 1789 Parliamentary Enquiry into the slave trade, and other accounts were published by Gomer Williams (*Liverpool Privateers*) in 1897.

15. On the credit system at Old Calabar, see A.J.H. Latham, "Currency, Credit and Capitalism on the Cross River in the Pre-Colonial Era," *Journal of African History*, 12 (1971), 600–05; and Lovejoy and Richardson, "Trust, Pawnship and Atlantic History," 333–55.

16. The holding of pawns as security is noted in James Berry's letter of April 3, 1763 (in Williams, *Privateers*, 533–35), List of Debts by King George, John Robin John, Otto Ephraim, and Orrock Robin John, August 22, [1767] concerning the boy named Assogua (Letter No. 2); Grandy King George, Old Town, January 13, 1773 (Letter No. 6); Otto Ephraim to Ambrose Lace, July 19, 1773 (Letter No. 7).

17. Ntiero Duke, "Diary," 35.

18. On 7 July 1785, Ntiero Duke reported that Captain Combesbock had "beg him to stay Little time about want get som prown out so I Did tak 2 Jar Brandy for I & Esin and I did send Optter antera for Enyong to trad of slave" (ibid., 87), that is, he wanted the captain "to stay a little longer … to get some pawns out" and hence Ntiero had sent an agent "to trade for slaves" to recover the pawns (Ibid., 35).

19. Lovejoy and Richardson, "Trust, Pawnship and Atlantic History," 347–49. Also see Lovejoy and Richardson, "The Business of Slaving: Pawnship in Western Africa, c. 1600–1810," *Journal of African History*, 41 (2000).

20. See, for example, the various case studies in Toyin Falola and Paul E. Lovejoy (eds.), *Pawnship in Africa: Debt Bondage in Historical Perspective* (Boulder, 1994).

21. According to Latham (*Old Calabar*, 29–30) *ekpe* was only introduced into Old Calabar in the middle of the eighteenth century, but based on our reading of the evidence, this is much too late. For a discussion of *ekpe*, also see A.E. Afigbo, "Peoples of the Cross River Valley and Eastern Niger Delta," in Obaro Ikime (ed.), *Groundwork in Nigerian History* (Ibadan, 1980), 61; Donald C. Simmons, "An Ethnographic Sketch of the Efik People," in Forde, *Efik Traders*, 1–26; U.N. Abalogu, "Ekpe Society in Arochukwu and Bende," *Nigeria Magazine*, 126/127 (1978), 78–97; P. Amaury Talbot, *In the Shadow of the Bush* (London, 1912), 37–48.

22. For descriptions of the *nsibidi* script and a discussion of its history and use, see Elphinstone Dayrell, "Some Nsibidi Signs," *Man*, 10 (1909), 113–14; J.K. MacGregor, "Some Notes on *Nsibidi*," *Journal of the Royal Anthropological Institute of Great Britain and Ireland*, 39 (1909), 209–19; Eliphinstone Dayrell, "Further Notes on 'Nsibidi Signs with their Meanings from the Ikom District, Southern Nigeria," *Journal of the Royal Anthropological Institute of Great Britain and Ireland*, 41 (1911), 521–40, plates lxv-lxvii.

23. See, for example, Keith Nicklin, "Skin-Covered Masks of Cameroon," *African Arts*, 12, 2 (1979), 54–59, 91; Ikwo A. Ekpo, "Ekpe Costume of the Cross River," *African Arts*, 12, 1 (1978), 73–75; Simon Ottenberg and Linda Knudsen, "Leopard Society Masquerades: Symbolism and Diffusion," *African Arts*, 18, 2 (1985), 37–95, 103–04.

24. Ntiero Duke, "Diary," 27.

25. On 24 December 1786, Ntiero Duke noted "we have Egbo Run for abou town and after 7 clock night wee Read Letter com to Willy Honesty about what Egbo monny theputt for Willy & tom Curcock 40 men first and 13 men mor for Cobham family in aqua Landing that"; that is "Ekpe running about town and after 7:00 PM we read a letter which had come to Willy Honesty about what Ekpe money they would put for Will and Tom Curcock; 40 men first and 13 men more for the Cobham family. In Aqua Landing that"; see "Diary," 102, 52.

26. Whereas pawns were used to secure debts in the 1780s, in later periods, letters of credit became common. See, for example, a letter of credit written by Duke Ephraim to L. Loiseau, captain of the French slave ship, *Le Charles*, in 1825: "I promest to Capt L. Loiseau, at the french brig Eugene to dispatch him at his Vessel, from this place for with his full cargo, at five hundred Slaves in the Current of three Months from Datte. Calbar July 7th 1825. Duke Ephraim," as quoted in Serge Daget, *Répertoire des Expéditions Négrières Françaises a la traite illégale (1814–1850)* (Nantes, 1988), 380.

27. Entry for 26 October 1786, Ntiero Duke, "Diary," 100. Translated as follows: "I heard that Ekpe was run and when I heard I walked up to Egbo Young. We saw Ekpe come down and the Ekpe men said that Sam Ambo and George Cobham had blown [*ekpe*] on Captain Fairweather. So all our family were damn angry about that blow and we sent to call Captain Fairweather to come ashore and break trade first with our family for about 15 slaves and we fired three guns on shore. At 3 o'clock in the afternoon we saw Eyo and Ebetim come down with Esin Ambo, and they went to Sam and George Cobham to make them settle with Captain Fairweather" (Ibid., 49).

28. It appears that, before 1807 at least, European merchants were not allowed to become members of *ekpe* and otherwise did not have access to its councils and therefore could not seek redress. By the 1820s, however, European merchants were allowed to join the highest grades of *ekpe*. For a discussion, see Lovejoy and Richardson, "Trust, Pawnship, and Atlantic History," 349, but see Latham, *Old Calabar*, 38, who speculates that European merchants may have been initiated into *ekpe* earlier.

29. Clarkson, *Essay on the Slavery*, 125–26, emphasis in the original.

30. John Adams, *Remarks on the Country Extending from Cape Palmas to the River Congo* (London, 1823), 144.

31. Ibid.

32. Aye and Law and Mann have concluded that the report dates to the period when Adams was at Old Calabar in the 1790s, but we think that the text is unclear and could apply to the period when Adams wrote his account, several years after British abolition in 1807. In any event there appears to have been a school at Old Calabar at least two decades before the first missionaries settled. See Aye, *Old Calabar*, 108; and Law and Mann, "West Africa in the Atlantic Community," 354 n70.

33. For a picture of a bell that is dated 1799, see the Cumberbeach bell of King Effiwatt, in Oku, *Kings and Chiefs*, 8; and Akak, *Palestine Origin*, vol. 3, 423. Also see R. Stewart-Brown, *Liverpool Ships in the Eighteenth Century* (Liverpool, 1932), 49, who reports a bell that was inscribed: "THE GIFT OF THOMAS JONES OF BRISTOL TO GRANDY ROBIN JOHN OF OLD TOWN OLD CALABAR 1770," as cited in Donald C. Simmons, ed., *Holman's Voyage to Old Calabar* [1828] (Calabar, 1959), 9.

34. Several ivory discs have survived and are located in the Merseyside Maritime Museum, Albert Dock, Liverpool. Inscriptions on five discs are as follows:

  1. "John Pepper Brig Highfield a good man"
  2. "Tom Buck of Grandy Bonny, an Honest Trader, he sold me 20 Slaves"
  3. "Calla Fubra of Grandy Bonny, an Honest Trader, he sold me 20 Slaves Ship Liverpool"
  4. "This Book given to Duke [missing piece] New Callabar by Rob[t] Boy'd of Liverp[ool] 65," which has on the reverse: "Duke Cullo Dash 60 Barrs, [piece missing] Gun, 1 Jackett, a lac'd Hatt & a [piece missing] His Fathers Dash [piece missing] 4 Bro[rs] 20, Wife 6, Mate 20 & his [piece missing] 30 Barrs"
  5. "The Gift of Captain Trousdall to Young West India of Grandy Bonny" and on the reverse, "West India of Grandy Bonney a Good Trader and a Honest Man: Sold the Alfred 30 Slaves."

We wish to thank Anthony J. Tibbles for providing us with plates of these discs.

35. Matthew, Penny and Norris, Letter from the Delegates from Liverpool, 83–84.

36. Ibid.

37. Account of Henry Nicholls, 1804–05, in Robin Hallet (ed.), *Records of the African Association, 1788–1831* (London, 1964), 195.

38. Ambrose Lace to Thomas Jones, 11 November 1773, in Williams, *Liverpool Privateers*, 541–42.

39. Lace to Jones, 11 November 1773, in Williams, *Liverpool Privateers*, 541–42. Nicholls, who was in Old Calabar in 1805, met Otto Ephraim and noted that he had "received his education in Liverpool; he speaks English very well"; see Nicholls' account in Hallet, *Records*, 203.

40. Matthew, Penny, and Norris, Letter from the Delegates from Liverpool, 84.

41. Ibid.

42. Behrendt, "Diary of Antera Duke."

43. However, there are some indications of limited sexual interaction, such as reference to the "families" of particular British traders, where kinship terms were being used to describe close friendships, and perhaps something more. However, unlike on other parts of the Guinea coast, there was no resident, mixed population, suggesting limited sexual interaction.

44. Alagoa, "Peoples of the Cross River Valley," 62–63; MacGregor, "Some Notes on Nsibidi," 209–19; Dayrell, "Further Notes on 'Nsibidi Signs," 521–43.

45. Hope Masterton Waddell, *Twenty-Nine Years in the West Indies and Central Africa* (London, 1863).

46. See, e.g., Paley, "Somerset." Also see the case of the *African Queen*, which sailed from Old Calabar to Montego Bay in 1793. The ship had on board "a Negro Boy of about 16 [who]... was put on Board on the Coast as a Pawn and we thought it advisable not to sell him" (John Cunningham and John Perry to James Rogers, 10 March 1793, PRO C 107/59).

"Remarkable Liberty"

Language and Identity in Eighteenth-Century Black Autobiography

Philip Gould

Human liberty cannot be bought or sold.

—Thomas Clarkson,
An Essay on the Slavery and Commerce of The Human Species (1786)

During the post-Revolutionary era the legal and social status of African Americans was at best precarious. Numerous historians have noted as much. Joanne Melish recently has argued that this period, which witnessed the gradual emancipation of black slaves, nevertheless left them in a liminal position, somewhere between being "freed" and truly "free." Such a position of course derived from the inability of whites to envision the reality of black citizenship. In this essay I wish to consider the literary and autobiographical ramifications of liberty. How did eighteenth-century black writers cultivate the claim to individual "freedom" or "liberty"? I address this question by considering the dynamic and complex relations between the changing ideas in the late eighteenth century about individual liberty and the rhetorical texture and transgressive identities in early black writing of this era. Such changes derived partly from the emergence of liberal ideology.[1] Most critics, however, dubiously view the relation between liberal ideology and black identity. Recent, influential work has argued that liberal, enlightened thinking left no real space for black participation; indeed, it militated against it.[2] In this essay I challenge such a premise and argue instead that black autobiographers pushed at the unstable semantic boundaries of the language of "liberty" in order to disrupt traditional norms of social subordination.

This argument is particularly relevant to autobiographies that were not written but "related" by black narrators to white editors. I focus on two autobiographies that were collaborative projects: *A Narrative of the Lord's Wonderful Dealings with John Marrant, a Black* (1785) and *A Narrative of the Life and Adventures of Venture, a Native of Africa* (1798). Unlike *The Interesting Narrative of the Life of Olaudah Equiano, or Gustavus Vassa, the African* (1789), these texts do not bear the claim "Written by Himself." They do not (yet) have the canonical cachet of Equiano's brilliant narrative, and their mode of literary production poses special problems to contemporary readers. As William Andrews has argued, narratives such as these raise the potential for "repression" and "restriction" by white editors upon their black subjects. If recent critics have qualified such skepticism, arguing instead for a more flexible understanding of the black author's "voice,"[3] I want to pursue Andrews' original insight that "the very language [of these autobiographical narratives . . . is of indeterminate origin" (35–6). Rather than see this as a disabling ambiguity of authorship, we might instead see it as an enabling ambiguity of black language that was forged in the very act of literary collaboration.

The Free Carpenter

The rhetorical complexity of early Black Atlantic autobiography derives in large part from social and economic changes that lent key political terms such as "liberty" and "slavery" new, fluid meanings. Historians of late–eighteenth-century America have emphasized the destabilization of traditional hierarchies during this era. "Throughout the eighteenth-century Anglo-American world," Gordon S. Wood has argued, "traditional authority was brought into question. . . . The social hierarchy seemed less natural, less ordained by God, and more man-made, more arbitrary" (*Radicalism* 145). In addition to the cultural importance of benevolence that Wood is describing, important economic changes helped to unsettle traditional assumptions about social order. The growth of agricultural exports, nascent industrial production, increases in population, urban growth and demographic movement, produced public debates about political economy that were accompanied by "discussion extolling voluntarism, free will, and the harmony of unfettered economic agents in a web of free markets" (Matson 119).[4] The antiauthoritarian impulses of modernizing society lay in both the "liberal vision of a society of undifferentiated competitors" (Appleby 183) and "the radical egalitarian strain within . . . commercial discourse" itself (Breen 488).

Notwithstanding these social movements, much of the period's antislavery writing by English and Americans actually belies a distinctly conservative posture towards the prospect of newly emancipated black slaves. For example, the noted English clergyman James Ramsay's *An Essay on the Treatment and Conversion of African Slaves in the British Sugar Colonies* (1784) railed against the brutality of the West Indies only in context of the "natural inequality, or diversity, which prevails among men that fits them for society" (3). His belief that there was "social servitude" even in the "freest state" (8) belies the hierarchical thinking in abolition movements, especially as they confronted the proslavery critique of its presumed radicalism that during the 1790s was associated with the revolutions in France and

Saint Domingue. Similarly, the dissenting minister Joseph Priestley urged a Birmingham antislavery audience in 1788 to consider "all distinctions among men as temporary, calculated for the ultimate benefit of all; and consequently that it is for the interest of the lower orders, as well as the highest, that such a subordination should exist" (vii). Such clerical conservatism, which can envision equality only in the safely removed space of heaven itself, is also highly self-conscious of the malleability of the language of "liberty." Conservative New Englanders who opposed slavery like the minister Jedidiah Morse, directly instructed African Americans to not pervert the meaning of "liberty" and thereby make it "a cloak for licentiousness" (18). The kind of Foulcauldian monitorship that Morse urged ("Many eyes are upon you") aimed to control the "liberty" that property theoretically afforded emancipated blacks. As the English antislavery leader Granville Sharp put it, those "negroes that are . . . not fit to be trusted, all at once, with liberty, might be delivered over to the care and protection of a county committee, in order to avoid the baneful effects *of private property in men*" (59). This context makes clearer the stakes of early black autobiography. It provides a rhetorical context for such language as "mastery," "liberty," "property," and "dependence" that is so prominent in the slave narrative. I would argue that the semantic slipperiness of such language allowed the black story-teller discursive space in which to assert striking yet subdued identities. Unlike the earlier *Narrative of the Uncommon Sufferings, and Surprizing Deliverance of Briton Hammon, a Negro Man* (1760), Marrant's *Narrative* denaturalizes (in Wood's terms) the fragile hierarchical norms of late–eighteenth-century Anglo-America.

Born into a free family in 1755, Marrant moved with his mother from New York to Florida, and then finally to Georgia, before he was sent at age eleven to live with his sister in Charleston, South Carolina and learn a respectable trade. Smitten at the age of fourteen by George Whitefield's preaching, Marrant embraced an evangelical Methodism that later facilitated the publication of his *Narrative*. Modeled on Bunyan's archetypal Christian, Marrant dramatizes his escape from his unconverted family as he went "on the road" into the South Carolina backcountry where he supposedly converted Cherokee Indians before returning to Charleston in the early 1770s. There his activities become even more uncertain. The *Narrative* claims that he was impressed into the British navy between 1775 and 1782; sometime soon afterwards, he arrived in London where he embraced the Calvinistic Methodism of the Countess of Huntington (who was Whitefield's correspondent as well as Phillis Wheatley's literary patron). Later, Marrant was ordained a minister at the Huntingdonian chapel in Bath, England, and traveled to Nova Scotia in the late 1780s to evangelize mixed audiences of whites, Native Americans and ex-slaves expatriated during the Revolution.[5]

Marrant's autobiography understandably has been read in the traditions of spiritual autobiography and Indian captivity narrative. It is, as one reader has put it, a tale of "rebirth and resurrection" (Montgomery 108). Such a reading certainly takes Marrant's white amanuensis, the English minister William Aldridge, at his word when he asks rhetorically, "Were the power, grace, and providence of God ever more eminently displayed, than in the conversion, success, and deliverances of John Marrant?" (Ed. Carretta 110). Moreover, Marrant's own penchant for biblical tropes reinforces the disciplinary context of his writing. His dramatic conversion, itinerant wandering, evangelical mission, as well as the plethora of typological identifications (including Paul, Daniel, Luke's story of the Prodigal Son, and the ancient Israelites of Exodus) all testify to the Methodist hand in its publication. In light of its evangelical conventions, some readers of Marrant allow for religion to displace antislavery politics, as Gates, for example, claims that Marrant does not "speak to the perilous condition of black bondsmen or even the marginally free" (145).

Recently, Nancy Ruttenberg has argued for the development of "democratic personality" in English and American religious culture in general and Whitefieldian evangelicalism in particular. As Ruttenberg claims, "The revolutionary self of the Whitefieldian convert was distinguished first and foremost by the aggressive uncontainability of his or her speech, underwritten by the reconceptualization of the self as a pure conduit for the expression of God's will" (118). Yet the problem with this account of the racial politics of religious conversion is not merely Whitefield's inability, as she acknowledges, "to contemplate the uncontainable enlargement of black Christians" (117), but the very premise that black speech in this case depends upon religious conversion. For the structural logic of Marrant's *Narrative* displays his socially transgressive self—and voice—long *before* his actual conversion. In this way, it subtly undermines the ostensible structure of spiritual autobiography, which on one level recounts the archetypal passage from sinner to saint. From the very outset, Marrant tells a story to Aldridge that—in light of the language we have seen in Priestley and Morse—stages a series of rebellions against various "masters" in order to gain a form of self-mastery whose secular and spiritual markers are always ambiguous. As a free black living in a slave society, Marrant epitomizes a larger reality in colonial America in which, as Joyce Appleby puts it, "the contrasting statuses of free and unfree, dependent and independent, came to represent stark alternatives" (144). As much as the reality of racial slavery looms over the *Narrative*, the political legacy of "slavery" as "dependence" takes on profoundly *social* meanings in a world where the brutality of chattel and indentured forms of labor bore striking resemblance (see Hofstadter). To this end, music suggests for Marrant not merely "voice" but the potential status of independence:

> [A]s I was walking one day, I passed by a school, and I heard music and dancing, which took my fancy very much, and I felt a strong inclination to learn the music. I went home, and informed my sister, that I had rather learn to play upon music than go to a trade ... [My mother] persuaded me much against it, but her persuasions were fruitless. Disobedience to God or man, being one of the first fruits of sin, grew out of me in early buds. Finding I was set upon it, and resolved to learn nothing else, she agreed to it, and went with me to speak to the man, and to settle upon the best terms with him she could. He insisted upon twenty pounds currency, which was paid, and I was engaged to stay with him eighteen months (112)

As it is expressed through his "fancy," Marrant's desire to avoid indentured servitude is coterminous with his dissent from parental authority. Regardless of Aldridge's editorial hand, the allusion in this case to Proverbs 10:16 ("The labour of the righteous tendeth to life; the fruit of the wicked to sin") introduces the Narrative's crucial theme of labor. This contrasts the state of being "free" as opposed to "enslaved"—whether the latter means spiritually "wicked" or socially dependent.

The apparent slippage in these alternative meanings of liberty and slavery enables the autobiography's simultaneous representations of both fallen sinner and ingenious individual. Indeed, Marrant's mother's failure to broker an advantageous deal makes her a foil in the protagonist's later successes. These successes derive from virtues that Marrant did not invent but reappropriated. In a rather Franklinian passage, his account of his work ethic confounds the Methodist conventions of the self's pre-converted iniquity:

> In the evenings after the scholars were dismissed, I used to resort to the bottom of our garden, where it was customary for some musicians to assemble to blow the French-horn. Here my improvement was so rapid, that in twelve-months time I became master both of the violin and of the French-horn, and was much respected by the Gentlemen and Ladies whose children attended the school, as also by my master. This opened a large door of vanity and vice, for I was invited to all the balls and assemblies that were held in the town. . . . I was a stranger to want, being supplied with as much money as I had any occasion for. (112)

Marrant's "labour" provides him with a newly claimed public identity commensurate with financial independence. He has property; he is "much respected." The moment is similar to one in the Interesting Narrative when Equiano proclaims, "In process of time I became master of a few pounds, and in a fair way of making more, which my friendly captain knew well" (Ed. Carretta 232).

Unlike the Interesting Narrative, however, which structurally places its protagonist's religious quest after the achievement of economic independence, Marrant's autobiography compresses them both—sometimes within the very same sentence. The above passage's oscillation between muted approval of self-mastery and open lament for the protagonist's enslavement "to every vice suited to my nature" (112) follows the dual imperatives of, on the one hand, Methodist conversion and, on the other, "a vision of society in which the rule of privilege is replaced by equal opportunity in which individuals, now masters of their destiny, are no longer the slaves of history, tradition, or birth" (Kramnick 5). Eventually, Marrant reverses the terms of mastery and dependence by manipulating a fragile colonial labor market: "The time I had engaged to serve my master being expired, he persuaded me to stay with him, and offered me any thing, or any money, not to leave him. His entreaties proving ineffectual, I quitted his service. . . ." (112). His second "master"—a carpenter—he similarly exploits through his economic value as a musician: "Accordingly I went, but every evening I was sent for to play on music . . . and I often continued out very late, sometimes all night, so as to render me incapable of attending my master's business the next day, yet in this manner I served him a year and four months, and was much approved of by him" (112–13).

What the *Narrative* thus dramatizes is the necessity of control over one's labor. The implicit value it places on rational calculation and individual acquisitiveness is especially significant in context of the historical effects commercial capitalism wrought on evangelical Methodism. The growth of the transatlantic book trade, the spread of advertising of print, and the increase in popular consumerism all served to commercialize eighteenth-century evangelical religion.[6] As evangelical religion gradually became a consumable commodity, "the intertwining of evangelical piety and lower-class claims to equal social consideration make it difficult to differentiate the language of Protestant salvation from that of secular liberalism" (Appleby 182). Hence readers often miss the entrepreneurial context of Marrant's "conversion." One should recognize that it comes at a precarious moment in his early life where his relatively free status is threatened with seven years of indentured servitude: "He [Marrant's second master] wrote a letter to my mother to come and have me bound, and whilst my mother was weighing the matter in her own mind, the gracious purposes of God, respecting a perishing sinner, were now to be disclosed" (113). Marrant's supposedly gracious confrontation with the voice of the "crazy man" Whitefield—presumably the vocal medium of black salvation and the vocal model of black expression—thus occurs at the very moment in which he stumbles uncertainly between "free" and "dependent" realms of labor and identity. Liberated from familial and indentured forms of authority, Marrant's spiritual conversion ensures a "liberty" that signifies uncertainly the emancipation from external and internal foes.

This rhetorical flexibility allows us to reconceive genre as well. Traditionally seen as an Indian captivity narrative (and included in modern anthologies of the genre), Marrant's work actually inverts the moral geography of Indian captivity. In the preface Aldridge describes the crucial passage "between the wilderness and the cultivated country" (111). But this movement might just as readily be read as the social empowerment of itinerancy that, as one historian has argued, "eroded the deferential boundaries, which subordinated 'private persons' . . . [and] also challenged the distinctions of parenthood, gender and race which eighteenth-century thinkers conceived of establishing a natural hierarchy" (Hall 56). Marrant's ingenious resourcefulness in this domain belies the providential explications he offers for his survival. For example, the spiritual distance he places between the Indian captor/partner and himself begins to show this sort of resourceful manipulation: "Having heard me praising God . . . he enquired who I was talking to? I told him I was talking to my Lord Jesus; he seemed surprized, and asked me where he was? For he did not see him there. I told him he could not be seen with bodily eyes" (116). The irony of this exchange begins to allow the possibility of reading the back country ("fifty-five miles and a half" from home) as both a spiritual wilderness and an arena of secular, or "bodily," virtues. In killing deer and drying their skins, the two together have to defend against "nocturnal enemies": "We collected a number of large bushes, and placed them nearly in a circular form, which uniting at the extremity, afforded us both a verdant covering a sufficient shelter from night dews. . . . A fire was kindled . . . and fed with fresh fuel all night, as we slept and watched by turns" (117).

The ingenuity and resourcefulness requisite in this new environment extends also to one's mastery of language. The two crucial passages that have received the most critical attention involve Marrant's spontaneous mastery of the spoken word as the means to personal "liberty." On the verge of being tortured by his Cherokee captors, the first of two miracles occurs: "I prayed in English a considerable time, and about the middle of my prayer, the Lord impressed a strong desire upon my mind to turn into their language, and pray in their tongue. I did so, and with remarkable liberty, which wonderfully affected the people" (118). Later, while on the verge of starvation, and again threatened with death, Marrant miraculously heals the king's daughter and converts both king and people to the Word:

> [T]he Lord appeared most lovely and glorious; the king himself was awakened, and the others set at liberty. A great change took place among the people; the king's house became God's house; the soldiers were ordered away, and the poor condemned prisoner had perfect liberty, and was treated like a prince. Now the Lord made all my enemies to become my great friends. . . . I had assumed the habit of the country, and was dressed much like the king, and nothing was too good for me. The king would take off his golden ornaments, his chain and bracelets, like a child, if I objected to them, and lay them aside. Here I learned to speak their tongue in the highest stile. (120)

Cast in the language of divine deliverance, these two scenes reveal the power of language for *both* protagonist and autobiographer. By narrating his story to Aldridge in a way that capitalizes upon the ambiguities of "liberty," Marrant fulfills at once the expectations of evangelical Methodism and the anti-authoritarian theme residing just below the narrative surface. This is not conventional captivity narrative. As opposed to, say, Mary Rowlandson's unintended adoption of "savage" ways, Marrant's newly acquired costume shows less the dangers of acculturation and more the inversion of social relations. Likening himself to a king, and the Cherokee king to a "child, Marrant stages yet another successful negotiation of masters.

These moments in Marrant's "captivity" provide a rhetorical key for the *Narrative*. As Gates influentially has argued, the motif of the "Talking Book" in early black autobiography suggests the self-conscious importance these autobiographers invested in literacy as the Enlightenment touchstone to reason and humanity. He reads these scenes as evidence of Marrant's revision of the trope found in the *Narrative of the Most Remarkable Particulars in the Life of James Albert Ukawsaw Gronniosaw, An African Prince* (1772). Yet by including Anglo-American discourses as the object of mimicry and parody, we might extend what Gates means by "signifying" as a rhetorical and political strategy. Marrant's typological identification with the biblical Daniel (the captive in Nebuchadnezzar's court) is as much as resourceful individualist as persecuted martyr. Rather than see his revisionary status only as the result of literacy—he can read the Bible as opposed to the Cherokee—we might see it simultaneously as an oral performance as well. His avowed manipulation of the "Indian tongue" (117), his mastery of it "in the highest stile," tropes the rhetorical logic of the *Narrative*, which engages a protean language of "liberty" and thereby allows for the black narrator's flexible response to the imposing presence of the white editor. Hence the *Narrative* refers to him as "the free Carpenter" (123).

THE VENTURE CAPITALIST

But what kind of "freedom" did this actually mean? I would argue that the questions itself turns on the deeper relation between race and liberal ideology. Critics of liberalism like Eric Cheyfitz, for example, have noted how the widespread influence of John Locke's *Second Treatise on Government* served to conceptually reduce humanity to property. "In the West, property, in that tangled space where the physical and metaphysical mix, is the very mark of identity, of that which is identical to itself: what we typically call a 'self' or an 'individual'" (50). (As one Revolutionary-era minister put it, "Property is prior to all human laws, constitutions and charters. *God hath given the earth to the children of men*" [Sherwood 398]). Perhaps the historian Winthrop Jordan has put the problem most succinctly in arguing that, "The absence of any clear disjunction between what are now called 'human' and 'property' rights formed a massive roadblock across the route to the abolition of slavery" (351).[7]

As black narrators, both Marrant and Venture Smith constructed identities that culminated in freedom, but did so in a historical period that still generally founded freedom on the possession of property. The comparison of Smith with Marrant only highlights the rhetorical problems for constructing racial identity that derived from the conflation of liberty and property. I would argue that it is the major problem and perhaps most interesting feature of Venture Smith's *Narrative*. The capacity for white antislavery writers to place this prickly issue into philosophical, and sometimes highly abstract, terms was simply not a luxury that black autobiographers enjoyed. They had to wage antislavery polemics through the gritty (albeit manipulable) details of their lives.[8]

Born sometime in the late 1720s in the region of Gangara, Broteer Furro (Smith's original name) was the son of a West African king and a member of the Dukandarra. At about the age of eight, Furro was captured by slave traders and taken to Rhode Island, and thereafter spent most of his life in Long Island and eastern Connecticut until he died in 1805. A more secular account than Marrant's *Narrative*, Smith's nevertheless was similarly transcribed by a white editor, Elisha Niles, a Connecticut schoolteacher and antislavery advocate, who published it over a six-week period in a local newspaper, *The New London Bee*. Republished in 1835 and 1897, Smith's text was accompanied by "Traditions of Venture" that provide legendary (and perhaps sensationalized) accounts of his physical strength and capacity for work. Even the first edition's preface, written by Niles, models its subject as a paragon of bourgeois virtue: "The subject of the following pages, had he received only a common education, might have been a man of high respectability and usefulness. . . . The reader may see here a Franklin and a Washington in a state of nature, or rather in a state of slavery. . . . This narrative exhibits a pattern of honesty, prudence and industry, to people of his own colour; and perhaps some white people would not find themselves degraded by imitating such an example" (369). Premised on the didactic potential of autobiography, Niles' preface signals the problem of Smith's representative status. Rather than see such hedging ("might," "perhaps") simply as the editor's irrepressible racism, I want to emphasize that it suggests the larger question of racial access to white, bourgeois ideology. In effect, Niles is struggling with the apparent incongruity of the black Ben Franklin. Do the values of "respectability and usefulness," his preface asks, erase or reify racial difference?

The cultural contexts for this issue are especially important in light of eighteenth-century discussions about the potential for black virtue. Certainly, the debates between proslavery and antislavery forces shaped this issue. For example, in the 1770s there occurred a heated exchange in print between the antislavery advocate Benjamin Rush and the West Indian planter, Richard Nisbet, in which Nisbet's reply to Rush's *An Address to the Inhabitants of the British Settlements in North America, upon Slave-Keeping* (1773) sardonically complained that Rush merely wanted to end West Indian slavery so that "that Africans might indulge their natural laziness in their own country" (10). Yet even outside the ranks of West Indian apologists there existed marked resistance to the growth of a free black population. Berlin has remarked that, "On the one hand, [white Americans] condemned newly freed slaves as dissolute wastrels whose unrestrained exuberance for freedom would reduce them to the penury they deserved. On the other hand, they mocked those who strove for respectability as feckless imposters." (225). Lest one imagine, however, that racial stereotyping was a proslavery possession in post-Revolutionary America, consider Noah Webster's commentary at the end of his *Effects of Slavery on Morals and Industry* (1793): "But I cannot believe that *all* the slaves in this country are so dull that motives of interest will make no impression on their minds, or that they are so unprincipled and ungrateful, that if set at liberty, they would turn their hands against their masters" (38).

In context of these prevailing sentiments, Smith cultivates an image of himself that racially embodies liberal values while avoiding the extremes of lassitude and libertinism. To this end, the *Narrative*'s ambiguous achievement describes a transformation from object to subject in a capitalist slave economy, a transformation that logically returns Smith to the status of property, which he then must reengage. Like Marrant's *Narrative*, Smith's shows the awareness of the importance of language to this process. The "social death" enacted by chattel slavery occurs first in the slave narrative's process of naming, for as Orlando Patterson argues,

"The slave's former name died with his former self" (55). Smith's *Narrative* accordingly invests thematic significance in the moment Broteer becomes Venture. "I was bought on board [the slave trading vessel] by one Robertson Mumford, steward of the said vessel, for four gallons of rum, and a piece of calico, and called VENTURE, on account of his having purchased me with his own private venture. Thus I came by my name" (374). If this summation wryly comments on the antislavery argument that the slave trade was a dangerously speculative form of commerce, it also introduces the theme of commodification that plagues the *Narrative*.

The capacity to effect such a change from object to subject in a slave economy narratively involves the creation of a proto-liberal persona. As we have seen, Niles' preface at once facilitates and undermines this project, introducing the black Ben Franklin who exists in a state of nature—or slavery. Does Niles' use of the epithet "native" for Smith suggest a state of nature associated with Africa? Or does he mean Smith's "native ingenuity and good sense"—virtues that might be accessible to all humans? (369). One meaning reifies racial difference; the other potentially displaces it. Smith pursues this later course, not to abandon his African origins, as Desrochers has shown, but to claim an individuated identity from the anonymity of slavery. Like Marrant's rhetoric of "liberty," Smith's persona of the venturesome capitalist achieves this goal. Early on, Smith demonstrates the virtues requisite to succeed in the competitive arena when he is betrayed by an indentured servant named Heddy during their planned escape: "I then thought it might afford some chance for my freedom, or at least a palliation of my running away, to return Heddy immediately to his master, and inform him that I was induced to go away by Heddy's address" (377). Like Marrant's mastery of the "Indian tongue," the *character* Venture Smith's manipulation of persona signals the self-consciousness with which the black autobiographer recognizes the forms of power that control chattel slavery and black writing alike. The *Narrative*'s persona is premised on this realization: "This [money] I took out of the earth and tendered to my master, having previously engaged a free negro man to take his security for it, as I was property of my master, and could not safely take his obligation myself. . . . By cultivating this land with greatest diligence and economy, at times when my master did not require my labor, in two years I laid up ten pounds" (380). In the scenes where Smith tills land, makes wise investments, lends money at interest, and bargains his time and labor wisely, he successfully negotiates the slave economy and, like Marrant, makes free labor (in the tradition of both Locke and Adam Smith) the key to free identity. This narrative process culminates in a scene where Smith exploits the paradox of liberty and slavery. After his new master Stanton puts him in shackles, he notes, "I continued to wear the chain peaceably for two or three days, when my master asked me with contemptuous hard names whether I had not better be freed from my chains and go to work. I answered him, No" (378). To be "free," then, is to exhibit an autonomous will, even if it means remaining in chains.

This inversion of liberty and slavery suggests the importance of rhetorical irony to the *Narrative*'s autobiographical and political design. Bakhtin's distinction between two forms of linguistic hybridity is useful in clarifying this design.

One is "intentional" where one discourse unmasks the other; the other "organic" where two cultural discourses unintentionally and unconsciously collide, mix, fuse and ultimately enable the historical evolution of language (Young 20–4). In this light, the *Narrative* ably manages the competing religious and economic meanings within the discourse of "redemption":

> What was wanting in redeeming myself, my master agreed to wait on me for, until I could procure it for him. I still continued to work for Col. Smith. . . .
>
>   Being encouraged by the success which I had met in redeeming myself, I again solicited my master for a further chance of completing it. The chance for which I solicited him was that of going out to work the ensuing winter. He agreed to this on condition that I would give him one quarter of my earnings. . . . I returned to my master and gave him what I received of my six months' labor. This left only thirteen pounds eighteen shillings to make up the full sum of my redemption. My master liberated me, saying that I might pay what was behind if I could ever make it convenient, otherwise it would be well. The amount of money which I had paid my master towards redeeming my time, was seventy-one pounds two shillings. The reason of my master for asking such an unreasonable price, was he said, to secure himself in case I should ever come to want. (380–81)

One might see the *Narrative*'s language of redemption as the "organic" process by which the late eighteenth century updated traditionally religious discourse to the ideological needs of commercial society. In context of an earlier scene in the *Narrative*, however, Smith's language bears out satiric intentionality. In this case, the young Smith justifies his defiance of his master's son by claiming that he is merely obeying his master's instructions. When the son becomes violently irate, Smith wryly summarizes the American slave's predicament: "This was to serve two masters" (376). By alluding to Christ's injunction to distinguish between spiritual and secular authority, Smith is able to call attention to the moral bankruptcy of slaveholding "Christianity"—a staple of the slave narrative apparent in later famous slave narratives by Frederick Douglass, Harriet Jacobs, and others. As a more openly secular account than Marrant's, Smith's *Narrative* simultaneously demystifies religious hypocrisy and sanctifies (through the religious connotations of "redemption") its protagonist's economic drives for freedom.

The value that Smith places on the self, however, signals the problem of commodification that characterized antislavery writing in general and early black autobiography in particular. The historian Shane White has described the achievement of slaves such as Venture Smith who labored for their emancipation: "Success in such negotiations [of slaves with their masters] and an early release from slavery were partly the result of luck, but the process also favored the most industrious, tenacious, and skilled of the slaves" (152). The necessity to demonstrate "individuality" within the cognitive contexts of the market serves to reconfigure humanity back into property. Succumbing to the epistemological trap endemic to slave capitalism, Smith commodifies even the most intimate of familial relations. Consider the account of his son's death:

> Solomon, my eldest son . . . I hired him out to one Charles Church, of Rhode-Island, for one tear, on consideration of his giving him twelve pounds and an opportunity of acquiring some learning. In the course of the year, Church fitted out a vessel for a whaling voyage, and being in want of hands to man her, he induced my son to go, with the promise of giving him . . . a pair of silver buckles, besides his wages. . . . [O]n my arrival at Church's, to my great grief, I could only see the vessel my son was in almost out of sight going to sea. My son died of the scurvy in this voyage, and Church has never yet paid me the least of his wages. In my son, besides the loss of his life, I lost equal to seventy-five pounds" (382).

While the episode dramatizes the seduction of Solomon in order to vilify white commercial relations, Smith's "grief" would seem to arise from a material rather than a sentimental economy. Solomon's value is "equal to" the amount paid to "redeem" him; accordingly, sentimental family relations are buried in the subordinate clause beginning with "besides." Thus Solomon is virtually reduced to the value he possessed *as a slave*. Similarly, Smith abruptly interrupts his lament about his daughter Hannah's "lingering and painful" death with financial concerns—"The physician's bills for attending her during her illness amounted to forty pounds" (383)—and then immediately returns to his ensuing business transactions.

The capacity for family members to stand as both persons and things expresses in Black Atlantic autobiography the cultural paradox blurring the ontological boundaries of property and humanity, one that was most explicitly written into early American political culture by James Madison in the *Federalist* #54. In order to rationalize the Constitution's Three-Fifths Compromise (which made the slave account for only part of a human being for purposes of state taxation and representation), Madison argued for "the mixt character of persons and property." Whereas Marrant sentimentalizes familial relations (chiefly through the biblical model of the Prodigal Son), Smith reduces them to the prosaic realities of the slave economy. In narrating his subjectivity out of the Madisonian paradox underwriting slavery, Smith nonetheless perpetuates the ideology of "value" endemic to slave capitalism. He makes liberty something that one literally owns.

To turn this dilemma into metacritical commentary about the nature of his own autobiography is perhaps the most striking achievement of Smith's *Narrative*. Rather than ultimately rejecting "his own success as a cultural identification" (521), as Robert Ferguson argues, Smith exploits this cultural role by commenting on the performative potential that one's status as "property" may afford. When he threatens his master, William Hooker, for example, Smith knows that by binding him

Hooker decreases his market value: "If you will go by no other measures, I will tie you down to my sleigh. I replied to him, that if he carried me in that manner, no person would purchase me, for it would be thought he had a murderer for sale. After this he tried no more, and said he would not have me as a gift" (379). Recognizing the uncertain cultural distinctions between humanity and property, Smith masters the symbolic economy of slave society. At crucial moments he takes control of his body as a symbolic commodity and redeploys its symbolic function. At one point he schemes with another white man, Hempsted Miner, to appear "discontented" during negotiations in order to lower his market value and thereby retaliate against his master Stanton. "[A]nd that in return he would give me a good chance to gain my freedom when I came to live with him. Not long after, Hemsted Miner purchased me of my master for fifty-six pounds lawful. He took the chain and padlocks from off me immediately after" (379). These moments lend irony to Smith's lament that Stanton wished to sell him only "to convert me into cash, and speculate with me as with other commodities" (379). For this sort of symbolic speculation is just what Venture Smith performs throughout the *Narrative*. To convert oneself from object to subject, the black autobiographer, like the black venture capitalist working his way to "freedom," must master the ideological and symbolic resources made available to him. Like the slave body, the slave narrative performs itself publicly within the context of such an exchange.

One of the more virulent attacks upon blacks during the Enlightenment came, as many critics today note, from the pen of the Scottish philosopher David Hume. Commenting on the poetry of Francis Williams, a free-born Jamaican who was later educated in England, Hume declared: "I am apt to suspect that the negroes and in general all other species of men . . . to be naturally inferior to the whites. . . . In Jamaica, indeed, they talk of one negroe as a man of parts and learning; but it is likely he is admired for slender accomplishments, like a parrot who speaks a few words plainly" (Ed. Eze 33). During a period of intensifying debate over the subject of West Indian slavery and the slave trade, proslavery apologists like Richard Nisbet and Edward Long cited Hume as gospel. In our own era, critics like Gates have responded to it in terms of the crisis of "originality" facing black writers— then as now. "Reacting to the questionable allegations made against their capacity to be original, black writers have often assumed a position of extreme negation, in which they claim for themselves no black literary antecedents whatsoever, or claim for themselves an anonymity of origins. . . ." (114). Rather than see the Humean commentary as a register for the challenge of articulating an African-American literary tradition, we might invert the trope of the parrot to consider instead how black writers like John Marrant and Venture Smith spoke within Anglo-American languages only to shape—and be shaped by—them. Rather than see these speaking autobiographers as victims to their white editors, we might see them truly as collaborators. During a period of social and cultural change, the nature of this collaboration depended in large part upon the black subject's ability to exploit the possible meanings of "rights," and "liberty." If, then, as John Sekora has suggested, reading black literature entails sifting through the "white envelope" for the "black message," reading the lives of these eighteenth-century autobiographers entails recognizing the fragile seams and fraying edges of the white envelope itself.

NOTES

1. I understand "liberalism" itself to be an ambiguous, inchoate ideology during this formative period. My use of the term recognizes the important connections between "rights" and "duties" in early modern philosophy and culture. For a discussion of this issue see Knud Haakonsen, "From Natural Law to the Rights of Man."

2. As Gilroy argues, the "rational, scientific, and enlightened Euro-American thought" that emerged in the eighteenth century was a source of "terror" for black writers, since the modern categories of race and nation implied "the supposedly primitive outlook of prehistorical, cultureless, and bestial Africans." See *The Black Atlantic*, 220. Saidiya Hartman similarly views the underside of ostensibly progressive thinking among nineteenth-century abolitionists: "Liberalism, in general, and rights discourse, in particular, assure entitlements and privileges as they enable and efface elemental forms of domination primarily because of the atomistic portrayal of social relations, the inability to address collective interests and needs, and the sanctioning of subordination and the free reign of prejudice in the construction of the social or the private." See *Scenes of Subjection*, 122.

3. Desrochers, for example, notes that "in assuming that whites consciously and effectively silenced the voices of the first black narrators, scholars too often limit themselves in search of a 'true' black voice of irreconcilable and discernible difference" (43). Rafia Zafar similarly argues that "domination by the white editor, no matter how significant, can never be complete" (54).

4. The literature about economic history and culture in early republican America is quite large. See Gilje, Rothen, and Vickers for interpretations that attempt to update the traditional view of a "moral economy" in this era. As Gilje has noted, one way of articulating the rise of capitalism is to "look for capitalistic behaviors and the adoption of core values rooted in individualism, competition, and the arbitration of market mechanisms" (2).

5. For biographical backgrounds see Carretta and Potkay and Burr. Carretta suggests that in South Carolina Marrant owned a slave. *The Black Loyalist Directory* lists "Mellia Marrant, 30, squat wench, B, ([Thomas Grigg]). Formerly the property of John Marrant, near Santee, Carolina; left him at the siege of Charleston." John and Millia Marrant's relations are shrouded in ambiguity; theirs may have been a sexual relationship, a master-slave one, or one based on indentured servitude—all of which turn on the rhetorical ambiguity of the word "master."

6. For historical backgrounds, see Hall and Lambert.

7. Anglo-American antislavery writers thus tried to disentangle the two. The Philadelphia Quaker Anthony Benezet, for example, drew upon George Wallis' *System of the Principles of the Laws of Scotland* to argue that "Men and their liberty are *not in Commercio*, they are not saleable or purchaseable" (30). Similarly, the Presbyterian minister Samuel Miller attacked the proslavery defense of property rights when he claimed that "The right which every one has to himself infinitely transcends all other human tenures" (15).

8. Smith's critics either admire or critique the substance of bourgeois ideology in the *Narrative*. See, for example, Desrochers and Melish for the former view and Zafar, esp. 91–3, 187, for the latter. Neither approach considers this context the formal and narrative ramifications for black autobiography.

"Property of Author"

Olaudah Equiano's Place in the History of the Book

Vincent Carretta

In the story of what is now commonly called "the history of the book," Olaudah Equiano (or Gustavus Vassa, as he almost always referred to himself in public and private) has been an invisible man, and the significance of his role in the publication and distribution of his autobiography, *The Interesting Narrative of the Life of Olaudah Equiano, or Gustavus Vassa, the African. Written by Himself* (London, 1789), has been largely overlooked.[1] For example, in an account of several late–eighteenth-century booksellers who published their autobiographies "to vindicate, to entertain, to sell, and usually to do all three," James Raven does not mention Equiano, though he certainly shared their motives for publishing and their interest in marketing books. Identifying John Dunton as "the founding figure of the genre" of bookseller-autobiography, Raven is mainly concerned with locating within that genre James Lackington, a London bookseller who published in 1791 the *Memoirs of the First Forty-Five Years* of his life.[2] Equiano was apparently well known among London's booksellers and publishers: Lackington was one of the original subscribers to Equiano's *Narrative*, as was John Almon, who published his bookseller-autobiography, *Memoirs of a Late Eminent Bookseller* (London), in 1790. Unlike Dunton, Lackington, and Almon, however, Equiano was not a professional bookseller of works by anyone other than himself. Consequently, the actual narrative of his life is not a primary source for the history of bookselling. Nor was Equiano the first self-published English-speaking author of African descent. That honor should probably go to Quobna Ottobah Cugoano, Equiano's friend and occasional collaborator, who published his *Thoughts and Sentiments on the Evil and Wicked Traffic of the Slavery and Commerce of the Human Species* in 1787.[3] But Equiano surpassed Dunton, Almon, Lackington, and Cugoano as a master of self-promotion through the book trade, and as someone who also used the telling and selling of his life as a means to non-autobiographical ends, such as the campaign to end the slave trade.[4]

Even before he proved himself to be a master of the commercial book market, Equiano had promoted himself and implicitly his forthcoming book in a number of letters, including book reviews, printed in the London newspapers. And he publicly made the right enemies, like the pseudonymous "Civis," who wrote defenses of slavery and the slave trade in the pro-ministerial *The Morning Chronicle and London Advertiser*, beginning with an essay "On the Slavery of the Blacks" in the February 5, 1788 issue. In his letter to the newspaper printed on August 19, 1788, "Civis" remarks, "If I were even to allow some share of merit to Gustavus Vasa [sic], Ignatius Sancho, &c. it would not prove equality more, than a pig having been taught to fetch a card, letters, &c. would shew it not to be a pig, but some other animal." As the comment of "Civis" indicates, Equiano was already known to his future reading public not only through his correspondence with the daily press but also through profiles printed in the press, including the laudatory one published in *The Morning Chronicle* (July 1, 1788) itself:

> *Gustavus Vasa*, who addressed a letter in the name of his oppressed countrymen [in *The Morning Chronicle*, June 27, 1788], to the author [Samuel Jackson Pratt] of the popular poem on Humanity [*Humanity, or the Rights of Nature*], which devotes several pages to that now universal subject of discussion, the Slave Trade, is, notwithstanding its romantick sound[,] the real name of an Ethiopian [that is, African] now resident in this metropolis, a native of Eboe, who was himself twice kidnapped by the English, and twice sold to slavery. He has since been appointed the King's Commissary for the African settlement, and besides having an irreproachable moral character, has frequently distinguished himself by occasional essays in the different papers, which manifest a strong and sound understanding.

Despite his bad intentions, "Civis"'s comment could only have helped to increase interest in the imminent publication of the *Narrative*, the first firsthand account in the slave-trade debate by a native African, former slave, and demonstrably loyal British subject. The notice given him by "Civis" acknowledges Equiano's prominence as the leading Black abolitionist. In 1787 Equiano had defended himself in the ministerial newspaper *The Public Advertiser* against charges of misconduct as Commissary for the Sierra Leone project for resettling the Black poor in Africa; in 1788 he had written scathing attacks on the proslavery publications of James Tobin, Gordon Turnbull, and the Reverend Raymund Harris; and on February 5, 1788 he had mentioned in print that he might soon "enumerate even my own sufferings in the West Indies, which perhaps I may one day offer to the public, [though] the disgusting catalogue would be almost too great for belief." The advertising ploy is almost too obvious. Even earlier, Equiano had actively intervened in the fight against the injustices of slavery: in 1774, as he tells us in the *Narrative*, he tried but failed to save John Annis from being kidnapped from London into West Indian slavery; and in 1783 he brought to the attention of the abolitionist

Granville Sharp the shocking story of how a cargo of 132 Africans were drowned to collect the insurance money on them. Equiano was already well known to many of his readers when his *Narrative* first appeared in 1789.

As surviving documents show, Equiano published his book both through open sale and by subscription, that is, by sale through booksellers and through public advertisement, as well as by convincing buyers to commit themselves to purchasing copies of his book prior to its publication, with booksellers effectively acting as his agents in accepting subscriptions, probably receiving a commission for doing so.[5] Subscribers typically received the book for a lower price than those who bought it at retail. During the eighteenth century the term *bookseller* was used to describe publishers as well as wholesale dealers and retail sellers of books, whose functions often overlapped in practice. No one involved in the book trade was normally keen to invest in an unknown author's first attempt at publication, especially if the author wanted to keep his or her copyright rather than sell it. Consequently, a would-be author sometimes sought subscribers, who promised to buy the finished product. With proof of a guaranteed market, the novice then either found a bookseller-publisher who would produce the book, paying the costs of publication plus a small sum to the author for the copyright, or the new author would pay the production costs and find bookseller-agents who would agree to distribute his or her work. If the book proved to have a market beyond its subscribers, the self-published author usually then sold his copyright to a bookseller-publisher at a premium price. Subscription publication had been used in England since the early seventeenth century, but by the end of the eighteenth it had become so unusual that John Murray, the first bookseller-agent listed in Equiano's subscription proposal and one of his principal distributors, noted in 1775, "That mode (which formerly was fashionable) is so much disliked now that the bare attempt is sufficient to throw discredit upon the performance."[6] Of the 1063 known works between 1768 and 1795 with which Murray was involved, only about twenty-five were published by subscription.

Equiano's recently discovered subscription solicitation tells us much about Equiano as a man of business and his role in the history of the book. Dated November 1788, the solicitation is the first known time Vassa identifies himself as Equiano. It shows that Equiano, unlike most authors near the end of the century, asked for advance payment from his subscribers, requiring partial payment in advance to cover living and production costs.[7] He probably had little choice because he apparently had enough confidence in his forthcoming book to want to try to keep as much of the profit as possible through self-publication rather than selling his copyright cheaply to a bookseller-publisher, assuming he could have found one willing to buy it. The publishers and retailers he approached about acting as his agents by taking in subscriptions for his *Narrative* and distributing it wholesale may have been understandably reluctant to risk investing more directly in a relatively inexperienced author. If so, at least three of them—James Lackington, Thomas Burton, and John Parsons—either had the economic foresight to subscribe for six copies each, or they received them as payment for acting as Equiano's agents, no doubt intending to sell the books for profit. A "Mr. W. Button," perhaps the agent-bookseller William Button, subscribed for one. Another bookseller, Charles Dilly, though not himself one of Equiano's agents, subscribed for two copies.

Even for subscribers, at seven shillings bound (six unbound) Equiano's *Narrative* was rather expensive for "a duodecimo, or pocket size . . . in two handsome volumes," when compared to the six shillings usually charged by John Murray for equivalent two-volume books.[8] Subscribers could buy a deluxe copy, for an unspecified higher price: "A few Copies will be printed on Fine Paper, at a moderate advance of price. It is therefore requested, that those Ladies and Gentlemen who may choose to have paper of that quality, will please to signify the same at subscribing." The pocket-book format, commonly used for novels, memoirs, and other works aimed at a relatively wide audience, was both fashionable and frequently profitable during the last quarter of the eighteenth century.[9] Equiano's use of "the Booksellers in Dover, Sandwich, Exeter, Portsmouth, and Plymouth" shows that he and they anticipated publishing success throughout southern England, especially in areas where the author had naval and personal affiliations. A further sign of Equiano's confidence in his investment was his registration of his copyright with the Stationers' Company. To avoid the expense of depositing the nine copies of a book required for registration, by the end of the eighteenth century many authors and publishers chose not to register their books with the Company. Equiano, however, decided to take the financial risk to protect his copyright. On March 24, 1789 he registered his 360-page, two-volume, first edition of his *Narrative* with the Company at Stationers' Hall as the "Property of Author," declaring his figurative as well as real ownership of his self.

The advertisement from the April 29 issue of *The Morning Star* tells us when Equiano first offered his book for public sale from his own address and through various booksellers, some of whom differ from those through whom he solicited his subscription copies, as well as from those listed on the title page of the book itself. For example, the name of the bookseller Humanitas Jackson first appears on the finished volume, and since he operated a circulating library as well as a press at his Oxford Street shop, the addition of his name may indicate another way Equiano found to distribute his *Narrative*. Comparison of the subscription proposal and the initial advertisement indicates that he decided to have a frontispiece for the second volume of the autobiography after the initial solicitation, and that subscribers received a relatively bargain price at seven shillings for a bound copy (six unbound), as opposed to the seven shillings asked for unbound copies from the public at large. The unbound copies most likely were the ones not subscribed for from the first printing. The appearance of the advertisement for them in *The Morning Star* further indicates the independent control Equiano exercised over the production and distribution of his book. The short-lived anti-ministerial *Morning Star* had been created in 1789 to subvert the ministerial *Star*, one of whose proprietors was Equiano's bookseller-agent John Murray.[10] The printer of Equiano's first edition is not certainly known, though he may have been the Thomas Wilkins identified in the imprint to the second edition of the *Narrative* (also 1789): "LON-

DON: printed and sold for the AUTHOR, by T. WILKINS, No. 23, Aldermanbury."
The second edition is the only one of the nine that identifies a printer.

In revising the solicitation into the advertisement, Equiano made several
stylistic and factual corrections, the latter probably reflecting the evolution of his
book from plan to product. Perhaps hoping to appeal to as wide an audience as
possible and to emphasize the extent to which the work is a spiritual autobiography, neither the proposal nor the newspaper advertisement describes *The Interesting Narrative* as in part a petition against the slave trade and a defense of Equiano's
role in the projected settlement of Sierra Leone. Potential buyers familiar with
Equiano's letters published in London newspapers during 1787 and 1788, however, would have known of his opposition to the slave trade. Thus they would not
have been surprised to find him say in his opening address in his *Narrative* "To the
Lords Spiritual and Temporal, and the Commons of the Parliament of Great Britain," that "the chief design of [the book] is to excite in your august assemblies a
sense of compassion for the miseries which the Slave Trade has entailed on my
unfortunate countrymen" (7). In the first edition, Equiano closes this opening
address with "Union-Street, Mary-le-bone, March 24, 1789." And now the book
"may be had of all the Booksellers in Town and Country."

Many elements in the book itself, not least the two illustrations, further demonstrate Equiano's genius for marketing and self-represention. Among the things
his proposal promises potential subscribers is "an elegant Frontispiece of the
Author's Portrait." Indeed this "elegant Frontispiece" is mentioned as the last of
the "Conditions," as if to emphasize the value it adds to the book's worth. But it
also adds value to Equiano's character and visually demonstrates his claim to *gentle*
status because it is "elegant" in subject as well as in execution.[11] We see an African
man dressed as an English *gentleman*, a figure who visually combines the written
identities of both Olaudah Equiano and Gustavus Vassa revealed in print beneath
the frontispiece, as well as on the title page opposite it. The Bible in his hand open
to Acts 4:12 illustrates his literacy and his piety. The frontispiece is "Published
March 1, 1789 by G. Vassa." All the evidence we have, such as Equiano's registering
his book in his own name at Stationers' Hall and marketing it himself, indicates
that he chose the artists to create and reproduce his likeness. The frontispiece was
painted ("pinx[i]t") by the miniaturist William Denton, about whom very little is
known beyond the fact that he exhibited portraits at the Royal Academy from 1792
to 1795. Denton's painting was reproduced ("sculp[si]t") in stipple and line en-
graving by Daniel Orme, at the beginning of what was to become a distinguished
career as a miniaturist portrait painter. Orme exhibited at the Royal Academy between 1797 and 1801 and was appointed engraver to King George III.

Equiano's decision to include a frontispiece for the second volume must have
been made later than November 1788 because it is not promised in the subscription proposal. The print of *Bahama Banks*, "a Plate shewing the manner the Author was shipwrecked in 1767," is after a painting by Samuel Atkins, who in 1789
had already begun to establish his reputation as a marine painter. His work was
exhibited at the Royal Academy in 1787–1788, 1791–1796, and 1804–1808. Read-

Olaudah Equiano's "elegant Frontispiece." The John Carter Brown Library at Brown University.

ers of the *Narrative* would soon discover the significance of the second frontispiece. It illustrates an incident in which Equiano, the natural leader of men, saved his White companions after a shipwreck. Equiano's selection of such talented artists as Denton, Orme, and Atkins, who, like Equiano himself, were at or near the beginning of their careers, reflects his business acumen as well as his artistic taste. Although engravers were frequently paid in kind with copies of the book, the presence of the names of the painters Atkins and Denton on the list of initial subscribers to Equiano's *Interesting Narrative* suggests that they donated their talents to what they considered a worthy cause, whose anticipated success would enhance their own reputations as well as that of the author.

The importance of Equiano's "elegant Frontispiece" in the first volume is underscored by comparing it to the only previously published frontispiece-portraits of present or former slaves: that of Phillis Wheatley (1753?-1784) in *Poems on Various Subjects, Religious and Moral* (London, 1773); and that of Ignatius Sancho (1729?-1780) in the posthumously published *Letters of the Late Ignatius Sancho, an African* (London, 1782).[12] Wheatley's was added to her book at the suggestion of her patron, the Countess of Huntingdon, and may have been engraved after a painting by Scipio Moorhead, the subject of her poem "To S.M. a Young *African* Painter, on Seeing his Works." The frontispiece displays the aspiring poet very modestly dressed as a domestic servant or slave, depicted in a contemplative pose. Her social status clearly inferior to that of most of her likely readers, she stares upward, to the viewer's left, as if hoping for inspiration for the pen she holds. The book on the table before her may be intended to represent her own poems, as well as to indicate that her literacy enables her to have been influenced by earlier writers. The artistic quality of her frontispiece is as modest as her status.

Sancho's frontispiece, on the other hand, vies with Vassa's in elegance of subject and execution. It was engraved by Francesco Bartolozzi in 1781, the year after Sancho's death, from a painting of the then-valet to the duke of Montagu hastily done by Thomas Gainsborough in an hour and forty minutes at Bath on November 29, 1768. Sancho is relatively well dressed, and as befits the servant of a nobleman, his attire enhances the status of his master more than his own. His pose, with his hand in his waistcoat, is the traditional expression of a reserved English gentleman.[13] At best, however, Sancho appears as a *gentleman's gentleman*. As was conventional in visual depictions of servants, neither Sancho nor Wheatley directly engages the gaze of the viewer, as does Equiano, the only one of the three who had any control over his visual representation. For the first time in a book by a writer of African descent, the author asserts the equality of his free social status with that of his viewers and readers by having himself shown as a *gentleman* in his own right, and by looking directly at them. The depiction of him pointing out to his readers a passage in Acts 4 that directs them to spiritual salvation indicates his moral equality, if not superiority, as well.

Unlike the frontispieces to the works of Wheatley and Sancho, Equiano's frontispiece clearly bears a thematic relationship to the text that follows. It is both the first and last illustration of the trope of the "talking book" the author uses to

Frontispiece from Phillis Wheatley's *Poems on Various Subjects, Religious and Moral*. Library of Congress.

Frontispiece from Ignacius Sancho's *Letters of the Late Ignatius Sancho, an African.*
Library of Congress.

emphasize the significance in his autobiography of literacy and acculturation.[14] From the reader's perspective, the frontispiece introduces the trope; from the perspective of the narrator's life, it marks the culmination of his development of the trope. Within the written text, the trope first appears when the child Equiano observes his master and comrade reading: "I had often seen my master and Dick employed in reading; and I had a great curiosity to talk to the books, as I thought they did; and so to learn how all things had a beginning: for that purpose I have often taken up a book, and have talked to it, when alone, in hopes it would answer me; and I have been very much concerned when I found it remained silent" (68). Later in the *Narrative*, having learned to read, the now-free adult Equiano demonstrates his mastery not only of books, but of *the* Book—the Bible. Faced with unruly, drunken Indians in Central America, he "thought of a strategem to appease the riot":

> Recollecting a passage I had read in the life of Columbus, when he
> was amongst the Indians in Jamaica, where, on some occasion, he
> frightened them, by telling them of certain events in the heavens, I
> had recourse to the same expedient, and it succeeded beyond my
> most sanguine expectations. When I had formed my determination,
> I went in the midst of them, and taking hold of the governor, I
> pointed up to the heavens. I menaced him and the rest: I told them
> God lived there, and that he was angry with them, and they must not
> quarrel so; that they were all brothers, and if they did not leave off,
> and go away quietly, I would take the book (pointing to the bible),
> read, and *tell* God to make them dead. This was something like
> magic [emphasis in original]. (208)

As the frontispiece illustrates, the fully acculturated Afro-British author of the *Interesting Narrative* intends to use his magic to make the Bible, as well as his own text, speak to his readers.

Readers of any of the first nine editions of Equiano's book were immediately confronted by the author's dual identity: the initial frontispiece presents an indisputably African body in European dress; and the title page offers us "Olaudah Equiano, or Gustavus Vassa, the African." To call him consistently by either the one name or the other is to oversimplify his identity, and one should point out that to choose to use the name Equiano rather than Vassa, as I and most contemporary scholars and critics do, is to go against the author's own practice.[15] Moreover, as the phrase "the African" reminds us, the author is very aware that his readers will assess him not just as an individual but as the representative of his race, as a type as well as a person. He is the first Anglophone writer of African descent to use the definite article to refer to himself: James Ukawsaw Gronniosaw (1710?-1772?) is "an African Prince"; Wheatley simply a "Negro Servant"; Sancho "an African"; John Marrant "a Black"; and Cugoano "a Native of Africa."[16]

Equiano's consciousness of being both African and British in identity is reflected in his decision to entitle his autobiography "The Interesting Narrative," a title not used earlier than 1789, according to the *Eighteenth-Century Short Title Catalogue* (*ESTC*). As Samuel Johnson's *Dictionary of the English Language* (London, 1755) reminds us, *to interest* meant "to affect; to move; to touch with passion; to gain the affections; as, this is an *interesting story*." It also meant "to concern; to affect; to give share in." As a noun, *interest* meant "concern; advantage; good." Equiano intended his *Narrative* to be received as *interesting* in all these ways, as the close of the first paragraph of his autobiography demonstrates. Assuming the pose of the humble author writing at the behest of his friends, he tells his readers,

> If, then, the following narrative does not appear sufficiently *interesting* to engage general attention, let my motive be some excuse for its publication. I am not so foolishly vain as to expect from it either immortality or literary reputation. If it affords any satisfaction to my numerous friends, at whose request it has been written, or in the smallest degree promotes the *interest* of humanity, the ends for which it was undertaken will be fully attained, and every wish of my heart gratified. Let it therefore be remembered that, in wishing to avoid censure, I do not aspire to praise. (31–32; emphasis added)

To the extent that his audience can sympathize or even empathize with his life because it is emblematic of the human condition, and to the extent to which his audience shares at least part of his cultural identity, his *Narrative* is interesting. But his *Narrative* is at the same time interesting in the more familiar modern sense of arousing curiosity and fascination because of his difference from his readers. He is at once Gustavus Vassa and Olaudah Equiano.

Purchasers of Equiano's *Narrative* familiar with the earlier published works of Wheatley, Sancho, and other Anglophone African writers probably noticed how distinctively Equiano identified and authorized himself on his title page. With the exception of Cugoano, the author of *The Interesting Narrative* was the first writer of African descent to present his work as self-authored and self-authorized, proudly announcing it on the title-page as "Written by Himself." The phrase "written by himself" appears in 1,110 titles of fiction and non-fiction listed in the ongoing *ESTC*,[17] almost always of works attributed to authors whose presumed levels of education and social status were likely to make readers suspect their authenticity. A familiar example is Daniel Defoe's *Robinson Crusoe* (1719), a fictional text to which Equiano's was compared early in the nineteenth century. Black authors faced greater suspicion than others. Cugoano and Equiano published their works without any of the authenticating documentation or mediation by white authorities that prefaces the works of Wheatley, Sancho, and other eighteenth-century Black writers to reassure readers that the claim of authorship is valid and to imply that their words have been supervised before publication. Wheatley's case represents the extreme: having failed to find a publisher in Boston, in part because of doubts about her ability to have written her poems, with the aid of the Countess of Huntingdon she published her works in London, prefaced by a statement from her owner and an "Attestation" signed by Boston worthies guaranteeing the authenticity of her literary achievement.

Equiano's equivalent "Attestation" is the list of the names of subscribers with which he prefaces every edition of his *Narrative*. From the first edition of 1789 on, every edition of the *Narrative* identifies more subscribers than the preceding one. By not selling his copyright to a publisher-bookseller after his book was a proven financial success and by continuing to seek subscribers for subsequent editions, Equiano was an atypical author who combined faith in his work with business acumen. By the ninth edition (1794), the original 311 subscribers (for a total of 350 copies) had increased to 804, with lists of English, Irish, and Scottish buyers. A second London edition also appeared in 1789, suggesting that the first edition was probably the standard run of 500 copies, including subscriptions.[18] Because publication by subscription, with its attendant lists, was itself traditionally a form of self-promotion, the lists must be approached with some caution and skepticism. Authors, publishers, and booksellers all clearly had motive for inflating the number and status of the names of subscribers. But the increasing number and repetition of names prefacing the multiple editions of Equiano's *Narrative* render them more credible, and thus more valuable, to the historian than they would be had they appeared in only one edition of an author's work.

A growing number of people wanted to be publicly associated with the *Narrative* and its author. Equiano's credibility and stature were enhanced by the presence of the names of members of the royal family, the aristocracy, and other socially and politically prominent figures, such as men prominent in trade and the arts, like the painter Richard Cosway or the potter Josiah Wedgwood. Elizabeth Montague and Hannah More, the leading bluestocking writers, were among the 11 percent of the original subscribers who were women. Furthermore, the list served to link Equiano to the larger movement against the slave trade by including names of others, like Thomas Clarkson, Thomas Cooper, William Dickson, James Ramsay, and Granville Sharp, all of whom had already attacked the invidious practice, in print or from the pulpit.

Moreover, the lists connected Equiano explicitly and implicitly with the African-British writers of the preceding fifteen years: Cugoano's name appears; Ignatius Sancho appears via his son William;[19] Gronniosaw and Phillis Wheatley by association with the Countess of Huntingdon; and John Marrant by association with his editor, the Reverend William Aldridge. Less directly, the presence of the name of his patron's heir, the current Duke of Montague, recalls the poem by Francis Williams, a free Black brought by the former Montague to England from Jamaica to be educated at Cambridge University earlier in the century.[20] By 1789, a recognized tradition of African-British authors had been established, with new writers aware of the work of their predecessors, and an African-British canon was being created by the commentators, who argued about which were the most representative authors and works. The publishing success of his predecessors gave Equiano cause for believing a market already existed for the autobiography of a Black entrepreneur.

The subscription lists also play a structural role in the *Narrative*, which is presented as a petition, one of the hundreds submitted to Parliament between 1789 and 1792, containing thousands of names of people asking the members to outlaw the slave trade. The *Narrative* is formally framed by a petition to the Houses of Parliament that immediately follows the list, and the book virtually closes with an appeal to Queen Charlotte. By placement and implication, the subscribers are Equiano's co-petitioners. Although like many of his subscribers, he was not qualified to vote, he thus declares himself a loyal member of the larger British polity, which can still effect change within the walls of Westminster. He effectively aligns himself politically with subscribing members of Parliament, like Sir William Dolben, George Pitt, George Rose, and Samuel Whitbread, who all opposed the trade.

Spiritual autobiography, captivity narrative, travel book, adventure tale, narrative of slavery, economic treatise, *apologia*, and petition against the slave trade, among other things, Equiano's *Narrative* was generally well received, and the author, saying he did so in self-defense, quickly employed the eighteenth-century version of the modern publisher's blurb by prefacing later editions of his book with favorable reviews from *The Monthly Review* and *The General Magazine and Impartial Review*, as well as with letters of introduction and support. He does not, however, include the extensive and influential review Mary Wollstonecraft wrote for *The Analytical Review* (May 1789). And, understandably, he omits the less favorable review that appeared in the June 1789 issue of *The Gentleman's Magazine*.

When the one-volume third edition was published, Equiano registered it at Stationers' Hall on October 30, 1790, depositing another required nine copies with the Company. The primary reason for moving from two volumes to one was probably economic: the latter sold for four shillings instead of seven, a very important consideration as the market for books and other luxury items declined in the shrinking national economy of the 1790s. The six subsequent editions were all single volumes: Dublin, 1791; Edinburgh, 1792; two London editions in 1793; Norwich, 1794; and London, 1794. Equiano's publication of several editions outside of London anticipated the nineteenth-century growth of the provincial press. For later editions, Equiano also conducted eighteenth-century versions of the modern book promotion tour throughout England, Ireland, and Scotland, speaking out against the slave trade while selling his book. As one of his few extant manuscript letters attests, he was a very successful salesman. He tells his correspondent in February 1792 that he "sold 1900 copies of my narrative" during eight and a half months in Ireland. During the eighteenth century selling five hundred copies of a book meant relative success and a thousand copies indicated a bestseller. Demand for his *Narrative* was great enough that Equiano decided to raise the price for his ninth edition to five shillings. The *Narrative* also found an international market during Equiano's lifetime: unauthorized translations appeared in Holland (1790), Germany (1792), and Russia (1794); and an unauthorized reprint of his second edition (1789) was published in the United States (1791).[21] Although he could of course neither do anything to stop them nor to profit directly from them, Equiano cleverly found a way to use them to further advertise the appeal of his book. In a passage added to his fifth (1792) and subsequent editions, Equiano acknowledged the international piracies he knew about: "Soon after[,] I returned to London [in 1791], where I found persons of note from Holland and Germany, who requested me to go there; and I was glad to hear that an edition of my Narrative had been printed in both places, also in New York" (235).

By acting as his own publisher, Equiano kept much of the profit margin for himself. Consequently, we can roughly estimate how much money he should have made on the sales of his *Narrative*. According to Samuel Johnson's calculations in 1776, the total profit margin on a book was about thirty percent of the retail price, the other seventy percent being the cost of production, including payment to the author for copyright. The total profit margin covered the costs and profits of the wholesaler and retailer, approximately 12.5 and 17.5 percent, respectively.[22] But complicating the calculation of Equiano's profits after his subscription proposal was his increasing control of the distribution of the *Narrative*—and thus of his own profit—by reducing in subsequent editions the number of bookseller-agents with whom he shared the profit margin. The proposal names thirteen booksellers-agents; the first edition twelve; the second eight; the third seven; the fourth one; the fifth one; the sixth two; and the seventh, eighth, and ninth each zero. If we assume, conservatively, that Equiano took half of the total profit margin of the first edition, he would have earned about one shilling on every seven-shilling book sold, approximately £25, if we assume only five hundred copies in the initial print-ing.[23] Sharing his margin with one third fewer bookseller-agents for the second edition, Equiano probably made at least £40 on it, substantially more if the number of copies printed increased, which is very likely given the success of the first edition. On each copy of the four-shilling, one-volume third edition, he might have made over one shilling, with number of sales more than compensating for the loss in per unit price. By that time he was probably having at least a thousand copies printed. The sale of more than 1,900 copies of the fourth edition at four shillings may have earned him more than £120.[24] Similar profits may be assumed for each of the fifth, sixth, seventh, and eight editions. And at five shillings retail for his last edition, with no sharing booksellers, he could have anticipated a profit of one and a half shillings per book. Equiano could easily have garnered more than a £1000 in total gross prof-its from the sale of the nine editions of his *Interesting Narrative*.

In large part due to the profits from selling his life, Equiano became prob-ably the wealthiest Briton of African descent living in England, when an annual income of £40 was sufficient to support a family of four modestly in London, and when a gentleman could live well on £300 per annum. By February 27, 1792, and before his income increased through marriage, Equiano was rich enough to have "Lent to a man, who [is] now Dying" £232, which he despaired of recovering. Whether or not he recovered that money, when he drew up his will on May 28, 1796, almost a year to the day before his own death, Equiano had "The Sum of Three hundred pounds at present undisposed of." Unlike the vast majority of his fellow Britons, Equiano was wealthy enough to justify having a will, making him one of the very few eighteenth-century African Britons in this position.[25] On her twenty-first birthday, in 1816, Equiano's surviving daughter, Joanna, inherited £950 from her father's estate, a sum roughly equivalent to £80,000 or $120,000 today. Equiano had achieved the fame and wealth he sought and deserved. Some of his wealth came to him through his marriage; much of it, however, was the result of his success as a self-published author who took advantage of the many personal contacts he had made during a life of varied adventures.

Despite evidence of growing demand for his profitable book, Equiano's ninth edition was his last, almost certainly for political and legal rather than economic reasons. On May 12, 1794 Equiano's friend Thomas Hardy was arrested and on November 5, 1794 tried and acquitted on a charge of high treason for his roles as a founder and first secretary of the London Corresponding Society. Hardy had helped establish the Society on January 25, 1792 as a radical working-class organization to promote the expansion of the electorate. Although Hardy was acquitted, the government's willingness to prosecute him frightened many in the reform move-ment into silence. Among the papers seized by the authorities at Hardy's arrest was a letter to him from Equiano, who had lived with Hardy while revising the fifth edition of his *Narrative*, and who had recruited or at least identified for Hardy potential members of the Society during his provincial book tours. The self-pub-lishing author Equiano apparently became self-censoring in response to the government's actions.

His probable self-silencing notwithstanding, as creator, producer, distribu-tor, and advertiser of his published life, Olaudah Equiano or Gustavus Vassa is indisputably the founder of the genre of modern Anglophone-African autobiog-raphy. In selling his life, Equiano was not only one of the earliest black writers, but also one of the earliest self-publishing entrepreneurs, who happened to be black. Recognition of his place in the history of the book is overdue.

NOTES

1. Quotations from Equiano's *Narrative*, correspondence, and will are taken from *The Interesting Narrative and Other Writings*, ed. Vincent Carretta (New York: Penguin Putnam Inc., 1995). James Green, "The Publishing History of Olaudah Equiano's *Interest-ing Narrative*," *Slavery and Abolition* 16 (1995), 362–375, includes a useful, albeit brief, preliminary discussion of the publication of Equiano's *Narrative* during his lifetime (363–365). I thank Paula McDowell and Eleanor Shevlin for their very helpful comments on an earlier version of my essay.

2. James Raven, "Selling One's Life: James Lackington, Eighteenth-century Booksell-ers and the Design of Autobiography," in O. M. Brack, Jr., ed. *Writers, Books, and Trade: An Eighteenth-Century English Miscellany for William B. Todd* (New York: AMS Press, 1994), 1–23; quotations from page 1. Although Equiano and Lackington were anticipated by the bookseller-autobiographer John Dunton in his self-justifying *The Life and Errors of John Dunton, Late Citizen of London: Written by Himself in Solitude* (London, 1705), Dunton's is a less coherent narrative of his life. Lackington was one of the original distributors of Equiano's autobiography.

3. Quobna Ottobah Cugoano (1757?-1791+), *Thoughts and Sentiments on the Evil and Wicked Traffic of the Slavery and Commerce of the Human Species, Humbly Submitted to*

the Inhabitants of Great-Britain, By Ottobah Cugoano, A Native of Africa (London, 1787) is reproduced in Quobna Ottobah Cugoano, *Thoughts and Sentiments on the Evil of Slavery and Other Writings* (New York: Penguin Putnam Inc., 1999), ed. Vincent Carretta. Cugoano and Equiano together published letters against the slave trade in London newspapers during the 1780s. Cugoano's polemical text is only briefly autobiographical. Unlike Equiano, Cugoano may have had the advantage of hidden patronage to support his apparent self-publication. One of his bookseller-agents was Thomas Becket, self-identified from 1786–1817 as "Bookseller to Prince of Wales." Cugoano's employer was the painter Richard Cosway, who had been appointed in 1785 *Primarius Pictor* (Principal Painter) to the Prince of Wales. Although in a private letter in 1786 Cugoano sought the patronage of his employer's patron, no record of the Prince's response has been found. The Prince's name heads the list of Equiano's original subscribers.

4. Michael Mascuch, *Origins of the Individualist Self: Autobiography and Self-Identity in England, 1591–1791* (Stanford: Stanford University Press, 1996), has recently constructed a history of the genre of autobiography that intersects with the history of the book. Lackington is the hero of Mascuch's narrative because he wrote, published, and distributed, as well as lived his life. Ignoring Equiano's *Narrative* and overstating Lackington's originality, Mascuch considers the publication of his *Memoirs* a turning point in the development of autobiography because it was "one of the earliest examples of popular modern autobiography in English, a work deliberately composed to represent to the public the authoritative ethos of its subject" (6).

5. Equiano's subscription proposal, newspaper advertisement, and other writings discovered since the publication of the Penguin Putnam edition of his *Narrative* are reproduced, with commentary, in Vincent Carretta, "More Letters by Gustavus Vassa or Olaudah Equiano?," in Robert Griffin, ed., *The Faces of Anonymity*, forthcoming. Dr. Mark Jones found the subscription proposal among the Josiah Wedgwood papers in the Keele University Library Special Collections, and very kindly brought it to my attention. Wedgwood was one of Equiano's original subscribers.

6. Letter to William Boutcher, December 30, 1775, quoted in William Zachs, *The First John Murray and the Late Eighteenth-Century Book Trade* (Oxford: Oxford University Press, 1998), 69. Zachs notes that Murray reiterates his opinion of publication by subscription in a letter to John Imison, August 27, 1784. Equiano may have been drawn to Murray as his primary bookseller-agent because he published the monthly *Political Magazine and Parliamentry, Naval, Military and Literary Journal* (1780–1791), in which both sides of the slave-trade debate were represented.

7. Green, "The Publishing History" (363) notes the relative rarity of asking for advance payment from subscribers.

8. My comment on the relative expense of Equiano's *Narrative* is based on comparison to comparable duodecimos published by Murray 1788–90: see entries 628, 632, 653, 655, 677, 687, 698, 699, 706, 721, 726, 746, 768, 777, 785, 795 in Zachs, *The First John Murray*, "A Checklist of Murray Publications, 1768–1795."

9. James Raven, *Judging New Wealth: Popular Publishing and Responses to Commerce in England, 1750–1800*, (Oxford: Clarendon Press, 1992), 52.

10. For the complex relationship between the two newspapers, see Lucyle Werkmeister, *The London Daily Press 1772–1792* (Lincoln: University of Nebraska Press, 1963), 219–316.

11. For a fuller discussion of how and why Equiano represents himself as a *gentleman* see my "Defining a Gentleman: the Status of Olaudah Equiano or Gustavus Vassa," forthcoming in *Languages Sciences*.

12. Wheatley's *Poems* was published in England and America at least four times by 1789. Her poetry, though not Wheatley herself, was known to Sancho, who calls her a "Ge-

nius in bondage" in a letter dated January 27, 1778: see *Letters of the Late Ignatius Sancho, an African*, ed. Vincent Carretta (New York: Penguin Putnam Inc., 1998), 111–112. Sancho's *Letters* went through four editions before Equiano's first edition.

13. Arline Meyer, "Re-dressing Classical Statuary: the Eighteenth-Century 'Hand-in Waistcoat' Portrait," *The Art Bulletin* 77 (1995), 45–64.

14. In his Introduction to the facsimile reprint of the two-volume first edition of *The Interesting Narrative* (London: Dawsons of Pall Mall, 1969), Paul Edwards first pointed out the trope of the book that does not speak to the illiterate and noted that it also appears in the writings of James Albert Ukawsaw Gronniosaw, John Marrant, and Quobna Ottobah Cugoano (see note 16 below). Henry Louis Gates, Jr., discusses the trope at length in *The Signifying Monkey: A Theory of African-American Literary Criticism* (New York: Oxford University Press, 1988). Neither Edwards nor Gates cites either the Central American incident or the frontispiece as examples of the "talking book" in Equiano's *Narrative*.

15. Periodically in the *Narrative*, the author reminds his readers that he exists on the boundary between his African and British identities. For example, at the beginning of Chapter IV, he tells us, "From the various scenes I had beheld on ship-board, I soon grew a stranger to terror of every kind, and was in that respect, at least, almost an Englishman." Several lines later he adds, "I now not only felt myself quite easy with these new countrymen, but relished their society and manners. I no longer looked upon them as spirits, but as men superior to us; and therefore I had the stronger desire to resemble them; to imbibe their spirit, and imitate their manners; I therefore embraced every occasion of improvement; and every new thing that I observed I treasured up in my memory."

16. Cugoano mentions Gronniosaw and Marrant in his *Thoughts and Sentiments* (1787): see Cugoano, *Thoughts and Sentiments*, ed. Vincent Carretta, 23–24. Gronniosaw's *A Narrative of the Most Remarkable Particulars in the Life of James Albert Ukawsaw Gronniosaw, an African Prince* (Bath, 1772) was published at least ten times in Britain and America before Equiano first published his autobiography. Marrant's *A Narrative of the Lord's Wonderful Dealings with John Marrant, a Black, (Now Going to Preach the Gospel in Nova-Scotia) Born in New-York, in North-America* (London, 1785), also a dictated text, went through at least fifteen London printings before 1790. Both texts were dictated to and revised by White amanuenses. The first edition of Gronniosaw's *Narrative* and the fourth edition of Marrant's *Narrative* are reproduced in *Unchained Voices: An Anthology of Black Authors in the English-Speaking World of the Eighteenth Century* (Lexington, University Press of Kentucky, 1996), ed. Vincent Carretta.

17. Another 135 titles claim to be "Written by Herself."

18. Green, "The Publishing History" (364–365), estimates that the size of the first edition was 750 copies. I think that as a good man of business Equiano probably limited his risk of having many unsold books left from a first printing, but that once the popularity of his work was clear he increased the number of copies for the second and subsequent editions. By the fourth edition he was selling 1900 copies.

19. Since William was only thirteen years old in March 1789 his name most likely appears because it enables Equiano to invoke his father's.

20. In his pro-slavery *The History of Jamaica* (London, 1774), 2:475–485, Edward Long published his hostile biography of Williams and reproduced "An Ode," Williams's one known poem. The poem and Long's comments on it and Williams are reproduced in *Unchained Voices*, ed. Carretta.

21. Green, "The Publishing History," 367–373, and Akiyo Ito, "Olaudah Equiano and the New York Artisans: The First American Edition of *The Interesting Narrative of the Life of Olaudah Equiano, or Gustavus Vassa, the African*," *Early American Literature* 32:1 (1997), 82–101, discuss the New York edition.

22. Johnson's March 12, 1776 letter to Nathan Wetherell, *The Letters of Samuel Johnson* (Princeton: Princeton University Press, 1992), 2:304–308; John Feather, *The Provincial Book Trade in Eighteenth-Century England* (Cambridge, Cambridge University Press, 1985), 53–59.

23. Green, "The Publishing History" 364–365, assuming that the first edition printed 750 copies and that Equiano received a quite generous three shillings per copy, estimates that he earned about £100 from the first edition alone.

24. I assume that at least 2000 copies of the fourth edition were printed because Equiano sold 1900 copies of it by February 27, 1792. The fifth edition was printed several months later: its address to the members of Parliament is dated "June 1792."

25. At least one other African Briton, John Scipio in 1760, had a will, in which he left £300 in cash legacies alone. See Kathy Chater, "Where There's a Will," *History Today* 50:4 (2000), 26–27. I thank Arthur Torrington for bringing Chater's work to my attention.

BIBLIOGRAPHY

Almon, John. *Memoirs of a Late Eminent Bookseller* (London, 1790).

Carretta, Vincent, ed. *Unchained Voices: An Anthology of Black Authors in the English-Speaking World of the Eighteenth Century* (Lexington, University Press of Kentucky, 1996).

Chater, Kathy. "Where There's a Will," *History Today* 50 (2000), 26–27.

Cugoano, Quobna Ottobah. *Thoughts and Sentiments on the Evil of Slavery and Other Writings* (New York: Penguin Putnam Inc., 1999), ed. Vincent Carretta.

Dunton, John. *The Life and Errors of John Dunton, Late Citizen of London: Written by Himself in Solitude* (London, 1705)

Equiano, Olaudah. *The Interesting Narrative of the Life of Olaudah Equiano, or Gustavus Vassa, the African. Written by Himself*, ed. Paul Edwards (London: Dawsons of Pall Mall, 1969).

Equiano, Olaudah. *The Interesting Narrative and Other Writings*, ed. Vincent Carretta (New York: Penguin Putnam Inc., 1995).

Feather, John. *The Provincial Book Trade in Eighteenth-Century England* (Cambridge, Cambridge University Press, 1985).

Henry Louis Gates, Jr., *The Signifying Monkey: A Theory of African-American Literary Criticism* (New York: Oxford University Press, 1988).

Green, James. "The Publishing History of Olaudah Equiano's *Interesting Narrative*," *Slavery and Abolition* 16 (1995), 362–375.

Gronniosaw, James Albert Ukawsaw, *A Narrative of the Most Remarkable Particulars in the Life of James Albert Ukawsaw Gronniosaw, an African Prince* (Bath, 1772).

Ito, Akiyo. "Olaudah Equiano and the New York Artisans: The First American Edition of *The Interesting Narrative of the Life of Olaudah Equiano, or Gustavus Vassa, the African*," *Early American Literature* 32:1 (1997).

Johnson, Samuel. *The Letters of Samuel Johnson* (Princeton: Princeton University Press, 1992), ed. Bruce Redford.

Lackington, James. *Memoirs of the First Forty-Five Years* (London, 1791).

Long, Edward. *The History of Jamaica* (London, 1774).

Mascuch, Michael. *Origins of the Individualist Self: Autobiography and Self-Identity in England, 1591–1791* (Stanford: Stanford University Press, 1996).

Marrant, John. *A Narrative of the Lord's Wonderful Dealings with John Marrant, a Black, (Now Going to Preach the Gospel in Nova-Scotia) Born in New-York, in North-America* (London, 1785).

Meyer, Arline. "Re-dressing Classical Statuary: the Eighteenth-Century 'Hand-in Waistcoat' Portrait" *The Art Bulletin* 77 (1995), 45–64.

Raven, James. *Judging New Wealth: Popular Publishing and Responses to Commerce in England, 1750–1800*, (Oxford: Clarendon Press, 1992).

Raven, James. "Selling One's Life: James Lackington, Eighteenth-century Booksellers and the Design of Autobiography," in O. M. Brack, Jr., ed. *Writers, Books, and Trade: An Eighteenth-Century English Miscellany for William B. Todd* (New York: AMS Press, 1994), 1–23.

Sancho, Ignatius. *Letters of the Late Ignatius Sancho, an African*, ed. Vincent Carretta (New York: Penguin Putnam Inc., 1998).

Werkmeister, Lucyle. *The London Daily Press 1772–1792* (Lincoln: University of Nebraska Press, 1963).

Zachs, William. *The First John Murray and the Late Eighteenth-Century Book Trade* (Oxford: Oxford University Press, 1998).

WORKS CITED

Andrews, William L.. *To Tell a Free Story: The First Century of Afro-American Autobiography, 1760-1865*. Urbana: U of Illinois P, 1986.

Appleby, Joyce. *Liberalism and Republicanism in the Historical Imagination*. Cambridge, MA.: Harvard UP, 1992.

Benezet, Anthony. *A Short Account of that Part of Africa, Inhabited by Negroes*. 1762. London: W Baker and J.W. Galabin, 1788.

Bender, Thomas, ed. *The Antislavery Debate: Capitalism and Abolitionism as a Problem of Historical Interpretation*. Berkeley: U of California P, 1992.

Breen, T.H. "Narrative of Commercial Life: Consumption, Ideology and Community on the Eve of the American Revolution." William and Mary Quarterly 3rd. series 50 (July 1993): 471-501.

Carretta, Vincent, ed. *Unchained Voices: An Anthology of Black Authors in the English Speaking World of the 18th Century*. Lexington: UP of Kentucky, 1997.

Cheyfitz, Eric. *The Poetics of Imperialism: Translation and Colonization from the Tempest to Parzan*. Philadelphia: U of Pennsylvania P, 1997.

Crowley, J.E. *This Sheba, Self The Conceptualization of Economic Life in Eighteenth Century America*. Baltimore: Johns Hopkins UP, 1974.

Davis, David Brion. *The Problem of Slavery in the Age of Revolution, 1770-1823*. Ithaca: Cornell UP, 1975.

Desrochers, Robert, Jr. "'Not Fade Away': The Narrative of Venture Smith, an African American in the Early Republic." Journal of American History 84 (1997): 40-66. .

Eze, Emmanuel Chukwudi. *Race and the Enlightenment: A Reader*. Cambridge, MA.: Blackwell, 1997.

Ferguson, Robert. "The Literature of Enlightenment." *The Cambridge History of American Literature*, Vol 1. New York: Cambridge UP, 1994.

Gates, Henry Louis, Jr. *The Signifying Monkey: A Theory of Afro American Literary Critacisria*. New York: Oxford UP, 1988.

Gilje, Paul; ed: *The Wages of Independence: Capitalism in the Early American Republic*. Madison: Madison House, 1997.

Gilroy, Paul. *The Black Atlantic: Modernity and Double Consciousness*. Cambridge, MA.: Harvard UP, 1993.

Haakonsen, Kud. "From Natural Law to the Rights of Man: A European Perspective on American Debates," in *A Culture of Rights: The Bill of Rights in Philosophy, Politics arid Law—1791 and 1991*. Eds. Michael J. Lacey and Knud Haakonsen. Cambridge: Cambridge UP 1991.

Hall, Timothy. *Contested Boundaries: Itineracy and the Reshaping of the Colonial American Religious World.* Durham: Duke UP, 1994.

Hartman, Saidiya V. *Scenes of Subjection: Terror, Slavery, and Self-Making in Nineteenth-Century America.* New York: Oxford UP, 1997.

Hofstader Richard. *America at 1750: A Social Portrait.* New York: Knopf, 1971.

Jordan, Winthrop D. *White Over Black: American Attitudes Toward the Negro, 1550- 1812.* Chapel Hill: U of North Carolina P, 1968.

Krarnmck, Isaac. *Republicanism and Bourgeois Radicalism: Political Ideology in Late Eighteenth-Century England and America.* Ithaca: Cornell UP, 1990.

Lambert, Frank. *"Peddlar in Divinity": George Whitefield and the Transatlantic Revivals, 1737-1770.* Princeton: Princeton UP, 1774.

Matson, Cathy D: "Capitalizing Home: Economic Thought and the Early National 'Economy.'" In Gilje. 117-136.

Melish, Joanne Pope. *Disowning Slavery. Gradual Emancipation and "Race" in New England 1780-1860.* Ithaca: Cornell UP, 1998.

Miller, Samuel: *A Discourse Delivered April 12, 1797, at the Request of and Before the New-York Society for Promoting the Manumission of Slaves.* New York: T and J Swords, 1797.

Montgomery, Benilde. "Recapturing John Marrant." *A Mixed Race: Ethnicity in Early America.* Ed. Frank Shuffelton. New York: Oxford UP, 1993. 105-115.

Morse, Jedidiah. *A Discourse Delivered at the African Meeting House, in Boston, July 14, 1808, in Grateful Celebration of the Abolition of the African Slave Trade by the Governments of the United States, Great Britain and Denmark.* Boston: Lincoln and Edmunds, 1808.

Nisbet, Richard. *Slavery Not Forbidden by Scripture. Or a defence of the West-India Planters, From the Aspersions Thrown out Against The, by the Author of the Pamphlet, Entitled, "An Address to the Inhabitants of the British Settlements in America upon Slave-Keeping."* Philadelphia, 1773.

Potkay, Adam and Sandra Burr, eds. *Black Atlantic Writers of the Eighteenth Century: Living the New Exodus in England and the Americas.* New York: St. Martins, 1995.

Priestley, Joseph. *A Sermon on the Subject of the Slave Trade; Delivered to the Society of Protestant Dissenters, at the New Meeting in Birmingham.* Birmingham: Pearson and Rallason, 1788.

Raboteau, Albert J. The Black Experience in American Evangelicalism: The Meaning of Slavery." *The Evangelical Tradition in America.* Ed. Leonard I. Sweet. Macon, GA.: Mercer UP, 1984.

Ramsay, James. *An Essay on the Treatment and Conversion of African Slaves in the British Sugar Colonies.* London: James Phillips, 1784.

Rothen, Winifred Barr. *From Market-Place to Market Economy: The Transformation of Rural,Massachusetts, 1750-1850.* Chicago: U of Chicago P, 1992.

Ruttenberg, Nancy. *Democratic Personality: Popular Voice and the Trial of American Authorship.* Stanford: Stanford UP, 1998.

Sekora; John; "Black Message/White Envelope: Genre, Authenticity and Authority in the Arttebellum-Slave Narrative." *Callalloo* 10 (1987): 482-515.

Shapiro, Ian. *The Evolution of Rights in Liberal Theory.* Cambridge: Cambridge University Press, 1986.

Sharp, Granvlle. *The Just Limitation of Slavery in the Laws of God, Compared with the Unbounded Claims of the African Traders and British American Slaveholders.* London: B. White, 1776.

Sherwood, Samuel. *Scriptural Instructions to Civil Rulers. Political Sermons of the American Founding Era, 1730-1805.* Ed. Ellis Sandoz. Indianapolis: Liberty Press, 1991.

Vickers, Daniel. "Competency and Competition: Economic Culture in Early America." *William and Mary Quarterly* 3rd. ser. 47 (1990): 3-29.

Webster, Noah. *Effects of Slavery on Morals and Industry*. Hartford: Hudson and Goodwin, 1793.

White, Shane. *Somewhat More Independent: The End of Slavery in New York City, 1770-1810*. Athens: U of Georgia P, 1991.

Wood, Gordon S. *The Radicalism of the American Revolution*. New York: Vintage, 1993.

Young, Robert J.C. *Colonial Desire: Hybridity in Theory, Culture and Race*. London: Routledge, 1995.

Zafar, Rafia. *We Wear the Mask: African Americans Write American Literature, 1760-1870*. New York: Columbia UP, 1997.

PART THREE

Language and the "Other" The Question of Difference

"Surprizing Deliverance"?

Slavery and Freedom, Language and Identity in the Narrative of Briton Hammon, "A Negro Man"

Robert Desrochers Jr.

Rule Brittania, rule the waves,
Britons never will be slaves.
> —James Thomson, "Rule Brittania," 1740

Briton Hammon spent a good part of Christmas Day 1747 on his feet, en route from the seaside town of Marshfield, Massachusetts, where he lived, to the docks of Plymouth just over ten miles south. The next day Hammon negotiated a berth aboard a trading sloop bound for "*Jamaica* and the *Bay*" of Campeche, where valuable logwood lay floating west of the Yucatan peninsula. Hammon, who had been to the West Indies at least once before, knew what he might be getting himself into. Disease and death, meager rations, the latent fury of nature and ruthless shipmasters. The eighteenth-century deep-sea mariner steeled himself in anticipation of all of these dangers and then some. Hammon left anyway, choosing the close quarters of a ship over service to John Winslow, an apparently paternalistic master of old and very distinguished Plymouth Colony stock, and in his own right one of the most respected military leaders in provincial Massachusetts.[1]

New Englanders would have found nothing particularly strange about this labor bargain between slave and master. Indeed, such work arrangements kept ice off the machinery of New England slavery in the months of cold and snow. But they also made it notoriously easier for some slaves to run, which may explain why Hammon recalled more than a decade later that this "Voyage to Sea" had been undertaken "with the leave of [his] Master." Significantly, though, Hammon also recalled that the cruise itself had been his "Intention," not Winslow's. Perhaps

Hammon decided that the dangers of the deep did not outweigh the relative autonomy that an eighteenth-century New England slave might enjoy aboard ship. Perhaps he had been lured by the high wartime wages many short-handed merchant vessels were offering in 1747, particularly for the notoriously dangerous Campeche run. Perhaps Hammon wanted only to beat a wet path away from the frosty Massachusetts winter. Whatever the case, when a six-month voyage to the Caribbean and back turned into a thirteen-year nightmare of shipwreck, captivity to Florida Indians, imprisonment in Spanish Havana, naval service under fire, and destitution in a London slum, Hammon sailed back to Massachusetts slavery with "his *good old Master.*"[2]

Hustled to press in Boston in late-June 1760, less than a month after Hammon returned from London, *A Narrative of the Uncommon Sufferings and Surprizing Deliverance of Briton Hammon* told of his extraordinary adventure.[3] The publication of the *Narrative* does not appear to have caused much public controversy in Boston, though it did earn Hammon pride of place as author of the first extant published work of any kind by a person of African descent in colonial British America. But that means more to us than it probably did to Hammon. The real significance of race and status in this seminal tale lies elsewhere, for instance in the relationship between Hammon and the anonymous white editor who committed it to paper and prepared it for press. That fact of publication raises thorny if familiar questions about the "authenticity" of the *Narrative*.[4] Did not Hammon's dependence on white patronage at every stage of the publishing process undermine his authority as a black autobiographer? Does this as-told-to *Narrative* speak for Hammon at all, or for a white amanuensis licensed to squelch his individuality, his black voice, when it diverged from social acceptability, and from popular literary models? After all, Hammon's story owed its print existence in no small measure to white New Englanders' hefty appetite for propagandistic invectives against French, Spanish, and Indian cruelty during the Seven Years War. It did not disappoint readers weaned on literary Puritanism and braced for warfare against Papist savages and savage Papists alike. In short, as literary scholar John Sekora wrote, Hammon's "black message" seems hopelessly entangled with, and often indistinguishable from, its "white envelope."[5]

Such healthy skepticism leaves us with very little understanding of what the *Narrative* might have meant to Hammon in his lifetime. What did Hammon stand to gain, and to lose, by its publication? How might the *Narrative*, and its subject, have been received by a reading audience comprised almost exclusively of white New Englanders, particularly in and around Boston? What does the *Narrative* reveal about the dynamic and politically charged process of self-fashioning faced by Hammon, a slave whose actions and literary presence reveal a man up to his neck in the mid–eighteenth-century Euro-Atlantic contest for empire. And how might Hammon's actions, and act of literary self-creation, have served to expand his long-term freedom possibilities even as both bound him closer in the short-term to Anglo-American slavery? This essay poses new questions, and tries to answer some old ones, about the production and historical significance of Hammon's *Narra-*

tive, a text that speaks to the possibilities and limits of language and freedom in late-colonial Massachusetts, and in the Atlantic world.

SLAVERY, FREEDOM, AND AUTHORITY IN THE ATLANTIC WORLD

In broad strokes the body of Hammon's *Narrative* sketches aspects of its subject's personal identity that must be taken into close account in the attempt to understand what the *Narrative* might have meant to a man in his shoes and shaped by his experiences. We first encounter Hammon in the guise of a sailor, a mobile occupation that allowed him to stretch the elastic bonds of New England slavery without breaking them. The mindset of a seafaring man may have stretched those bonds in another way. In November 1747, just a month before Hammon set out on his fateful journey, some 300 "Seamen Servants [and] Negroes" speaking a common language of liberty rioted for three days in the name of fellow sailors netted by the press gangs of the Royal Navy. Boston witnessed no larger civil disturbance than the Knowles Riot, as the incident became known, before the Stamp Act; the British admiral who lent his name to the proceedings remarked that "a Spirit of Rebellion" coursed through the veins of seamen in Boston. But rowdy Boston tars were part of a larger maritime culture that fostered powerful resistance to authority on both sides of the rail, and on both sides of the Atlantic. Forged by seamen in the crucible and confinement of the ship, where the autocratic control of shipmasters rivaled that of slavemasters, Atlantic maritime culture flowed with egalitarian undercurrents that mediated the ways race worked aboard ship. Not always for the better, to be sure. In 1788, for instance, Prince Hall petitioned the Massachusetts General Court on behalf of Boston's free black mariners, claiming that "maney of us who are good seamen are oblidge to stay at home thru fear" of being kidnapped and sold into slavery. Nevertheless, sailors' oppositional culture and the collective nature of seafaring work made ships workplaces where color "might be less a determinant" of social status than it was shore-side, where slaves found themselves competing with laboring whites for scarce jobs in mid-century Massachusetts. In the cramped space of the ship, in portside taverns, and at times in the streets, slave sailors like Hammon rubbed shoulders with whites who cherished fragile "liberty" almost as much as they did, and who resisted attempts to deprive them of it. In 1736 a white sailor was asked by the captain of another ship to explain why he and his shipmates threatened mutiny in response to the harsh punishment meted out to a "Brother Tar." The man replied that "they would not be serv'd so, [that] no Man shou'd confine any of them, for they were one & all resolved to stand by one another."[6]

Instances of such rough-hewn egalitarianism and anti-authoritarianism appear only briefly in Hammon's *Narrative*, a text that by its own admission "omitted a great many Things." They appear often enough, however, to demonstrate that staying alive at sea and in the Atlantic world at the very least taught Hammon to challenge authority. As we pick up the narrative, Hammon and his shipmates have enjoyed a "pleasant Passage" of "about 30 Days" from Plymouth to the Caribbean. It is on the return trip that their sloop runs upon a reef on "*Cape-Florida*." Cast away about five leagues from shore and "destitute of every Help," no one knew "what to do or what course to take in this our sad Condition." Meanwhile, the sloop's captain, John Howland, seemed more concerned with the bottom line than the bottom of the ocean. The crew tried to set him straight: "The Captain was advised, intreated, and beg'd on, by every person on board, to heave over but only 20 Ton of the *Wood*, and we should get clear, which if he had done, might have sav'd his Vessel and Cargo, and not only so, but his own Life, as well as the Lives of the Mate and Nine hands." Had the majority ruled – a unanimous party made up, it should be stressed, of eight white hands, one "Negro Man" (Hammon), and one "Molatto" – Captain Howland might have lived to tell the tale himself. Instead, two days later he "order'd the Boat to be hoisted out" and "ask'd who were willing to tarry on board?" Again, "the whole crew" reached the decision that none would stay. The lone boat could "not carry 12 Persons at once," however, so three people would have to remain behind. We are not privy to the deliberations that ensued. We do know that only one of the three souls who went down with the ship was a common hand (the odd man out, probably), and that he was neither the "Negro Man" nor the "Molatto," Moses Newmock. The two others ambushed on the sloop were Howland himself and "a Passenger" from Jamaica, both of whom agreed to linger on, we read, in order "to prevent any Uneasiness" with a crew that had made up its collective mind to get ashore, come hell or high water.[7]

Only a party of Florida Indians spoiled their escape. From a distance, Hammon and his comrades thought they saw "an *English Colour*" hoisted in one of twenty canoes advancing toward them, "at the Sight of which" they "rejoiced." Rescued at last, or so it seemed. By the time the crew realized to their "very great Surprize" that they had been duped by an Indian subterfuge, they "could not possibly" escape. The "Sixty" Indians had already shot three of the nine men in the boat when Hammon "jump'd overboard, chusing rather to be drowned, than to be kill'd by those barbarous and inhuman Savages." After killing everyone else, the Indians "padled after" Hammon, "hawled" him in, and beat him "most terribly with a Cutlas." When Hammon's new masters "ty'd [him] down" his subjugation was complete.[8]

Predictably, the *Narrative* evinces little love lost between Hammon and his Indian captors, observing that he initially feared that they "intended to roast me alive." In the end, though, Hammon reports that the Indians "were better to me than my Fears." They may have slaughtered everybody else, but the *Narrative* relates that, reputations and expectations aside, for the duration of Hammon's five-week stay the Indians "us'd [him] pretty well, and gave [him] boil'd Corn, which was what they often eat themselves." Eventually, they even "unbound" him. Nevertheless, Hammon's text reveals no desire on his part to live forever among a people cast in the *Narrative* as "Villains." When Spanish authorities arrived to inquire about English prisoners, Hammon bargained his way aboard their schooner and sailed for Havana, whence the Indians soon appeared and demanded the return of their prisoner. When Governor Francisco Antonio Cagigal de la Vega purchased

Hammon from the Indians for a ten-dollar bounty, he passed to his fourth "master" in five pages.[9]

Not surprisingly, the "matters of fact" presented in the *Narrative* about Spanish Catholicism amounted to poison darts aimed at an as-yet undefeated military and religious enemy. We read that in Havana the Bishop "is carried (by Way of Respect) in a large two-arm Chair . . . lin'd with crimson Velvet, and supported by eight Persons." Hammon got a long look at this chair near the end of his time in Cuba, when he helped carry it and its rider on a seven-month missionary tour into the countryside. If evocations of such pomp and pageantry did not excite Protestant passions back home, the *Narrative* also observed that the Bishop received "large Sums of Money" for bringing false religion to the natives, a perversion of Christian charity that gave Massachusetts clergymen enough sermon fodder for one Sunday. On the other hand, though, Hammon's derision of popery, like his disdain for Indians, paled in comparison to the animus displayed by most other white-authored captivity tales of the day. For one thing, the carping about the Bishop's mobile throne, itself mild in any event, appeared only as a footnote at the bottom of the page. Even more important, before leaving the subject Hammon's *Narrative* added that he "lived very well" those months with the Bishop. Quality of life again gets the last word.[10]

Though the political implications of Anglo-Protestant allegiance figure enormously in Hammon's tale, the language of Protestant Christianity itself does not. Perhaps that is to be expected: men of the sea were notoriously irreligious, and Christianity made relatively few slave converts in colonial New England at any rate. Whatever the reasons, we can attribute two out of only four references in the *Narrative* to the "Divine Goodness" of God to editorial imposition. Whereas most attempts to isolate Hammon's authorial voice from that of his amanuensis end up engaging in racial presupposition, the preface and postscript offer instances in which we can see the handiwork of an editor who took it upon himself to attach appropriately pious introductory and closing remarks: a typical prefatory disclaimer in which authorial self-effacement and avowals of truth cleared the way for the heirs of the Puritans to ponder their abject dependence upon a vengeful God; and a concluding reference to Psalm 107 that celebrated Hammon's having been "freed" from "captivity" (without mentioning that he had really traded one captivity for another). Save for those two bookends the rest of Hammon's *Narrative* is decidedly less devout, which is another way to put literary scholar Alice A. Deck's observation that editors of slave narratives often reserved the first and last word for themselves. As for the two remaining, brief references to "the Providence of God" and to "kind Providence," the words of Sir Thomas Overbury are instructive. Even seamen, Overbury wrote in the eighteenth century, could "pray, but 'tis by rote, not faith."[11]

Ironically, it is to a portion of Psalm 107 not attached to Hammon's *Narrative* that we might look in order to grasp the nature of his relationship not only with Florida Indians and Spanish Havanans but with a world that sought to bind him at every turn. Verses ten through fourteen of Psalm 107 say this: "They dwelt in darkness and gloom / bondsmen in want and in chains / . . . And he led them forth from darkness and gloom / and broke their bonds asunder." In the event Hammon took upon himself the task of breaking his bonds asunder, or at least, and more realistically, controlling who held the key and, whenever possible, under what terms. The *Narrative* itself avoids the language of enslavement, depicting a man neither comfortable with nor ready to submit to his own servility. We read on two separate occasions, for instance, that Hammon "liv'd with the [Spanish] Governor." We also read that, although Hammon found himself "confined" for a spell after a thwarted escape from Havana, "in a short Time I was set at Liberty." The use of the slippery language of liberty here is most intriguing. Did it connote something beyond Hammon's release from temporary incarceration? The Spanish variety of New World slavery held out freedom possibilities recognized by whites and blacks throughout the British Atlantic. In 1773 a group of Boston slaves, emboldened by the imperial crisis, petitioned that even "the *Spaniards*, who have not the sublime ideas of freedom that Englishmen have . . . allow [their slaves] one day in a week to work for themselves, to enable them to earn money to purchase" liberty. In fact, the common wind of this Spanish system of *coratacion* blew into New England ports with slave-sailors like Hammon, who had felt it up close, and who thus contributed to the evolution of diasporic consciousness in the region. In short, Hammon may have struck a freedom bargain with de la Vega, who at the very least granted him "Liberty to walk about the City, and do Work for my self." If so, the *Narrative* wisely failed to mention it. White New Englanders clearly would have looked upon any such agreement as a deal with the enemy, if not a pact with the devil. Regardless of the exact nature of Hammon's labor arrangement with de la Vega, the point to be stressed is that in at least one important respect it resembled his work relationship with John Winslow in Massachusetts. In each situation Hammon enjoyed broad "liberty" to move. Indeed, the relative ease with which Hammon rambled about Havana eventually alerted him to the presence of the English man-of-war *Beaver* in port, and enabled him to learn from its crew that the ship would set sail in a few days. After that Hammon "had nothing left to do, but to seek an Opportunity how I should make my Escape," which he did within days.[12]

Hammon's *Narrative* derives thematic unity above all else from sentences like the one just excerpted, in which Hammon's acts of resistance to successive attempts to restrict his freedom of choice and movement become pivots upon which the reconstructed moments of his life turn. We read of two failed escape attempts before Hammon finally gave de la Vega the slip for good in December 1758. Furthermore, Hammon's resistance to Spanish subjugation went beyond answering an emphatic "no" to slavery (or freedom) in Havana, where he also ran up against a Spanish press gang. Stolen off the street along with "a Number of others," Hammon was "ask'd" to "go on board the King's Ships" bound for Spain. Like the Boston sailors in 1747, Hammon rejected impressment, and paid a steep price for asserting his English allegiance. He spent the next "*Four Years and seven months*" in a "close Dungeon," and remained there until the captain of a merchantman from Boston interceded with de la Vega on behalf of his "Relief and Enlargement."[13]

From Hammon's spirited resistance to the Spanish press gang and his subsequent jailing emerges a portrait of a man struggling to maintain and extend personal sovereignty under less than ideal circumstances. The same can be said about Hammon's refusal to be bound by the Florida Indians. Long after initial fears of "immediate Death" at the hands of barbarous Indian cannibals proved irrational, prospects of confinement remained, prospects for which Hammon apparently had no stomach, notwithstanding that Indian captivity was not nearly as bad as he thought it would be. Ultimately it seems to have mattered less to Hammon that the Indians "us'd" him "pretty well" than it did that they "us'd" him at all. Moreover, Hammon's Indian captors may have "unbound" him, but from them he had freed himself. In saltwater parlance, we might say that when the Spanish schooner arrived from St. Augustine, Hammon "deserted" the Indians for what he hoped would be a better "berth" among another of Britain's, but not necessarily Briton's, enemies. The "relief and enlargement" to which the *Narrative* referred was less a faint hope of Hammon's than a strategy he pursued from one locale and one page to the next.[14]

How, then, to explain Hammon's re-enslavement of himself in London to "*good old Master*" Winslow, the man whose service he temporarily abandoned to go the voyage that began his Atlantic odyssey? First, it must be remembered that, unlike countless slaves who absconded to the sea, Hammon's sanctioned voyage had never been an attempted escape from slavery so much as an effort to achieve a greater level of freedom within slavery. Then there was the more pressing matter of what the *Narrative* called Hammon's "very poor Circumstances" in London. Like many black sailors whose seaborne quasi-freedom gave way to sordid life and often death in Atlantic ports, in London Hammon found himself penniless after a "Fever" "confin'd" him for six weeks to a public sickbed, his second hospital stay in a matter of months. His health failing, his money "expended," small wonder that Hammon claimed to have been struck speechless by the "happy sight" of Winslow aboard ship. Sincerely surprised, he might have felt heartened besides. And so Hammon, a man with a demonstrated knack for staying alive and optimizing personal security and relative freedom in an Atlantic world governed by hierarchies of servitude, returned to Massachusetts with a master from whom he probably expected nothing less than generous treatment, and who had indulged him before.[15]

Significantly, the flow of events in the *Narrative* makes clear that the decision to return with Winslow, like the original decision to leave Marshfield, had indeed been Hammon's choice, not that of his master. One night in early 1760 Hammon heard "a Number of Persons" in a London tavern "talking about Rigging a Vessel bound to *New-England*," and inquired whether the ship "did not want a Cook." Informed that it did, Hammon begged off a voyage on a slaver bound for Africa and instead shipped himself "at once" aboard the Boston-bound merchantman. This all transpired some time before Hammon's "remarkable" shipboard reunion with Winslow; it was "almost Three Months" later, we read, that Hammon, "one Day being at Work in the Hold," overheard "some Persons on board mention the Name of *Winslow*, at the name of which I was very inquisitive."

Very inquisitive indeed, given the prospect that the master he had not seen in thirteen years might be on the same ship! Hammon asked "what *Winslow* they were talking about," and was told "it was *General Winslow* . . . one of the Passengers." Hammon suspected then that "it must be *Master*." Any remaining doubt vanished when the two men spotted each "a few days" later. Emphatically, then, Hammon had decided to sail for Boston alone; what he intended to do upon arrival we will never know. Perhaps Hammon meant to seek out his long-lost master, post haste. If so, Winslow's appearance must have seemed fortuitous, even "Providential." If not, Winslow's physical proximity presented Hammon with a drastically different set of alternatives. He could reveal himself and take his chances, or jump ship. Choosing the former, Hammon assumed the role of the prodigal slave, gratified to be "miraculously preserved, and delivered" from the clutches of Indians and Spaniards, back into bondage in what the *Narrative* called his "own Native land" of Massachusetts. What had Hammon opted into? How did the short- and long-term state of slavery and race relations in Massachusetts, and the general mood and outlook of the colony in the summer of 1760, shape not only his present and immediate future, but also the past his *Narrative* restored and rearranged?[16]

SLAVERY, PRINT, AND THE POLITICS OF IDENTITY AND ALLEGIANCE IN LATE-COLONIAL MASSACHUSETTS

Following several years of unprecedented expansion beginning in the late 1720s, by the end of the 1730s the trajectory of slavery's development in Massachusetts was still one of slow growth fueled by small but fairly regular influxes of mainly West Indian slaves. In the next two decades, however, the landscape of slavery and of slave trading in Massachusetts underwent fundamental change. Even as the black population of colonial Boston peaked at about 1,400 souls in the early 1740s, war and declining economic fortunes, particularly in the carrying trade, dealt a double blow to the supply of imported slaves and to local demand for slave labor in the 1740s and 1750s. In contrast to the fifteen years before 1740, when newly imported slaves comprised at least forty and perhaps more than seventy percent of all slaves advertised for sale in the *Boston Gazette*, from 1745 to 1759 recent imports made up no more than about ten percent of slaves for sale. Almost entirely internal, the newspaper slave trade in Massachusetts was in one respect also decidedly dull for most of the 1740s and 1750s. Not until the late 1760s did *Gazette* ads repeat longer on average than in the 1740s, and slaves sold slowly for most of the 1750s as well. One master touted his slave's unmatched prowess "with a Scythe, Ax, and Teem" for an unprecedented nine straight weeks from March through June, 1758. Despite slow sales, Massachusetts masters demonstrated a clear resolve to part with their slaves by placing 226 different slave-for-sale notices in the *Gazette* in the 1740s, the most in any decade (and many issues from 1742 have been lost). Another 195 ads followed in the 1750s, by which time the slave population of Massachusetts had entered permanent decline.[17]

In part the critical weakness of the paper money Massachusetts had issued in piles since early in the century helps explain these developments.[18] As the colony's long-simmering fiscal crisis boiled to a head, "want of cash," as a number of slave sellers described their predicament, convinced many masters to fetch a going price for their slaves. But underemployed and idle slaves posed an even thornier problem than masters' financial difficulties. An ad from March 1740 anticipated many that appeared in the next twenty years, offering "a likely Negro Girl about 18" not because her master needed money yesterday, not because she was "addicted to anything ill," but rather on account of her "Owner having no Occasion for her." Though seasonal fluctuation in slave employment had always been the rule in Massachusetts, no previous seller had rationalized a slave sale that way; in the years after 1740 dozens of masters in town and country alike explained that lack of steady work had forced their hand. If anything employment prospects for slaves worsened in the 1750s. Forty-four out of fifty-three sellers who provided a reason for proposed slave sales in the 1750s cited "want of employ," a phrase that became both mantra and lament of slave sellers in the *Gazette*. Fully a quarter of all ads from the 1750s included words to the effect that slaves were out of work.[19]

At the same time, the increasingly shrill complaints about slave competition and occasional turns to violence of white artisans and laborers who, by 1760, had also been feeling the pinch of underemployment for almost a generation, made slave labor even more problematic around mid-century. Economic problems became social ones in the masculine workplace, where the growing and cultivated versatility of the local slave workforce pitted unprecedented numbers of blacks against whites in a fight for scarce jobs. Meanwhile, as urban and rural masters alike struggled to keep slaves and keep slaves working in the 1740s and 1750s, ads indicate that they exacerbated racial tensions by resorting with increasing frequency to the controversial practice of hiring out slave labor. "Letting" slaves offered an attractive alternative to outright sale, allowing hard-pressed masters to retain nominal ownership of slaves they did not need or could not afford to support, and perhaps line their pockets at the same time. Hiring held important benefits for slaves too. As more and more slaves came to realize the value of their labor in market terms, they also gained a degree of autonomy and mobility that connected Afro-New Englanders to one another and to the currents of black life in the larger Atlantic world, and that subtly undermined masters' control. A Boston slave named Cesar, for example, though "frequently seen" in "some of the neighbouring Towns," prevented being taken up "as a Runaway" in 1761 by telling people "he was there Working for his Master." In short, hiring created as many problems as it solved for Massachusetts masters, as slaves like Cesar – and Briton Hammon—parlayed the social capital they gained on the job into dynamic new understandings of their own subservience, the patron-client relations that ordered their working lives, and the possibilities for freedom.[20]

As the Massachusetts economy failed to keep black hands and minds busy for much of the 1740s and 1750s, white apprehension about what slaves did with their time intensified, and found expression in the enactment and frequent reenactment of curfews and various regulations designed to control black behavior.

But passing new laws and strengthening old ones failed to make any of them more effective, or to smooth over white concerns about "great Disorders committed by Negroes." No strangers to slave mischief, whites in mid–eighteenth-century Massachusetts were equally accustomed to reading about it in newspapers that early on assumed the role of slave watchdogs, reinforcing negative public perceptions of slaves, heightening concerns about slave behavior, and exacerbating fears about inversions of the racial and social order. A rarity in print were slaves like the "Honest Negro" who offered to return to its owner, for "a suitable Reward" and the cost of a newspaper ad, a "Gold Ring" found on the common in September 1738. On the other hand, reports of slave violence and black unrest were staples of colonial newspapers, and not just in Massachusetts. For instance, when a slave from southern Maine tossed his master's child down a well "where it perished" in August 1755, the news traveled south to newspapers in Boston, New Haven, New York, Philadelphia, and finally Annapolis within three weeks. The regular flow of slave news in the other direction helped cast a paranoid shadow as big as the Atlantic world on slave troubles in Massachusetts, where by the end of the 1730s five weeklies kept close tabs on slave doings at home and abroad. In the 1740s and 1750s, as war and economic downturn challenged whites' commitment to slavery in Massachusetts, the press in sharp didactic hues chronicled a present and prophesied a future ripe with black unrest. In September 1745, for instance, at least two Boston papers reported that a slave from Mendon, Massachusetts, had killed his mistress with a hatchet. A year later, constables forcibly prevented a Boston slave from allegedly carrying out a similar plan to kill his master's family. And in March 1747, just months before the Knowles Riot, a "Molatto Fellow" waved a gun around the streets of Boston before shooting at a woman and her daughter in a second-story window. In short, by the summer of 1749, when "a young Negro Girl" supposedly "instigated . . . by one or more Negro Men" confessed to igniting the last of three suspicious blazes in Charlestown, it might have seemed like the coals of slave rebellion glowed hot.[21]

They continued to smolder and flare in the 1750s. In January 1751, in Boston, a sixteen-year-old "Slave to an Apothecary" named Phillis was accused of poisoning her master's child "by putting Arsenick . . . into what it drank." Four months and at least five newspaper reports preceded her execution; a printed execution sermon followed it. Four years later, in July 1755, Captain John Codman of Charlestown, across the Charles River from Boston, was murdered by two of his slaves, "a Quantity of Poyson" found undissolved in his dissected corpse. After a long and sensational trial, both slaves went to the gallows in September, "attended by the greatest Number of Spectators ever known on such an Occasion." Phillis was "burnt to Death"; Mark, her co-conspirator, was "hanged by the Neck" and left to rot on Charlestown Common. A broadside poem commemorating the event counseled slaves that they could avoid a similar fate by remaining "in their own Place" and serving their masters "with Fear." For years Mark's chained skeleton stood as a more grisly reminder, bore gruesome testimony to white vengeance, and temporarily appeased white bloodlust. But in the long run slave executions, like the printed accounts that accompanied them, probably did little either to ease racial tensions or quell white nervousness. They may have had the opposite effect. Indeed, before Mark and Phillis died they further alarmed the entire region by implicating in Codman's murder six other slaves from Charlestown and Boston.[22]

And so it went, as time and again Boston's hyperactive press shined a harsh, teleological light on local slaves, while also enabling whites to locate their behavior within an inter-colonial continuum of resistance that did not inspire much confidence in the system. The press played a vital role in the creation of an expansive, anxious, and reactionary community of New England slavery; it tended to blur regional differences in Anglo-Atlantic slavery, portraying slaves everywhere and with very few exceptions as a troublesome if not deadly element. When, for example, the initial advertisement for Hammon's *Narrative* ran in Green & Russell's *Post-Boy* on June 30, 1760, it shared space with panicky reports of black revolt as near as Lancaster County, Pennsylvania, and as far away as Jamaica. Perhaps whites worried with good reason. Perhaps, as Herbert Aptheker and other scholars have suggested, the mid-eighteenth century witnessed a wave of slave unrest in the British North American colonies about which Massachusetts whites knew and to which worldly slaves like Hammon contributed knowledge if nothing else. The salient point to be made is that the press gave every appearance that no less was true, and thus helped create an atmosphere in which slave "disorders" could be construed as a problem that rivaled in its seeming intractability doubts about the institution as a viable system of labor.[23]

As a moment in the print history of New England slavery, Hammon's *Narrative* was, then, like its subject something of an anomaly. It contradicted familiar roles of blacks in print as chattel to be sold, runaways to be apprehended, and rebels and malcontents to be alternately quashed and feared. On one level it even quelled specific concerns about black allegiance during wartime, concerns given voice in 1755, when the Massachusetts legislature made it a capital crime in "the Time of Alarm or Invasion" for any slave to venture a mile or more from an owner's "Habitation or Plantation." Among the members of the General Court that passed this drastic measure, which gave whites license to "shoot or otherwise destroy" alleged offenders "without being impeached, censured or prosecuted," had been none other than Hammon's master, John Winslow, "Esq.," representative from Marshfield. In a broader sense, Hammon's *Narrative* mitigated long-term white anxieties about their faltering slave system, offering a model of all that a good master and a good slave could be, a primer that may have been aimed as much at slaves as whites. For if, as two Georgia planters told John Adams in 1775, slaves had a remarkable way of "communicating intelligence among themselves," whites grudgingly accepted that print information ranked among that which buzzed along the black grapevine. James Dwyer of Portsmouth, New Hampshire, certainly thought as much. In a fugitive notice from August 1757, Dwyer directly addressed his runaway slave, Scipio, advising the man that if he returned "of his own Accord" and without putting his master to the charge of a reward, he would "be kindly received, and . . . forgiven." And in Massachusetts whites had a history of using the press in a calculated effort to influence black behavior. In 1718, for instance, the *Boston Newsletter* reported the castration by passersby of a black man who allegedly attempted to rape an "English Woman" he met on the road, offering the news "as a caveat for all Negroes meddling with any White Women, least they fare with the like Treatment."[24]

More an archetype than an admonition, Hammon's *Narrative* actually appeared at the only time in the history of colonial Massachusetts after about 1740 during which the grinding gears of slavery lurched forward. Those gears had been lubricated by high war casualties in the Seven Years' War, by low rates of white emigration that might have made up for the loss, and, significantly, by the optimistic mood with which whites greeted the imminent subjugation of French Canada. With homegrown leaders like "brave" Winslow leading New England's "warlike Bands," as Abiezer Peck described them in his 1756 poem "On the Valiant *New-England* General," victory seemed at hand in July 1758, when a parcel of African slaves ushered in the most intense period of importation since the 1730s. This last gasp for slave importing in Massachusetts involved nowhere near the numbers of slaves as did the colony's largest importing cycle of the late-1720s and early-1730s. Nor did most of the slaves imported in the late 1750s and early 1760s arrive from the West Indies, as most had before; instead, most came direct from West Africa. Clearly, though, slaves from "Guinea" and elsewhere fit the rebuilding plans of a people who thought their lives had been fractured by imperial war for the last time, who looked forward to peace and prosperity following two decades of neither. A construction boom in the months following the Great Fire that leveled much of Boston in March 1760 created additional short-term demand for manpower, and helps explain why in 1761 not a single slave seller in the *Gazette* complained that "want of employ" had influenced their decision. That had not happened since 1749.[25]

By the late 1750s and early 1760s a number of slave sellers in the *Gazette* appear to have been less concerned with finding work for slaves than with finding the right slave for the job. In March 1762, for instance, one *Gazette* patron offered "a likely Negro girl, between fourteen and fifteen Years of Age . . . only [for] the want of a larger Negro." Heightened demand for slaves is also indicated by a sharp rise in the number of ads placed by patrons looking to buy slaves instead of sell them, including two eager buyers who placed ads that expressed willingness to "give a good price" to obtain the slaves they wanted. In the short-term, then, Hammon's *Narrative* appealed in obvious ways to white readers who cut their literary teeth on the Bible, *Robinson Crusoe*, and captivity literature, and who wanted to put the past behind them. It evoked optimism about the future in general, and about the future of slavery specifically, at a pivotal moment in the history of the institution in Massachusetts when the resumption of slave importing and the increased presence of strange new Africans made whites simultaneously hopeful and nervous. For, despite slavery's revitalization in the confident days surrounding the fall of French Canada, there were indications that the institution still stood on weak legs. Many Massachusetts whites, less quick, perhaps, than others to forget the lessons of the previous twenty years, simply did not share the renewed enthusiasm. For others the honeymoon ended almost before it began. But if whites dimly sensed the masquerade of their awkward dance with slavery in the summer of 1760, they did not let it stop them from basking in the triumphant glory of being British, of being integral members of the most powerful empire in the world. As white New Englanders awaited the golden age of Britain's colonial adventure in America, they felt more self-consciously British, and more proud of it, than ever before.[26]

Hammon's tale captured the ultra-patriotic mood of the moment, evincing and encouraging a strong sense of English nationalism among whites and blacks alike as the curtain lowered on the northern theater of the Seven Years' War. But nobody needed to push the buttons of British nationalism for Hammon, whose political sensibilities had been razor-sharpened by wide experience, and whose *Narrative* offered some ruminations of its own on just what it meant to be British, and on who was or could become English. All the "true Englishmen" in Hammon's story were people who helped him secure "relief and enlargement," as if he was one of their own. In Havana an Englishwoman named Betty Howard proved a worthy "Friend" and liaison. On two separate occasions "Mrs. Howard" interceded on Hammon's behalf, including when he made his final escape. It had also been Howard who related Hammon's "deplorable Condition" to the Boston ship captain who got him out of the "miserable" dungeon, and whose good deed did not go unnoted in print, albeit anonymously. Other names did not escape publication, including that of the English captain who ruined Hammon's initial attempt to flee Havana. It had been "Captain *Marsh*" who, fearing de la Vega's displeasure, sent ashore Hammon and "a Number of others," stowaways on his man-of-war. The difference between Marsh and a true Englishman is made abundantly clear later in the *Narrative*, when Hammon, again with "a Number of others," successfully escaped aboard the *Beaver*, a captured French privateer. "The *Spaniards* came alongside" the *Beaver* "and demanded" Hammon, just as they had of Captain Marsh, and just as the Indians had demanded Hammon's return from the Spanish. But because Captain Edward Gascoigne of the *Beaver* was "a true *Englishman*" he "refus'd them, saying he could not answer it, to deliver up any *Englishmen* under *English* Colours."[27]

The subtle transformation here of Hammon into an Englishman with rights protected, at least aboard ship, by other "true" Englishmen is not unlike one described by Olaudah Equiano later in the century. Equiano recalled in his famous *Narrative* that once he found his sea legs he "began to long for an engagement" in which to prove himself; after three years of getting his wish Equiano had come to consider himself "in that respect at least, almost an Englishman." By Equiano's criteria, so was Hammon, who following his escape from Cuba, served on a succession of Royal Navy warships in the late 1750s before landing in London in October 1759. In one "smart Engagement" aboard the *Hercules*, seventy British sailors died in an eighty-four-gun onslaught at the hands of the French. Hammon himself suffered wounds to the head and an arm, "country marks" of sorts that served, in a manner not unlike ritual African scars, to locate him within an English culture club the motto of which appeared in abbreviated form in a Boston newspaper in 1756: "true Britons love fighting." But even as almost-Englishmen like Equiano and Hammon identified and shrewdly pressed the levers of patronage and allegiance in Anglo-American society, at the same time they transcended notions of identity rooted in race and nation. Like the Atlantic creoles described by historian Ira Berlin, men like Hammon and Equiano parlayed familiarity with the dynamics of Atlantic life into survival and sometimes freedom as they crisscrossed and tested the limits of national, colonial, imperial, and racial boundaries. Such cosmopolitanism and the forging of personal ties it promoted played a vital role in Hammon's *Narrative*, not least when he made his escape from the Indians. Hammon gained passage aboard the Spanish getaway schooner in the first place largely because he already knew its commander, Captain Romond, quite well. Hammon had made the acquaintance of "this Gentleman" during the War of Jenkins' Ear, when he was in Jamaica (presumably with Winslow, who helped lead the unsuccessful attack on Cartagena in 1740) and Romond was brought there as a prisoner of war.[28]

Finally, if experience opened up new possibilities for Hammon, so too did language. We should take with a heavy dose of salt the narrative's prefatory note "TO THE READER," in which a voice that purports to be Hammon's proclaims that, since his "Capacities and Condition of Life are very low," he will relate only "Matters of Fact" and leave interpretation to his betters. As noted above, those words were not his, but rather were a formulaic insertion made by his editor; in any event the bold testament to creative survival undermined any suggestion that Hammon would be a nonentity in his own text. On another level, though, the prefatory plea for readers to make sense of Hammon's experiences for him requires close consideration for what it reveals about the overall nature of this text. Hammon's *Narrative* is what John Fiske, a student of popular culture, has called a "producerly" text: it does not shock readers with a sense of stark difference from other texts; it does not demand that readers rewrite it in ways that deviate from the dominant meaning or ideology. It does, however, quite explicitly offer itself up to popular production, and by inviting readers' active participation in the construction of meaning opens itself to voices and meanings that escape and even subvert control. Fiske's observations about the multiplicity of meaning in popularly produced texts are a slightly different way to make a point about the subtleties of language familiar enough to students of black Anglophone literature that it can be stated briefly. Hammon had little choice, of course, but to posture meekly, to don the mask, before whites at whose discretion his literary career proceeded. As such he faced an authorial challenge similar to that of antebellum slave narrators, who found themselves restricted by abolitionist pressures to depict the horrors of 'slavery as it is.' Like those later authors, however, Hammon could carve a meaningful space in between the gaps of the affirmation that the *Narrative* meant nothing to him; the preface in fact encouraged readers to search for obscured meanings, while allowing them to think they figured it all out for themselves. Thus do we arrive at a grand irony, that the author-evacuated language of Hammon's preface presented to him opportunities not precluded even by the fact that the words were not his own.[29]

Folklorist and historian William D. Piersen has observed that eighteenth-century Afro-New Englanders, like other transplanted Africans, nurtured and maintained lively oral and storytelling traditions steeped in symbolic wordplay that adapted well to the page and to the needs of early black authors. Surely some communicative wires crossed or short-circuited in the translation from mouth to pen. And yet, as literary historian Frances Smith Foster has observed, the earliest black authors in colonial British America did not "abandon the discourse of indirection" that characterized "their folk tales . . . and, especially, their daily interactions with whites . . . simply because they were writing instead of speaking." Instead, vernacular language styles that made effective use of obliquity, wit, and metaphor – the roots of which stretched as far as West Africa – guided the transition in ways that made the space between that much more viable, that much more fertile. For their part, eighteenth-century whites recognized their limited control over language, print, and slaves at least as clearly as do modern scholars. Such was their frequent lament in runaway ads. William Johnson, a smooth-talking Connecticut slave who told people he was a free black from Amboy, New Jersey, was deemed "very apt to tell any lie to serve his own turn" by the master whose service he quit in June 1784. For fugitives like Johnson, saying the right thing to the right people at the right time could mean the difference between freedom and capture. The ability to "tell an ample story for being [away] from home" helped Bristo, a thirty-year-old sailor and fiddler from Middletown, Connecticut, avoid capture for at least two months in the spring of 1769. As for fugitives like Johnson and Bristo, for Hammon the opportunity to assert agency, self, and meaning out of the materials, linguistic and otherwise, of oppression depended in large measure on his ability to craft "an ample story." On one hand that meant a story that met the needs and expectation of his white audience in Massachusetts, where God was definitely Protestant and most likely English. But if Hammon operated within Anglo-American social, cultural, and literary forces that pushed his individuality to the edges, the sophisticated nature of both language and the man made it easier to work around them, as well. In his *Narrative*, Briton Hammon beat Ralph Ellison's fictional Invisible Man by two centuries to the recognition that there is room to maneuver at the margins.[30]

CODA—NEW BEGINNINGS

Ellison's anonymous protagonist could have savored the irony of Hammon's "descent" back into bondage. *Invisible Man* also ends in descent, with the literal movement of Ellison's hero underground. But he will not stay there forever and neither should we assume will Hammon, whose story does not end in 1760, but begins again. What did Hammon do with his fresh start? On June 3, 1762, almost two years to the day after he returned to Massachusetts, "Britain Negro Servt of Genl Winslow" was joined in marriage to "Hannah Servt of Mr Hovey" in Plymouth's

First Church. Hannah had been a member of the First Church of Plymouth in full communion since 1748, and in 1760 was one of only two women out of 140 total Church's members described as a "Negro." About her we know little else. Neither do we know when Hammon and Hannah first met, which raises the possibility that he returned to Massachusetts for love of her and not at all of slavery or the beneficent Winslow. Following the marriage Hammon appears to have settled into family life with Hannah in Massachusetts, his desire to ply his seafaring skills dampened, perhaps, by memories of that ill-fated voyage of late-1747. The couple remained together for many years, and had at least one child, which died tragically in early-June 1776, possibly of an outbreak of smallpox that claimed the lives of thirteen Plymouth Church members in the last eight months of that year. After the death of this child Briton Hammon vanishes from the print record.[31]

Or does he? During the American Revolution a "negro" named Briton Nichols enlisted at the rank of private at least four times between August 1777 and July 1780 for short stints in Massachusetts regiments out of Hingham and neighboring Cohasset. Nichols appears in the print record again in the federal census of 1790, according to which he was a free black, head of a household of three in Hingham, and also the only identifiably non-white man in the entire state with the forename "Briton," variously spelled. There is reason to believe that Briton Nichols of Hingham, Massachusetts, was in fact the man of shifting identities formerly known as Briton Hammon. When "*good old Master*" Winslow died in April 1774 he resided at Hingham with his sister Bethia and her husband, Roger Nichols. At this point we can only speculate that sometime after Winslow's death Hammon became tied to the family of his old master's brother-in law, relocated to Hingham, and adopted the Nichols surname to announce the change and perhaps a shift in his patriotic loyalties. We do know that when the showdown with Britain came to blows John Winslow's heirs, including his wife, sons, brother, and nephew, sided with the British and left Massachusetts when they evacuated Boston in 1776, some of them before. The men of the Nichols family all fought well and often for the cause of liberty and freedom.[32]

Other clues point to the common identity of Briton Nichols and Briton Hammon, and suggest that in some ways black freedom remained no less conditional at the end of the eighteenth century than it had been in the middle. The name of a white woman identified only as "Mrs. Hammond" appeared in the Hingham census return just two lines above the aforementioned record for Briton Nichols.[33] Was this Mrs. Hammond of the same family from which Briton Hammon's surname derived? Since the pages of data compiled by census-takers on a door-to-door basis would resemble neighborhood grids if plotted on a map, we can presume that Briton Nichols and Mrs. Hammond lived close to and knew one another. One wonders on what terms. Did Nichols not live near but actually with Mrs. Hammond, like the one in three ex-slaves in post-revolutionary Massachusetts who resided in a white household? In short, was Briton Hammon's brief *Narrative* not the finished account of a black prodigal after all, but a chapter in an unfinished book of a pilgrim's progress toward freedom? We are left for now with as many questions as answers. Perhaps it is only fitting, however, that Briton Hammon continues to elude us, nearly two-and-a-half centuries after his first and apparently only appearance on the public stage.[34]

NOTES

Epigraph from James Thomson, "Rule Brittania," in J. Logie Robertson, ed., *The Complete Poetical Works of James Thomson* (Oxford, 1908), 420.

1. Briton Hammon, *A Narrative of the Uncommon Sufferings and Surprizing Deliverance of Briton Hammon* (Boston, 1760), 3–4.

2. Hammon, *Narrative*, 1, 3. Fugitive slave notices in the *Boston Gazette* suggest that running away in Massachusetts may have become more prevalent around the time of Hammon's departure. An annual average of just three runaway slave ads appeared in the *Gazette* from 1719 through 1744; in the last half of the 1740s, at the height of King George's War, the average jumped to just under nine notices per year. On race and autonomy aboard ship, see W. Jeffrey Bolster, *Black Jacks: African American Seamen in the Age of Sail* (Cambridge, MA, 1997). On seamen's wages in 1747, during wartime, and for the Campeche run, see Marcus Rediker, *Between the Devil and the Deep Blue Sea: Merchant Seamen, Pirates, and the Anglo-American Maritime World, 1700–1750* (Cambridge, Eng., 1987), 32, 139, 305; and Gary B. Nash, *The Urban Crucible: Social Change, Political Consciousness, and the Origins of the American Revolution* (Cambridge, MA, 1979), 167.

3. On June 2, 1760, Green & Russell's *Boston Post-Boy and Advertiser* announced the arrival of "General Winslow, belonging to Marshfield," aboard a ship that entered from London sometime after May 26. The *Boston Gazette* did the same in its edition of June 2. Neither paper announced the homecoming of the slave accompanying him. That happened on June 30, when Green & Russell's *Post-Boy* ran the first of four consecutive weekly advertisements for Hammon's *Narrative*. Ads for Hammon's *Narrative* also ran in the *Boston Evening-Post* throughout July 1760 (July 7, 14, 21, 28). See Vincent Carretta, ed., *Unchained Voices: An Anthology of Black Authors in the English-Speaking World of the Eighteenth Century* (Lexington, 1996), 24.

4. Since the days of U. B. Phillips the authenticity debate has shifted from reservations about slave narratives as history to questioning slave narratives as voices of the black experience. For recent critical exchanges, see Charles T. Davis and Henry Louis Gates, Jr., eds., *The Slave's Narrative* (New York, 1985); Henry Louis Gates Jr., "The Master's Pieces: On Canon Formation and the African-American Tradition," *South Atlantic Quarterly*, 89 (Winter 1990), 89–111; Henry Louis Gates, Jr., "'Authenticity,' or the Lesson of Little Tree," *New York Times Book Review*, November 24, 1991; Graham White, "Inventing the Past?: The Remarkable Story of an African King in Charleston," *Australasian Journal of American Studies*, 12 (1993), 1–14; Jean Fagan Yellin, "*Written by Herself*: Harriet Jacobs' Slave Narrative," *American Literature*, 53 (November 1981), 478–86.

5. The engaging and innovative ideas of literary scholars William L. Andrews and John Sekora sparked my interest in early black autobiography, and have shaped the field. See William L. Andrews, "The First Fifty Years of the Slave Narrative, 1760–1810," in John Sekora and Darwin T. Turner, ed., *The Art of Slave Narrative: Original Essays in Criticism and Theory* (Macomb, IL, 1982), 6–24; William L. Andrews, *To Tell a Free Story: The First Century of Afro-American Autobiography, 1760–1865* (Urbana, 1986), 1–60; and three articles by John Sekora: "Black Message/White Envelope: Genre, Authenticity, and Authority in the Antebellum Slave Narrative," *Callaloo*, 10 (1987), 482–515; "Is the Slave Narrative a Species of Autobiography?," in James Olney, ed., *Studies in Autobiography* (New York, 1988),

99–111; and "Red, White, and Black: Indian Captivities, Colonial Printers, and the Early African-American Narrative," in Frank Shuffelton, ed., *A Mixed Race: Ethnicity in Early America* (New York, 1993), 92–104.

6. Peter Linebaugh and Marcus Rediker, "The Many-Headed Hydra: Sailors, Slaves, and the Atlantic Working Class in the Eighteenth Century," *Journal of Historical Sociology*, 3 (Sept. 1990), 233; "Protest Against Kidnapping and the Slave Trade," in Herbert Aptheker, ed., *A Documentary History of the Negro People in the United States*, 2 vols. (New York, 1951), I, 21; Bolster, *Black Jacks*, 75; Rediker, *Between the Devil and the Deep Blue Sea*, 109. On the Knowles Riot, see John Lax and William C. Pencak, "The Knowles Riot and the Crisis of the 1740's in Massachusetts," *Perspectives in American History*, 10 (1976), 163–214. On seamen and Atlantic maritime culture, see Jesse Lemisch, "Jack Tar in the Streets: Merchant Seamen in the Politics of Revolutionary America," *William and Mary Quarterly*, 3d ser., 25 (July 1968), 371–407; and Peter Linebaugh, "All the Atlantic Mountains Shook," *Labour/Le Travailleur*, 9 (Autumn 1982), 87–121.

7. Hammon, *Narrative*, 4, 6, 14.

8. Hammon, *Narrative*, 5–6.

9. Hammon, *Narrative*, 6–7. It is unclear whether the Florida Indians repaired to Havana in order to negotiate a bounty for Hammon, to collect payment of one, or to assert that he belonged to them.

10. Hammon, *Narrative*, 10.

11. Alice A. Deck, "Whose Book is This?: Authorial Versus Editorial Control of Harriet Jacobs' *Incidents in the Life of a Slave Girl: Written by Herself*," *Women's Studies International Forum*, 10 (1987), 36; Overbury quoted in Rediker, *Between the Devil and the Deep Blue Sea*, 175. On editorial imposition in Hammon's *Narrative*, see Sekora, "Black Message/White Envelope," 488, and "Red, White, and Black," in Shuffelton, ed., *A Mixed Race*. On Christianity among slaves in New England, see William D. Piersen, *Black Yankees: The Development of an Afro-American Subculture in Eighteenth-Century New England* (Amherst, MA, 1988), 49–86; and Lorenzo J. Greene, *The Negro in Colonial New England* (1942; reprint New York, 1974), 257–89.

12. *The New American Bible* (New York, 1970), 107; Hammon, *Narrative*, 8–10; [Petition of Peter Bestes, Sambo Freeman, Felix Holbrook, and Chester Joie,] in Dorothy Porter, ed., *Early Negro Writing, 1760–1837*, (1971; reprint Baltimore, 1995), 254. In addition to the knowledge imparted by well-traveled slaves like Hammon, the presence in Massachusetts of Spanish slaves, most of them war captives, brought the possibilities of Spanish slavery close to home. In October 1741, for instance, "five Spanish Negroes lately brought in" to Boston convinced a local slave to accompany them in an unsuccessful attempt "to get to St. Augustine." Cosmopolitan Havana had a special reputation among fugitive slaves, particularly in the southeast. Slaves from French Louisiana sang songs like the following as they escaped to Havana: "Oh General Fleuriau! It's true they cannot catch me! There is a schooner out at sea. It's true they cannot catch me!" *Boston Gazette*, Oct. 5, 1741; Gwendolyn Midlo Hall, *Africans in Colonial Louisiana: The Development of Afro-Creole Culture in the Eighteenth Century* (Baton Rouge, 1992), 146–47.

13. Hammon, *Narrative*, 8–10.

14. Hammon, *Narrative*, 6–7.

15. Hammon, *Narrative*, 12–13. Life in black London probably sharpened Hammon's sense of the possibilities and limits of freedom. As Sir John Fielding noted in 1768, blacks "no sooner come over [to England], but the Sweets of Liberty and the Conversation with free Men . . . enlarge their Minds" until they became "intoxicated with Liberty." And London's growing community of color, made up significantly of seamen like Hammon, offered some support. But, as historian Gretchen Gerzina observed, "[for blacks] there was a real possi-

bility of starvation and homelessness in England." Peter Fryer, *Staying Power: Black People in Britain Since 1504* (Atlantic Highlands, NJ, 1984), 71; Gerzina, *Black England: Life Before Emancipation* (London, 1995), 19.

16. Hammon, *Narrative*, 12–14. A life-long military man, Winslow was made general for leading New England's forces in the Seven Years War. For a brief and whiggish summary of Winslow's career, see Lorenzo Sabine, *Biographical Sketches of Loyalists of the American Revolution*, 2 vols. (Boston, 1864), II, 439–44. Winslow's gallantry was immortalized by Abiezer Peck of Rehoboth, Massachusetts, in a laudatory poem "On the Valiant *New-England* General" (broadside, n.p., 1756; reprinted in Ola Elizabeth Winslow, *American Broadside Verse, From Imprints of the 17ᵗʰ and 18ᵗʰ Centuries* [New Haven, 1930]), 122–23. On Winslow's military exploits, see especially Francis Parkman, *Montcalm and Wolfe*, (1884; New York, 1984); and Fred Anderson, *A People's Army: Massachusetts Soldiers and Society in the Seven Years' War* (Chapel Hill, 1984). Winslow's military *Journal* (1754–58), on 2 microfilm reels, can be consulted at the Massachusetts Historical Society, Boston.

17. [1742 census], *Report of the Records Commissioners of the City of Boston, Containing the Selectmen's Minutes from 1736 to 1742* (Boston, 1886); *Boston Gazette*, Mar. 20, 1758. The discussion of slaving trends in this and the ensuing paragraphs is based on a close analysis of slave-for-sale ads in the *Gazette*, Boston's longest-lived and most advertising-friendly weekly newspaper. 1,103 different slave-for-sale ads appeared in the roughly 3,200 issues of the *Gazette* printed following its inception in December 1719 through 1781, when slave trading in its pages ended for good. In all close to 2,000 slaves, and, counting repeat ads, 2,300 slave-for-sale notices appeared in the *Gazette*. Thus did three out of four editions of one local newspaper alone document the important and highly visible role of slaves and slave labor in eighteenth-century Massachusetts. Untold other slaves appeared for sale in others of Boston's multiple weeklies. See Robert E. Desrochers, Jr., "Every Picture Tells a Story: Slavery, Freedom, and the Printed Word in Eighteenth-Century New England" (Ph.D. diss., The Johns Hopkins University, 2000).

18. Massachusetts began printing paper money in order to underwrite costly wars, finance a poor balance of trade, and offset deeper (if only dimly understood) structural disadvantages of a volatile regional economy in which much depended on the foreign sector, especially the carrying trade. By 1746, when Charles Apthorp, venerable slave importer and one of the richest men in Boston, observed that "our Currency is very bad and I think must be worse," and despite efforts to stabilize provincial fiscal policy, the value of hyperinflationary Massachusetts' paper money had plummeted to crisis levels. See Nash, *The Urban Crucible*, esp. 112–13, 136–38, 173–75, 212–16; Carl Bridenbaugh, *Cities in the Wilderness: Urban Life in America, 1625–1742* (1938; reprint New York, 1964), 205, 360–61, and *Cities in Revolt: Urban Life in America, 1743–1776* (1955; reprint New York, 1971), 90–92 (Apthorp quote 91); G. B. Warden, *Boston 1689–1776* (Boston, 1970), esp. 102–48; Herman Belz, "Paper Money in Colonial Massachusetts," *Essex Institute Historical Collections* (1965), 149–63; and John J. McCusker, *Money and Exchange in Colonial America, 1600–1775: A Handbook* (Chapel Hill, 1978), 125–37.

19. *Boston Gazette*, Mar. 3, 1740. Unemployment affected some owners and some slaves more clearly than it did others. For example, the long-term decline of shipbuilding in Boston probably had a lot to do with the impending sales of four separate slave ship carpenters, each of whose masters parted with them, they said, for lack of work. *Boston Gazette*, July 18, 1749, Jan. 29, 1754, Apr. 16, 1754, Aug. 28, 1758. For slaves with seafaring skills, wartime expansions of the maritime work force helped offset the generally shrinking employment opportunities for blacks in the 1740s and 1750s.

20. *Boston Gazette*, Sept. 21, 1761. On white unemployment and the scapegoating of slaves, see *Boston Evening Post*, Apr. 2, 1750 (report of widespread joblessness); Nash, *The*

Urban Crucible, 187, 227, 241–42; Edgar J. McManus, *Black Bondage in the North* (Syracuse, 1973) 44; and Lawrence William Towner, *A Good Master Well Served: Masters and Servants in Colonial Massachusetts, 1620–1750* (New York, 1998), 225, 227 n11. In 1756 a "Trades-man" complained in a letter to the *Gazette* that white workingmen suffered "great Want of Employ," and railed against employers who adopted the "very ill practice" of advertising jobs so as to hire "*him who will work cheapest*," which everybody knew meant slaves. Competition from slaves, the argument went, stole jobs from and undercut the wages of a "whole Class" of "poor industrious" white laborers. *Boston Gazette,* Mar. 1, 1756.

21. Robert C. Twombly, "Black Resistance to Slavery in Massachusetts," in William O'Neill, ed., *Insights and Parallels: Problems and Issues of American Social History* (Minneapolis, 1973), 26: "curfews and prohibitions [aimed at Massachusetts blacks] . . . reached their peak in the 1740s and 1750s;" *Boston Evening-Post,* July 14, 1740; *Boston Gazette,* Sept. 18, 1738; David A. Copeland, *Colonial American Newspapers: Character and Content* (Newark, DE, 1997), 139–40, 147; Charles E. Clark, *The Public Prints: The Newspaper in Anglo-American Culture, 1665–1740* (New York, 1994), 267–68; *Boston Evening-Post,* Sept. 16, 1745; *Boston News-Letter,* Sept. 20, 1745; *Boston Evening-Post,* Jan. 20, 1746; *Boston News-Letter,* Mar. 26, 1747; *Boston Gazette,* Aug. 8, 1749.

22.*Boston Gazette,* Jan. 22, Mar. 5, Apr. 9, 16, May 21, 1751 (Phillis); July 7, Aug. 11, 25, 1755; *Boston News-Letter,* Sept. 25, 1755 (Mark and Phillis). Mather Byles, *The Prayer and Plea of David, to be delivered from Blood and Guiltiness, Improved in a Sermon at the ancient Thursday-Lecture in Boston, May 16, 1751. Before the Execution of a Young Negro Servant, for Poisoning an Infant* (Boston, 1751); "A few Lines On Occasion of the untimely End of *Mark* and *Phillis,* Who were Executed at *Cambridge, September* 18th for Poysoning their Master, Capt. *John Codman* of *Charlestown* (broadside, Boston, 1755).

23. David Paul Nord, "Teleology and News: The Religious Roots of American Journalism, 1630–1730," *Journal of American History,* 77 (June 1990), 9–38; Patricia Bradley, *Slavery, Propaganda, and the American Revolution* (Jackson, MS, 1998), 8–13, 27; Herbert Aptheker, *American Negro Slave Revolts* (1943; reprint New York, 1993), 196; Peter H. Wood, "'I Did the Best I Could for My Day:' The Study of Early Black History during the Second Reconstruction, 1960 to 1976," *William and Mary Quarterly,* 3d ser., 35 (Apr. 1978), 216; Philip D. Morgan and George D. Terry, "Slavery in Microcosm: A Conspiracy Scare in Colonial South Carolina," *Southern Studies,* 21 (1986), 121.

24. *Boston Evening-Post,* Mar. 10, 1755; *Boston Gazette,* June 4, 1754 (election results); Charles Francis Adams, ed., *The Works of John Adams,* 10 vols. (Boston, 1850–1856), II, 428; *Boston Gazette,* Aug. 8, 1757; *Boston Newsletter,* Feb. 24, 1718. On white northerners' fears of slave insurrection during wartime, see McManus, *Black Bondage in the North,* 126–27; and Arthur Zilversmit, *The First Emancipation: The Abolition of Slavery in the North* (Chicago, 1967), 21.

25. Peck, "On the Valiant *New-England* General," in Winslow, *American Broadside Verse,* 122–23; *Boston Gazette,* July 3, 1758. As much as ninety-four percent of the 2,500 New England troops raised in 1756 called Massachusetts home; only about half the colony's soldiers emerged from armed service "present and fit," many did not return at all. Anderson, *A People's Army,* 231. Bernard Bailyn has shown that only 77 of 9,364 emigrants from Britain to the colonies in the years before the Revolution made Massachusetts their final destination. Bailyn, *Voyagers to the West: A Passage in the Peopling of America on the Eve of the Revolution* (New York, 1986), 205, 209. On African importation in the era of the Seven Years' War, see Jay Coughtry, *The Notorious Triangle: Rhode Island and the African Slave Trade, 1700–1807* (Philadelphia, 1981); Gary B. Nash, "Slaves and Slaveholders in Colonial Philadelphia," *William and Mary Quarterly,* 3d ser., 30 (1973), 229; Darold D. Wax, "Africans on the Delaware: The Pennsylvania Slave Trade, 1759–1765," *Pennsylvania History,* 50

(1983), 40; Wax, "Black Immigrants: The Slave Trade in Colonial Maryland," *Maryland Historical Magazine*, 73 (1978), 36–37; James G. Lydon, "New York and the Slave Trade, 1700–1774," *William and Mary Quarterly*, 3d ser., 35 (1978), 381; and Elizabeth Donnan, *Documents Illustrative of the Slave Trade to America*, 4 vols. (1932; reprint New York, 1969), III: *New England and the Middle Colonies*, and IV: *The Border Colonies and the Southern Colonies*.

26. *Boston Gazette*, Mar. 22, 1762, June 23, 1760, May 25, 1761. A third of all the 'slave wanted' ads that appeared in the *Gazette* from 1719 through 1781 clustered around the nine years between 1756 and 1764. On the other hand, following the brief hiatus in 1761, under- and unemployment of slaves returned with a vengeance in 1762, when nine sellers (the most in any single year) rationalized slave sales due to "want of employ." Nine more slave sellers cited "want of employ" in each of the next two years, followed by another six in 1765, and eight more in 1766. On the growth of English nationalism, or, perhaps more accurately, patriotism in New England around the time of the Seven Years' War see T. H. Breen, "An Empire of Goods: The Anglicization of Colonial America, 1690–1776," *Journal of British Studies*, 25 (1986), 467–99; John M. Murrin, "Anglicizing an American Colony: The Transformation of Provincial Massachusetts" (Ph.D. diss., Yale University, 1966); Nathan O. Hatch, "The Origins of Civil Millennialism in America: New England Clergymen, War with France, and the Revolution," *William and Mary Quarterly*, 31 (July 1974), 407–30; and Jack P. Greene: "The Seven Years' War and the American Revolution: The Causal Relationship Reconsidered," *Journal of Imperial and Commonwealth History*, 8 (1980), 85–105.

27. Hammon, *Narrative*, 8–11. Gascoigne is identified in Carretta, ed., *Unchained Voices*, 25fn20. Among a number of recent works on English nationalism and identity, I have found most useful Linda Colley, *Britons: Forging the Nation, 1707–1837* (New Haven, 1992). For a turn-of-the-eighteenth-century satirical view on the subject, see Daniel Defoe, *The True Born Englishman* (London, 1700).

28. Olaudah Equiano, *The Interesting Narrative of the Life of Olaudah Equiano, or Gustavus Vassa, the African. Written by Himself,* Vincent Carretta, ed. (New York, 1995), 70, 77; *Boston Gazette*, May 17, 1756; Hammon, *Narrative*, 7. On Atlantic creoles, see Ira Berlin, "From Creole to African: Atlantic Creoles and the Origins of African-American Society in Mainland North America," *William and Mary Quarterly*, 53 (April 1996), 279–82; and *Many Thousands Gone: The First Two Centuries of Slavery in North America* (Cambridge, MA, 1998). On the martial aspects of English nationalism and identity, see Colley, *Britons*.

29. Hammon, *Narrative*, 3; John Fiske, *Understanding Popular Culture* (London, 1989), esp. 103–5.

30. William D. Piersen, "Puttin Down Ole Massa: African Satire in the New World," *Research in African Literatures*, 7 (Summer 1976), 166–80, and *Black Yankees: The Development of an Afro-American Subculture in Eighteenth-Century New England* (Amherst, 1988), esp. 106–13, 155–58; Frances Smith Foster, *Witnessing Slavery, The Development of Ante-Bellum Slave Narratives* (2d ed., Madison, WI, 1994), xxviii; [New London] *Connecticut Gazette*, June 11, 1784; [Hartford] *Connecticut Courant*, May 3, 1769; Ralph Ellison, *Invisible Man* (1947; reprint New York, 1995). For similar observations about language, see for example Lawrence W. Levine, *Black Culture and Black Consciousness: Afro-American Folk Thought from Slavery to Freedom* (New York, 1977); Charles Joyner, *Down by the Riverside: A South Carolina Slave Community* (Urbana, 1984), esp. ch. 6; Claudia Mitchell-Kernan, "Signifying," in Alan Dundes, ed., *Mother Wit From the Laughing Barrel: Readings in the Interpretation of Afro-American Folklore* (Englewood Cliffs, NJ, 1973), 310–28; Raymond Hedin, "Muffled Voices: The American Slave Narrative," *Clio*, 10 (1981), 129–42; and Henry Louis Gates, Jr., *The Signifying Monkey: A Theory of African-American Literary Criticism* (New York, 1988). On the persistence of vernacular forms, see also Gilbert Osofsky, "A

Note on the Use of Folklore," in *Puttin' On Ole Massa: The Slave Narratives of Henry Bibb, William Wells Brown, and Solomon Northrup* (New York, 1969), 45–48.

31. *Plymouth Church Records 1620–1859*, 2 vols. (New York, 1923), I, 469, II, 406, 493, 528. The reference here and on the title page of the *Narrative* to Hammon as Winslow's "Negro Servt" suggests that Hammon was not a free black laborer, as some scholars have assumed, but rather Winslow's personal slave. In colonial Massachusetts the linguistic distinction between "free Negro" and "Negro servant" was as clear as it was important, with the difference being that the latter meant the same as slave, a term that white New Englanders rarely employed, especially before the imperial crisis aroused fears of their own "slavery." The distinction becomes clearer upon examining the language used to describe hundreds of marriages between and among slaves and free blacks in *A Volume of Records Relating to the Early History of Boston, Containing Boston Marriages From 1752 to 1809* (Boston, 1903).

32. E. Victor Bigelow, *A Narrative History of the Town of Cohasset, Massachusetts: Massachusetts Soldiers and Sailors of the Revolutionary War* (Cohasset, 1898), 298, 308; *Heads of Families at the First Census of the United States Taken in the Year 1790: Massachusetts* (Spartanburg, S.C., 1982), 168, 201; *History of the Town of Hingham*, 3 vols. (Hingham, 1893).

33. The name between was "Marsh Lewis." I have been unable to link Marsh Lewis to Mrs. Hammond or to Briton Hammon (Nichols). The Lewis and Winslow families, however, had been related since Isaiah Lewis married into the Winslow family in the late seventeenth century. *Heads of Families at the First Census of the United States Taken in the Year 1790: Massachusetts*, 148; Samuel Deane, *History of Scituate, Massachusetts, From Its First Settlement to 1831* (Boston, 1831), 304.

34. Gary B. Nash, "Forging Freedom: The Emancipation Experience in the Northern Seaport Cities, 1775–1820," *Slavery and Freedom in the Age of the American Revolution*, ed. Ira Berlin and Ronald Hoffman (1983; reprint Urbana 1986), 31. I second historian Erik R. Seeman's observation that "the raw materials for work on African Americans in colonial New England are relatively abundant." Persistence and the assistance of other scholars can and will answer some of the questions raised here, even as new ones emerge as scholars continue to explore the possibilities of this text. Seeman, "'Justice Must Take Plase': Three African Americans Speak of Religion in Eighteenth-Century New England," *William and Mary Quarterly*, 3d ser., 56 (Apr. 1999), Appendix 1, available on the worldwide web, http://www.wm.edu/oieahc/Seemanp1.html.

ON HER OWN FOOTING

Phillis Wheatley in Freedom

Frank Shuffelton

When Phillis Wheatley wrote in 1770 to the Countess of Huntingdon, presenting a copy of her elegy on George Whitefield, the Countess's chaplain, she opened a connection to an imperial public sphere that paid off handsomely for a self-styled "untutored African." By the early autumn of 1773 Wheatley had become a figure of public note in Boston and London, made an almost triumphal visit to the imperial capital, published her poems in a handsome volume, and, perhaps most importantly, gained her freedom upon her return to Boston. She wrote a "short Sketch" of her trip to Col David Wooster of New Haven, expressing her pleasure in the "kindness, Complaisance, and so many marks of esteem and real Friendship" that were extended to her there, including visits with the Earl of Dartmouth, the Earl of Lincoln, "who visited me at my own Lodgings with the Famous Dr. Solander, who accompany'd Mr. Banks in his late expedition round the World," Benjamin Franklin, and Granville Sharp, "who attended me to the Tower & Show'd the Lions, Panthers, Tigers, &c." Sharp seems to have given her an extensive tour of the Tower, also showing her "The Horse Armoury, Small Armoury, the Crowns, Sceptres, Diadems, the Font for christ[en]ing the Royal Family," all the paraphernalia of monarchy that was exhibited for the edification of provincial subjects visiting the metropolis. Although Wheatley was supposedly sent on an ocean voyage for her health, she was in London as a poet and for the purpose of assisting in the publication of her volume of poems. Because doubts had been raised earlier in London about the authenticity of her writings, her presence was useful to her publisher, no doubt, to establish her credentials as well as to generate interest in the book that was in the press; Wheatley's visit to London was in effect a very early, if not the first, author's publicity tour. She proudly described to Wooster the books given to her by Lord Dartmouth and by Brook Watson, signs of "Complaisance" that also attested to her status as a remarkable woman of letters, and concluded her account by linking her manumission to the "real Friendship" she had developed in the imperial center: "Since my return to America my Master has at the desire of my friends in England given me my freedom, The Instrument is drawn, so as to secure me and my property from the hands of the Exec[utors,] administrators, &c of my master, & secure whatsoever Should be given me as my Own, a copy is Sent to Isr[ael] Mauduit Esqr. F.R.S."[1] Publication of her poetry had guaranteed Wheatley the respect that distinguished her from slavery's anonymity, but in making public the instrument of her manumission, both in the letter to Wooster and the communication to Mauduit, she consequently demanded the equal recognition that Charles Taylor has identified as the basis for an authentic modern freedom.[2] "I am now upon my own footing," she wrote Wooster, and requested him to look out for her business interests in New Haven.

An unmarried African woman in white Boston in the 1770s, however, would have found it difficult to be truly independent, to be on her own footing in any absolute sense, because the economic opportunities for single free black women were extremely limited. Wheatley continued to live with John Wheatley's family, even after the death of Susanna Wheatley, her strongest supporter, but the Wheatley family was itself undergoing the changes that often mark transition from one generation to the next. The Wheatley children were going their separate ways in the world; Mary Wheatley and the Rev. John Lathrop of Providence had married in 1771, and Nathaniel, who had accompanied Phillis to London, stayed there and married in the following November. Susannah Wheatley's death in 1774 left her husband alone with the family servants in their Boston house, but within little more than a year both he and Phillis would be refugees from British-occupied Boston. Phillis would have found herself on new and unstable ground as she simultaneously lost her first patrons and discovered that the imperial world that had done so well by her was itself being transformed. The plaudits of Phillis Wheatley's London acquaintances might have had considerable cultural prestige among the Wheatley family's acquaintances before 1775, but in revolutionary Boston the relevance of London friends would have become more questionable. The belletristic discourse of the tea table was for the moment subordinated to the political and military concerns of a new social order. Wheatley needed to reconstruct her role as a poet in this changing society, and she would do it by developing a more complex, pluralistic sense of audience than shown in the 1773 collection of her work. In a shifting and unstable world Wheatley positioned herself aesthetically in terms of the Atlantic civilization of the old empire, patriotically within the context of an emergent national culture, and politically in the possiblity of a new community of free people of color in New England. No one of these worlds could in itself give her a sure home: her friends were Bostonians, not empire loyalists; the new nation, for all its talk about universal human liberties and rights, was emphatically a nation of white people, and the community of free people of color in New England was only at that moment in the process of defining itself. As she attempted to negotiate her way among these different discursive possibilities, however, she explored the new potential of the black Atlantic world.[3]

If her connections to the Countess of Huntingdon were primarily defined by religious concerns, they nonetheless always seem to have been, on Wheatley's

side at least, entangled in complex ways with discourses about slavery and freedom. Although Wheatley has been accused by twentieth-century critics of
"think[ing] white" and being "not sensitive enough to the needs of her own people
to demonstrate a kinship to Blacks in her life or writings," she insisted upon her
African identity in poem after poem in the 1773 volume, be it as the "Ethiop" who
admonished the students at Harvard, the "refin'd" Negro brought from Africa to
America, the "vent'rous *Afric*" undertaking to write a poem about memory, or the
speaker "snatch'd from *Afric's* fancy'd happy seat" who addresses the Earl of
Dartmouth.[4] Lest there was any doubt about the significance of her racial identity,
half-heartedly mystified on the title page of the volume by identifying her as a
"servant," the attestation made it clear that she was "under the Disadvantage, of
serving as a Slave in a Family in this Town." These interpellations and others like
them would seem to require her readers to have some sense of the irony implicit,
surely intentional, in lines like those addressing King George III after the repeal of
the Stamp Act, "And may each clime with equal gladness see / A monarch's smile
can set his subjects free!" The freedom hinted at here is more extensive, applicable
in all climes and not only New England, than a mere liberation from intolerable
taxes; the optative "may" yearns for freedoms not yet granted, possibilities still
only dreamed of. Similarly, the lines in the poem to Dartmouth, who had been
appointed Secretary of State for North America only a few months before Wheatley
composed her address to him, express hope for improved relations with the colonies that resonate beyond the most narrow reading of their political message:

> No more, *America,* in mournful strain
> Of wrongs, and grievance unredressed complain,
> No longer shalt thou dread the iron chain,
> Which wanton *Tyranny* with lawless hand
> Had made, and with it meant t' enslave the land.[5]

Wheatley's description of America's case is no more exaggerated than a great deal
of the patriot rhetoric of the time, but it evokes the actual experience of the middle
passage as much as it does the polemical reality of 1772 Boston. She enforces this
reading by announcing in the next lines that her own love of freedom sprang from
her "seeming cruel fate" of being stolen from her parents and sold into slavery as a
child. If passages like these obviously register what John Shields has described as
"Wheatley's continued chronicling of America's freedom struggle," they also clearly
speak to struggles closer to herself, struggles against slavery, the slave trade, and
disrespect for Africans caught up in the "iron chain."[6]

Several critics have responded effectively to the charges that Wheatley was
merely an accommodationist with no care for the situation of her African compatriots in slavery, first by calling attention, as I have just done, to overt expressions
of her racial identity and her desire for a freedom yet to come and, second, by
revealing patterns of resistance and critique in her poetic practice, particularly her
mobilization of the sublime, her use of biblical allusion, and her use of an ambigu-

ous, disruptive rhetoric.[7] Many of them confess, however, that these forms of poetic resistance seem to have gone unrecognized in Wheatley's time. After demonstrating Wheatley's subversive practice, one writer notes ruefully, "The mystery here is that it took more than 210 years to recognize the subversive mode in this author." Another comments, "Readers quite likely missed the play of Wheatley's racial and ontological ambiguities due to the absence of any preexisting generic codes for a poetic practice such as Wheatley's."[8] Yet few critics have noticed the historical context of her writing that would have provided for her readers' codes, less generic than historical and political, and that would have enabled her contemporaries to assess her subversive potential more accurately than we assume they did—and incidentally would offer a better answer to the charges of accommodationism than exercises in advanced hermeneutics.

During Wheatley's career as a public woman of letters, slavery was overthrown in Massachusetts through the efforts of white and black reformers, and in the British Empire the abolitionist movement began that would eventually end the slave trade and slavery in the West Indies. Before she wrote to Dartmouth in 1772, a diffuse and loosely organized movement to end slavery in Massachusetts was afoot that manifested itself in individual lawsuits, petitions to the House of Representatives, and the drafting of laws, although to refer to the pressure to abolish slavery as being the result of a movement is almost to overstate the case. There was no explicit organization dedicated to abolition nor were there dedicated, single-minded leaders such as William Lloyd Garrison would be in the next century; Jeremy Belknap reported in 1795 that slavery and slaveholding were not discountenanced in any "publick and formal manner" but by the slow and steady growth of "public opinion." Massachusetts passed no laws in the eighteenth century explicitly abolishing slavery but simply let it wither away as judges and juries refused to uphold slave owners' claims to a property interest in their slaves.[9] The emerging public opinion against slavery was no passive phenomenon, however, but was shaped and led by public debate; in Massachusetts, especially in the revolutionary decade of the 1770s, Wheatley's comments about slavery and the oppressed state of Africans would have been inevitably read within the context of this struggle.[10]

The energies of black men and women in New England were directed first of all towards obtaining their own freedom and that of their compatriots, and beginning with Jenny Slew's action in November, 1766, against John Whipple for having "restrained her of her liberty," they initiated in the courts a number of suits for the liberty of individual slaves. Slew lost her case but won on appeal when the jury of the superior court found for her a month later.[11] Other liberty suits were filed over the next fifteen years, often successfully, until Chief Justice William Cushing's charge to the jury in the Quok Walker vs. Nathaniel Jennison case established the unconstitutionality of slavery in Massachusetts.[12] Blacks adopted a second tactic in January, 1773, by petitioning to the House of Representatives for relief from "their unhappy State and Condition." A second, more forceful petition followed in April, stating, "We expect great things from men who have made such a noble stand against the designs of their *fellow-men* to enslave them," and further petitions arrived in May, 1774, and in March, 1777, each in succession arguing in more compelling and explicit terms for the abolition of slavery.[13] The earlier suits for liberty obtained freedom a plaintiff at a time, but the petitioners looked toward a general abolition in Massachusetts based upon universal terms of humanity and justice. The discourse of lawyers was crucial for Jenny Slew, but Phillis Wheatley's neoclassical language that dealt with enlightened and Christian tropes of universal freedom offered more support to the petitioners' quest for a general, principled emancipation.

Blacks' efforts to secure their freedom found support from white abolitionist efforts to end the slave trade, and at the same time their demands for freedom may have refocused abolitionist attention to the immediate and specific problem of emancipation at home. Throughout the eighteenth century sporadic voices were raised against slavery, but in the later 1750s and 1760s John Woolman carried on an extensive mission against slavery among the Quakers, and Anthony Benezet carried on an effective opinion-shaping campaign outside the Quaker community. In the year after Jenny Slew's suit for liberty, Boston merchant Nathaniel Appleton published *Considerations on Slavery, in a Letter to a Friend*, and the legislature considered a bill "to prevent the *unwarrantable and unusual* Practice or Custom of inslaving Mankind in this Province, and the importation of slaves into the same."[14] After two readings this bill was tabled in favor of discussing a bill "laying an Impost on the Importation of Negro and other Slaves" in order to discourage the slave trade. This also failed to pass, but in 1771 the legislature passed "An Act to prevent the Importation of Negro Slaves into this Province" that was rejected by Governor Thomas Hutchinson, acting under instructions to disapprove "any Laws of a new and unusual nature." Coming on the heels of the non-importation associations, Hutchinson seems to have suspected the professedly moral motives of the law's proponents as a mere cover for an attack upon imperial trade, but in the following year James Swan, a Scottish merchant resident in Boston, argued in *A Dissuasion to Great Britain and the Colonies from the Slave Trade* that all "*wellwishers of the British Empire*" ought to be "*consequently enemies* to Slavery."[15] When the "many slaves living in the Town of Boston, and Other Towns in the Province" presented their January 1773 petition, they submitted with it a revised edition of Swan's pamphlet, and the author of a subsequent pamphlet urging legislative action to abolish slavery and the slave trade began his appeal with reflections on Swan and concluded it by reprinting the petition along with an appeal from "The Sons of Africa."[16] At the Harvard commencement in July Theodore Parsons and Eliphalet Pearson, bachelor's candidates, debated "whether the slavery, to which Africans are in this province, by the permission of law, subjected, be agreeable to the law of nature?" The legislature declined to act until 1774 when it passed "An Act to prevent the importation of Negroes or other Persons as Slaves into this Province; and the purchasing them within the same," a law left unapproved by Governor Hutchinson in the last desperate days before his departure for England. Given the public nature of the campaign to abolish slavery through the legal cases, petitions, propagandizing, and legislation, readers of Wheatley's lines to Dartmouth could hardly miss her intent, nor could they fail to suspect at least some intimations of a political purpose to her frequent denotations of herself as an African. They would not have remarked on her writing as subversive because she was echoing antislavery sentiments shared by both blacks and whites, even if they experienced the import of these sentiments very differently.

The abolition movement of the 1770s in Massachusetts blurred the distinctions between black suffering and white sympathy with a veil of sentiment that tended to obscure the very real differences that divided blacks and whites in a society in which racist distinctions flourished, despite a growing antipathy to the institution of slavery. None of the legislative acts actually freed any slaves but were directed toward the abolition of the slave trade. Certainly many if not most of the laws' supporters intended these acts to lead to a termination of slavery in Massachusetts, but the laws they passed stopped short of depriving Massachusetts citizens of property. The black petitioners, on the other hand, were less intent upon the comparatively remote question of the slave trade and more focused upon immediate relief of their own condition. This strategic difference between black and white abolitionists in Massachusetts also figured in the differences between white opponents of the slave trade in the colonies and in the imperial center. English reformers in the context of a relatively small population of blacks tended to identify the problem of slavery in terms of the ethics and conduct of slaveowners, whereas the colonists, particularly those in locations with much larger slave populations, saw the problem as a function of the slave trade.[17] There was some tendency for each side of the Atlantic to blame the other; thus Jefferson's deleted article in the Declaration blaming George III for being "Determined to keep open a market where MEN should be bought and sold" and Samuel Johnson's indignant question, "How is it that we hear the loudest *yelps* for liberty among the drivers of *negroes?*"[18]

When Phillis Wheatley went to London in 1773, at the height of the antislavery debate in Boston, she found among the friends of the Countess of Huntingdon men and women whose interest in evangelical Christianity facilitated their antagonism to slavery and their interest in improving the conditions of blacks. During her six-week stay in England, she was unable to meet the Countess, who was at her estate in Wales, but she expressed by letter "her very great satisfaction to hear of an African so worthy to be honour'd with your Ladiship's approbation & Friendship as him whom you call your Brother."[19] James Albert Ukawsaw Gronniosaw's *Narrative* had been published the year before under the Countess's patronage, and Wheatley's 1773 *Poems* were a further contribution to what might have seemed to be a budding school of African writers in English. Wheatley might also have expected the Earl of Dartmouth, a friend of the Countess's who probably assisted in the publication of *Poems*, to be a supporter of the growing British antislavery interest, but in this she was as mistaken as she was in hoping for him to be a friend to America. Perhaps her most significant encounter in London may have been with Granville Sharp, who in 1772 had overseen the successful handling of the Somerset case in which Judge Mansfield ruled that slave owners could not force the return of slaves to the colonies. Although this had no effect on the status of slavery in the colonies, it was widely celebrated as a major victory for the humanitarian conscience, and, as Vincent Carretta has pointed out, it may have been of considerable personal significance for Wheatley.[20] If, as she wrote David Wooster, she gained her freedom "at the desire of my friends in England," Sharp's success in the Somerset case would have given the weight of precedent and moral authority to their "desire." In Boston as a protégé of Susannah Wheatley, Phillis's status as a slave was mystified behind that convenient term "servant," but in London the reviewer in the *Gentleman's Magazine* of her *Poems* saw things rather differently: "Youth, innocence, and piety, united with genius, have not yet been able to restore her to the condition and character with which she was invested by the Great Author of her being. So powerful is custom in rendering the heart insensible to the rights of nature, and the claims of excellence!"[21]

In London, then, Wheatley found among the Countess of Huntingdon's connection friends who embraced the Christian beliefs she had learned from Susanna Wheatley and augmented them with desires to see the end of slavery. In their most generous and idealistic moments of self-definition people like Granville Sharp offered a genuinely cosmopolitan world view that was based on Christian principle: "[U]nder the glorious Dispensation of the Gospel," Sharp announced, "we are absolutely bound to consider ourselves as *Citizens of the World;* that every Man whatever, without any *partial distinction* of Nation, Distance, or Complexion, must necessarily be esteemed *our Neighbour,* and *our Brother,* and that we are absolutely bound in Christian Duty to entertain a *Disposition* towards *all Mankind* as charitable and benevolent, *at least,* as that which was required of the Jews, under the Law, towards their *national Brethren.*"[22] Among the verses written before the publication of *Poems* in the late summer of 1773, she had occasionally trafficked in passages of political rhetoric, but the patriotic sentiments of a piece of whig bombast like "On the Death of Mr. Snider Murder'd by Richardson" (not included in her book) did not reflect her most powerful yearnings for transcendence, flight, or power over herself. In London, however, where Granville Sharp seemed to share the goals of the Sons of Africa who were petitioning for their freedom in Boston, Wheatley might have seen with greater clarity the possiblity of speaking more boldly and explicitly about issues of slavery and race. Soon after her return to Boston she wrote a famous letter to Samson Occom, supporting his "Reasons respecting the Negroes . . . offer[ed] in Vindication of their natural Rights" that was widely published in New England newspapers in March, 1774, as the latest act abolishing the slave trade lay waiting the governor's approval. Wheatley hailed "the glorious Dispensation of civil and religious Liberty, which are so inseparably united, that there is little or no Enjoyment of one without the other; . . . for in every human Breast, God has implanted a Principle, which we call Love of Freedom; it is impatient of Oppression, and pants for Deliverance; and by the Leave of our modern Egyptians I will assert, that the same Principle lives in us" And echoing the English critique of new world slave owners, she concludes, "How the Cry for Liberty, and the reverse Disposition for the exercise of oppressive Power over others agree,—I humbly think it does not require the Penetration of a Philosopher to determine."[23]

But the world of cosmopolitan friendship envisioned by Granville Sharp was a remote ideal in the Boston of the mid-1770s. Susannah Wheatley, Phillis's chief protector and patroness, died within three weeks of the composition of the letter to Occom, and she began to learn, as she wrote one of her London friends, "The world is a severe Schoolmaster, for its frowns are less dang'rous than its Smiles and flatteries, and it is a difficult task to keep in the path of Wisdom. I attended, and find exactly true your thoughts on the behaviour of those who seem'd to respect me while under my mistress's patronage: you said right, for Some of those have already put on a reserve."[24] Wheatley was being reminded of what she undoubtedly had long known: although many Bostonians opposed slavery and the slave trade on principle, at least as many if not more held Africans in contempt and inflicted daily humiliations on them. She found herself "on her own footing," bereft of her strongest supporter, just as Boston was coming under increasing pressure to submit to imperial authority in the form of occupation by British troops and closure of its port. Within six months of writing to her London friend, and this is the last surviving letter to any of her English acquaintance, she had joined the flight from besieged Boston, apparently taking refuge with Mary Wheatley Lathrop and her husband, Thomas, in Providence. Imperial connections were of little value to a black Bostonian in the years after 1774 unless she were willing to join the Loyalist forces when they left Boston, and, deprived of her most supportive patrons, she lost the relatively easy access to publication she had heretofore enjoyed.

Furthermore, the paradigm of the English antislavery critique, the immediate attack on slave owning rather than the attack on the slave trade, could no longer be used in the same way she once had because the professed enemies of slavery were now openly hostile to the Americans to whom the blacks would have to look for relief. Formerly, Wheatley could speak in the preferred poetic modes of the Boston literati, where critical approval from the imperial center supported local judgment, but in the revolutionary decade following the London publication of her *Poems* she would have to realign herself from a position in an imagined imperial order to one in an equally imagined revolutionary order in which she hoped to follow other Americans, both black and white, in the passage from political subject to citizen. For Wheatley this self-transformation led her to construct within the framework of her acquired poetic skills a pluralist, tolerant, vision of America after the empire.

The difficulties in making this realignment in imaginative loyalties, as well as one strategy for reinventing a new position for herself, appear in a poetic exchange between the "*young Affrican of surprising genius*" and "*a gentleman of the navy*" that appeared in the pages of the *Royal American Magazine* in 1774 and 1775. The recipient was apparently a Lieutenant Rochfort, attached to the occupying British naval forces under Vice-Admiral Samuel Graves and possibly billeted in the Wheatley household; he apparently had previously served on the African coast. In the opening lines Wheatley asks the "Celestial muse" for "true poetic fire" to inspire her verses for Rochfort, but she situates herself in a very different position from what she seems to desire for her adressee: "For here, true merit shuns the glare of light, / She loves oblivion, and evades the sight." Darkness and obscurity had earlier been for Wheatley preferred sites for the activities of imagination and recollection ("Thoughts on the Works of Providence," "On Recollection," "Hymn to Evening"), but her self-positioning in this poem ironically affirms both the power of "oblivion" to energize poetic "true merit" as well as its psychic cost, the price for her of being "here" in Boston. She goes on to play out the role of captive woman in emotionally charged lines that play with the idea of the British naval lieutenant as her possible rescuer:

> Paris, for Helen's bright resistless charms,
> Made Illion bleed and set the world in arms.
> Had you appear'd on the Achaian shore
> Troy now had stood, and Helen charm'd no more.
> The Phrygian hero had resign'd the dame
> For purer joys in friendship's sacred flame,
> The noblest gift, and of immortal kind,
> That brightens, dignifies the manly mind.

In Wheatley's Homeric simile "friendship" has for the moment replaced sexual passion, civility has replaced eros as a redemptive force. This turns out to be only a dream, however, as the actual implications of the British naval presence in the Atlantic world are brought back to mind. "[A]ncient Albion" exists among the violent "roarings of the sacred deeps," and her fleets bring "dread" to distant worlds where "The trembling natives of the peaceful plain / Astonish'd view the heroes of the main." Wheatley's imperial vision of civilized exchange was threatened by the intrusion of the raw power that it had sought both to control and to mystify, by the violence of rapine, rebellion, and armed force, but she for the moment continues to hope in the power of "the muse" to bring "These blooming sons of Neptune's royal race" to "virtue's cause," to "Celestial friendship and the muse's care." The fundamental incoherence of violence and civility, of "The thirst of glory that burns each youthful breast" and the mutuality of friendship, creates a dissonance that Wheatley's final appeal, a rhetorical urgency without historical or narrative support, cannot resolve.[25]

Rochfort's answer, published in the same issue of the *Royal American Magazine*, sang the praises of "The lovely daughter of the Affric shore," fantasized about the pastoralized Africa which gave Wheatley birth, sought to enroll her in the pantheon of "Britain's glory" that included Isaac Newton and John Milton, but finally regretted that "this blissful clime, this happy land . . . Nor more can boast, but of the power to kill, / By force of arms, or diabolic skill." The conclusion of Wheatley's poem had asked the "Cerulean youths" to reverence virtue "more than mortal fair," but "The Answer" ignores that injunction, professing to find in "Wheatly's song, for Wheatly is the fair," no more than "softer strains" which can relieve the grim boasts of war and violence. In the next issue of the magazine Wheatley's "Reply to the Answer" struck out in directions signalling a realignment of her public poetic voice that established new relationships with both her audience of white Boston readers and an obscured, repressed audience of black readers.

Stepping forward into the light "For one bright moment," she bids "Rochford, attend. Beloved of Phoebus! hear, / A truer sentence never reach'd thine ear." She responds with polite deference to the exaggerated compliments of Rochfort's poem by professing poetic inferiority to him but also by allowing him to "fix the humble Afric muse's seat / At British Homer's and Sir Isaac's feet." She recognizes Milton's sublime poetic, his imaginative freedom to explore the great depth "Of nature, . . . Thro' earth, thro' heaven, and hell's profound domain, / Where night eternal holds her awful reign." She concludes, however, by announcing, "But lo! In him Britania's prophet dies, / And whence, ah! ah whence, shall other *Newton's* rise?"[26] If "Rochford's matchless pen" displays "The charms of friendship," he might become the "muse's darling," but this promise seems idle flattery after her revolutionary announcement of the end of "Britania's glory," particularly in view of the fact that Milton was her "prophet," and in this poem Wheatley takes over the prophetic voice, becoming an exemplar of a resistant American poetic. In the tense days prior to the outbreak of hostilities at Concord and Lexington, she remains hopeful about the power of friendship to preserve the imperial fabric, but she is also keenly aware of the limits of friendship amid the contingencies of nature and history. Her playfully seductive address to the royal naval officer would have charmed the loyalist friends who signed the attestation of *Poems*, but prophesying the end of "Britania's glories" would have evoked a more enthusiastic response from the patriot signers.

Yet the revolutionary heart of this poem occurs in the lines where she responds to Rochfort's description of the "guilded shore . . . where cancers torrid heat the soul inspires; with strains divine and true poetic fires: (Far from the reach of Hudson's chilly bay)." Her lines here are the first by a black American writer to offer such a romantic, longed-for vision of Africa as a lost homeland of pleasure, love, and song:[27]

> Charm'd with thy painting, how my bosom burns!
> And pleasing Gambia on my soul returns,
> With native grace in spring's luxuriant reign,
> Smiles the gay mead, and Eden blooms again,
> The various bower, the tuneful flowing stream,
> The soft retreats, the lovers golden dream,
> Her soil spontaneous, yields exhaustless stores;
> For phoebus revels on her verdant shores.

It matters little that Wheatley may in fact have had few, if any, precise memories of her life in Africa; her poetic construction of recollection, her validation of the power

of memory for the Afric muse, energizes her prophetic voice. The affirmation of
African origin, coming as a rhetorical disruption of the conversation about British
tradition, enables her consequent post-colonial skepticism about "Britania's glories." If the series of poems taken as a whole skillfully repositions herself within
the community of white readers as a refined speaker with a patriot heart, the evocation of "pleasing Gambia" spoke to the yearnings of a repressed, silenced community of black readers. If it was a very much smaller community in 1774 and 1775, it
was perhaps also still largely an envisioned possibility of the prophet as Afric muse.

If these poems are charged with the tensions of occupied Boston, they are
also charged with the energies of the Massachusetts antislavery debates in the 1770s
and with the explosive force of the revolutionary moment in Boston. Black petitioners continued to send in appeals even after the passage of the March, 1774, Act,
submitting another petition in May and another six weeks later. White sympathiz-
ers to the antislavery cause argued for the logical consistency of liberty for both
black and white in Massachusetts, as "A Son of Africa" had asked in the *Massachusetts Spy* of February 10, 1774, "You are taxed without your consent, (I grant that a
grievance,) and have petitioned for relief, and cannot get any. . . . Are not your
hearts also hard when you hold men in slavery who are entitled to liberty by the
law of nature, equal as yourselves?"[28] And on October 25th of the same year "Mr.
Wheeler brought into [the first Provincial] Congress a letter directed to Doct.
Appleton, purporting the propriety that while we are attempting to free ourselves
from our present embarassments, and preserve ourselves from slavery, that we also
take into consideration the state and circumstances of the negro slaves in this province."[29] Wheeler's statement might also have been in response to rumors current
the month previous of "a conspiracy of the negroes" that Abigail Adams reported
centered on "a petition to the Governor [now General Thomas Gage] telling him
they would fight for him provided he would arm them, and engage to liberate
them if conquered."[30] In this context the editorial introduction printed above
Wheatley's "To a Gentleman of the Navy" points to the complex signifying of the
ensuing exchange. "By this single instance may be seen, the importance of education.—Uncultivated nature is much the same in every part of the globe. It is probable *Europe* and *Affrica* would be alike *savage* or polite in the same circumstances;
though, it may be questioned, whether men who have no *artificial* wants, are capable of becoming so ferocious as those, who by faring *sumptuously every day,* are
reduced to a habit of thinking it necessary to *their* happiness, to plunder the whole
human race." The argument for the universality of human nature supports the
recognition of the natural rights of black slaves to liberty, but at the same time the
exchange between a black woman and an officer of the resident British military
force might encourage the anxieties about a "conspiracy among the negroes."
However, the insistence upon the importance of education as a counterweight to
savagery as well as the patriotic turn of Wheatley's argument would also seem to
reassure those who feared for the local loyalty of Massachusetts' black residents.
Looked upon in this way, Wheatley's poem is less subversive than it is skillfully
addressed to at least three different audiences with different, recognizable implica-

tions for each of them: a white loyalist readership, a white patriot readership, and a black readership implied by her coded African presence.

In 1774 and 1775, as Abigail Adams's report of fears about black loyalty suggests, the shadowy, still undefined black audience occupied an ambiguous ground between loyalist and patriot audiences. Each of the audiences for the exchange of poems with the naval gentleman, at least in Wheatley's polite construction of them, shares an imagined antagonism to slavery, although their experiences with slavery are very different. Yet their differing levels of respect for the black race drive the apologetic undertone of these poems and their introduction that hints at differences not fully comprehended by the poet's respondents and readers. Arguing against the slave trade and against slavery itself was in Massachusetts of the 1770s much less dificult than overcoming the racist failure to recognize the fundamentally equal humanity of its African residents. The suits for liberty and the petitions had attacked the legal institution of slavery and the economic motive of the slave trade, and in late 1775 individual black men addressed the third issue of emancipation by demanding recognition of their right to serve in the Continental armies besieging Boston. Debates during the fall and early winter in the Continental Congress and in the army itself on the propriety of enlisting blacks were inconclusive, although the practical consensus was to keep both free blacks and slaves out of the army, partaly because of the fear of allowing arms to come into the hands of slaves, partly because of the belief that blacks would not be adequate soldiers. George Washington's general orders for November 12, 1775, seemed to list them among the incompetent: "neither negroes, boys unable to bear arms, nor old men unfit to endure the fatigues of the campaign, are to be enlisted." Free black soldiers protested at the army headquarters in Cambridge the decisions that forbade their re-enlistment, and Lord Dunmore's proclamation in Virginia offering freedom to slaves who would desert their masters and fight for the ministerial cause gave an even more compelling reason to reopen the question of enlisting black soldiers in the Continental armies besieging Boston.[31]

Before Washington's order of December 30, 1775, which reversed this policy against black enlistment, he had received a different testimony of black ability when Wheatley's poem addressed to him arrived in the middle of that month. Wheatley could safely assume by this time that her black identity would be immediately recognized, and neither the poem nor its covering letter calls attention to this, submerging her identity into a universalized patriot voice that speaks to "Columbia's scenes of glorious toils." Yet even here her Miltonically-colored description of the soldiers in the American army, "thick as leaves in Autumn's golden reign, / Such, and so many, moves the warrior's train," seems to have a double-edged significance in the context of the ongoing debates about enlisting and re-enlisting black soldiers. "In bright array they seek the work of war," says Wheatley, "Shall I to Washington their praise recite? Enough thou know'st them in the fields of fight." Coming to the point, she goes on more peremptorily, "Thee, first in place and honours,—we demand / The grace and glory of thy martial band." No small part of the poem's strategy in these lines is a clever shift of reference that moves without any sense of disruption from addressing the Muse to imploring Washington's aid, collapsing the two addresses and in effect making Washington a mythic spirit presiding over the American enterprise. More important, however, Wheatley's rhetorical strategy insists on equal respect for black poet and for black soldiers by downplaying racial difference, coding all soldiers, black or white, as equally patriotic agents of "Columbia's arm," yet at the same time her established fame as the African poet particularizes the demand for Washington's "guardian aid" in terms of the more specific requests that had been made by black soldiers denied re-enlistment. Wheatley's "we" in "we demand / The grace and glory of thy martial band" is simultaneously a patriotic "we" and a specifically black collective for whom she speaks. When the poem and the covering letter were published in the following spring in Williamsburg and Philadelphia, they were identified for readers in those markets, perhaps less familiar with her poetry and racial identity, as the work of "the famous *Phillis Wheatley*, the African poetess."

The poem to Washington was not published in Boston, which remained in British hands until the following spring, and Wheatley published only four more new poems prior to her death in 1784, although poems on the capture of General Lee and the death of General Wooster survive in manuscript.[32] The poem to Washington, however, signals a possible new direction for her poetic career with its constellation of black and white desires, of the hopes of American patriots for a valorous and virtuous leader and of African American demands for "grace and glory." At the same time, however, its appearance suggests some of the difficulties Wheatley faced in a revolutionary culture. Her inability to get the poem published in Boston perhaps foreshadows her apparent inability to gain the same access to the press as she had enjoyed at the beginning of the 1770s. Her 1779 proposal for a new volume of poetry, despite appearing in six different issues of the Boston *Evening Post*, did not attract enough subscriptions to warrant publication. The Washington poem also marks a new theme for her in its engagement in public issues, particularly military ones, where she had to identify with a "warrior's train" rather than to flirt in print with one of the warriors. The manuscript poems on Generals Lee and Wooster show her willingness to explore the possibilities of contemporary events and patriotic concerns as do the titles of lost poems such "Thoughts on the Times." The outbreak of the revolution, however, shifted the arena of cultural crisis from the public sphere of print discourse and polite conversation to the battlefield, and in so doing it brought forward old gender barriers. In spite of the demurrers of writers like Abigail Adams and Mercy Otis Warren, the Revolution understood as military crisis gave priority to masculine heroics; if it resulted in the feminized understanding of virtue, which Ruth Bloch has described, it did so by reconstructing a separate sphere for women and women's expression.[33] In this world Phillis Wheatley was perhaps technically on her own footing for only a brief moment in March, 1778, in the two weeks between the death of John Wheatley and her marriage to John Peters. The items she proposed in 1779 for her new volume nevertheless demonstrate her intention to occupy a ground that had room for poems to George Washington and "Lt. R—— D—— of the Navy," for letters to the Earl of

Dartmouth as well as to Benjamin Rush, signer of the Declaration of Independence and author of an abolitionist tract. In 1784 Wheatley died alone and in poverty in a Boston made unfamiliar and unfriendly to her by the forces of revolution, but the world she imagined in the proposed volume of 1779 was cosmopolitan, multiracial, and free. If the real world of Boston failed to find a place for her, her imagined world held out promise to the free people of color who created a community there for themselves in the years following her death.

NOTES

1. Letter to Wooster in Julian Mason, ed. *The Poems of Phillis Wheatley* (Chapel Hill: Univ. Of North Carolina Press, 1989), 195–97.

2. Charles Taylor, *The Ethics of Authenticity* (Cambridge: Harvard, 1991), 23.

3. Paul Gilroy cites Wheatley as the first black American traveller to have her "perceptions of American and racial domination shifted as the result of her experiences" in Europe. *The Black Atlantic: Modernity and Double Consciousness* (Cambridge: Harvard, 1993), 17.

4. Eleanor Smith. "Phillis Wheatley: A Black Perspective," *Journal of Negro Education* 43(1974), 403.

5. Wheatley, 83. Note this is stronger than in the earlier mss. version.

6. John Shields, "Phillis Wheatley's Struggle for Freedom in Her Poetry and Prose" in Shields, ed. *The Collected Works of Phillis Wheatley* (New York: Oxford Univ. Press, 1988), 234.

7. For examples of these respective approaches, see John C. Shields, "Phillis Wheatley and the Sublime" in William Robinson ed. *Critical Essays on Phillis Wheatley* (Boston: G. K. Hall, 1982), 189–205; Sondra O'Neale, "A Slave's Subtle War: Phillis Wheatley's Use of Biblical Myth and Symbol," *Early American Literature* 21(1986), 144–65; Russell Reising, "The Whiteness of the Wheatleys: Phillis Wheatley's Revolutionary Poetics" in *Loose Ends: Closure and Crisis in the American Social Text* (Durham, NC: Duke Univ. Press, 1996), 73–116.

8. John C. Shields, "Phillis Wheatley's Subversive Pastoral," *Eighteenth-Century Studies* 27(1994), 632; Reising, 114.

9. Belknap, "Queries Respecting the Slavery and Emancipation of Negroes in Massachusetts, . . . " *MHS Collections*, 1st ser. 4(179?), 193; For the end of slavery in Massachusetts, see Arthur Zilversmit, "Quok Walker, Mumbet, and the Abolition of Slavery in Massachusetts," *William and Mary Quarterly* 25(1968), 614–24; Robert C. Twombly, "Black Resistance to Slavery in Massachusetts" in Paul Finkelman, ed. *Slavery in the North and the West* (New York: Garland, 1989), 389–411; Arthur Zilversmit, *The First Emancipation* (Chicago: Univ. of Chicago Press, 1967).

10. There were earlier protests against slavery, like Sewall's *Selling of Joseph*, but the widespread and continuous agitation against slavery and the slave trade began in Massachusetts in the 1760s. George H. Moore, *Notes on the History of Slavery in Massachusetts*, (New York: Appleton, 1866), 111–12.

11. Moore, 113–14.

12. Zilversmit, "Quok Walker," 615.

13. . Petitions in Herbert Aptheker, ed. *Documentary History of the Negro People in the United States* (New York: Citadel, 1951), 6–9.

14. Moore, 126.

15. On Hutchinson, Moore, 131–32; Swan, in Roger Bruns, ed. *Am I Not a Man and a Brother* (New York: Chelsea House, 1977), 201.

16. *The Appendix: Or, Some Observations on the Expediency of the Petition of the Africans* ... Boston, 1773.

17. David Brion Davis, *The Problem of Slavery in the Age of Revolution, 1770–1823* (Ithaca: Cornell Univ. Press, 1975), 343–45.

18. Thomas Jefferson, *Writings* (New York: Library of America, 1984), 22; Samuel Johnson quoted in Philip S. Foner, *Blacks in the American Revolution* (Westport, CT: Greenwood Press, 1976), 33.

19. Wheatley, 195.

20. On the Somerset case, Davis, 480–501; Vincent Carretta, to my knowledge, is the only person to have pointed out the possible significance of Sharp's meeting with Wheatley. See his *Unchained Voices: An Anthology of Black Authors in the English-Speaking World of the 18th Century* (Lexington: University Press of Kentucky, 1996), 68.

21. Quoted in William H. Robinson, *Phillis Wheatley: A Bio-Bibliography* (Boston: G. K. Hall, 1981) 23–24.

22. Sharp, *The Law of Retribution* . . .1776, quoted in J. C. D. Clark, *Language of Liberty, 1660–1832: Political Discourse and Social Dynamics in the Anglo-American World* (Cambridge: Cambridge University Press, 1994), 20.

23. Wheatley, 203–4.

24. Wheatley, to John Thornton, Oct. 30, 1774. 210.

25. Instructive here might be Reising's notion of "loose ends," where we recognize "the internal conflicts and referential instabilities of . . . works when, by virtue of their endings, they emerge as an alternative and supplementary referential grid capable of displacing what had been established by various generic and conventional practices as the works' dominant thematics." *Loose Ends*, 22.

26. One wonders could she have known of John Newton, the former slave trader and now friend of abolition, and eventual author of "Amazing Grace"?

27. Mukhtar Ali Isani, "Far from 'Gambia's Golden Shore': The Blacks in the Late Eighteenth-Century American Imaginative Writing," *William and Mary Quarterly* 36(1979), 353–72.

28. Foner, 28–29.

29. Quoted in Moore, 144.

30. *Letters of Mrs. Adams*, ed. Charles Francis Adams. Boston: Little and Brown, 1840. 24.

31. Benjamin Quarles, *The Negro in the American Revolution* (Chapel Hill: University of North Carolina Press, 1961), 15, 23. Permission to enlist in the army could be seen, given the rhetoric of a people's army, as an implicit recognition of citizenship for blacks, and in New England states that did not abolish slavery until after the Revolution, emancipation was a frequently promised reward for faithful army service..

32. Also in manuscript is the recently discovered poem entitled "Ocean," although it seems likely that this was written during or just after her trip to London. See, Julian D. Mason, Jr., "'Ocean': A New Poem by Phillis Wheatley," *Early American Literature* 34(1999), 78–83.

33. Ruth Bloch, "The Gendered Meanings of Virtue in Early America," *Signs* 13 (1987), 37-58.

"THOU HAST THE HOLY WORD"

Jupiter Hammon's "Regards" to Phillis Wheatley

Rosemary Fithian Guruswamy

In the early pages of her seminal work, *Jupiter Hammon and the Biblical Beginnings of Black American Literature*, Sondra O'Neale makes an incontrovertible case for Hammon's existence as a textual protester of slavery based on his use of the Bible as a metaphorical vehicle for masked articulation of his dissent.[1] Hammon's occupation as a slave exhorter[2]—a class of itinerant, often illiterate African-American preachers—suggests such an alliance with antislavery protest. Whereas contemporaneous Protestant texts place these men on the lunatic fringe, their evangelical stance allied them in the eyes of their own community with the powerful African cultic priest, the shaman, who himself was often uneducated and illiterate.[3] These exhorters' use of the Bible, biblical symbols, and theological discourse to encourage revolt was done in the tradition of the African *nommo*.[4] As with all shamans, the African-American slave exhorter specialized in the cohesion and mobilization of the community through inventive use of language, often specifically by freeing biblical text from its context and applying it to the actual lives of a congregation as a way to give them a spiritual history that would act as a source of power. This reinterpretive use of the Bible would sometimes involve covert communication through the use of the double entendres familiar to African oral narratives, which would reveal the truth to some but mask it from others. This would give the exhorter freedom to convey his message only to those at whom his sermons were targeted.[5] Often survival tactics such as "subterfuge, sabotage, fraud, [and] trickery" were communicated, what Gayraud Wilmore calls "a kind of psychological guerilla warfare" and Theophus Smith calls "a collective strategy" posing as an embrace of otherworldliness that misled the slaveholders and has also managed to trick many twentieth-century critics of slave poets.[6]

Biblical language, while often used in the dominant discourse to justify slaveowning, was semiotically flexible enough also to cement the community of African Americans that slaveholders were constantly trying to fragment. Religious

empowerment discourse in the late eighteenth century coupled the Bible with political demands even in mainstream discourse. Because of the double Enlightenment appeal to the tenets of Christianity and the existence of natural law that
spoke for the essentiality of freedom, African Americans were able to participate
openly in a related thread about "black uplift." Through biblical discourse, revolutionary America offered blacks more "room to maneuver" than before or after,
both linguistically and practically.[7] Thus, Hammon could have a document like
"An Address to the Negroes in the State of New York" published in 1787, because
the unity of African descendents that he calls for is subordinated to the emerging
national identity.[8] And, in "A Winter Piece," he could write that the biblical Israel
was actually a type of the colonial African nation, implying that its antitype could,
like Israel, expect deliverance in a country committed to liberty.[9]

Recent scholars have charted ways in which these biblically based discursive
practices inform both Hammon's and Wheatley's writing. But since both of them
write mainly poetry, the biblical text and its exegetical popular tradition that they
would relate to the most would be the Book of Psalms. Those critics who find
Hammon's poetry to be derivative of hymnology—a pejorative claim, in most
cases—are probably sensing its closeness to psalmic prosody and language, since
psalmody and hymnology were closely identified with one another during
Hammon's lifetime and served as two major influences on the development of the
African-American spiritual.[10] Like the later African-American poet A.A. Whitman,
Hammon's use of the hymn stanza and the call-and-response technique that
O'Neale identifies in "An Evening Thought" suggests a comparison between the
state of African-American life under slavery and the oppression of the Israelites,
with both producing "Zion's songs" of longing and liberation.[11] The tendency of
seventeenth- and eighteenth-century religious poets to identify with David the
psalmist parallels Hammon's identification of the enslaved man with Christ, both
being "God's Bondservant," which O'Neale sees in "An Evening's Improvement."[12]
If the oppressed slave Christian is a contemporary antitype of Christ, then surely
the lamenting, supplicating, thankful black Christian poet is an antitype of David
in the Psalms. Hammon strengthens this identification by defining David as an
exhorter, like himself, in "An Evening's Improvement."[13]

In this prose piece and in "A Winter Piece," Hammon also uses David as the
meditative example for his readers, in the tradition of devotional manuals that
reaches back to fifteenth-century Europe. Specifically, he cites David as he who,
though imperfect and oppressed, puts trust in God and depends on God's mercy.[14]
But David also becomes to Hammon the maker of images, whose metaphorical
language inspires the Christian: "Let us not forget the words of holy David: 'man is
but the dust, like the flower of the field' (Ps. 103:15)."[15] Later, he urges his readers
to "adopt the language of David" and use their tongues for seeking forgiveness and
praising rather than sinning.[16]

But something different happens with Hammon's psalmic allusions when
he writes a poem, particularly one addressed to another poet, specifically "An Address to Miss Phillis Wheatly [sic], Ethiopian Poetess." Vernon Loggins has noted

that the biblical citations—the majority of which are from the Book of Psalms—
which Hammon puts to the right of the lines of this poem have a "fairly logical
and exact" association with the meaning of the lines.[17] Most of these citations deal
with central evangelical themes, such as thankfulness for God's mercy and supplication for His help, and on the surface, the poem appears to be an exhortation to
the slave poetess to be as Christian as she can possibly be, in response perhaps to
her thoughts expressed in "On Being Brought from Africa to America."[18]

A closer look at Hammon's language, however, reveals some semantic slide
operating around the image of "his holy word." In the first verse, Hammon seems
to be urging Wheatley to admire God's wisdom in making her literate in English.
In succeeding allusions to the word, then, ambiguity of phrasing makes it possible
to see "the holy word" as the Bible, which Wheatley could now read, or the poetry
she herself is writing. Her God-given possession of this word, he continues, makes
her "a pattern . . . / to youth of Boston town" in both her writing and her religious
witness. As verse 13 says:

> Thou, Phillis, when thou hunger hast,
> Or pantest for thy God;
> Jesus Christ is thy relief,
> Thou hast the holy word.[19]

These lines indicate, through their ambiguity and a kind of parallelism not unlike
that found in the Book of Psalms, an equalization between Christianity and poetic
language in their power to satisfy Wheatley's needs and those for whom she serves
as a pattern.[20] What William Robinson has called a "long and wearisome" poem
possesses some surprises if one reads it carefully.[21]

Indeed, deeper investigation that looks at the entire chapters from which
Hammon's verse citations of the Psalms come reveals an even more subversive
meaning for the poem. In every case, the exact verse citation Hammon uses, which
relates so closely to mainstream evangelical themes, is surrounded in the Bible by a
context that places that particular Psalm in the biblical discourse targeted by African Americans for their liberation theology. The regularity with which this happens strongly suggests the deliberate creation of a puzzle available for the canny
reader to unravel.[22] That the chapter and verse of the biblical text Hammon cites
and the context from which it comes are so often a coupling of innocuous Christianity and startling liberation theology suggests a deliberate coding technique.[23]

The practice of signifying comes immediately to mind, with its mixture of
the appropriation of text, the donning of masks, techniques of repetition, and deliberate use of irony. Several critics have exposed and discussed the signifying
present in African-American spirituals and songs as a masked critique of the rul-
ing class and a deliberate attempt to upset hierarchical givens. African-American
cultural practices such as the New York pinkster festivities and the later Louisiana
carnival have roots in African carnivalesque tribal practices that employed signifying as a social leveling device.[24] These cultural activities, furthermore, have an ana-

logue in language use itself and the relation between black and white utterance and intentionality. The verbal indirectness that is a hallmark of signifying creates a linguistic safety valve since the singer, speaker, or writer can always plead ignorance or lack of intention and escape confrontation or punishment.[25]

This juxtaposition of culture and language naturally reaches its apotheosis in the creation of literature, such as the 1820 text *Mystery Developed* by Lemuel Haynes that signifies on the Puritan captivity narrative to expose the injustices of slavery.[26] The existence of a double-voiced discourse that embeds slave protest in allusions to Scripture and consequently obscures deep meaning while destabilizing the status quo has been suggested by readers of Phillis Wheatley's poetry.[27] William Scheick even suggests that Wheatley uses the exact contextualizing technique that Hammon appears to be using in his address to her. When Hammon uses it, though, the signifying occurs mostly on the Book of Psalms.[28]

The psalmic citations attached to Hammon's verses 11, 13, 14, 18, and 21 come from praise psalms, in which David declares his intention to praise or to sing, to use his language in holy ways. Although a religious poet identifying himself with David was totally conventional by the time Hammon was writing, its application to an African-American woman would still have been transgressive.[29] Scheick has speculated that Wheatley herself identified with David, a parallel she exposes particularly in her poem "Goliath of Gath," although she is not overt about the parallel. Many aspects of David's biblical personality would have appealed to the poetic Wheatley: obviously his status as God's poet and psalmist; his warrior role against overwhelming odds, as depicted in the battle with Goliath; his lowly occupation as shepherd enhanced by Christ's metaphorical assumption of the same task; and God's choice of David as subsequent king of Israel.[30] Hammon, in writing to and about Wheatley in this poem, appears to cast Wheatley in the role of David via the contextualization of his marginal citations from the Book of Psalms. As Scheick has indicated, David's dual roles of warrior and writer construct him as using his enemies' own weapons against them. For the latter role, those weapons are words. Scheick sees Wheatley often using "double-edged language, inspired by Scripture" in her poems based on the Bible, one layer to please the authorities and the other to undercut them.[31] Hammon appears not only to be encouraging Wheatley to practice this strategy, but to be doing it himself. For example, Psalm 34:1–3 attached to Hammon's verse 11 relates to songs David sings about God's relief to the poor and His deliverance of them, and Psalm 89:1 attached to Hammon's verse 10 is followed in the psalm by a verse that says, "The north and the south, thou hast created them" and a subsequent differentiation between the righteous and the wicked. Both of these hidden contexts suggest liberation themes that Wheatley might imitate from David's writing. Indeed, the citation from Ecclesiastes 12:1 that accompanies Hammon's first verse is in a chapter that includes the line, "all the daughters of music will be brought low." Perhaps the "pattern" Wheatley is to model—which O'Neale suggests burdens her with the task of telling the truth about slavery even within its constraints—is that of the sweet singer of the original oppressed Israel.[32] Looking into Psalm 16, from which Hammon selects verses 10 and 11 to attach to his own verse 14, we read another verse that may have been meant to prophesy to Wheatley about the Davidic expectations for her poetry: "The lines are fallen unto me in pleasant places; Yea, I have a goodly heritage."

Perhaps the most satisfying use of biblical discourse to encode a protest theme surrounding Wheatley's identity as a poet, however, relates to Hammon's use of Matthew 7:7–8 appended to his own verse 9. Hammon writes:

> Come you, Phillis, now aspire,
> And seek the living God,
> So step by step thou mayst go higher,
> Till perfect in the word,

again conflating her religious duties and her poetic abilities. The lines from Matthew that Hammon associates with this verse contain the well-known "Ask, and it shall be given you . . . knock, and it shall be opened" passage. What is not immediately obvious, however, are the lines that precede this in the same Gospel chapter: "Give not that which is holy unto the dogs, neither cast your pearls before the swine, lest haply they trample them under their feet, and turn and rend you," a subtle suggestion to Wheatley about her choice of subjects and audiences if she wishes to be "perfect" in her words. How could Hammon risk such protest among white Christians? As he says in "A Dialogue, Entitled, the Kind Master and Dutiful Servant," "The only safety that I see / Is Jesus' holy word."[33]

Other antislavery protests that surface when whole Psalms, rather than just cited verses, are read include the "How long, O Lord, how long" discourse found in the psalms of lamentation and appropriated widely in African American spirituals. Psalm 13, appended to Hammon's verse 13, and Psalm 89, used to gloss Hammon's verse 10, both contain this ubiquitous psalmic line.[34]

The theme of the righteous triumphing over the encroaching wicked runs throughout the Book of Psalms. John Lovell points out the pertinence of this theme to the Bible-reading slave who would see the use of God's power in his behalf that would result in the doom of his enemies.[35] When the psalmist refers to this theme, he often uses the language of redemption and deliverance from oppression that so intrigued the newly Christianized slaves. Psalm 34, whose verses are attached to Hammon's verses 8 and 11; Psalm 1, appended to Hammon's verse 3; and Psalm 116, glossing Hammon's verse 18, all contain versions of this discourse. Psalm 116, whose innocuous verse 15 ("Precious in the sight of the Lord is the death of his saints") is cited by Hammon, continues with the uncited lines, "O Jehovah, truly I am thy servant; / I am thy servant, the son of thy handmaid; / Thou hast loosed my bonds," interpreted Christologically to be a reference to Christ and thus falling into the Christ-as-servant identification so precious to African-American Christians.

Finally, several Psalms contain verses relating to the Exodus story of the deliverance of Israel, and many of these are used by Hammon to gloss the poem to Wheatley, even though the exact verses he cites do not carry the clearest liberation message. The shepherd image Hammon uses in his verse 12 is clearly related to Psalm 23, where the Lord is David's shepherd, but also appears in Psalm 80, where God is called "the Shepherd of Israel."[36] The verses Hammon cites are very positive—God the Shepherd shines and saves—but later in Psalm 80, David describes the "vine out of Egypt" as an oppressed and ravaged people under the thumb of cruelty. Psalmic messages about the cruelty of the Egyptians, the suffering of the enslaved Israelites, and the deliverance and redemption of the Lord also appear in Psalm 103, whose verses 1–4 gloss Hammon's verse 4, and Psalm 126, whose verses 1–3 are appended to Hammon's verse 2.

What "An Address to Miss Phillis Wheatly [sic], Ethiopian Poetess" appears to be, then, when the psalmic and other biblical glosses are decoded by a reading of complete chapters, is much more than the "wearying broadside" Robinson sees.[37] Hammon is, in Smith's words, "conjuring with Scripture." By signifying on the relationship between the word and its mainstream signification, Hammon critiques white religious meaning and intentions. In doing so, he creates the beginning of what Katherine Clay Bassard refers to as the discourse of "African Americanism," a discourse empowered by a self-conscious consideration of "both the possibilities and the risks in written language."[38] Using his knowledge of the Book of Psalms and psalmic exegesis and the techniques of the underground slave church, he creates a liberation discourse meant to empower his fellow slave poet with a sacred identification for herself as a writer and a heavenly commission to write on antislavery themes, even if she—like him—has to cloak them in hidden codes and patterns.

NOTES

1. Sondra A. O'Neale, *Jupiter Hammon and the Biblical Beginnings of African-American Literature* (Metuchen, NJ: Scarecrow Press, 1993), 1–2. Lonnell E. Johnson, "Portrait of the Bondslave in the Bible: Slavery and Freedom in the Works of Four Afro-American Poets" (Ph.D. diss., Indiana University, 1986), 33, also calls for a re-examination of Hammon in light of his use of Christianity "to mediate a stronger response to slavery."

2. Oscar Wegelin, "Biographical Sketch of Jupiter Hammon," in *America's First Negro Poet: The Complete Works of Jupiter Hammon of Long Island*, ed. Stanley Austin Ransom (Port Washington, NY: Kennikat Press, 1970), 24, and Vincent Carretta, ed., *Unchained Voices: An Anthology of Black Authors in the English-Speaking World of the Eighteenth Century* (Lexington: University of Kentucky Press, 1996), 31, confirm Hammon's status as an itinerant preacher of this kind. He was probably affiliated with the Methodist Episcopal movement, as the presence of the Anglican Society for the Preservation of the Gospel in Foreign Parts on Long Island in the eighteenth century was pervasive, according to Frank J. Klingberg, *Anglican Humanitarianism in Colonial New York* (Philadelphia: Church Historical Society, 1940), 158–59.

3. O'Neale quotes Joseph Tracy, in his 1842 history of the Great Awakening, as calling slave exhorters "a heinous invasion of the ministerial office" (*Biblical Beginnings*, 83). Gayraud S. Wilmore, *Black Religion and Black Radicalism* (Garden City, NY: Doubleday, 1972), 46, 69, also indicates that "cultural despisers" of black religion, especially slaveholders, tried to portray these men as "fools and buffoons."

4. Theophus Smith, *Conjuring Culture: Biblical Formations of Black America* (New York: Oxford University Press, 1994), 160. The *nommo* is defined by modern diasporic scholars as "the properly spoken word that results in appropriate action," a feature of religious activity traced to the Dogon and Yoruban religions that, when used by early African-American preachers, legitimatized the use of "linguistic inventiveness" in conjunction with the Bible in the African-American religious experience (Charles Joyner, "'Believer I Know': The Emergence of African-American Christianity," in *African-American Christianity: Essays in History*, ed. Paul E. Johnson [Berkeley: University of California Press, 1994], 26–27). The Christian slave exhorters may have been encouraged to practice nommistic strategy with the Bible because of the evangelical movement's view of the Bible as interpretatively diverse (Vincent L. Wimbush, "The Bible and African Americans: An Outline of an Interpretative History," in *Stony the Road We Trod: African American Biblical Interpretation*, ed. Cain Hope Felder [Minneapolis: Fortress Press, 1991], 86.)

5. David T. Shannon, "'An Antebellum Sermon': A Resource for an African American Hermeneutic," in *Stony the Road We Trod: African American Biblical Interpretation*, ed. Cain Hope Felder (Minneapolis: Fortress, Press, 1976), 103–04, 121, 123; Smith, *Conjuring*, 125; Gilbert Osofsky, ed., *Puttin' on Ole Massa: The Slave Narratives of Henry Bibb, William Wells Brown, and Solomon Northup* (New York: Harper and Row, 1959), 26. John Lovell, Jr., reports on the use of Christian and biblical double entendre in African-American spirituals to protect the African Americans against whites and to bind them together. He points out the poetic effect of these songs in *Black Song: The Forge and the Flame* (New York: Macmillan, 1972), 190–92. See also Sidney Finkelstein, *Composer and Nation: The Folk Heritage of Music* (New York: International Publications, 1960), 19; R. Nathaniel Dett, "Preface to *Religious Folk-Songs of the Negro as Sung at Hampton Institute*," in *The Social Implications of Early Negro Music in the United States*, ed. Bernard Katz (New York: Arno Press, 1969), xlii. The early African-American preacher Lemuel Haynes actually preached about the fittingness of employing religious double entendre (John Saillant, "'Remarkably Emancipated From Bondage, Slavery, and Death': An African-American Retelling of the Puritan Captivity Narrative, 1820," *Early American Literature* 29 (1994): 128).

6. Wilmore, *Black Religion*, 72–73; Smith, *Conjuring*, 115. Lovell discusses the "grapevine telegraph" that existed among slaves and is discussed in the early pages of Booker T. Washington's autobiography, an enigmatic means of communication among mostly illiterate slaves whose source remains a mystery (*Black Song*, 121, 181). For a twentieth-century writer who does not penetrate Hammon's disguise, see Houston Baker, Jr., *The Journey Back: Issues in Black Literature and Criticism* (Chicago: University of Chicago Press, 1980), 3.

7. Phillip M. Richards, "Nationalist Themes in the Preaching of Jupiter Hammon," *Early American Literature* 25 (1990): 124; O'Neale, *Biblical Beginnings*, 28; Arthur J. Raboteau, "Martin Luther King, Jr., and the Tradition of Black Religious Protest," in *Religion and the Life of the Nation: American Recoveries*, ed. Rowland A. Sherrill (Urbana: University of Illinois Press, 1990), 48–49; Lester B. Scherer, *Slavery and Churches in Early America, 1619–1819* (Grand Rapids, MI: W.B. Eerdmans, 1975), 106, 107; Ira Berlin, "The Revolution in Black Life," in *The American Revolution: Explorations in the History of American Radicalism*, ed. Alfred F. Young (DeKalb: Northern Illinois University Press, 1976), 363.

8. Richards, "Nationalist," 124, 126. St. Clair Drake, among others, sees this text as a capitulation to white desire for slaves to concentrate on their spiritual fate as an antidote to their physical slavery. He notes that Hammon and Wheatley are more privileged and thus less resistant to white control (*The Redemption of Africa and Black Religion* [Chicago: Third World Press, 1970], 27–28). I find this attitude frankly puzzling, since Hammon clearly expresses disappointment in the "Address" that the Revolution had not clued in the whites to the need for African-American liberty and also urges those he addresses to learn to read,

a clearly subversive message (see Sondra A. O'Neale, "Jupiter Hammon," in *Dictionary of Literary Biography: Afro-American Writers before the Harlem Renaissance*, ed. Trudier Harris [Detroit: Gale, 1986], 162–63).

9. Richards, "Nationalist," 127, 135.

10. Critics who see Hammon's poetry as connected to hymnology include Roger Whitlow, *Black American Literature: A Critical History* (Chicago: Nelson Hall, 1973),19; Benjamin Brawley, *Early Negro American Writers* (New York: Dover, 1970), 9; Johnson, "Portrait," 43; Bernard W. Bell, "Afro-American Writers," in *American Literature, 1764–1789: The Revolutionary Years*, ed. Everett Emerson (Madison: University of Wisconsin Press, 1977), 177; Lovell, *Black Song*, 94; and Jon Michael Spencer, *Black Hymnody: A Hymnological History of the African-American Church* (Knoxville: University of Tennessee Press, 1992), 191–92.

11. Ernest M. Bradford, "Biblical Metaphors of Bondage and Liberation in Black Writing: A Study of the Evolution of Black Liberation as Mediated in Writing Based on the Bible," (Ph.D. diss., University of Nebraska at Lincoln, 1976), 149; O'Neale, "Jupiter Hammon," 158.

12. O'Neale, *Biblical Beginnings*, 149; "Jupiter Hammon," 156.

13. O'Neale, *Biblical Beginnings*, 161.

14. Ibid., 98, 102, 104, 107, 162, 164, 167.

15. Ibid., 104.

16. Ibid., 111, 161, 162, 168, 169.

17. Vernon Loggins, "Critical Analysis of the Works of Jupiter Hammon," in *America's First Negro Poet: The Complete Works of Jupiter Hammon of Long Island*, ed. Stanley Austin Ransom (Port Washington, NY: Kennikat Press, 1970), 41. See also Oscar Wegelin, *Jupiter Hammon: American Negro Poet: Selections from His Writings and a Bibliography* (Miami, FL: Mnemosyne Publishing Co., 1969), 40.

18. Carretta, *Unchained*, 5.

19. O'Neale, *Biblical Beginnings*, 77. All citations from Hammon's poetry are from this edition.

20. O'Neale, "Jupiter Hammon," 158, sees Hammon's call to Wheatley to be a pattern as a request for her, like him, to use poetry as a "prophetic call to report the truth despite the restraining circumstances of their enslavement."

21. William H. Robinson, *Phillis Wheatley in the Black American Beginnings* (Detroit: Broadside Press, 1975), 32. See also Wegelin, *Jupiter Hammon*, 20–21.

22. I have deliberately adapted my description here from the language Claudia Mitchell-Kernan uses in "Signifying," in *Mother Wit from the Laughing Barrel: Readings in the Interpretation of African-American Folklore*, ed. Alan Dundes (Jackson: University Press of Mississippi), 318, to describe signifying as an art form. Smith, *Conjuring*, 67, also notes that African-American spirituality "creatively transform[s] [texts] at the same time it thoroughly appropriates them." All such criticism suggests a deliberate use of the signifying technique by these early African-American writers. William J. Scheick, *Authority and Female Authorship in Colonial America* (Lexington: University of Kentucky Press, 1998), 126, notes that no evidence exists that any of Wheatley's contemporaries would detect her encoded protest. However, the fact that Hammon is using the same technique in a poem addressed to her seems to be at least a strong suggestion that some sharing of transgressive undertones was occurring. Katherine Clay Bassard, *Spiritual Interrogations: Culture, Gender, and Community in Early African American Women's Writing* (Princeton: Princeton University Press, 1999), 25–26, also indicates, with a nod to William Robinson, that African-American slaves who were able to communicate with one another would necessarily bear the burden of a lack of privacy. Encoded messages using systems familiar to all, such as the Bible and related Christian discourse, could solve such a problem.

23. Scheick, *Authority*, 114, sees similar contextual encoding, using the Bible as linguistic device, in Wheatley's own verse paraphrase of "Isaiah LXIII.1–8." Dawn Henwood, "Mary Rowlandson and the Psalms: The Textuality of Survival," *Early American Literature* 32 (1997), 174, also sees Rowlandson's use of the Psalms in her captivity narrative as employing the same contextual encoding to allow her expression of negative emotions normally forbidden to a Puritan woman.

24. Sterling Stuckey, "Through the Prism of Folklore: The Black Ethos of Slavery," in *Black and White in American Culture: An Anthology from "The Massachusetts Review,"* eds. Jules Chametzky and Sidney Kaplan (Amherst: University of Massachusetts Press, 1969), 178; Henry Louis Gates, Jr., *Figures in Black: Words, Signs, and the "Racial" Self* (New York: Oxford University Press, 1987), 49; Lovell, *Black Song*, 45–46, 223; James Eights, "Pinkster Festivities in Albany Sixty Years Ago," *Collections on the History of Albany* 2 (1867): 323–27.

25. Henry Louis Gates, Jr., *The Signifying Monkey: A Theory of Afro-American Literary Criticism* (New York: Oxford University Press, 1987), 45; Mitchell-Kernan, "Signifying," 318; Marcyliena Morgan, "The Africanness of Counter-language among Afro-Americans," in *Africanisms within Afro-American Language Varieties*, ed. Salilioko S. Mufwene (Athens: University of Georgia Press, 1993), 424–25.

26. Saillant, "'Remarkably Emancipated,'"124.

27. Gates, *Figures*, 52–53; William J. Scheick, "Subjection and Prophecy in Phillis Wheatley's Verse Paraphrases of Scripture," *College Literature* 22 (1995): 124; Mitchell-Kernan, "Signifying," 311, 314; Smith, *Conjuring*, 148. Gates, *Monkey*, xxv-xxvi, defines this particular use of double-voicedness as "tropological revision."

28. Scheick, "Subjection," 124, 127; *Authority*, 123. Loggins, "Critical," 37–38,and A. Robert Lee, "Selves Subscribed: Early Afro-America and the Signifying of Phillis Wheatley, Jupiter Hammon, Olaudah Equiano, and David Walker," in *Making America/Making American Literature* (Amsterdam: Rodopi, 1996), 290, both note Hammon's use of the signifying technique of incantatory repetition. Henry Edward Krehbiel, *Afro-American Folksongs: A Study in Racial and National Music*, 4th ed. (Portland, ME: Longwood Press, 1976), 140–41, cites the finding of Henry T. Fowler that Israelite songs of triumph have relationships to the African-originated satire or "taunt" song. Both have their roots in the carnival tradition.

29. Equally transgressive were later identifications with Moses by such African-American women leaders as Harriet Tubman and Sojourner Truth (Smith, *Conjuring*, 69). Sondra O'Neale, "Jupiter Hammon and His Works: A Discussion of the First Black Preacher to Publish Poems, Sermons, and Essays," *Journal of the Interdenominational Theological Center* 9 (Spring 1982): 107, also states that, in his poem to Wheatley, Hammon parallels her trip from Africa with Christ's trip to earth via the Incarnation. A comparison of an African-American woman and Christ would be even more transgressive.

30. Scheick, "Subjection," 124–25; *Authority*, 110–14. See also George B. Cheever, *The Guilt of Slavery and the Crime of Slaveholding, Demonstrated from the Hebrew and Greek Scripture* (Boston: John P. Jewett & Co., 1860), i-ii; Lovell, *Black Song*, 253–54, 256.

31. Scheick, *Authority*, 113.

32. O'Neale, *Biblical Beginnings*, 68.

33. Ibid., 207. See also Baker, *Journey*, 5.

34. See Sidney Kaplan, *The Black Presence in the Era of the American Revolution, 1770–1800* (Washington: Smithsonian Institution Press, 1973), 173.

35. Lovell, *Black Song*, 230.

36. O'Neale, *Biblical Beginnings*, 70.

37. William H. Robinson, *Critical Essays on Phillis Wheatley* (Boston: G.K. Hall, 1982), 7.

38. Bassard, *Spiritual Interrogations*, 29.

IGNATIUS SANCHO'S LETTERS

Sentimental Libertinism and the Politics of Form

Markman Ellis

Over nearly two years between July 1766 and March 1768, a correspondence, and subsequently a friendship, blossomed between Ignatius Sancho—"a Negro, a Butler, and a Grocer"—and Laurence Sterne, a clergyman, a novelist, and a literary celebrity.[1] To their contemporaries, such a connection was unusual enough to appear a kind of wonder of the age, not only crossing firmly demarcated boundaries of status, education and race, but also revealing what they shared: an enthusiasm for, and ambition within, the cultural elite of London society. The fame of their association, feted and analyzed both by contemporaries and twentieth-century historians and critics, has however served to occlude the exceptional qualities of Sancho's writing. Sancho's contemporaries understood that the conception, publication and reception of his posthumous collection, entitled *The Letters of the Late Ignatius Sancho, an African,* in 1782 was determined by Sterne's writings: a form of imitation that verged on mimicry. However, while much has been made of Sancho's debt to Sterne, recent work has lost sight of what Sterne meant to Sancho's contemporaries, and in so doing, has overlooked the dangerous and subversive aspects of Sancho's deployment (or appropriation) of the Shandean method and its associated discourses of sensibility and libertinism. By re-examining the politics of Shandean form, modern readers of Sancho can recover the radicalism of Sancho's writing, and as such, revise the critical assumption first offered in the 1960s that amongst all the African writers in English of the late eighteenth century, he represents the most complete example of "assimilation" to English culture.

The approach by historians and literary scholarship in the 1960s and 1970s to eighteenth-century African writing in English was not simply a rediscovery of a forgotten body of writing, but also rightly perceived as an opportunity to host debates about race and culture in the modern era. To these scholars of literature and history, with their own intellectual allegiances and debts, Sancho's Shandean and sentimental epistolary strategies were difficult to reconcile with the period's rapidly changing and radicalizing black politics (both in Britain and America). The confessional strategies and explicit arguments of slave narratives such as those of Olaudah Equiano, written against the controversialist politics of the Abolition movement, seemed a more eloquent contribution to the modern debate. In his introduction to the first modern edition of Sancho's *Letters*, published in 1968, Paul Edwards described the letters as "those of a man thoroughly assimilated into the middle-class English society of his day."[2] James Walvin remarked in 1973 that Sancho was "one of the most obsequious of eighteenth-century Blacks,"[3] and in 1985 Paul Edwards restated his opinion that Sancho was "a man largely assimilated to English middle-class society, good-natured, easy-going, patriotic, liberal and devoué both attached to, and detached from, the English values of his time."[4] The question of Sancho's "assimilation" has an analogy in the debate within literary studies on how much Sancho "owed" to Sterne, and whether Sterne had been influenced by Sancho's plea for the novelist to address the topic of slavery in his letter of 21 July 1766. Most Sterne scholars, determining this question through an examination of Sterne's works, plumb for the novelist's genius as the origin of his subsequent interest in the theme of slavery.[5]

Subsequent interdisciplinary critical approaches have continued to examine Sancho's deployment of sensibility. In 1988, Keith Sandiford argued that Sancho's sentimentalism allowed him to adopt "the language of the heart, identifying himself passionately with the cult of benevolism and religious enthusiasm"; yet he sees this sentimentalism as a "weak-spirited, temporising rhetoric" that subverts Sancho's development of a rigorous antislavery position.[6] Paul Edwards's "Introduction" to his edition in 1994 described his "sentimentality of expression" as a fashionable and "self-indulgent" weakness that palliates the "impassioned voice of angry and outraged feeling." It is this literary failing, the recourse to "sentimentality," that "gives the impression" that Sancho was "almost wholly assimilated into the lifestyle and values of polite eighteenth-century English society."[7] In recent years the status of sensibility has remained at the heart of the central critical (and historiographical) debate about Sancho, not only in my own *The Politics of Sensibility* (1996), but also in essays by James Walvin, Vincent Carretta and Sukhdev Sandhu.[8]

The terms sensibility and sentimentalism are notoriously difficult for modern readers to measure. There is a long tradition amongst scholars of sentimentalism that sentimental means "'engaged in moral reflections,' 'moralising,' 'sententious.'"[9] But the term, which enjoyed an astonishing vogue in the literature and thought of the mid-eighteenth century, more often has another connotation, suggesting a mode of writing that engages the sympathies or affections of the reader, advertising virtuous and benevolent conduct by repeatedly displaying scenes of feeling and distress. These scenes engage the emotions of the reader by exhibiting the work of emotions in the characters, who often make a luxurious display of their tears, blushes and faintings. These scenes had an instructive, moral dimension, by disseminating the theory of benevolent action and thought. In the period of Sancho's first recorded writings, the mid-1760s, the most notorious exponent of this oft-derided literary mode was Laurence Sterne, despite the eccentricity of his sentimentalism. In *Tristram Shandy* (1759–1767), four volumes of sermons (1760–1766) and *A Sentimental Journey* (1768), he established a name for himself and his distinctive prose and idiosyncratic narrative strategies. The Shandean or Shandyism, as it was often called, offers the reader a complex and sophisticated version of the sentimental, freely mixing the sincerity of emotional spectacle with a different strain of writing, somewhere between satirical irony and desiring libertinism.

Sancho's writings first found a public through Sterne's literary fame. After Sterne's death in 1768 a large number of supplementary publications satiated a continued demand for the Shandean. Amongst these works were legitimate editions and collections of his letters, but also spurious continuations, imitations and parodies, and 'beauty-book' collections of excerpts from his work. The publication of Sancho's work can be located against this shoal of secondary Shandean texts. The first work of Sancho's to appear in print was his correspondence with Sterne, comprising his letter to Sterne, and three letters in reply, which appeared in the *Letters of the Late Rev. Mr. Laurence Sterne, To his most intimate Friends,* published posthumously in 1775 by Sterne's daughter, Lydia de Medalle.[10] The correspondence between Sancho and Sterne was greatly admired: it would not be unfair to say that Sterne's correspondence with Sancho was Sterne's (rather than Sancho's) most celebrated exchange of letters. The Sancho exchange showed the celebrated writer in a better light than many of his other letters, confirming him as a benevolent philanthropist rather than a rakish libertine, whose "delicate sensibility," in the words of William Wilberforce, was "applied to the pernicious purposes of corrupting the national taste, and lowering the standard of manners and morals."[11] The review of Medalle's edition of Sterne's *Letters*, in *The Gentleman's Magazine* (January 1776), even reprinted the letter to Sterne from "honest Sancho," describing him as a "sooty correspondent" of "sensibility and delicacy" who "though black as Othello has a heart as humanized as any of the fairest about St. James's."[12]

Sancho's own publication waited until early 1782, more than a year after his death on 14 December 1780. To advertise "that a collection of his Letters is preparing for the publick," an anonymous correspondent sent a copy of one of "the same "good-hearted" Negro'[s]" letters to *The Gentleman's Magazine* on 5 April 1781.[13] The collection was published in 1782 as *The Letters of the Late Ignatius Sancho, An African*, in two volumes, with a brief biography by Joseph Jekyll, published by a prestigious group of booksellers under John Nicholls. It was the first substantial volume published in English by a man of African descent. As well as a splendid portrait frontispiece engraved by Bartolozzi from a Gainsborough oil sketch, the book had a remarkable subscription list comprising 1,216 names, including a parade of nobility. In her prefatory introduction, the supposed editor, Frances Crew, stated that the letters were not "originally written with a view to publication."[14] *The Gentleman's Magazine* of August 1782 found Crew's humility risible, complaining that few of the letters were "more than common-place effusions, such as many other Negroes, we suppose, could, with the same advantages, have written, and which there needed 'no ghost to come from the grave,' or a black from Guinea, 'to have told us.'"[15] Although the sequence of events is unclear, the letters were presumably gathered from friends, although Sancho may have kept copies of some or all of them. The tenor of the prefatory material implies that the project of publishing the letters should be located within the emergent agitation against the slave trade, through the volume's eloquent contribution to the contested question of African "arts and learning" in contemporary discourse. Crew stated her motive for publishing the *Letters* as "the desire of shewing that an untutored African may possess abilities equal to an European; and the still superior motive, of wishing to serve his worthy family."[16] Jekyll added that the reader will perceive that "the perfection of the reasoning faculties does not depend on a peculiar conformation of the skull or the color of a common integument."[17] Nonetheless, amongst the most controversial aspects of Sancho's *Letters* to contemporary readers was the nature of Sancho's imitation of Sterne.

Sancho's imitation of Sterne was not a matter of slavish copying. The stress on spontaneous originality in the post-Romantic period has lent a pejorative sense to the term imitation that it may not have had for Sancho. In neo-classical aesthetics, by contrast, imitation (derived from Latin *imitatio* and Greek *mimesis*) was an elevated ambition for writers: not merely copying the style and devices of a great writer, but emulating their project (or spirit). Rather than a falling away from his own voice, imitation is a kind of inspiration, the mask that allows Sancho's voice to be heard. Given the forces ranged against his utterance, contesting the ability of the African Englishman to write, imitation here can be seen to be a powerful force. In the critical terms of his own period, then, the issue around Sancho was not that he imitated, but whether what he imitated was appropriate. In Sancho's case, the choice of Sterne as his literary model was little less than scandalous, and, in its own way, a disturbing, even subversive gesture.

Sancho's Shandean manner aroused the censure of his first critics, who questioned the propriety of Sterne's mode to Sancho's condition and status. An early review of Sancho in *The European Magazine* (September, 1782) noted that these letters were written by a "self-tutored" "negroe." Their publication countermanded those philosophers (such as David Hume) who claimed that Africans were not capable of "arts and letters." Nonetheless, the pleasure granted to readers by the confirmation of "the common elevation of the human race," gave way to anxieties about the form of the letters, which it characterises as "the naked effusions of a negroes heart . . . glowing with the finest philanthropy, and the purest affections." The reviewer, swinging between a language of sensibility and libertinism, categorizes Sancho's correspondence as a kind of familiar letter: "They have the ease of epistles written in the openness of nature, and in the playful familiarity of friendship. They breathe unaffected piety—and have the ardour of genuine patriotism." But the reviewer warns that "it must not be expected that these letters are taken as models of this species of writing. They have more warmth than elegance of diction, and more feeling than correctness."[18] He hints that this dangerous warmth and feeling (again a libertine language) is related to Sterne, who is the subject of a

warm encomium in the letter quoted in the review (Letter LIII, to Mr. S——
[Stevenson], dated October 24, 1777).[19] Indeed, the reviewer suggests that the "stile
in which he chiefly indulged himself" gave him "a licence for expressions light and
frivolous."[20] That the Shandean mode was contentious was reiterated in Ralph
Griffiths's review in *The Monthly Review* (1783). He praised Sancho's "merry vein"
of "pleasantry" but rejected the appropriateness of the Shandean model. As to
Sancho's "epistolary style," Griffiths says, "it bears in general, some resemblance to
that of his admired Sterne—with his breaks—and dashes—which, by the way, are,
in this wild, indiscriminate use of them, an abomination to all accurate writers
and friends to sober punctuation."[21] Griffiths (himself a practised Shandean imi-
tator) notes with concern that the looseness of Sterne's punctuation seemed irre-
vocably connected to the looseness of his morals. The Shandean signalled its
libertinism in its liberty with dashes: it is, according to Griffiths, "a *vicious* practice."[22] The American Thomas Jefferson, in his *Notes on the State of Virginia* (1785),
argued that Sancho's *Letters* had some "merit in composition," as they "breathe
the purest effusions of friendship and general philanthropy." But his Shandean
style was a matter for concern: "He is often happy in the turn of his compliments,
and his stile is easy and familiar, except when he affects a Shandean fabrication of
words. But his imagination is wild and extravagant, escapes incessantly from every
restraint of reason and taste, and, in the course of its vagaries, leaves a tract of
thought as incoherent and eccentric, as is the course of a meteor through the sky."[23]
These reviewers, then, express unease when Sterne's dashing manner, tolerable in
his own hands, is deployed by Sancho.[24] Sukhdev Sandhu has argued that the relation between the writing of Sancho and Sterne is identifiable in a verbal manner
given to puns, word play, and double entendre, and a typographical eccentricity,
given to dashes, digression and hesitancy.[25] Sancho's imitation of Sterne's variety
of sentimentalism is also a matter of content, of thematic and ethical parallels.
Sancho finds creative potential in Sterne's mode of the gentle Horatian satire against
the follies of learned society—as is seen in Sancho's squib on hairdressers for the
General Advertiser of April 29, 1780.[26] Furthermore, Sancho also pursues a Shandean
mode of sentimental libertinism.

One of the signature strategies of Sterne's novels is to interweave a layer of
licentious innuendo within the detailed physiological description congenital to
the mode of sensibility. This strategy is endemic to both *Tristram Shandy* and *A
Sentimental Journey*, and had long attracted the attention of the critics, who felt
that Sterne's writing contained a vein of indecency and licentiousness that was
potentially obscene, and certainly inappropriate in a clergyman. Even John Cleland,
author of *The Memoirs of a Woman of Pleasure* (1748) thought Sterne's bawdy was
"too plain" or explicit.[27] In short, in the 1770s and 1780s, while the term sentimental had come to represent a dangerously immoral quality, the notion of Shandy
and the Shandean signalled this libertine mode in its vicious extreme. An example
here, typical if obscure, is the anonymous two-volume collection of short fictions
attributed to William Russell, called *Sentimental Tales*, published in 1771, which
asserts its allegiance to Sterne on its title-page by quoting the defense of the pas-

sions from *A Sentimental Journey*: "Ye whose clay-cold heads and luke-warm hearts can argue down, or mask your passions—tell me, what trespass is it that man should have them?—"[28] These short tales, which occasionally allude to Sterne and Yorick, are explicitly libertine. In "The Progress of Love, or, The Effects of Familiarity: a sentimental tale," the characters Sophia and Modestus fall in love, despite the fact that Sophia is promised to Sir Thomas Goodville. Their uncontrollable passion leads them to secret assignations, at which kissing turns to lubricious fondling (and a long section admiring her breasts), and finally to sexual intercourse. After luxuriating in passion for a period, Modestus grows tired of Sophia and they break off their amour. The story is framed and expressed as a moral lesson on the effect of familiarity and the transience of passion, in the orthodox language of virtuous sentimentalism, but simultaneously it positions the reader as a voyeur, in a manner which is clearly libertine.

The unease of Sancho's first critics about his Shandean imitation also reflected contemporary notions of the elevation of the familiar letter, to which Sancho's low status—as an African, an uneducated man, and a man of trade—was incommensurate. A form of writing that was traced back to classical precedents, the familiar letter implied and nurtured a practice of sociability, manners and politeness that embedded it within the new sentimental and domestic ideology of the mid-century. The classical sources of the theory of the familiar letter were the examples of Cicero, Pliny and Seneca. Despite their disparate interests, these writers were understood by their eighteenth-century readers to have found in the letter form "an escape from formality, a release from the sort of rules associated with higher kinds of literature."[29] In the informal structure of the letter, writers might give loose to informal thoughts in informal diction, while still aiming at a lucid and organized disposition of material. To the eighteenth century, then, the familiar letter was a form in which the writer expressed thoughts with candor and spontaneity (the one guaranteed by the other). Pope, whom Sancho invokes in his first letter, claimed that his letters conveyed "thoughts just warm from the brain without any polishing or dress." Although the quest for a natural and artless mode of expression was pursued by writers throughout the period, polish was nonetheless also valued. The requisite civility of the familiar letter was a balance between "freedom" and "ceremony." Techniques of letter-writing proliferated: writers were advised to make rough drafts in a letter-book, before revising and copying out the letter in their best hand. George Seymour argued that "A fine letter does not consist in saying fine things, but expressing ordinary ones in an uncommon manner. It is the *propria communia dicere*, the art of giving grace and elegance to familiar occurrences that constitutes the merit of this kind of writing."[30] As many writers noticed, the familiar letter was allied on one side to the occasional essay, and on the other, to polite conversation. The essay, as modelled on the example of *The Spectator*, contributed an urbane and congenial approach to issues of philosophical, cultural and social note (ideas, sentiment and gossip). Conversation contributed its anecdotal strategies and the easy immediacy of spoken discourse, although in the letter (where only one voice speaks) this conversation becomes a kind of conversation with one's self. The implied conversational model here was an informed and mannered colloquy between acquaintances who share a common view of culture and society.

From the middle of the eighteenth century there was a significant increase in the number of texts offering practical guidance for letter-writing. Works such as the anonymous *Complete Letter-Writer: or, New and Polite English Secretary. Containing Directions for writing Letters on all Occasions, in a polite, easy, and proper Manner* (1755) ran to more than forty editions by the end of the century. Letter-writing instruction manuals offered practical advice about the epistolary method, providing examples upon which the student might model his or her own correspondence, concerning topics that might be raised in everyday life, such as "Business, Duty, Amusement, Affection, Courtship, Love, Marriage, Friendship, &c."[31] The desired effect of such letter-writing manuals was to render the correspondence of the reader into, as the title page has it, a "polite, easy, and proper manner." This project of mannered reform allies the letter-writing manual with the kinds of practical advice about social life and manners contained in contemporary conduct books. Considered in this light, the letter-writing manuals of the latter half of the century increasingly offer themselves as part of a much wider discourse on the reform of manners. As such, they shift away from merely offering directions or instructions for secretaries and clerks (servants), towards the zone occupied by the conduct books, which aim to mould the manners and conduct of young women and men in the middle station of life (or rather, those who would fashion themselves as such). Like the conduct books then, the letter-writing manuals establish a set of desirable characteristics which are identified as natural or innate, and then detail the way in which they might be acquired or affected. The letter-books, like the conduct books, encode both a stable set of rules, and a mode of cultural dynamism.

Reviews of Sterne's correspondence suggest that it was not clear to contemporaries that his eccentric letters adequately conformed to the model of polite propriety associated with the letter-writing manuals. His letters lacked the requisite signs of organization and seemed to scorn notions of finish and polish. Moreover, the vein of libertine obscenity encountered in Sterne's letters (even those addressed to married women) signalled, if not depravity, then at least that he had invested insufficient reflection on his topics.[32] But defenders of Sterne, of course, could counter that all these attributes only underlined the manner in which Sterne had managed to catch the evanescent and fleeting character of thought: that these were the spontaneous outpourings of his mind, delivered both with candor and a just quality of benevolent sentiment (especially, for example, in the case of his letters to Sancho). Once identified as eccentricities allowable to a writer of "greatness," the irregularity of Sterne's letters could be described as a kind of epistolary accomplishment. Although many readers continued to execrate his formal and moral reversions, Sterne's letters were offered as a model in their own right—and so were Sancho's. The sixteenth edition of the enormously popular letter-writing manual *The Complete Letter-Writer: or, Polite English Secretary,* published in 1778, offered amongst its range of model letters drawn from the best practitioners, a selection of

Sterne's correspondence. Responding to the vogue for Sterne's letters, these were inserted into the section called "Elegant Letters on Various Subjects, to improve the Style and Entertain the Mind, from eminent authors."[33] As well as two letters to his daughter, the editor included the entirety of the Sancho-Sterne correspondence: not only Sancho's letter of 1766 and its reply of 1766, but also the two subsequent letters sent by Sterne to Sancho on more prosaic matters of business.[34] To this letter-writing manual, then, not only Sterne's but also Sancho's epistles are exemplary as "Elegant Letters."

Sterne's eccentricities as a correspondent, of course, further demonstrated the unique and original quality of his creative genius. The signal attributes of Sterne's letters—their spontaneity, sincerity, and naturalness—were of course the product of much art: Sterne used the letter-book technique to draft and plan his letters (as is testified by the differences between the several transcribed and sent versions of his own, and indeed Sancho's, letters). He advised his daughter Lydia, "never let your letters be studied ones—write naturally, and then you will write well."[35] The danger was that the artlessness of Sterne's letters might appear as a genuine lack of art rather than the appearance of its lack. Though his manner was easy to imitate and parody (as evidenced by the flood of such imitations), his epistolary style could only be earned by careful endeavor, by demonstration of ability in other areas, by being an established figure. The content of Sterne's letters accrued further symbolic capital: the heady mixture of sentimental effusions and exemplary benevolence together with his amiable and ingratiating letters to the great and good accumulated a specially innovative kind of status. Even the libertine turn of Sterne's letters marked their location in the culture of an exclusive group of urban rakes such as John Hamilton Mortimer, John Hall Stevenson, and John Wilkes. In short, Sterne's letters, and his manner of writing in general, possessed a particular kind of high status: urban and urbane, Whiggish and libertine, fashionable and exclusive.

Sancho's imitation of Sterne approaches both his sentimentalism and his libertinism through the mode of the familiar letter. It might seem to modern readers that benevolent and virtuous sentimentalism was the more natural ally of the emergent discourse of antislavery, and as such ought to have attracted Sancho. Certainly, sensibility and abolition have long been considered fellow travellers.[36] Nonetheless, there are compelling reasons why the politics of libertinism were attractive to Sancho too, especially in the 1760s and 1770s. In assessing Sancho's *Letters*, critics and historians have debated extensively the nature of his comments on slavery, race and cultural allegiance: it has been noted above that Walvin concluded that he was "obsequious," and Edwards that he was "almost wholly assimilated" to polite English society. A comprehensive assessment of Sancho's politics may be impossible now, and the *Letters*, the primary record, is a slippery medium upon which to base speculations. In large measure it does not always help to gauge Sancho against the self-consciously abolitionist politics of later writers such as Equiano or Cugoano, not simply because of Sancho's personal eccentricities, nor because his work is written prior to the emergence of a public antislavery discourse in the 1780s debate on abolition, but rather, because of this question of form. Sancho's politics are articulated most clearly in his chosen mode of address, the Shandean familiar letter, and in particular his peculiar interpolation of the sentimental-libertine discourse. In this way it is not rewarding to ask how much Sancho was an abolitionist: rather, the early history of public discourse against slavery might be revealed by an enquiry into the kinds of politics to which Sancho bears allegiance.

As Vincent Carretta has shown, Sancho was the only man of African descent known to have voted in a British parliamentary election in the eighteenth century. Sancho's right to vote depended on the unusual franchise governing the Westminster electorate where he lived. Open to all inhabitants paying "scot and lot," the franchise was essentially open to all male property-owning residents required to pay the poor-rate. With over twelve thousand electors, it was by far the largest elector-ate in the country. It was also a highly active electorate, whose elections after 1769 were influenced by the volatile radicalism of the nearby electorates of the City of London and Middlesex. In 1774, Sancho voted for Hugh Percy (Earl Percy) and Lord Thomas Pelham Clinton, the candidates of the North administration (thus opposing the radical interest backed by Wilkes). In 1780, however, Sancho sup-ported the radical ticket, voting for George Brydges Rodney (Admiral Rodney) and Charles James Fox—who, Sancho remarks, gave him the honor of thanking him personally.[37] Sancho's inconsistent voting pattern indicates that he was un-willing to be cast as an orthodox member of any particular party faction (and may reflect no more than a mercenary attitude to electoral allegiance). In a letter dated 4 May 1778, to Jack Wingrave, he disengenously remarks that "I say nothing of politics—I hate such subjects;—the public papers will inform you of mistakes—blood—taxes—misery—murder—the obstinacy of a few—and the murder and villainy of a many."[38] His distrust of faction, however, should not obscure his en-during concern with the politics of language and the languages of politics.

Sancho's letters on the Gordon Riots of 1780 to John Spink (Volume II, Let-ter LXVII to LXXI) serve as a case in point.[39] In themselves, his letters are an his-torically important description of events: as an eye-witness account they have a charming immediacy, and written by a man of property, they are ideologically invested in the outcome. Sancho's self-ironizing horror at the destructions of the mob—"worse than Negro barbarity"—and approving description of efforts to re-store order have usually been read as conservative and patriotic. However, the crowd of the Gordon Riots, animated by anti-Catholic sentiment and violent xenopho-bia (if not racism), was no friend of an African chandler, even if trial records indi-cate that there were several black participants in the riots.[40] He describes his justifiable fear at the appearance of "two thousand liberty boys swearing and swag-gering by with large sticks—thus armed in hope of meeting with the Irish chair-men and laborers." The vengeful blood-thirsty mob, he concludes ironically, articulate their sectarian bigotry in the loyalist discourse of liberty: "This—this—is liberty! genuine British liberty!"[41] His letters approvingly relate the measures taken by authority against the "anarchy": after noting that "martial law is this night to be declared," he expects the soldiers to do "terrible work," before noting that the "tumult begins to subside."[42] Here, as elsewhere, Sancho explores the parameters of the common-law notion of personal liberty so deeply ingrained in the English constitution. In doing so, he demonstrates that there is no easy way to map the popular politics of liberty in the mid-eighteenth century onto the concerns of liberation and emancipation in the late twentieth century.

The libertine turn in Sancho's *Letters* thus rounds out, and subverts, the picture of Sancho as a conservative and patriotic Whig. As a political language, libertinism was particularly associated with the Whig faction led in turn by Wilkes and Fox. As Kathleen Wilson has argued, libertine masculinity offered a mode of personal behavior as a radical political expression.[43] The libertine Whigs like Fox and Wilkes made extensive claims for the liberty of the English subject, a liberty which they defended from encroachment by both royal corruption and executive tyranny. This Wilkes-ite defense of the liberty of the English subject, in Wilson's construction, combined natural rights language with notions of historical resistance (celebrated in appeals to the "people's" actions in 1648 and the events of 1688). Sancho's patriotism establishes and elaborates his status as an English subject, to whom liberty is not accidental but essential. In this way Sancho's patriotism, often derided by recent observers who argue he ought to be more critical of nation and empire, is arguably a canny reading of the political field. In the period before abolition, the Whiggish notion of English liberty was the only viable political defense of his freedom (and indeed, it played an important role in the Mansfield decision in 1772 that restricted the rights of slave-owners). Libertine personal politics manifests this platform in a "manly patriotism" of which Wilkes was the prime example—a gendered self-fashioning in the libertine mode that Wilson argues was used "to naturalise claims to political subjectivity." "The model of manly patriotism simultaneously defined and solicited a particular version of masculinity to be put at the call of patriotism that marginalized and opposed non-resisting and hence 'effeminate' others. It defined the true patriot as the austere, forceful, and independent masculine subject who would resist, often at considerable personal cost, the illegitimate powers that threatened to overtake the polity."[44] Political liberty could thus be manifested in the "phallic adventuring" of libertine rakes. As Wilkes understood, his political cause was complicit with his performance as a rake: seen clearly in his production of pornography (the notorious *An Essay on Woman* (1762–1763),[45] a fondness for liaisons with women (affairs and mistresses), a perverse pride in personal indebtedness and high-stakes gambling, and excessive consumption of alcohol and food.

Sancho's reading of Sterne does not, of course, have recourse to the vulgar licentiousness (and libidinal coarseness) of libertine writings like those of Wilkes, Cleland or the *Sentimental Tales* of William Russell. Equally, there is no evidence that Sancho was a Wilkes-ite, nor was he a debauched libertine: indeed, he seems unusually faithful to his wife, his family and the cozy scene of domesticity in Charles Street. His letters are not sprinkled with "warm scenes," and he wasn't a member of a Hell-Fire Club.[46] Nonetheless, the quality of Sancho's friendships with men, his jokey masculine dilettantism, his predilection to excessive consumption, his love of luxury foods, his ironic respect for his gout and obesity, even his propensity to indulge the pathetic scene, might be called a kind of libertine masculinity. Perhaps this is no more than a stylistic turn: occasionally but repeatedly, Sancho allows his language to become libertine in this Wilkes-ite manner, without of course producing the explicitly rakish behaviour associated with and described by it.

Striving, like Sterne, for a lithe and fluid miscellaneity, Sancho's engagement with libertine discourse in the *Letters* is pervasive but inconsistent. With the appropriately named Mrs Cocksedge (perhaps the governess of Frances Crew),[47] Sancho adopts a playful mode of teasing flirtation. In Letter XXV (August 14, 1775), commenting on her excursion to the fashionable spa Bath, Sancho coquettishly imagines himself as her lover: "I imagine I see you rise out of the waves another Venus—and could wish myself Neptune, to have the honour of escorting you to land."[48] With John Meheux, a clerk or public official in the India Board, Sancho affects the swaggering brand of rakish masculinity, associating himself with excess drinking, the company of lewd women, and gout. Sancho was happy to appear the reformed rake too. Sancho's biographer, Joseph Jekyll, suggests that Sancho had enjoyed the dissipated life of the libertine following his receipt of the Duchess of Montagu's bequest in 1751. "Freedom, riches, and leisure, naturally led a disposition of African texture into indulgences; and that which dissipated the mind of Ignatius completely drained the purse. In his attachment to women, he displayed a profuseness which not unusually characterises the excess of the passion."[49]

A model for Sancho's libertine years is perhaps provided by the experiences of another Black servant in London in the 1770s, Julius Soubise, to whom Sancho addressed a number of concerned letters.[50] Brought to London from the West Indian colony of St Kitt's as a slave aged 10, Soubise had, like Sancho, attracted the benevolent attention of a noble patron, in his case the Duchess of Queensberry. The main record of Soubise's exploits are from a distinctly unreliable "whores biography" entitled *Nocturnal Revels* (1779), anonymously published by a minor pornographer, M. Goadby, and pretending to be by a "Monk of the Order of St. Francis," which is to say, a member of the burlesque Order of St. Francis assembled by the notorious libertine Sir Francis Dashwood at Medmenham Priory.[51] Two chapters of this miscellaneous work are devoted to the Soubise scandal, offering a "*Sketch of an extraordinary Black Character*" and a survey of "*His good fortune in England*" and "*His Success with the Fair Sex.*"[52] Having been educated by the Duchess in fencing and riding (high-status pursuits traditionally associated with the education of noblemen), Soubise became known as "The Mungo Macaroni": in short, a fop.[53] The generosity of the Duchess also allowed him to fashion himself the personal identity of a nobleman: he styled himself "Prince Ana—Ana—maboe" and was noted as "a very extraordinary personage parading the streets of the Town, in an elegant equipage, servants in superb liveries, and drawn by fine dun horses."[54] To the status of fop (with its connotations of fashionable effeminacy), Soubise added fame as a rake and a libertine (which carried connotations of fashionable masculinity):

> *Mungo* indulged in all the gaiety and extravagance of the Town. His
> face was very well known in the Fleshmarket at the Play-houses; he
> constantly frequented the Masquerades at the Pantheon and
> Cornelys,' where he has very naturally, and much in character, played
> the part of *Mungo*, by which name he was afterwards called. He was
> soon initiated at all the Nunneries in *King's Place* and the New
> Buildings; and the Nuns have frequently done the honour of taking
> an airing in his carriage in Hyde-Park and elsewhere. Mrs L—w—
> gt—n, Miss B—t—n, Miss K—g, Miss H—ph—ys, Miss K—y, and
> even Miss Emily C—lth—st herself, thought it no dishonour to have
> yielded to the intreaties of his Highness. His pocket was always well
> replenished; his carriage was always at their service; and the Ladies
> gave him the best of characters for his manly *parts* and *abilities*.[55]

Soubise's masculinity, the proper expression of his performative libertinism, gave
him the freedom of the town, measured in his attendance at fashionable resorts
and brothels. In society he was free to be a rake, as long as his sexual virility gave
him access to the ladies and prostitutes. But for contemporaries, Soubise's liberty
was troubling, an illusory freedom dependent upon the financial resources of his
female patron, with whom he was accused of sexual complicity. Indeed, like Jekyll's
description of Sancho's libertinism, Soubise's rakish exploits were made the occasion of further physiological stereotyping: as "his constitution was as warm as his
complexion," it is the vaunted virility of black masculinity that ensures his popular "freedom," which has no foundation outside female concupiscence.[56]

But although Soubise's life might give us a sense of Sancho's libertine past,
Sancho's letters to Soubise deploy a tone of pious morality more akin to conduct-
book discourse and the reforming language of the sermon. Sancho's first letter to
Soubise, written in 1772 when Soubise still enjoyed the benefits of his noble patron's
benevolence, cautions him to follow the path of virtue, a lesson Sancho underlines
by inviting Soubise to compare his station in life with that of his enslaved fellow
countrymen:

> Look round upon the miserable fate of almost all of our unfortunate
> colour—superadded to ignorance,—see slavery, and the contempt of
> those wretches who roll in affluence from our labours superadded to
> this woeful catalogue—hear the ill-bred and heart-racking abuse of
> the foolish vulgar.—You, S[oubise], tread as cautiously as the
> strictest rectitude can guide ye—yet must you suffer from this—but
> armed with truth—honesty—and conscious integrity—you will be
> sure of the plaudit and countenance of the good.[57]

The second letter was written after a space of six years, in the course of which
Soubise had gained his considerable notoriety in the lists of fashionable debauch,
and so dissipated his good fortune and name. His fall was complete. After years of

consorting with known courtesans and prostitutes, Soubise had been accused of raping one of the maids of the Duchess of Queensberry. He departed for Calcutta as a riding instructor on 15 July 1777, a week before a report of the rape was published in *The Morning Post* on 22 July.[58] Soubise was aware of his precarious position, as signalled by "a very penitential letter" that Sancho received from Soubise, probably sent from Portsmouth (noted in a letter to Mr Meheux, Letter XLIII, July 23, 1777). But Sancho continued to worry about the quality of Soubise's reformed "sensibility."[59] Sancho's second letter to Soubise offered sterner counsel. Sancho advised him to use his East Indian exile to embark on a course of moral and commercial penitence:

> It has pleased God to take your props to himself—teaching you a lesson at the same time, to depend upon an honest exertion of your own industry—and humbly to trust in the Almighty.
> You may safely conclude now, that you have not many friends in England—be it your study, with attention, kindness, humility, and industry, to make friends where you are—industry with good-nature and honesty is the road to wealth.—A wise oeconomy—without avaricious meanness—or dirty rapacity will in a few years render you decently independent.[60]

Sancho proposes that Soubise should endeavour to repay his outstanding debts to London tradesmen, so that on his return Soubise may "create" a "better name." This conversion is expressed as a spiritual transformation, but it also proposes to reform Soubise from the excesses of libertinage towards a more homely domestic virtue clearly associated with the honest poverty of the tradesman, a man who stands independently on his own credit and name (Sancho remarks on his poverty, "'tis an honest poverty—and I need not blush or conceal it").[61] Ironically Soubise's libertine freedom, Sancho proposes, is revealed as a kind of slavery (slave to fashion and sexual intrigue, or more teasingly, a sexual slave of his white female mistresses). Disturbingly, then, Soubise's libertine slavery exposes the insecurities of Sancho's own freedom, especially as it is asserted through the same libertine language of liberty.

By rendering distinctions between high and low culture unstable and unclear, Sancho's *Letters* possess within their mode of address a dangerous subversive quality. In this way, Sancho's *Letters* are arguably more adventurous than Equiano's slave narrative, whose allegiance to low prose genres ironically serves to confirm, for resistant readers such as Jefferson, Equiano's place, status and subjectivity. Sancho's deployment of Sterne's style translates a literary infelicity into a political scandal, because Sterne's style celebrates Sancho's exceptional status. Sancho's *Letters* are a species of category error that confirms Sancho's own confusion of hierarchy and order. The Shandean and sentimental form of his letters exposes to Jefferson and others the irredeemable incongruity between Sancho the Anglo-African man (racially different) and his status in life (enfranchised, property-owning and fêted in elite circles). By delicately and elegantly elaborating a digressive biography of Sancho's London life, locating him at the centre rather than the margin of webs of culture and commerce, patronage and gossip, Sancho invites speculation on matters of status and subjectivity, toying with his self-representation, and invoking inconsistency. Rather than being an example of assimilation, obsequiousness or mimicry, as many of Sancho's recent critics have contended, the form and substance of Sancho's *Letters* repeatedly declare a culturally combative exceptionalism that makes his book both transgressive and radical.

NOTES

I am grateful to the following for their advice and assistance in the preparation of this essay: Rebecca Beasley, Brycchan Carey, Vincent Carretta, Dierdre Coleman, Lyn Innes, Chris Reid, Vanessa Smith and Helen Thomas.

1. Ignatius Sancho, *The Letters of the Late Ignatius Sancho, an African*, ed. Vincent Carretta (London: Penguin, 1998), 7. All references to this edition unless otherwise specified.

2. Ignatius Sancho, *The Letters of the late Ignatius Sancho*, ed. Paul Edwards (London: Dawsons of Pall Mall, 1968), i.

3. James Walvin, *Black and White: The Negro and English Society, 1555–1945* (London: Allen Lane, 1973), 61.

4. Paul Edwards, "Black writers of the eighteenth and nineteenth centuries," in David Dabydeen, ed., *The Black Presence in English Literature* (Manchester: Manchester University Press, 1985), 52, 53.

5. See for example David Thomson, *Wild Excursions: The Life and Fiction of Laurence Sterne* (London: Weidenfeld and Nicholson, 1972), 252; Melvyn New, *Notes*, in Laurence Sterne, *The Life and Opinions of Tristram Shandy, Gentleman*, ed. Melvyn New and Joan New, 3 vols (Gainesville, Florida: University Presses of Florida, 1978–84), 532, n. 747.1ff; and Arthur H. Cash, *Laurence Sterne: The Later Years* (London and New York: Methuen, 1986), 255.

6. Keith Sandiford, *Measuring the Moment: Strategies of Protest in Eighteenth-Century Afro-English Writing* (London and Toronto: Associated University Presses, 1988), 75–76.

7. Paul Edwards, "Introduction," in Ignatius Sancho, *Letters*, ed. Paul Edwards and Polly Rewt (Edinburgh: Edinburgh University Press, 1994), 6–7, 3. See also Paul Edwards, "Unreconciled Strivings and Ironic Strategies: Three Afro-British Authors of the Georgian Era; Ignatius Sancho, Olaudah Equiano, Robert Wedderburn," *Occasional Papers*, No. 34 (Edinburgh: Centre of African Studies, Edinburgh University, 1992), unpaginated.

8. Markman Ellis, *The Politics of Sensibility: Race, Gender and Commerce in the Sentimental Novel* (Cambridge: Cambridge University Press, 1996), 57–64, 79–86; James Walvin, "Ignatius Sancho: The Man and his Times" in *Ignatius Sancho: An African Man of Letters*, ed. Reyahn King (London: National Portrait Gallery, 1997); Sukhdev Sandhu, "Ignatius Sancho: An African Man of Letters," in *Ignatius Sancho: An African Man of Letters*, ed. Reyahn King (London: National Portrait Gallery, 1997); Vincent Carretta, "Introduction" in *The Letters of the Late Ignatius Sancho, an African*, ed. Vincent Carretta (London: Penguin, 1998), ix-xxxii; Vincent Carretta, "Three West Indian Writers of the 1780s Revisited and Revised," *Research in African Literatures*, Special Issue "The African Diaspora and its Origins," 29, 4 (1998), 73–77; Sukhdev Sandhu, "Ignatius Sancho and Laurence Sterne,"

Research in African Literatures, Special Issue "The African Diaspora and its Origins," 29, 4 (1998), 88–106.

9. Eric Erämetsä, *A Study of the Word "Sentimental" and of Other Linguistic Characteristics of the Eighteenth-Century Sentimentalism in England*, Annales Academiae Scientiarum Fennicae, Series 13, No. 74 (Helsinki: Helsingen Liike Kinjapaino Oy, 1951), 29. See also Edith Birkhead, "Sentiment and Sensibility in the Eighteenth-Century Novel," *Essays and Studies*, 11 (1925), 92–116.

10. Lydia de Medalle (ed.), *Letters of the Late Rev. Mr. Laurence Sterne, To his most intimate Friends. With a Fragment in the Manner of Rabelais. To which are prefix'd, Memoirs of his Life and Family. Written by Himself. And Published by his Daughter, Mrs. Medalle*, 3 vols (London: T. Becket, 1775), 22–36.

11. William Wilberforce, *A Practical View of the Prevailing Religious System of Professed Christians, in the Higher and Middle Classes, Contrasted with Real Christianity* (London: T. Cadell, Jun. and W. Davies, 1797), p. 203.

12. *The Gentleman's Magazine*, XLVI (January 1776), 27, 29.

13. *The Gentleman's Magazine*, LI, (April 1781), 162. Carretta suggests the letter (to William Stevenson, dated August 31, 1779) was sent by Frances Crew, in Sancho, *Letters*, xv.

14. Sancho, *Letters*, 4.

15. [Review of Sancho's *Letters*], *Gentleman's Magazine*, LII, (August 1782), 437–439, 437.

16. Sancho, *Letters*, 4.

17. Ibid., 9.

18. "[Review of Sancho's *Letters*]," *The European Magazine*, II (September, 1782), 199–201, 199.

19. Sancho, *Letters*, Carretta ed., 101–4.

20. *European Magazine*, II (September, 1782), 199.

21. Ralph Griffiths, "Art. X [Review of Sancho's *Letters*]," *The Monthly Review; or, Literary Journal*, LXIX, (December, 1783), 492–97, 493.

22. Griffiths, *Monthly Review*, LXIX, 1783, 493.

23. Thomas Jefferson, *Notes on the State of Virginia* (London: J, Stockdale, 1787); repr. ed. William Peden (New York: Norton, 1954), 140–141.

24. Sancho, *Letters*, 214–15.

25. Sandhu, "Ignatius Sancho and Laurence Sterne," 96–97.

26. James Boswell, conversation with Cleland in his journal entry for 13 April 1779, in *Private Papers of James Boswell from Malahide Castle*, ed. Geoffrey Scott and Frederick A. Pottle, xiii ([New York: W.E. Rudge], 1932), 220.

27. [William Russell], *Sentimental Tales, in two volumes*, 2 vols bound and paginated as one (Dublin: James Williams, 1771); Laurence Sterne, *A Sentimental Journey Through France and Italy by Mr. Yorick*, 2 vols (London: T. Becket and P.A. DeHondt, 1768), II, 100.

28. Russell, *Sentimental Tales*, 7–79.

29. Howard Anderson and Irvin Ehrenpreis, "The Familiar Letter in the Eighteenth Century: Some Generalisations," in Howard Anderson, Philip B. Daghlian, and Irvin Ehrenpreis (eds), *The Familiar Letter in the Eighteenth Century* (Lawrence: University of Kansas Press, 1966), 271.

30. George Seymour, *The Instructive Letter-Writer, and Entertaining Companion: containing Letters On the Most Interesting Subjects, In an Elegant and Easy Style; Most of which are wrote by the following Royal and Eminent Personages, and the Best Authors, Antient and Modern, viz. Cicero, Brutus, Trajan, Pliny, Plutarch [. . .] Locke, Addison, Steele, Pope, Gay, Atterbury, Mr. & Mrs. Rowe, Richardson, Coleman, Murphy &c. With Forms of Messages for Cards* (London: G. Kearsley, 1763), 8.

31. *The Complete Letter-Writer: or, New and Polite English Secretary. Containing Directions for writing Letters on all Occasions, in a polite, easy, and proper Manner; with a great Variety of Examples, from the best Authors, on Business, Duty, Amusement, Affection, Courtship, Love, Marriage, Friendship, &c. And at the End some elegant Poetical Epistles. To which is prefix'd, an easy and compendious Grammar of the English Tongue. With Instructions how to address Persons of all ranks*, 2nd ed. (1755, London: S. Crowder and H. Woodgate, 1756).

32. The publication of Sterne's *Letters* (1775) by his daughter Lydia Medalle in 1775 reconfirmed his allegiance to a peculiar brand of English libertine sentimental writers. Like the *Letters from Yorick to Eliza* (London: W. Johnston, 1773, reprinted 1775), the *Letters* (1775) hinted that Sterne's ambiguous affairs with women in the 1760s had a passionate and physical dimension.

33. *The Complete Letter-Writer: or, Polite English Secretary. Containing Familiar Letters on the most common Occasions in Life.* 16th edition (first ed. 1755; London: S. Crowder and Benj. Cha. Collins, 1778), 167–256.

34. *Complete Letter-Writer* (16th ed., 1778) No. XLVII. "*From* Ignatius Sancho *(a Black) to Mr.* Sterne" [u.d.], 249–250; No. XLVIII. "*From Mr.* Sterne, to Ignatius Sancho," [u.d.], 251–52; No. XLIX. "*To the same*," [u.d.], 252; No. L. "*To the same*," [u.d.], 252–53.

35. Laurence Sterne, *Letters of Laurence Sterne*, ed. Lewis Perry Curtis (Oxford: Clarendon, 1935), 302.

36. See for example Thomas Haskell, "Capitalism and the Origins of the Humanitarian Sensibility, Part I," *American Historical Review*, 90, 2 (April 1985), 339–361; and "Part II," 90, 3 (June 1985), 547–66; and by contrast Ellis, *Politics of Sensibility*, 87–128; and George E. Boulukos, "Maria Edgeworth's 'Grateful Negro' and the Sentimental Argument for Slavery," *Eighteenth-Century Life*, 23, 1 (1999), 12–29.

37. Carretta, in Sancho, *Letters*, 321–22. Carretta's source is the published poll-books for the Westminster elections of that year. The 1776 election was unopposed.

38. Sancho, *Letters*, 116.

39. Ibid., 217–26.

40. Peter Linebaugh, *The London Hanged: Crime and Civil Society in the Eighteenth Century* (London: Allen Lane, 1991), 336.

41. Sancho, *Letters*, 217–18.

42. Ibid., 220, 221, 222.

43. Kathleen Wilson, *The Sense of the People: Politics, Culture and Imperialism in England, 1715–1718* (Cambridge: Cambridge University Press, 1995). See also John Sainsbury, "John Wilkes, Debt, and Patriotism," *Journal of British Studies*, 34 (April 1995), 165–96; James G. Turner, "The Properties Of Libertinism," *Eighteenth-Century Life*, 9, no. 3 (1985), 75–87; Brian Cowan, "Reasonable Ecstasies: Shaftesbury and the Languages of Libertinism," *Journal of British Studies*, 37 (April 1998), 111–38; Randolph Trumbach, "Erotic Fantasy and Male Libertinism in Enlightenment England" in *The Invention of Pornography*, ed. Lynn Hunt (New York: Zone Books, 1993), 253–82.

44. Wilson, *Sense of the People*, 219.

45. Adrian Hamilton, *The Infamous 'Essay on Woman'* (London: Deutch, 1972).

46. Betty Kemp, *Sir Francis Dashwood* (London: Macmillan, 1967), 101–57; D.P. Mannix, *The Hell-Fire Club* (New York: Ballantine, 1959).

47. Carretta, in Sancho, *Letters*, 255n.

48. Sancho, *Letters*, 61.

49. Jekyll in ibid., 6.

50. Sancho's letters to Soubise: (i) Richmond, Oct. 11, 1772, I, Letter XIII, 46–47; (ii) Charles Street, Westm., Nov. 29, 1778, II, Letter XIII, 147–49. Another letter (I, Letter I, 27–28), to Mr. Jack Wingrave in Bengal, India, Charles Street, Feb. 14 1768 [actually 1778],

relates Soubise's departure to India to seek his fortune (and escape public scandal); about which see also Carretta note p. 258. Sancho also comments on how to advise Soubise in a letter to Meheux (II, Letter II, July 26, 1778, 134).

51. *Nocturnal Revels: or, The History of King's Place, and other Modern Nunneries. Containing their Mysteries, Devotions, and Sacrifices. Comprising also, The Ancient and Present State of Promiscuous Gallantry: with their Portraits of the most Celebrated Demireps and Courtezans of this Period: as well as Sketches of their Professional and Occasional Admirers. By a Monk of the Order of St. Francis*, 2 vols, 2nd ed. (London: M. Goadby, 1779).

52. Ibid., 210.

53. Soubise was so named in the caricature *A Mungo Macaroni*, a visual satire published by Matthew and/or Mary Darly on 10 September 1772. Mungo was a commonplace name for a black slave, from Isaac Bickerstaffe's comic opera *The Padlock* (1769), in which Mungo was a ridiculous and officious servant who was willing to undertake any service for his employers. A macaroni was a fashionable fop.

54. *Nocturnal Revels*, 210–11.

55. Ibid., 216–17. The women are all courtesans or prostitutes.

56. Ibid., 216.

57. Sancho, *Letters*, 46.

58. Carretta, in Ibid., 257. Soubise died in India after a fall from a horse on 25 August 1798.

59. Ibid., 85.

60. Ibid., 147–48.

61. Ibid., 148.

BIBLIOGRAPHY

"[Advertisement for Sancho's *Letters*]." *The Gentleman's Magazine* LI (April 1781): 162.

Anderson, Howard, Philip B. Daghlian, and Irvin Ehrenpreis, eds. *The Familiar Letter in the Eighteenth Century*. Lawrence: University of Kansas Press, 1966.

Birkhead, Edith. "Sentiment and Sensibility in the Eighteenth-Century Novel." *Essays and Studies* 11 (1925): 92–116.

Boulukos, George E. "Maria Edgeworth's 'Grateful Negro' and the Sentimental Argument for Slavery," *Eighteenth-Century Life* 23, 1 (1999): 12–29.

Boswell, James. *Private Papers of James Boswell from Malahide Castle*. Ed. Geoffrey Scott and Frederick A. Pottle. 18 vols. [New York: W.E. Rudge], 1932.

Carretta, Vincent. "Three West Indian Writers of the 1780s Revisited and Revised." *Research in African Literatures*, Special Issue "The African Diaspora and its Origins" 29, 4 (1998): 73–77.

Cash, Arthur H. *Laurence Sterne: The Later Years*. London and New York: Methuen, 1986.

The Complete Letter-Writer: or, New and Polite English Secretary. Containing Directions for writing Letters on all Occasions, in a polite, easy, and proper Manner; with a great Variety of Examples, from the best Authors, on Business, Duty, Amusement, Affection, Courtship, Love, Marriage, Friendship, &c. And at the End some elegant Poetical Epistles. To which is prefix'd, an easy and compendious Grammar of the English Tongue. With Instructions how to address Persons of all ranks. 2nd ed. London: S. Crowder and H. Woodgate, 1756.

The Complete Letter-Writer: or, Polite English Secretary. Containing Familiar Letters on the most common Occasions in Life. 16th ed. London: S. Crowder and Benj. Cha. Collins, 1778.

Cowan, Brian. "Reasonable Ecstasies: Shaftesbury and the Languages of Libertinism," *Journal of British Studies* 37 (April 1998): 111–38.

Edwards, Paul. "Black writers of the eighteenth and nineteenth centuries." Ed. David Dabydeen. *The Black Presence in English Literature*. Manchester: Manchester University Press, 1985.

Edwards, Paul. "Unreconciled Strivings and Ironic Strategies: three Afro-British Authors of the Georgian Era; Ignatius Sancho, Olaudah Equiano, Robert Wedderburn." *Occasional Papers*, No. 34. Edinburgh: Centre of African Studies, Edinburgh University, 1992.

Ellis, Markman. *The Politics of Sensibility: Race, Gender and Commerce in the Sentimental Novel*. Cambridge: Cambridge University Press, 1996.

Erämetsä, Eric. *A Study of the Word "Sentimental" and of Other Linguistic Characteristics of the Eighteenth-Century Sentimentalism in England*. Annales Academiae Scientiarum Fennicae, Series 13, No. 74. Helsinki: Helsingen Liike Kinjapaino Oy, 1951.

The Gentleman's Magazine and Historical Chronicle. London, D. Henry and R. Cave, 1731–1907.

Griffiths, Ralph. "Art. X [Review of Sancho's *Letters*]." *The Monthly Review; or, Literary Journal* LXIX (December, 1783): 492–97.

Hamilton, Adrian. *The Infamous 'Essay on Woman.'* London: Deutch, 1972.

Haskell, Thomas. "Capitalism and the Origins of the Humanitarian Sensibility, Part I." *American Historical Review*, 90, no. 2 (April 1985): 339–361; and "Part II." 90, no. 3 (June 1985): 547–66.

Jefferson, Thomas, *Notes on the State of Virginia*. London: J, Stockdale, 1787. Repr. ed. William Peden. New York: Norton, 1954.

Kemp, Betty. *Sir Francis Dashwood*. London: Macmillan, 1967.

King, Reyahn, ed. *Ignatius Sancho: An African Man of Letters*. London: National Portrait Gallery, 1997.

Linebaugh, Peter. *The London Hanged: Crime and Civil Society in the Eighteenth Century*. London: Allen Lane, 1991.

Mannix, D.P. *The Hell-Fire Club*. New York: Ballantine, 1959.

Medalle, Lydia de, ed. *Letters of the Late Rev. Mr. Laurence Sterne, To his most intimate Friends. With a Fragment in the Manner of Rabelais. To which are prefix'd, Memoirs of his Life and Family. Written by Himself. And Published by his Daughter, Mrs. Medalle*. 3 vols. London: T. Becket, 1775.

Nocturnal Revels: or, The History of King's Place, and other Modern Nunneries. Containing their Mysteries, Devotions, and Sacrifices. Comprising also, The Ancient and Present State of Promiscuous Gallantry: with their Portraits of the most Celebrated Demireps and Courtezans of this Period: as well as Sketches of their Professional and Occasional Admirers. By a Monk of the Order of St. Francis. 2 vols. 2nd ed. London: M. Goadby, 1779.

"[Review of Sancho's *Letters*]." *Gentleman's Magazine*. LII (August 1782): 437–439.

"[Review of Sancho's *Letters*]." *The European Magazine*. II (September 1782): 199–201

"[Review of Sterne's *Letters*]." *The Gentleman's Magazine*. XLVI (January 1776): 27–29.

Russell, William. *Sentimental Tales, in two volumes*, 2 vols bound and paginated as one. Dublin: James Williams, 1771.

Sainsbury, John. "John Wilkes, Debt, and Patriotism." *Journal of British Studies* 34 (April 1995): 165–96.

Sancho, Ignatius. *Letters*. Ed. Paul Edwards and Polly Rewt. Edinburgh: Edinburgh University Press, 1994.

———. *The Letters of the Late Ignatius Sancho, an African.* Ed. Vincent Carretta. London: Penguin, 1998.

———. *The Letters of the late Ignatius Sancho.* Ed. Paul Edwards. London: Dawsons of Pall Mall, 1968.

Sandhu, Sukhdev. "Ignatius Sancho and Laurence Sterne." *Research in African Literatures.* Special Issue "The African Diaspora and its Origins." 29, no. 4 (1998): 88–106.

Sandhu, Sukhdev. "Ignatius Sancho: An African Man of Letters." *Ignatius Sancho: An African Man of Letters.* Ed. Reyahn King. London: National Portrait Gallery, 1997.

Sandiford, Keith. *Measuring the Moment: Strategies of Protest in Eighteenth-Century Afro-English Writing.* London and Toronto: Associated University Presses, 1988.

Seymour, George. *The Instructive Letter-Writer, and Entertaining Companion: containing Letters On the Most Interesting Subjects, In an Elegant and Easy Style; Most of which are wrote by the following Royal and Eminent Personages, and the Best Authors, Antient and Modern, viz. Cicero, Brutus, Trajan, Pliny, Plutarch [. . .] Locke, Addison, Steele, Pope, Gay, Atterbury, Mr. & Mrs. Rowe, Richardson, Coleman, Murphy &c. With Forms of Messages for Cards.* London: G. Kearsley, 1763.

Sterne, Laurence. *Letters of Laurence Sterne.* Ed. Lewis Perry Curtis. Oxford, Clarendon, 1935.

Sterne, Laurence. *The Life and Opinions of Tristram Shandy, Gentleman.* Ed. Melvyn New and Joan New. 3 vols. Gainesville, Florida: University Presses of Florida, 1978–84.

Thomson, David. *Wild Excursions: The Life and Fiction of Laurence Sterne.* London: Weidenfeld and Nicholson, 1972.

Trumbach, Randolph. "Erotic Fantasy and Male Libertinism in Enlightenment England." *The Invention of Pornography.* Ed. Lynn Hunt. New York: Zone Books, 1993: 253–82

Turner, James G. "The Properties Of Libertinism." *Eighteenth-Century Life.* 9, no. 3 (1985): 75–87.

Walvin, James. *Black and White: The Negro and English Society, 1555–1945.* London: Allen Lane, 1973.

Walvin, James. "Ignatius Sancho: The Man and his Times." *Ignatius Sancho: An African Man of Letters.* Ed. Reyahn King. London: National Portrait Gallery, 1997.

Wilberforce, William. *A Practical View of the Prevailing Religious System of Professed Christians, in the Higher and Middle Classes, Contrasted with Real Christianity.* London: T. Cadell, Jun. and W. Davies, 1797.

Wilson, Kathleen. *The Sense of the People: Politics, Culture and Imperialism in England, 1715–1718.* Cambridge: Cambridge University Press, 1995.

BENJAMIN BANNEKER'S REVISION OF THOMAS JEFFERSON

Conscience vs. Science in the Early American Antislavery Debate

William Andrews

On August 19, 1791, Benjamin Banneker, a Maryland farmer, surveyor, and astronomer nearing his sixtieth birthday, wrote a letter to forty-eight-year-old Thomas Jefferson, United States Secretary of State in George Washington's first administration. Banneker was not in the habit of writing to national political figures, but he had reason to believe that Jefferson would not regard a letter from him as an impertinence. After all, earlier that year Jefferson had approved of Banneker's appointment to the team of surveyors charged by President Washington with laying out the District of Columbia (Bedini, 108). Banneker also may have known that he shared a number of intellectual interests in common with Jefferson. They were both curious about the natural world and calculating its mechanisms. Meteorology was a matter of serious study for Jefferson (Richard B. Davis, 195). For years Banneker kept a journal in which he recorded the atmospheric phenomena he observed (Bedini, 232–33). Banneker's fascination with clocks and their construction—he first became famous in his region for the clock he constructed out of wooden parts when he was twenty-two years old—had real affinities with Jefferson's lifelong obsession with time[1]. Although farming provided each man his livelihood, both preferred the life of the mind.

Banneker, however, was a black man, the freeborn son of a mixed-race mother and a formerly enslaved African father, raised on a modest tobacco farm in Baltimore County.[2] Jefferson, by contrast, was a Virginia aristocrat, born and reared at Shadwell in the Virginia upcountry, the son of a prosperous plantation owner and slaveholder. Both men showed unusual intellectual aptitude early on. But as a rural free Negro Banneker had little opportunity for instruction beyond his own family. Jefferson's position at the top of the Virginia socioeconomic order awarded him the best that the colony could afford its favorite sons. Until he wrote his letter to Jefferson, Banneker had passed his adult life in comparative isolation and anonymity, a moderately successful farmer who lived alone, distinguished to a small group of local whites whom he impressed by his devotion to the study of astronomy. Jefferson, on the other hand, figured prominently in national affairs as early as the mid-1770s, and was celebrated for his authorship of the *Declaration of Independence*, his crucial diplomacy as the American revolutionary government's minister to France, and his book *Notes on the State of Virginia* (1785), probably the most important scientific and political book written by an American up to that time. No wonder Banneker began his letter by assuring the Secretary of State that he was "fully sensible of the greatness of that freedom, which I take with you on the present occasion; a liberty which Seemed to me Scarcely allowable, when I reflected on that distinguished, and dignifyed station in which you Stand; and the almost general prejudice and prepossession which is so prevalent in the world against those of my complexion."[3] Among the limited freedoms available to a quasi-free man of color in Maryland was not the liberty to address an august white gentleman (who had invited no such presumption upon his time), unless of course Banneker wanted to express his gratitude for the appointment the Secretary of State gave him to the District of Columbia surveying team.

But Banneker did not write to thank Jefferson for anything. Intoning words of humility and hesitancy even as he took liberties "scarcely allowable" to a man of his caste and class position, Banneker approached Jefferson sending mixed signals, at once respectful and challenging, earnest and ironic. The tonal tensions in the black man's opening paragraph—instanced in oxymoronic formulations such as "allowable freedom"—surface repeatedly in Banneker's ostensibly deferential mode of address, making his letter among the most rhetorically provocative short texts in early African American literature. How could such an imposition, such a seizure of freedom bordering on license, be justified, given the popular notion, as Banneker bluntly summarized it, that "we are a race of Beings . . . considered rather as brutish than human, and Scarcely capable of mental endowments" (152)? The answer, Banneker blandly asserted, lay not in his apparent audacity but in Jefferson's reputed magnanimity.

"Sir, I hope I may Safely admit, in consequence of that report which hath reached me, that you are a man far less inflexible in Sentiments of this nature [i.e., about black inferiority], than many others; that you are measurably friendly and well disposed towards us, and that you are willing and ready to Lend your aid and assistance to our relief from those many distresses and numerous calamities to which we are reduced" (152). More than mere flattery, this characterization of Jefferson by Banneker was essential to the rhetorical relationship the free man of color wanted to cultivate with the formidable white statesman. By appealing to the Virginia aristocrat's noblesse oblige, the free Negro gave himself the opportunity to call attention to the fact that for African Americans the post-Revolutionary era had brought little hope for a better future. Many African Americans had fought and some had died in the belief that liberation from Great Britain would bring about a more general emancipation from slavery (Quarles, 291–294). But as

Banneker wrote his letter, the white leadership of his Chesapeake Bay region, exemplified by statesmen-slaveholders (such as Jefferson) who had once proclaimed their libertarian ideals, showed no disposition to engineer a national emancipation movement (Dunn, 49; Nash, 11–12). In the aftermath of the war, the great revolutionary leaders of the Chesapeake "made few legal and institutional changes in their slave system. They closed the slave trade, restricted entry of slaves from other states, and permitted individual manumission, but they squelched every move toward general abolition" (Dunn, 51–52). The Constitution of 1787 cemented into law the refusal of Jefferson's generation of revolutionaries to extend to African Americans the "self-evident truths" of equality and liberty promised white Americans in the *Declaration of Independence*. In response, free black men and women, particularly in the North, set to work building schools, churches, fraternal organizations, and other mutual aid alliances to promote their socioeconomic development and to resist caste alienation (Franklin and Moss, 98–104; Berlin, 62–78). Benjamin Banneker's solitary disposition and scholarly temperament, along with his relative isolation as a free black man in a slave state, kept him on the fringes of collective African American self-improvement efforts. Still "the most accomplished black in the early national period" (Franklin and Moss, 95) was not indifferent to his people's strivings. His contribution would be to attempt to re-enlist Thomas Jefferson himself in the cause of freedom.

The Secretary of State may have wondered about Banneker's ambiguous reference to a "report" that had convinced him that Jefferson was much less "inflexible" in his racial views than many other whites. Although we are unlikely ever to know for certain what this report was, the most widely circulated evidence of Jefferson's notions about race, and particularly about the "mental endowments" of black people, had been available in the United States since 1788, when the first American edition of the *Notes on the State of Virginia* was published in Philadelphia (*Notes*, xxiii). The *Georgetown Weekly Ledger* was familiar enough with Jefferson's *Notes* and its discussion of African American intellectual capacity that in reporting the arrival of the surveying commission for the new District of Columbia in March 1791, it singled out "Benjamin Banneker, an Ethiopian whose abilities as surveyor and astronomer already prove that Mr. Jefferson's concluding that race of men were void of mental endowment was without foundation" (Jordan, 450). If Banneker had not read the *Notes* by then, such a public linking of himself to that already controversial book would surely have pricked his curiosity about it. Since its initial appearance in French and British editions, the *Notes* had received a great deal of attention throughout the United States. Although written in response to a French man of letters' queries about everything from Virginia's state boundaries to its people's manners and customs, what the *Notes* said about slavery and the mental and moral capacities of African Americans earned its author a most unwanted notoriety (Jordan, 441). Defenders of the Negro took issue with what they saw as Jefferson's disparagement of black intellectual potential; proslavery writers decried the *Notes*'s disposition in favor of gradual emancipation (Jordan, 435, 442–444). Regardless of one's racial attitudes, *Notes on the State of*

Virginia served as the inescapable text of reference on the Negro until well into the middle of the next century (Jordan, 429, Fredrickson, 1–2).

Congratulating Jefferson on his reputed flexibility on race was only a prelude, however, to Banneker's real purpose, which was to induce Jefferson to take a further step into the racial arena, a step that would inevitably face up to the controversies that the *Notes* had helped to kindle. *If* you are as liberal as you are reported to be, the black man observed, "I apprehend you will readily embrace every opportunity to eradicate that train of absurd and false ideas and oppinions [sic] which so generally prevail with respect to us" African-descended people (153). Thus Banneker laid the groundwork for a disarmingly simple proposal: that Jefferson join him, in effect, in a common cause against ignorance and prejudice about race.

This high-minded invitation contained its own implicit challenge, of course. Jefferson was being asked to justify the reputation Banneker had already half-granted him as open and fair-minded on matters of race. But because Jefferson was who he was—the culture hero of enlightened thinking in the new republic, the great articulator of American Revolutionary ideals in the *Declaration of Independence*—Banneker's challenge extended beyond Jefferson the man. Jefferson symbolized the slaveholding southern aristocrat as professed democrat, meritocrat, and champion of human rights. Since his days in the Virginia legislature in the mid-1770s, Jefferson had been publicly identified as antislavery. But after the new nation achieved its freedom in 1783, he had been conspicuous by his silence on specific abolition measures.[4] To prompt Jefferson to speak once again, Banneker decided to confront him directly through correspondence, widely utilized among gentlemen of the eighteenth-century South as a means of engaging in respectable intellectual discourse on politics (Hubbell, 101–102, 133). A personal letter would be a discreet yet direct way for a free black man of the South to approach a liberal white southerner on a topic of considerable sensitivity. In an effort to reach a middle ground with Jefferson, Banneker would adapt the terms of his discourse to Jefferson's own, citing especially the grand public generalizations of the *Declaration*. But the pretext of Banneker's effort not just to appeal to Jefferson, but to engage him in a dialogue, was probably the *Notes*. Therein lay ample evidence of a personal struggle of mind and moral equilibrium in an archetypal American, a slaveholding democrat who seemed anxious to find a way out of the desperate contradictions of democracy on the one hand and human bondage on the other.

Since its publication *Notes on the State of Virginia* has furnished readers and analysts much contradictory evidence about what its author really believed about race vs. environment, about slavery vs. emancipation, and about the natural rights of individuals vs. society's obligation to guarantee equality for all. If, having perused the *Notes*, Benjamin Banneker was perplexed by its tentative and tortuous reasoning on these issues, he was certainly not alone among his countrymen then or now. As John P. Diggins has shown in his survey of major twentieth-century examinations of Jefferson's ideas about slavery, race, and equality, no one has yet been able to reconcile Jefferson's philosophy with his prejudices. Both were based in paradoxes that lay at the heart of the so-called Enlightenment, of which Jefferson was both a creator and a creation.

Some of these paradoxes were hardly subtle. As we shall see, Benjamin Banneker had no difficulty pointing out the most obvious ones in his letter to Jefferson. But a man of Banneker's caste would not have taken the liberty to do so unless he felt not only a moral responsibility on his own part but also a receptiveness in Jefferson. In part Jefferson's frequent espousal of environmentalism rather than racial determinism as a basis for judging the potential and achievement of various peoples in the human family made the author of the *Notes* seem like a man open to reason on this topic (Shuffelton, 274–75). In addition readers of the *Notes* have often alluded to the remarkably personal tone of portions of that text, labeling it "Jefferson's unintentional self-portrait" (Tauber), calling attention to passages in which "the passionate underpinnings of his feelings were laid bare" (Jordan, 458), and detecting the anxieties of white subjectivity intimated throughout Jefferson's discourse on race and slavery (Nelson, 20; Simpson, "Ferocity of Self," 76). Since much of the self-reflective quality of the *Notes* inheres in Jefferson's writing about race, and especially about blackness, it was not surprising that Banneker, who "freely and Chearfully acknowledge[d]" to Jefferson "that I am of the African race, and, in that colour which is natural to them of the deepest dye" (153–154), would feel personally engaged by the *Notes*.

Benjamin Banneker was as proud of his freedom as he was of his race, and he made certain that Thomas Jefferson knew it. "I am not under that State of tyrannical thraldom, and inhuman captivity, to which too many of my brethren are doomed; . . . I have abundantly tasted of the fruition of those blessings which proceed from that free and unequalled liberty with which you are favoured," he informed Jefferson (154). Such a freeman would have strongly endorsed the *Notes*'s categorical condemnation of slavery as "this great political and moral evil" (*Notes*, 87). Jefferson's catalogue in Query XVIII of the *Notes* of the many evils attendant to slavery must have impressed Banneker, the son of a former slave. Perhaps Banneker heard Jefferson deprecating himself in the statement, "And with what execration should the statesman be loaded, who permitting one half the citizens thus to trample on the rights of the other, transforms those into despots, and these into enemies, destroys the morals of the one part, and the amor patriae of the other" (*Notes*, 162–63). More evidence of Jefferson's antislavery feelings arose in his eloquently dire prophecy: "Indeed I tremble for my country when I reflect that God is just: that his justice cannot sleep for ever: that considering numbers, nature and natural means only, a revolution of the wheel of fortune, an exchange of situation, is among possible events: that it may become probable by supernatural interference! The Almighty has no attribute which can take side with us [whites] in such a contest" (163). If, as the culmination of Query XVIII stated, Jefferson sincerely hoped that "under the auspices of heaven" a "total emancipation" would come about "with the consent of the masters, rather than by their extirpation" (163), Banneker was prepared to offer his guidance toward that end, especially to a statesman who seemed anxious to rid his country and himself of the dreadful stigma of slaveholding.

The problem was that the author of the *Notes* seemed to throw up his hands in helplessness when he touched the nub of the issue: what, exactly, to do to rid Virginia of slavery? The issue, Jefferson worried, was too big, too complex, and too distressing for the white majority to face up to. "It is impossible to be temperate and to pursue this subject through the various considerations of policy, of morals, of history natural and civil. We must be contented to hope they will force their way into every one's mind" (163). What made it "impossible" for Jefferson to work out a rational mechanism for emancipating the slaves was not his affection for slavery, which he unequivocally condemned in Query XVIII as fatal to the American experiment in democracy and free government. What set Jefferson's intellect and psyche so uncharacteristically at odds with each other in this matter was his profoundly conflicted view of black people, who seemed to him on the one hand the undeserving victims of slavery, yet who on the other hand appeared to be incapable of appreciating the benefits of liberty.

In Query XIV of the *Notes*, entitled "Laws," Jefferson conducts a quasi-anthropological comparison of black people, American Indians, and white people as he has observed them. He finds black equality with whites in only a few areas, but most notably in "the heart," by which Jefferson meant the perception of "moral right and wrong" and the capacity to live accordingly. "We find among them [black people] numerous instances of the most rigid integrity, and as many as among their better instructed masters, of benevolence, gratitude, and unshaken fidelity" (143). Given Jefferson's observation on another occasion that "the general existence of a moral instinct" constitutes "the brightest gem with which the human character is studded" (*Writings*, vol. 5, 143), the quiet respect with which the *Notes* characterized the African American conscience testifies to Jefferson's ability to rise above the racial prejudices rife among eighteenth-century whites, North and South, who interpreted blackness as nature's mark of the Negro's baseness and wickedness (Jordan, 257–8, Davis, *Problem of Slavery*, 447–49). On the matter of the equal moral perspicacity of whites and blacks, Jefferson did indeed write like a man of liberal outlook and open mind, at least when compared to the vast majority of thinkers about race in his era.[5] But the moral instinct exists in balance with the mental faculties, Jefferson believed (Scheick, 225–26), and the latter had the task of regulating the former in every person. With regard to "the faculties of reason and imagination," black people gave little evidence, as far as Jefferson was concerned, of their having reached that standard of rational self-regulation that white Americans pronounced as their peculiar qualification for freedom.[6] Jefferson cited Phillis Wheatley, the first internationally recognized African American writer, as proof of his contention that a black might be inspired by religious fervor, but could not, or at least had not, produced intellectually sophisticated poetry. On this basis he dismissed Wheatley's verse as "below the dignity of criticism" (140). Similarly, Jefferson granted "strong religious zeal" to the writing of Ignatius Sancho, a British nobleman's servant who was born on a slave ship and whose witty letters had been published posthumously in 1782. Nevertheless, the heart-felt sentiments of Sancho's letters lacked "restraint of reason and taste"; they "do more honour to the heart than the head" (140). Of blacks in general Jefferson concluded: "never yet could I find that a black had uttered a thought above the level of plain narration; never see even an elementary trait of painting or sculpture" (140). By contrast, "among the Romans, their slaves were often their rarest artists. They excelled too in science, insomuch as to be usually employed as tutors to their master's children. Epictetus, Diogenes, Phaedon, Terence, and Phaedrus, were slaves. But they were of the race of whites" (142). Hence, Jefferson's conclusion about black people: "It is not their condition then, but nature, which has produced the distinction" between them and white people, a distinction most obviously manifest in white superiority "in the endowments of the head" (142).

If this had been the sum total of Jefferson's commentary on black people's capacities in *Notes on the State of Virginia*, Banneker would have had no basis for supposing the Virginian "far less inflexible" than other whites when it came to deciding whether blacks were, in Banneker's words, "capable of mental endowments." But another vein ran through Jefferson's discourse on blacks and whites, which traced apparently racial differences to the environment of each race rather than to its inbred "nature." "It will be right," Jefferson observed in Query XIV, "to make great allowances for the difference of condition, of education, of conversation, of the sphere in which they [African Americans] move" (139). In particular, "that disposition to theft with which they have been branded, must be ascribed to their situation, and not to any depravity of the moral sense. The man, in whose favour no laws of property exist, probably feels himself less bound to respect those made in favour of others. . . . That a change in the relations in which a man is placed should change his ideas of moral right and wrong, is neither new, nor peculiar to the colour of the blacks" (142).

Once he had postulated the moral equality of black and white people in the realm of the heart, Jefferson felt obliged to back away from his awarding of "natural" intellectual superiority to whites, which he had proposed earlier in Query XIV. "The opinion, that they [black people] are inferior in the faculties of reason and imagination, must be hazarded with great diffidence," Jefferson warned. "To justify a general conclusion, requires many observations," he continued, invoking the scientific method (143). A judgment that "would degrade a whole race of men from the rank in the scale of beings which their Creator may perhaps have given them" could not be made rashly. "I advance it therefore as a suspicion only, that the blacks, whether originally a distinct race, or made distinct by time and circumstances, are inferior to the whites in the endowments both of body and mind" (143).

Although a "suspicion" was closer to a prejudice than a hypothesis, Banneker probably regarded remarks of this sort in the *Notes* as reason enough to hope that Jefferson had not closed his mind to argument and evidence on racial matters. But as Jefferson's most recent critics have pointed out, although he could assume scientific objectivity when speaking of the American Indian as potentially improvable enough to intermix with whites, he could maintain no such equanimity when he trained his mind's eye on African Americans, whose very color repelled him[7].

Lacking "the fine mixtures of red and white" evident in the color of his own race, blackness in Jefferson's gaze betokened the presence of an unnerving "eternal monotony," an "immovable veil of black which covers all the emotions of the other race," thus rendering them not only alien, but disturbingly unknowable (*Notes*, 138).[8] Remarkably, although Banneker made certain that Jefferson knew of his pride in his race and color, his letter does not signal offense over the white man's projection of his own guilty fears onto the black man. Ignoring this side of Jefferson, Banneker addressed the man who refused dogmatically to ascribe blackness as nature's imprint of inferiority, who seemed to be open to, indeed asking for, more convincing evidence of the Negro's intellectual capacity and achievements.

This Jefferson, the scientist and objective seeker of new knowledge, the man "far less inflexible" in his racial attitudes than most of his white countrymen, Banneker hoped to influence by presenting him with a tangible demonstration of African American intellectual sophistication: "a copy of an Almanack which I have calculated for the Succeeding year" (156). This almanac, the first in a series that Banneker published annually from 1791 to 1796 (Bedini, 379–384), was not just another compendium of weather predictions, domestic lore, farming advice, practical wisdom, and popular journalism got up to satisfy a substantial American market for almanacs, such as those that helped to make famous Benjamin Franklin's Poor Richard. *Benjamin Banneker's Pennsylvania, Delaware, Maryland, and Virginia Almanack and Ephemeries, for the Year of Our Lord, 1792* featured *the Motions of the Sun and Moon, the true Places and Aspects of the Planets, the Rising and Setting of the Sun, and the Rising, Setting and Southing, Place and Age of the Moon, &c.*, in other words, a completely calculated ephemeris done entirely by Banneker himself. This was a notable mathematical achievement for anyone in the United States. It was an unprecedented accomplishment for a black man in a slaveholding state.

As if to underline his intellectual credentials, Banneker represented himself to Jefferson as a self-reliant autodidact. "Having long had unbounded desires to become Acquainted with the Secrets of nature, I have had to gratify my curiosity herein thro my own assiduous application to Astronomical Study, in which I need not to recount to you the many difficulties and disadvantages which I have had to encounter" (156). The black astronomer went on to apprize Jefferson pointedly of the fact that a Philadelphia printer wanted to publish his almanac. These comments show Banneker building a case for common intellectual ground with Jefferson as both a scientist and an author. Yet a black astronomer and mathematician in eighteenth-century America could go only so far before he had to concede to a suspicion that informed not only Jefferson's but the larger culture's thinking with regard to black "endowments of body and mind." "You may have the opportunity of perusing it [the Almanac] after its publication," Banneker assured Jefferson, "yet I chose to sent it to you in manuscript previous thereto, that thereby you might not only have an earlier inspection, but that you might also view it in my own hand writing" (156).

With this remark Banneker acknowledged his awareness that unless he sent Jefferson a manuscript copy of the almanac in his own hand, his claim to authorship would be open to doubt. As Henry Louis Gates, Jr., has shown, European philosophers such as Hume, Kant, and Hegel had taught thinkers of the American Enlightenment that Africa signified its absence of cultural and historical self-consciousness in its failure to develop the arts of writing (*Figures*, 25–28). Predispositions against accepting the genuineness of black creativity, particularly when it was expressed through literacy and authorship, had compounded Wheatley's effort to publish her *Poems on Miscellaneous Subjects* in 1773. She had been subjected to an oral examination from a committee of white Bostonians intent on discerning whether she could prove herself the author of her own book (Wheatley, "To the Publick," *Poems*, no pag.). Bowing to white American culture's demand for such proofs must have galled Banneker. But he said nothing to Jefferson about it. Perhaps the black man reflected on the inherent duplicity of any exchange of scientific evidence that proceeded from an assumption that one scientist had the right to question the integrity, as well as the intelligence, of the other simply because the latter was of a different and suspiciously inferior color. Perhaps it was resentment over being put into this supplicating position, even as he attempted to affirm commonality with Jefferson on higher scientific ground, that accounts for Banneker's failure—or refusal—to press the argument represented by his gift of a manuscript copy of his almanac and ephemeris.

Implicit in the gift, of course, was its creator's claim to individual intellectual recognition on a par with that of white scientists of his era. By inference, the almanac should also have signified the right of African Americans to be viewed as comparably intellectually endowed with American whites. But Banneker made no such claims. He constructed his letter in such a way that the gift of the almanac came almost as an afterthought, postponed until Banneker could unburden himself of something that was closer to his heart than his own desire for recognition and respect. He would be content to leave implicit his personal claim to intellectual equality with whites in order to make urgently explicit his enslaved brothers and sisters' moral claim to political equality with the white citizenry of the newly freed and independent United States.

At the heart of Banneker's letter to Jefferson was the black man's determination to press the white statesman toward a personal engagement with the morality of the enslavement of African Americans in the freshly constituted United States. Despite its recommendation of scientific open-mindedness with regard to race and environment, despite its denunciation of slavery as subversive of democracy, *Notes on the State of Virginia* did not provide Banneker the terms he needed to move from the head to the heart, from the intellect to the conscience, in confronting this evil. The predominantly rational (and rationalizing) tone of the *Notes* allowed Jefferson to speculate about African American difference as though it were merely a "subject of natural history" that required contemplation "with the eye of philosophy" (*Notes*, 143). Even when the gaze of the philosopher failed him and he conjured up visions of white degeneration and black revolution as a consequence of slavery, Jefferson still shrank from moral decisiveness. To push the white man toward genuine accountability for slavery and for the means of its destruction, Banneker resolved to compel the tentative, temporizing author of the *Notes* to answer to the bold, self-assured human rights idealist who wrote the *Declaration of Independence*. Jefferson, in effect, would be thrust into a dialogue with himself.

"Sir," Banneker announced, "Suffer me to recall to your mind that time in which the Arms and tyranny of the British Crown were exerted with every power-ful effort, in order to reduce you to a State of Servitude" (154). Thomas Jefferson reduced to slavery? Though the notion may sound absurd today, Banneker was by no means exaggerating. Since the 1750s a generation of American agitators, Jefferson prominent among them, had labored to stir up the passions of their white coun-trymen by accusing the British King of treating them, "freeborn Englishmen," as though they were an alien breed of contemptible slaves (Foner, 439–440). As more than one intellectual historian has shown, slavery was the standard metaphor of revolutionary America's political discourse whenever the egregious relationship of the colonies to England was broached (Robinson, 60–65). The idea that Ameri-cans were in danger of falling under the control of an arbitrary power that con-nived to wrest away their just property and their abstract rights "appears in every statement of political principle, in every discussion of constitutionalism or legal rights, in every exhortation to resistance," from Massachusetts to Georgia (Bailyn, 232–33). A year before the *Declaration of Independence*, a Continental Congress had drawn up a resolution of "the Causes and Necessity for Taking up Arms" against England, based in the representatives' determination "to die freemen rather than live slaves" (Jensen, 847). The *Declaration* of 1776 did not go so far as to call the King an outright enslaver of the American colonies, although if Jefferson had had his way George III would have been publicly branded the premier Atlantic slave trafficker and the American colonists the unfortunate victims of his lust for hu-man flesh.[9] Instead, the final edited version of Jefferson's *Declaration* presented the American colonies' grievances against George III as a morality play in which "a FREE people" had been compelled to defend their "inalienable right" to liberty against the depredations of a "tyrant" bent on placing them "under absolute despotism" (Jefferson, *Life*, 22). But in the summer of 1774 in what one biographer calls "his first major political statement" (Randall, 211), Jefferson had portrayed the Crown's policy toward the colonies as nothing less than "a deliberate, systematical plan of reducing us to slavery" (Jefferson, *Life*, 290). These incendiary words had been published later that year in *A Summary View of the Rights of British America*, which quickly became one of the most widely read pamphlets of the revolutionary era.

The blatant, self-serving hypocrisy of this appropriation of slavery by middle- and upper-class white revolutionaries, many of whom were themselves slaveowners, could not have been lost on a free man of color. What Banneker remembered of white America's pre-revolutionary rhetoric of resistance to enslavement he was determined that Jefferson should not conveniently forget. "This, Sir, was a time in which you clearly saw into the injustice of a State of Slavery, and in which you had Just apprehensions of the horrors of its condition" (154). "It was now Sir, that your abhorrence thereof was so excited, that you publickly held forth this true and

invaluable doctrine, which is worthy to be recorded and remembered in all Succeeding ages. 'We hold these truths to be Self evident, that all men are created
equal, and that they are endowed by their creator with certain inalienable rights,
that amongst these are life, liberty, and the persuit of happiness'" (154–55).

This re-evocation of the occasion of the *Declaration* was designed to jostle
Jefferson into a historical consciousness that Banneker felt was sorely lacking in
white southern revolutionaries now safely ensconced in their own independence.
The implicit aim of the *Declaration* had been, as Lewis Simpson states, "the creation of a modern secular state in the image of the rational, lettered, free mind"
("The Ideology of Revolution," 63). The willed secularism of Jefferson's view of
the American state had freed it from royal domination and from traditional European justifications for hierarchy as the divinely sanctioned blueprint for political
order. Sweeping away these historical and religious norms, the American Revolution instituted (as Jefferson's *Notes* implicitly acknowledged) a society that found
its reason for existence and its ordering principle in "the rational, sovereign self's
will to freedom" (Simpson, "Ferocity of Self," 75). What troubled Banneker, however, was the quickness with which post-revolutionary white Americans construed
their "inalienable rights" of "life, liberty, and the pursuit of happiness" without
reference to the *Declaration*'s stated origin of those rights in "their creator." One
reason for reciting to Jefferson his revolutionary generation's former abhorrence
of slavery was to remind the inventor of the modern secular state that (to use
Jefferson's own terms in the *Declaration*) neither "the laws of nature" nor "of nature's
god" could be made to justify the corporate selective memory that, in the post-
Constitutional era, was steadily divorcing white America's claim to freedom from
the Creator's endowment of such rights in "all men."[10]

Banneker's reiteration of the most famous sentence Jefferson ever wrote registered the black man's anxiety about what Winthrop Jordan has called "the secu-
larization of equality" in the politics of late–eighteenth-century North America.
Although at the time of the Revolution "the concept of natural rights was still
suffused with religious feeling," and "the right to religious liberty was normally
spoken of as God's gratuitous gift to mankind," by the end of the century "an
intellectual shift of major proportions" had rendered God's role in the revolutionary enterprise increasingly peripheral (Jordan, 294). This shift toward "a political,
even legalistic, conception of proper social relations" between persons in the new
republic could be helpful to those who asserted the brotherhood of humankind
not only in the hereafter but also in their "natural" condition on earth. Nevertheless, "*by itself* this legalistic view of men afforded dangerously weak leverage against
such a massive institution as Negro slavery" (Jordan, 295; emphasis added). It was
possible simply to argue that slaves, as unsocialized beings occupying the margins
of the new sociolegal order, had no claim to the rights of those who defined freedom in accordance with their prior membership in that order (295).[11]

Responding to these trends, Banneker's antislavery thesis reinvoked a presumed pre-Revolutionary balance between political imperative and moral obligation implicit in the *Declaration*'s linkage of "the laws of nature" and of "nature's

god." Re-historicizing the colonies' victory over the British empire, the black man found the outcome of the Revolution so unlikely as to point to a supernatural moral principle decisively at work. Reflect on "the variety of dangers to which you were exposed" during the Revolution, Banneker urged Jefferson, when "every human aide appeared unavailable," and "you cannot but be led to a Serious and grateful Sense of your miraculous and providential preservation" (154). Indeed, "you cannot but acknowledge, that the present freedom and tranquillity which you enjoy you have mercifully received, and that it is the peculiar blessing of Heaven" (154). Summoning up the idea of American exceptionalism nascent in this notion of freedom as the "peculiar blessing of Heaven" gave Banneker what he needed to argue that Jefferson and his white revolutionary compatriots had become eligible for liberty not through legalistic or political means (or because they had declared themselves worthy of it on July 4, 1776), but because they had done God's work in history.

Readers of today may be bothered by Banneker's invocation of the myth of American exceptionalism to explain the success of the Revolution of 1776. But Banneker seems to have been convinced that the only way to reclaim the antislavery ideals of the Revolution from the laissez-faire ideology of the Constitution was to treat the victory of the colonies as a manifestation of God's moral investment in the politics of freedom. If the Creator awarded freedom to the colonies because Jefferson's document had declared their dedication to those rights which the Creator had endowed in all humankind, then the colonies, once liberated, had a peculiarly moral as well as political obligation: to extend "the blessing" of freedom to those who continued to suffer under "the injustice of a State of Slavery" (154).

Banneker's moral reading of the Revolution and of the key human rights passage in the *Declaration of Independence* ushered in the first influential revisionist reading of Jefferson's text in African American literature.[12] The black writer's central point—that freedom incurred a moral obligation to others even as it conferred a political opportunity on the self—spoke directly to the delicate balance in the *Declaration* between freedom for the individual and equality among the social group. For Banneker, as for more famous antislavery heroes such as Douglass and Lincoln, linking freedom to equality meant empowering politics with religion in such a way that the national myth of America could only be justified and fulfilled by a firm adherence to the universal doctrine of human brotherhood.[13] No people whose freedom was contingent on their having become "fully convinced of the benevolence of the Father of mankind, and of his equal and impartial distribution of those rights and privileges which he had conferred upon them [mankind]" could renege on their moral debt, Banneker warned Jefferson (155). In his capacity as Secretary of State, therefore, as well as author of the *Declaration*, Jefferson had a special duty to the nation. To countenance a retreat from the equalitarian responsibility of freedom would be to perpetrate a hypocrisy more outrageous than the arrogance that let George III treat the American colonists as fit candidates for "a State of Servitude."

The urgency of Banneker's convictions about Jefferson's and America's moral responsibility to freedom intensified his tone and personalized his manner of address as the black man pushed toward the climax of his antislavery argument. Jefferson the Secretary of State, hitherto treated with propriety in accordance with the dignity of his office, gives way to a new Jefferson, the slaveholder, toward whom Banneker the gentlemanly interlocutor, the celebrator of America's moral mission, turns aggressively in a new posture, that of the prosecutor. Not once, not twice, but three times in successive paragraphs Banneker rehearses how eloquently and touchingly the Virginian had championed liberty before the Revolution, when his own welfare had been jeopardized. After the third rendition of Jefferson's past devotion to the cause of freedom, Banneker can no longer contain the bitter irony of it all: "Here, Sir, was a time in which your tender feelings [one can almost hear the dramatic pause] *for your selves* engaged you thus to declare, you were then impressed with proper ideas of the great valuation of liberty" (155, emphasis added). The unabashed sarcasm of Banneker's reference to "your tender feelings for your selves" warns of the moral coup de grace that the black man, no longer humbly deferential, is poised to deliver. "But Sir how pitiable is it to reflect, that altho you were so fully convinced of the benevolence of the Father of mankind, and of his equal and impartial distribution of those rights and privileges which he had conferred upon them, that you should at the Same time counteract his mercies, in *detaining by fraud and violence so numerous a part of my brethren under groaning captivity and cruel oppression*, that you should at the Same time be found *guilty of that most criminal act, which you professedly detested in others, with respect to yourselves*" (emphasis added, 155).

With this statement—or rather, indictment—Benjamin Banneker deliberately transgressed southern caste decorum, going well beyond accusing the Virginia aristocrat of arrant hypocrisy. By repeating the phrase "at the Same time" and twice capitalizing "Same," Banneker created a homology between the slavery Jefferson opposed in George III and the slavery Jefferson himself practiced in his own personal life as a slaveholder. Thus from the black man's morally egalitarian perspective, American revolutionary and British tyrant were one. Jefferson the slaveholder was as guilty as George III of "cruel oppression," of "fraud and violence," of rank, indefensible criminality. Jefferson's moral degradation from apostle of freedom to slaveholding tyrant might be "pitiable," but it remained a disgrace both individually and collectively (hence the references to "your selves") to the new Republic's corporate self-image as the land of the free. Such an attack on the personal as well as political integrity of a major white American hero by a black man was unprecedented in American as well as southern history.[14] No African American, free or slave, could have made these charges face to face or in a public forum in the South without taking a significant risk. Banneker got away with it, in effect, because he chose to upbraid Jefferson through a letter, a means uniquely suited to bridging the chasms of southern caste that kept black people's voices separate and largely unheard by the southern elite, except on its own terms. Through a letter, which required no access to or acceptance by the white-controlled publishing media, a southern man of color could make his presence felt, quite literally, in places where he himself could never enter, let alone be allowed to speak. He could confront a southern white man frankly and personally and still keep a safe distance. He could privately challenge a white southerner's integrity without publicly insulting his honor.

The logic of Banneker's case against Jefferson led inevitably, it would seem, to a demand that the white man acknowledge his hypocrisies and demonstrate his true dedication to freedom and equality by first emancipating his own slaves and then marshalling his political power to bring about the "total emancipation" he had called for in the *Notes*. Surprisingly, however, Banneker required nothing explicit or immediate from Jefferson in response to his own complicity in slavery. Almost as surprising as Banneker's daring indictment of Jefferson was his subsequent refusal to "presume to prescribe methods" by which the white leader was to right the wrongs he had done to enslaved African Americans in particular and to the cause of freedom in general. Instead, the black prosecutor donned a minister's robes, counseling Jefferson "as Job proposed to his friends 'Put your Souls in their [the slaves'] Souls' stead." "Thus shall your hearts be enlarged with kindness and benevolence towards them, and thus shall you need neither the direction of myself or others in what manner to proceed herein" (155).

Did Banneker really think that having brought Jefferson to justice, he could trust the white man to decide how best to serve his sentence? Was Banneker's unwillingness to seize the moral advantage he had claimed over Jefferson in the climax of his letter due to his naivete? Or did he truly worry that to dictate moral behavior to so powerful a white man was one freedom *not* allowable to a black man in the slaveholding South in 1791? It may be that Banneker's reticence stemmed from a belief that Jefferson already knew well enough how to dispose of slavery (in an appendix to the *Notes* Jefferson had proposed a scheme for abolition in Virginia by the end of 1799),[15] so that further directives toward this end were unneeded. Even more likely, given the moral and religious basis on which his letter's critique of Jefferson is founded, Banneker probably felt that the most important thing he could do as an individual black man confronting an individual white man was to impress upon the slaveholder the fact of his inalienable common humanity with black people, even those he held as chattel. In this respect, Banneker was following an already established practice of the late–eighteenth-century antislavery movement, as epitomized in its widely-known emblem of a manacled slave in a supplicant posture with an underlying inscription, "Am I Not a Man and a Brother?" (Andrews, 1, 47, 61–62). The key thing to note about Banneker's plea for the brotherhood of "Souls" between black folk and white folk, however, is that his letter did not abide by the rhetoric of supplication, except as a gambit. Instead Banneker staked out a middle ground where the mind and the heart, intellectual analysis and moral evaluation, freedom and equality, could be brought into a balanced perspective on racial difference, independent of the established parameters of social hierarchy and caste privilege.

In the junction on the color line that Banneker carefully engineered through his letter, he neither allowed Jefferson his accustomed priority nor claimed it, ultimately, for himself. He spoke instead in Jefferson's own language of the self-evident truth of their equality before their creator and history. He warned Jefferson of the indefensible moral equivalence of his position vis-a-vis his slaves and that of George III vis-à-vis the North American colonies. But Banneker closed by underlining what he shared with Jefferson—faith in humanity's God-given capacity to liberate itself from mental and moral enslavement. Then Banneker witnessed to that faith by leaving the Virginian to the direction of his own "enlarged heart" and conscience in his future dealings with slavery.

Four days after he received Banneker's letter and the copy of his almanac, Jefferson responded to both in a brief letter from his Philadelphia office on August 30, 1791. The Secretary of State thanked the Maryland astronomer, avowing, "No body wishes more than I do to see such proofs as you exhibit, that nature has given to our black brethren, talents equal to those of the other colors of men, and that the appearance of a want of them is owing merely to the degraded condition of their existence, both in Africa & America" (*Writings*, V, 377). Doubtless Banneker was encouraged to see Jefferson refer to the almanac as a "proof" of a notion advanced only tentatively in the *Notes*, namely, that apparent differences between the races derived from their condition, not from an unequal distribution of abilities from nature. In speaking of "our black brethren," Jefferson also seemed to be taking a step forward toward the middle ground of common humanity to which Banneker's letter had invited him.

Turning to the vexed matter of what to do about "the degraded condition" of African Americans, the white man assured his black correspondent: "no body wishes more ardently to see a good system commenced for raising the condition both of their body & mind to what it ought to be, as fast as the imbecility of their present existence, and other circumstances which cannot be neglected, will admit" (377–78). This statement required more than a little decoding. Jefferson seemed to be ready to endorse a change in the condition of black people, but he also had reservations that raised doubts as to how and to what extent such a change could be effected. What "ought to be" the proper condition of African Americans, mentally and materially, in the United States? Jefferson offered no hint of the norm he felt should be applied. Who or what was responsible for "the imbecility of their present existence"? Jefferson skirted this moral issue even as he left ambiguous the antecedent of "their." Was he referring to the "imbecility" of the slaves' condition or to that of African Americans in general? The veiled reference to "other circumstances which cannot be neglected" envisioned any number of additional difficulties, if not outright impediments, to efforts to raise the condition of African Americans.[16] Was it significant that even as he talked about "raising the condition" of black Americans, the Virginia slaveholder did not mention emancipation specifically as a "good system" of effecting that goal?

In this ambiguous sentence, which balanced a statement of liberal sentiments with a set of questions and contingencies that carefully hedged the writer's commitment to enacting those sentiments, Jefferson said all he was going to say to Banneker about the key issue raised in the black man's letter, i.e., the white man's obligation to the moral and political ideal of freedom. The Secretary of State took no notice whatever of the freeman's challenge to his conscience over the matter of his individual moral responsibility for slaveholding and slave liberation. This crucial silence in Jefferson's reply to Banneker signaled the white man's retreat from the junction on the color line that at the beginning of his letter he seemed to be reaching for. It was as though Jefferson's mind had opened, and his heart desired, but his conscience felt no compulsion to find a way to act. He was prepared, intellectually at least, to embrace the "proofs" of human equality that Banneker's example represented. His heart "ardently" longed to see a means of elevating black Americans out of their degradation. But he stopped short of acknowledging to Banneker any moral necessity to move beyond thinking and hoping, beyond gathering evidence and desiring change. Instead of joining Banneker in a common effort to articulate a morally and socially viable ideal of human liberty and equality, Jefferson opted instead to act as the freeman's intellectual patron, offering him what he never asked for—the promotion of his personal reputation as a black scientist.

"I have taken the liberty," Jefferson announced, winding up his letter on a note of personal support, "of sending your Almanac to Monsieur de Condorcet, Secretary of the Academy of Sciences at Paris, and member of the Philanthropic society, because I considered it as a document to which your whole colour had a right for their justification against the doubts which have been entertained of them" (378). This gesture may well have gratified Banneker. But in proclaiming the black astronomer an intellectual prodigy to a skeptical white world, Jefferson was also muffling the fundamental motive of Banneker's letter, which was not self-advertisement for an individual intellectual but moral activism on behalf of an oppressed people. Assuring the black man of his "great esteem," Jefferson closed his letter by subscribing himself "your most obedt humble servt" (378). The courtesy of this closing, albeit conventional, echoed the phrasing Banneker had adopted in his closing to Jefferson,[17] and seemed to put the white man at the freeman's disposal. But Banneker could hardly mistake the fact that Jefferson was offering his services to Banneker as a scientist-mentor, not a partner in the cause of emancipation.

Jefferson made good on his promise to Banneker to send news of his achievement to Condorcet, one of the most influential *philosophes* in the foremost society of scientific learning in France. In his letter to Condorcet, the Virginian represented Banneker as a boon to scientific progress and enlightenment on the racial front, causes with which Jefferson took some pains to identify himself: "I am happy to be able to inform you that we have now in the United States a negro . . . who is a very respectable mathematician. . . . he made an Almanac for the next year, which he sent me in his own hand writing, & which I inclose to you. I have seen very elegant solutions of Geometrical problems by him. Add to this that he is a very worthy & respectable member of society. He is a free man. I shall be delighted to see these instances of moral eminence so multiplied as to prove that the want of talents observed in them is merely the effect of their degraded condition, and not proceeding from any difference in the structure of the parts on which intellect depends" (*Writings*, V, 379). In these remarks Jefferson reiterated the liberal sentiments he articulated to Banneker, although to a white man he would not go so far as to say Banneker's case was a "proof" of racial equality, only that such cases, sufficiently "multiplied," could ultimately provide a proof.

No one knows how Banneker reacted to the letter Jefferson sent him or to the information that the Virginian had transmitted the almanac to Condorcet. We do know that Banneker felt strongly enough about his letter to Jefferson and Jefferson's reply that he contemplated publishing them as a preface to his first almanac (Bedini, 168). When it came out in Baltimore in late December 1791 or early January 1792 (Bedini, 174), however, Banneker's almanac did not contain the correspondence, the printer having decided instead to publish as an afterword a letter from a well-known Maryland antislavery figure, U.S. Senator James McHenry. In his letter, McHenry went well beyond Jefferson, concluding from Banneker's intellectual attainments that whites and blacks shared a common origin and hence were equal in intellectual capacity, and that such evidence as the almanac provided would spur "the progress of humanity, which, meliorating the condition of slavery, necessarily leads to its final extinction" (Bedini, 181). Perhaps McHenry's linkage of Banneker's individual achievement to the extinction of slavery was sufficiently straightforward that the almanac-maker himself was content to postpone the publication of his exchange of correspondence with Jefferson. In any case, the exchange was made public within the year in a Philadelphia pamphlet and in two northern magazines, and in the 1793 edition of *Benjamin Banneker's Almanack*.[18]

During the next half-century Banneker's achievement and significance to the cause of antislavery and civil rights in the United States spread widely. In the South as well as the North, in England as well as the United States, the reputation of the African American intellectual from Maryland flourished. Members of the Maryland Society for Promoting the Abolition of Slavery heard Banneker praised publicly as early as 1791 (Bedini, 386). Sketches of his life and work circulated in the Maryland Historical Society and found their way into print early in the nineteenth century, becoming the bases for accounts of Banneker in venues as politically divergent as the *Maryland Colonization Journal* and the *Southern Literary Messenger* on the one hand and Bishop Henri Gregoire's *De la litterature des Negres* (1808), Wilson Armistead's *A Tribute for the Negro* (1848), and William G. Allen's *Wheatley, Banneker, Horton* (1849) on the other.[19] These and other antebellum efforts to publicize Banneker's intellectual feats usually highlighted his antislavery letter to Jefferson, prompting one historian of early African American literature to conclude that "perhaps no other protest against slavery written by an early Negro was so often used as antislavery propaganda down to the time of the Civil War" (Loggins, 39).[20]

More than one southern political contemporary denounced Jefferson for his dialogue with Banneker once the record of their exchange became generally known. Congressman William Loughton Smith of South Carolina wondered about a Secretary of State "thus fraternizing with negroes, writing them complimentary epistles, stiling them *his black brethren*, congratulating them on the evidences of their *genius*, and assuring them of his good wishes for their speedy emancipation" (Bedini, 280). Another South Carolina political adversary, Henry William De Saussure, fulminated against Jefferson's reply to Banneker, charging that it disclosed the Virginian's covert sympathies with abolitionism (Jordan, 452). Such reactionary readings of the Banneker-Jefferson exchange did not bode well for future literary junctions on the southern color line, especially for white men like Jefferson who wanted to pursue public careers. Enduring these attacks stoically, Jefferson learned never again to leave himself so exposed on the increasingly volatile issues of race and slavery.

Maybe it was exasperation over the way his personal dialogue with a black man had been politicized by both antislavery and proslavery factions that soured Jefferson's memory of Banneker later in his life. Perhaps as he got older and the South's commitment to slavery hardened, Jefferson felt freer to voice a skepticism about black potential and achievement that he had long harbored, though would not commit to print after the *Notes*. In any event, in the fall of 1809 after receiving from Bishop Gregoire a copy of his *De la litterature des Negres*, Jefferson unburdened himself of his final judgment of Banneker and of efforts such as Gregoire's to exploit the record of accomplished blacks like the Maryland astronomer as an argument for their human rights. This time Jefferson's correspondent was a white political confidant, Joel Barlow, with whom the Virginian felt comfortable airing his impatience with zealous racial liberals like Gregoire. "I believe him a very good man," Jefferson said of the Frenchman, "with imagination enough to declaim eloquently, but without judgment to decide. He wrote to me also on the doubts I had expressed five or six and twenty years ago, in the Notes of Virginia, as to the grade of understanding of the negroes, and he sent me his book on the literature of the negroes. His credulity has made him gather up every story he could find of men of color. . . . The whole do not amount, in point of evidence, to what we know ourselves of Banneker. We know he had spherical trigonometry enough to make almanacs, but not without the suspicion of aid from Ellicot, who was his neighbor and friend,[21] and never missed an opportunity of puffing him. I have a long letter from Banneker, which shows him to have had a mind of very common stature indeed. As to Bishop Gregoire, I wrote him, as you have done, a very soft answer. It was impossible for doubt to have been more tenderly or hesitatingly expressed than that was in the Notes of Virginia, and nothing was or is farther from my intentions, than to enlist myself as the champion of a fixed opinion, where I have only expressed a doubt" (*Writings*, IX, 261–62).

We may wonder if this dismissal of Banneker represents what Jefferson really felt all along about the Maryland freeman who had had the temerity to upbraid him about the hypocrisy of his position vis-à-vis slavery. Were the liberal sentiments and scientific open-mindedness of Jefferson's letters to Banneker and Condorcet merely a mask, carefully managed expressions of the politic, self-protective "very soft answer" that the master of Monticello sent to the importunate French bishop? Were the encouraging words and professed appetite for further data in the letters to Banneker, Condorcet, and Gregoire calculated not only to conceal Jefferson's deep-seated "suspicion" of black intellectual capacity but also to postpone forever the necessity of his ultimately having to take some sort of public stand on the matter? Perhaps it was convenient for Jefferson to keep the jury out, as this would forestall his ever having to render another public judgment on racial equality or slavery.

To paraphrase Jefferson, it is impossible to entertain a "fixed opinion" about this, though we are entitled to "express a doubt" as to whether Jefferson ever wanted to make himself clear, assuming that he ever was clear himself about it. The political and moral justification that accrued to such deliberate indecision, however, does seem clear, especially for a white defender of the South and of its right to decide how and when to dispose of its peculiar institution—in other words, for Thomas Jefferson during the rest of his life (Miller, 247). Regardless of what he "really" thought about the likes of Benjamin Banneker, the sage of Monticello could and did maintain, with absolute scientific equanimity, that with regard to race as far as the white South was concerned, a true intellectual liberal would have to be a social conservative. Dialogues on race were welcome as long as decisions could be indefinitely deferred.

The need for such face-saving paradoxes as the liberal conservative, the slaveholding opponent of slavery, the human rights champion asking for proof of his own "self-evident truths" would steadily decline in the South after Jefferson's death in 1826. An increasingly unapologetic proslavery leadership rejected the relativism and straddling of the issue that many Revolutionary-era southerners had entertained (Faust, 9), declaring fealty instead to a nineteenth-century anthropology of racism whose "scientific" authority fixed black inferiority well beyond the "doubt" and "suspicion" that Jefferson hazarded (Fredrickson, 49–50, 70–74). That "science" would end up buttressing rather than undermining the South's entrenched racial hierarchies was an irony of history apparently unforeseen by Jefferson. A bigger unforeseen irony emerged from the abolition movement's attempt, led by the likes of William Lloyd Garrison, Theodore Parker, and John Quincy Adams, to rehabilitate Jefferson into "the prime mover of the antislavery movement" (Peterson, 171–72). Despite the glaring inconsistencies of Jefferson's private complicity with a system he publicly deplored, despite his doubts about black equality with whites, despite his support of emancipation only on condition of forced emigration (anathema to radical abolitionism), the reputation of Jefferson as an antislavery prophet thrived in the first half of the nineteenth century (Peterson, 188–89). An image of Jefferson as Banneker wished him to be—"far less inflexible" than his southern contemporaries on matters of race, "measurably friendly and well disposed towards us [black people]" (Bedini, 152)—was reinforced every time the story of the dialogue between the Virginia slaveholder and the Maryland freeman was retold. Thus the attention that this dialogue received in the antislavery press benefited not only Banneker as black intellectual exemplar; Jefferson, representing the white South's liberal tradition and incipient open-mindedness about race, also appeared to advantage. In dialogue together, the white man apparently primed to be convinced by the black man of racial equality and hence of the indefensibility of slavery, Jefferson and Banneker represented the fondest hope of those who wanted to believe that the problem of slavery could yet be ameliorated, and ultimately resolved, through a meeting of the minds.

NOTES

1. Banneker built his striking clock on his own after studying the construction of a friend's watch, an achievement that earned him a regional reputation as an intellectual and mechanical prodigy (Bedini, 43–44). As Mechal Sobel points out, Jefferson had a "passion for clocks," designed and oversaw their construction, and had them placed throughout his home at Monticello in an effort to ensure that everyone would be conscious of the proper use of time (57–59).

2. For biographical details about Banneker and for the text of his letter to Jefferson, I am indebted to Bedini's biography.

3. All references to Banneker's letter to Jefferson are taken from the version reprinted in Bedini's *Life of Benjamin Banneker*, pp. 152–57.

4. In 1770–1772, as a Virginia attorney, Jefferson tried to defend and further the rights of mixed-race clients. He attacked the international slave trade and condemned the King of England for its perpetuation in his 1774 pamphlet, *A Summary View of the Rights of British America*, and in his draft of the *Declaration of Independence*. Shortly after the adoption of the *Declaration of Independence* he drafted a constitution for the state of Virginia that stipulated the gradual abolition of slavery, although the legislature did not approve it. In 1778 Jefferson successfully saw into law a bill in the Virginia legislature that prohibited the further importation of slaves into the state. See Miller, 5–8, 16–18, 21–22; *Life and Selected Writings*, 40, 51.

5. An early American thinker more prepared than Jefferson to recognize African American mental and moral equality with whites was Benjamin Rush, author of an *Address to the Inhabitants of the British Settlements in America upon Slave-Keeping* (Philadelphia, 1773).

6. As Ronald Takaki has demonstrated, Jefferson basically agreed with his colleagues among the American nation builders on the predication of republican freedom on individual rational and virtuous self-control. Without an external authority such as the British King to preside over them, the new American democrats called for individual self-regulation to keep the passions under the surveillance of the reason. What distinguished nonwhite peoples from Anglo-Americans was the failure of African Americans and American Indians to manage their instinctual life in a way that qualified them for full admission into the democratic experiment (9–15). See also Winthrop Jordan's discussion of the early American association of bodily color with emotional license and moral degeneracy (222–249) and Henry Louis Gates's review of efforts to combat this notion (*Figures*, 61–72).

7. For Jefferson's attitudes toward the American Indian vs. the African American, see Sheehan, Shuffelton, 273–74, Jordan, 478–81, Gossett, 42–43, and Takaki, 58–59.

8. For a discussion of the political implications of Jefferson's aesthetic critique of blackness, see Fliegelman, 192–94.

9. In Jefferson's well-known draft of the Declaration of Independence, he accused George III of waging "cruel war against human nature itself, violating its most sacred rights of life and liberty in the persons of a distant people who never offended him," a construction that, as Jay Fliegelman has noted, seems on first reading to refer to the American colonists, until one discovers, "captivating and carrying them into slavery in another hemisphere." This attack on George III as the king of the slave traders who bore direct

responsibility for the continuing existence of slavery and its attendant horrors in North America was not approved by the Continental Congress in the summer of 1776 and was not a part of the document published as the Declaration of Independence. See Jefferson, *Life*, 25; and Fliegelman, 140–43.

10. All quotations from *The Declaration of Independence* are taken from the version in Garry Wills's *Inventing America*, pp. 374–79.

11. Not only was it possible to make this argument that slaves were not eligible for freedom and independence until they "enter into a state of society"; as Jordan shows, such an argument was advanced and prevailed at the Virginia Convention of 1776 over the objection of George Mason, who maintained unequivocally that "all men are by nature equally free and independent." The "far-reaching implications" of predicating freedom on entrance into "a state of society" may not have "become truly apparent until after the Revolution," as Jordan submits, but observers such as Banneker could easily have predicted how such legalistic thinking could serve to postpone indefinitely African American claims to freedom and equality in the new republic.

12. In "Preface to Blackness," Henry Louis Gates, Jr., has shown how influential Jefferson's comments on African character in the *Notes* were on the development of a discourse on blackness in late–eighteenth- and early–nineteenth-century American, British, and European literature (46–48). The impact of the *Declaration of Independence* on African American literature of the eighteenth and nineteenth centuries has not been systematically examined as yet, although the influence of the Declaration as the justifying text of the Revolution of 1776 cannot be underestimated in its impact on the development of African American literature (Andrews, 14; Fishkin and Peterson, 193–195, Sundquist, 31–36).

13. See Garry Wills's discussion of Lincoln's evocation of the *Declaration of Independence* for both the prosecution of an antislavery Civil War and the idealization of America as a missionary state that promised, in Lincoln's words, "'that in due time the weights would be lifted from the shoulders of all men, that all should have an equal chance. This is the sentiment embodied in the *Declaration of Independence*'" (ix-xx).

14. Compare Phillis Wheatley's October 26, 1775 letter to George Washington, which prefaces her poem, "To His Excellency General Washington," in which the poet wishes the "Generalissimo of the armies of North America. . . all possible success in the great cause you are so generously engaged in" (*Poems*, 185), which is, according to the poem, leadership of "the land of freedom's heaven-defended race" (*Poems*, 146). In this letter from a black correspondent to a white Virginian, nothing is said about Washington's being a slaveholder, and no question is asked or implied about which race enjoys heaven's defense in "the land of freedom." In a 1774 letter Wheatley did express her impatience with the "absurdity" of slaveholding America's protests in the name of freedom, but her correspondent was the Mohegan Indian minister, Samson Occom (*Poems*, 177).

15. See Jefferson's "Draught of a Fundamental Constitution for the Commonwealth of Virginia, *Notes on the State of Virginia*, pp. 209–222, which forbids the introduction of slaves into the state "or the continuance of slavery beyond the generation which shall be living on the thirty-first day of December, one thousand eight hundred" (214). This was "the only definite record of a formal proposal by Jefferson for gradual emancipation," although in 1784 Jefferson also "urged Congress to exclude slaves from the Western territories" (Davis, *Was Jefferson an Authentic Enemy of Slavery?*, p. 8).

16. Among the "other circumstances which cannot be neglected" Jefferson may have referred to the question of how to compensate slaveowners for their emancipated human property, or the question of what to do with African Americans once emancipated. On the latter issue, Jefferson was quite explicit in the *Notes*: "Among the Romans emancipation required but one effort. The slave, when made free, might mix with, without staining the

blood of his master. But with us a second is necessary, unknown to history. When freed, he is to be removed beyond the reach of mixture" (143). For more on Jefferson's belief that emancipation and the expulsion of former slaves from the U.S. went hand in hand, see Miller, 60–64, 207.

17. Banneker's closing sentence to Jefferson was, "And now Sir, I shall conclude and Subscribe my Self with the most profound respect, Your most Obedient humble Servant Benjamin Banneker" (Bedini, 156).

18. See *Copy of a Letter from Benjamin Banneker, to the Secretary of State, with his Answer*. Philadelphia: David Lawrence, 1792; "Letter from the Famous Self-Taught AS-TRONOMER, BENJIMIN BANNEKER, a Black Man, to THOMAS JEFFERSON, Esq. Secretary of State, *Universal Asylum and Columbian Magazine*, 2 (October 1792), pp. 222–224; and "From a Virginia Newspaper to the Printer," *Providence Gazette and Country Journal*, November 3, 1792, p. 1. Bedini notes that Lawrence's pamphlet sold out its first edition and a reprint (187–88).

19. See John H. B. Latrobe, "Memoir of Benjamin Banneker, Read Before the Historical Society of Maryland," *Maryland Colonization Journal*, 2 (May 1845): 353–64; and Moncure Conway, "Bannaker [sic], The Black Astronomer," *Southern Literary Messenger* 23 (July 1856): 65–66. Banneker was also prominently featured in two internationally popular antislavery texts, Gregoire's *De la litterature des Negres, ou, Recherches sur leur facultes intellectuelles* (Paris, 1808) and Armistead's *A Tribute for the Negro* (Manchester, England 1848). William G. Allen's *Wheatley, Banneker, and Horton* (1849), a biographical anthology, represents the first effort by an African American scholar-activist to enlist Banneker's example in the service of antislavery and civil rights work.

20. One indication of Banneker's continuing importance and appeal is the popularity of the biography of him that Shirley Graham Du Bois authored for young readers in 1949 and the illustrated *Dear Benjamin Banneker* by Andrea Davis Pinkney, a Children's Book-of-the-Month Club featured selection in 1994.

21. Jefferson probably refers to George Ellicott, Banneker's neighbor and longtime friend, who encouraged and aided him in his study of astronomy (Bedini, 69–83).

Works Cited

Allen, William G. *Wheatley, Banneker, and Horton.* Boston: Daniel'iLaing, 1849.

Andrews, William L. *To Tell a Free Story: The First Century of Afro-American Autobiography, 1760-1865.* Urbana: U of Illinois P, 1986.

Armistead, Wilson. *A Tribute for the Negro.* Manchester: William Irwin, 1848.

Bailyn, Bernard. *The Ideological Origins of the American Revolution.* Cambridge, MA: Harvard U P, 1967.

Bedini, Silvio. *The Life of Benjamin Banneker.* New York: Scribner's, 1972.

Berlin, Ira. *Slaves Without Masters.* New York: Pantheon, 1974.

Conway, Moncure D. "Bannaker [sic], The Black Astronomer." *Southern Literary Messenger* 23 (July 1856): 65-66.

Davis, David Brion. *The Problem of Slavery in Western Culture.* Ithaca, NY: Cornell U P, 1966.

———. *Was Thomas Jefferson an Authentic Enemy of Slavery?* Oxford: Clarendon Press,1970.

Davis, Richard Beale. *Intellectual Life in Jefferson's Virginia, 1790-1830.* Chapel Hill: U of North Carolina P, 1964.

Diggins, John P. "Slavery, Race, and Equality: Jefferson and the Pathos of the Enlightenment." *American Quarterly* 28 (1976) : 206-228.

Du Bois, Shirley Graham. *Your Most Humble Servant.* New York: Julian Messner, 1949.

Dunn, Richard S. "Black Society in the Chesapeake 1776-1810" in *Slaavery and Freedom in the Age of the American Revolution,* ed. Ira Berlin and Ronald Hoffman. Charlottesville: U Press of Virginia, 1983, pp. 49-82.

Faust, Drew Gilpin, ed. *The Ideology of Slavery.* Baton Rouge: Louisiana State U P, 1981.

Fishkin, Shelley Fisher and Carla L. Peterson. "'We Hold These Truths, to Be Self-Evident': The Rhetoric of Frederick Dough s's Journalism." *Frederick Doualass: New Literary and Historical Essays.* Ed. Eric J. Sundquist. Cambridge: Cambridge UP, 1.990; pp. 189-204.

F.liegelman, Jay. *Declaring Independence.* Stanford: Stanford U P, 1993.

Foner,, Eric. "The Meaning of Freedom in the Age of Emancipation." *Journal of, American History* 81 (Sept. 1994): 435-460.

Frankln, John Hope and Alfred A. Moss, Jr. *From Slavery to Freedom: A History of African Americans.* 7th ed. New York: Knopf, 1994.

Frederickson, George M. *The Black Image in the White Mind.* New York: Harper & Row, 1971.

Gates, Henry Louis Jr. *Figures in Black.* New York: Oxford UP, 1985.

———. "Preface to Blackness: Text and Pretext." *Afro-American Literature: The Reconstruction of Instruction.* Ed. Dexter Fisher and Robert B. Stepto. New York: Modern Language Association, 1978, pp. 44-69.

Gregoire, Henri. *De la litterature des Negres, ou, Recherches sur leur facultes intellectuelles.* Paris: Chez Maradan, 1808.

Hubbell, Jay B. *The South in American Literature.* Durham, N.C.: Duke University Press, 1954.

Jefferson, Thomas. *The Life and Selected Writings of Thomas Jefferson.* Ed. Adrienne Koch and William Peden. New York: Random House, 1944.

———. *Notes on the State of Virginia.* Ed. William Peden. New York: Norton, 1972.

———. *The Writings of Thomas Jefferson.* Ed. Paul Leicester Ford. 10 vols. New York: G. P. Putnam's Sons, 1892-99.

Jensen, Merrrill, ed. *American Colonial Documents to 1776.* Vol. 9 of *English Historical Documents.* Ed. David C. Douglas. 12 vols. London: Eyre and Spottiswoode, 1955.

Jordan, Winthop D. *White Over Black: American Attitudes toward the Negro, 1550-1812.* Chapel Hill: U of North Carolina P, 1968.

Latrobe, John H. B. "Memoir of Benjamin Banneker, Read Before the Historical Society of Maryland." *Maryland Colonization Journal* 2 (May 1845): 353-64.

Loggins, Vernon. *The Negro Author: His Development in America to 1900.* New York: Columbia UP, 1931.

Miller, John Chester. *The Wolf by the Ears: Thomas Jefferson and Slavery.* New York: Free Press, 1977.

Nash, Gary B. *Race and Revolution.* Madison, WI: Madison House, 1990.

Nelson, Dana. *The Word in Black and White.* New York: Oxford U P, 1991.

Peterson, Merrill D. *The Jefferson Image in the American Mind.* New York: Oxford U P, 1962.

Pinkney, Andrea Davis. *Dear Beniamin Banneker.* New York: Harcourt Brace & Company, 1994.

Quarles, Benjamin. "The Revolutionary War as a Black Declaration of Independence." *Slavery and Freedom in the Age of the American Revolution,* ed. Ira Berlin and Ronald Hoffman. Charlottesville: U Press of Virginia, 1983, pp. 283-301.

Randall, Willard Sterne. *Thomas Jefferson.* New York: Henry Holt, 1993.

Robinson, Donald L. *Slavery in the Structure of American Politics, 1765-1820.* New York: Harcourt Brace Jovanovich, 1971.

Rush, Benjamin. *An Address to the Inhabitants of the British Settlements in America upon Slave-Keeping*. Philadelphia: the author, 1773.

Sancho, Ignatius. *Letters of the Late Ignatius Sancho*. Introd. Paul Edwards. London: Dawsons, 1968.

Scheick, William J. "Chaos and Imaginative Order in Thomas Jefferson's *Notes on the State of Virginia*. *Essays in Early Virainia Literature*. J. A. Leo Lemay, ed. New York: Burt Franklin, 1977, pp. 221-34.

Sheehan, Berhard W. *Seeds of Extinction: Jeffersonian Philanthropy and the American Indian*. Chapel Hill: U of North Carolina P, 1973.

Shuffleton, Frank. "Thomas Jefferson: Race, Culture, and the Failure of Anthropological Method." *A Mixed Race: Ethnicity in Early America*. New York: Oxford U P, 1993, pp. 257-277.

Simpson, Lewis P. "The Ferocity of Self: History and Consciousness in Southern Literature." *South Central Review* 1 (1984): 67-84.

———. "The Ideology of Revolution." *The History of Southern Literature*. Ed. Louis D. Rubin, et al. Baton Rouge: Louisiana State U P, 1985. Pp. 57-67.

Sobel, Mechal. *The World They Made Together: Black and White Values in Eighteenth-Century Virainia*. Princeton: Princeton U P, 1987.

Sundquist, Eric J. *To Wake the Nations: Race in the Making of American Literature*. Cambridge: Harvard U P, 1993.

Takaki, Ronald T. *Iron Cages: Race and Culture in 19th-Century America*. New York: Knopf, 1979.

Tauber, Gisela. "Notes on the State of Virginia: Thomas Jefferson's Unintentional Self-Portrait." *Eighteenth-Century Studies* 26 (1993): 635-648.

Wheatley, Phillis. *The Collected Works of Phillis Wheatley*. Ed. John Shields. New York: Oxford U P, 1988.

Wills, Garry. *Inventing America: Jefferson's Declaration of Independence*. New York: Doubleday, 1978.

Fifth of July

Nathaniel Paul and the Construction of Black Nationalism

Robert S. Levine

The opening decades of the nineteenth century, we sometimes forget, were a hopeful time for African Americans in the northern states. Strong black communities emerged in Philadelphia, New York, and other cities, and black leaders became increasingly vocal in calling for emancipation. With the New York legislature's relatively late decision to abolish slavery in the state effective 4 July 1827, many African Americans came to believe that they would be able to achieve equal status with whites as enfranchised citizens, and that slavery might even come to an end within their lifetimes. Among those buoyed by the prospects of emancipation, according to an article in *Freedom's Journal*, the first African American newspaper, were the free blacks of Albany. At a formal "meeting of the people of colour, of the city of Albany, held at the African meeting-house, March 27, 1827, for the purpose of taking into consideration the expediency of celebrating the abolition of slavery in the state of New-York, which is to take place on the 4th day of July, 1827," Nathaniel Paul, the charismatic and highly respected pastor of the First African Baptist Church in Albany, delivered a "short but pertinent address" instructing New York's blacks on "a just sense of their own rights and the duties which they owe to the community." Paul also offered a resolution that was resoundingly adopted by the group: "Resolved, That whereas slavery by the laws of this state is ABOLISHED on the 4th of July next, we deem it a duty to express our gratitude to Almighty God and our public benefactors, by publicly celebrating the same." Though grateful for emancipation, Paul was hardly naive about the difficulties facing poor, illiterate blacks, and he also supported the group's more ironically conceived resolution which pointed to the limits of New York's emancipation act in a nation in which slavery remained the law of the land: "Resolved, That whereas the 4th day of July is the day that the National Independence of this country is recognized by white citizens, we deem it proper to celebrate the 5th."[1]

This essay explores the efforts of the relatively obscure but highly influential

Nathaniel Paul (?-1839) to construct a black nationalist politics that would help African Americans to secure full rights to citizenship in the United States. I will be focusing in particular on what could be termed the contradictory transnational and even postnational dimensions of Paul's abolitionist and antiracist work on behalf of U.S. blacks. Born in New Hampshire during the 1790s (in all likelihood), Paul probably attended the Free Will Academy in Hollis, New Hampshire, an integrated school which trained future ministers. In 1820 he became pastor of the First African Baptist Church of Albany, New York. By the mid-1820s he had emerged as a highly regarded antislavery voice in the community, so it is not surprising that he should have assumed a leadership position among Albany's blacks by 1827. But rather than remaining in Albany to fight for blacks' rights in the U.S., he moved to Canada in 1830 to experiment with the newly formed black community at Wilberforce, and then made a notably successful (and extended) antislavery tour in Britain from 1832 to 1836, before eventually returning to Albany. Unlike Frederick Douglass, who never relinquished his project of attempting to bring about African Americans' elevation in the U.S., Paul, in somewhat improvisatory fashion, committed himself for a while to an alternative black community which he apparently believed had the potential to develop a black nationality, if not in the U.S., then in the Americas. In this regard, Paul anticipated, and may have influenced, the thinking of William Wells Brown and Martin R. Delany, who, while beginning their antislavery careers in the mode of Douglass (preaching the importance of black uplift in the U.S.), also for a relatively short period of time supported the development of separatist black communities in Canada and the southern Americas as part of their commitment to developing a black nationalist politics in the Americas.[2]

Sterling Stuckey has usefully defined black nationalism in the U.S. as a consciousness among African Americans "of a shared experience of oppression at the hands of white people," and as a program that "emphasized the need for black people to rely primarily on themselves in vital areas of life."[3] As Stuckey and others have pointed out, black nationalism could embrace a range of sometimes competing and conflicting options—black uplift, separatism, emigration, and so on—and had to be constructed and reconstructed in response to different exigencies and contexts. One large context that has received considerable attention of late is what Paul Gilroy refers to as "the black Atlantic." In his influential study, Gilroy has urged cultural historians to consider black experiences in relation to the figure of "ships in motion across the spaces between Europe, American, Africa, and the Caribbean," insisting that "themes of nationality, exile, and cultural affiliation accentuate the inescapable fragmentation and differentiation of the black subject."[4] There are certainly such moments of fragmentation, differentiation, and motion in the career of Nathaniel Paul, whose evolving politics at times can seem to renounce, or transcend, the categories of nation and race. But even as Paul develops truly radical visions of social change that challenge categories of nation and race, he never abandons a consciousness of his connections to black people, and he never completely abandons the idea of the nation-state.

What ultimately holds Paul's career together, I want to argue, is the meta-phor of the Fifth of July, which speaks to the differentiation and fragmentation of the African American subject in the U.S., while at the same time implying the po-tential for allegiance and wholeness. And yet the metaphor of the Fifth of July also speaks to the contradictions of Paul's career (contradictions that had much to do with the nation's absurd racial realities). Emerging from a black oppositional poli-tics, the metaphor of the Fifth of July, even as it attempts to hold U.S. nationalism to its ideological promises, ultimately skews U.S. nationalism. Literally postnational, the figure of the Fifth of July raises important questions about location, for the figure suggests that black nationalism could be regarded as no longer within the U.S. but more complexly sometimes inside and sometimes outside, moving from within the self to within the community, to outside and then beside, a gesture of critical parataxis. This essay, then, will explore Paul's contradictory, sometimes in-coherent, yet eminently pragmatic sense of transnational nationality, showing how the diasporic tendencies of his thinking allowed him creatively to construct a poli-tics of black nationalism that could make adjustments and redefinitions in response to new challenges and situations. But because the Fourth of July remained the implicit foundational term of his Fifth of July politics, he ultimately never relin-quished his hopes for a transformed (or redeemed) U.S. nationalism that was just, equitable, and racially inclusive.

Paul's hopes for such a transformation were powerfully enunciated in his eloquent Fifth of July speech, *An Address, Delivered on the Celebration of the Aboli-tion of Slavery, in the State of New-York, July 5, 1827*. Like Frederick Douglass in his equally eloquent Fifth of July speech, "What to the Slave Is the Fourth of July?" (1852), which may have been influenced by Paul's, Paul addressed head-on what he referred to as "the medley of contradictions which stain the national charac-ter." Locating the national contradictions in the nation's failure to live up to the egalitarian ideals of its founding documents, a failure that exposes the hypocrisy of Fourth of July celebrations, he declares to his auditors: "[P]aradoxical as it may appear to those acquainted with the constitution of the government, *or* who have read the bold declaration of this nation's independence; yet it is a fact that can neither be denied or controverted, that in the United States of America, at the expiration of fifty years after its becoming a free and independent nation, there are no less than fifteen hundred thousand human beings still in a state of uncondi-tional vasalage [*sic*]." But despite the persistence of slavery in the new republic, Paul, speaking at the optative moment of 1827, sees great possibilities for the nation's blacks, particularly the free blacks of New York state, and much of his speech is devoted to encouraging the free blacks to take on the burden of their own self-elevation. Sharing the views of many other black leaders of the time, Paul argues that the best possible refutation of proslavery arguments would be for the free blacks to demonstrate their ability to rise in northern market culture. Regarding black nationalism at this point in his career as demanding internal work by blacks within the borders of the free states, he places a large burden on the shoulders of New York's free blacks: "This day commences a new era in our history; . . . new duties devolve upon us; duties, which if properly attended to, cannot fail to improve our moral condition, and elevate us to a rank of respectable standing with the community; or if neglected, we fall at once into the abyss of contemptible wretchedness."[5]

But even as Paul calls for black elevation, he remains acutely aware that white racist practices present huge barriers to black progress in the United States. He is also aware that the experience of slavery and racism has made U.S. blacks into what Martin Delany would later refer to as "a nation within a nation."[6] In declaring, for example, that he and his auditors "will tell the good story" of the abolition of slavery in New York "to our children and to our children's children, down to the latest posterity," Paul establishes from the outset of his speech that blacks constitute an ethnic community that has very different experiences from whites, in large part because blacks were forcibly brought to the nascent nation as slaves. One of the more fascinating aspects of Paul's 1827 speech is his patriotic willingness, in the tradition of Jefferson's *Declaration of Independence*, to blame England for the origin of slavery in North America. In this formulation, slavery preceded the making of the U.S.: "It was before the sons of Columbia felt the yoke of their oppressors, and rose in their strength to put it off that this land became contaminated with slavery. . . . It was by the permission of the British parliament, that the human species first became an article of merchandize among them." While Paul blames Britain for the presence of slavery in the U.S., he notes that the principal abolitionists of the past thirty years have been British, praising "the immortal Clarkson" and "the immortal Wilberforce" for having consecrated themselves "to the holy purpose of rescuing a continent [Africa] from rapine and murder."[7] Paul thus brings to the forefront of his sometimes U.S. nationalistic address the transatlantic context that, as Gilroy and others have argued, threatens to undercut the very concept of the autonomous nation-state. Insisting that a revolution against a (waning) slave power that brings forth a new slave power is a false revolution, Paul presents the U.S. as not so separate or special after all.

Africa, too, has an important place in Paul's Fifth of July speech. It is crucial to note that Paul is speaking approximately ten years after the formation of the American Colonization Society (ACS), a white "philanthropic" organization, championed by Henry Clay, Lyman Beecher, and many others, that claimed that the "natural" place for blacks was Africa. The large goal of the ACS was to ship the free blacks back to their putative homeland in Africa, specifically to the ACS's colony of Liberia, and in this way bring about the end of slavery and ensure that the U.S. would be a white nation. Most African Americans of the period vigorously opposed the ACS, though John Russwurm, the editor of *Freedom's Journal*, eventually came to support the colonization project. In his Fifth of July speech, Paul, though opposed to the ACS, seems somewhat conflicted about Africa, and this conflict points to his complex thinking about black nationalism in 1827. Arguing that blacks deserve citizenship in the U.S., he nonetheless depicts blacks as different from whites, not only because of their shared experience of slavery and racism in the U.S. but also because of their shared genealogical connection to Africa and their links to the historical trauma of the Middle Passage. In a particularly compelling moment in his speech, Paul in visionary fashion describes blacks being taken from "the shores of Africa" and suffering the horrors of the Middle Passage: "I view them casting the last and longing look towards the land which gave them birth, until at length the ponderous anchor is weighed . . . ; I behold those who have been so unfortunate as to survive the passage, emerging from their loathsome prison, and landing amidst the noisy rattling of the massy [sic] fetters which confine them." For Paul, the question remains as to why a benevolent God would allow such an awful practice to occur, and he concludes, as Alexander Crummell would conclude several decades later, that God wanted to "bring good out of evil" by exposing blacks to western Christianity and science. He proclaims: "the glorious light of science is spreading from east to west, and Afric's sons are catching the glance of its beams as it passes; its enlightening rays scatter the mists of moral darkness and ignorance." According to Paul, the ultimate result of this historical movement will be that "Afric's sons," and hence Africa, will be redeemed, and that Africa itself will "take her place among the other nations of the earth."[8]

What begins, then, as a call for black uplift that draws on U.S. nationalistic ideals quickly enlarges to a vision of the education of "Afric's sons," the redemption of Africa, and the advent of a revolutionary moment that will bring about universal enlightenment and the end of slavery. Paul imagines this emancipatory moment less in American revolutionary terms than in transnational terms, in which restive slaves throughout the world rise up against antiquated slave powers: "I declare that slavery will be extinct," for "the recent revolution in South America, the catastrophe and exchange of power in the Isle of Hayti, the restless disposition of both master and slave in the southern states, the constitution of our government" all point to the eventuality that slavery will "be forever annihilated from the earth." Not only does he link African Americans to British abolitionism, Haitian revolutionism, and a redeemed Africa, but by proclaiming in the midst of his speech the Biblical notion that "God . . . has made of one blood, all nations of men," Paul celebrates egalitarian ideals from a monogenetic, religious point of view and challenges the idea of the racially "pure" nation as it was understood in the U.S. in 1827 by the colonizationists and other white racists.[9] All that said, Paul in his Fifth of July speech remains mostly optimistic about blacks' prospects in the U.S. and about the promises of U.S. nationalism.

Paul is less hopeful about those promises in his 1829 Sixth of July speech, *An Address, Delivered at Troy, on the Celebration of the Abolition of Slavery, in the State of New York, July 6, 1829.—Second Anniversary*. Though he makes an effort in the speech to underscore blacks' relationship to U.S. nationalism, he laments what now seem to him the nearly insurmountable obstacles in the way of black uplift in the foreseeable future, proclaiming that "although the shackles of slavery are broken, and we are no longer under bondage; yet many circumstances have combined to render our condition in many things, far behind our more highly favored countrymen." But as despairing as he is, Paul in his Sixth of July address does not relinquish the July Fourth ideals which implicitly inform his Fifth of July speech. Still committed to bringing about black elevation in the U.S., he tones down the vision of African redemption that had such an important place in his 1827 address, characterizing the American Colonization Society's project of ridding the U.S. of its black population "as utterly chimerical and absurd." Convinced that the ACS agenda makes it all the more urgent for blacks to insist upon the legitimacy of their claims to U.S. citizenship, he invokes the deeds of black American Revolutionary fighters, declaring in no uncertain terms: "We claim this as *our country*, as the land of our nativity, and to achieve its independence, our fathers faced her enemies on the field of battle, and contended even unto death." (William C. Nell would make a similar argument for black citizenship in *The Colored Patriots of the American Revolution* [1855].) Despite the fact that he seems less hopeful about African Americans' immediate prospects, he concludes his 1829 Sixth of July address with a vision of the end of racism in the U.S. at "some more distant period," a time when "prejudices, however long their standing or deeply rooted, will be eradicated, and distinctions shall be known no more."[10]

Paul must have imagined such quixotic harmony emerging in the U.S. at a *very* distant period, for less than a year after delivering this speech, he decided to abandon his pastorate in Albany (and his commitment to doing internal work within U.S. borders) and move to the reformist black community of Wilberforce in Upper Canada. Named in honor of the great British abolitionist William Wilberforce, the community of Wilberforce, near what is now Lucan, Ontario, was established between late 1829 and 1831 in response to an 1829 decision by Cincinnati's legislators to enforce the state's Black Codes of 1804 and 1807, which among other things required that blacks display their freedom papers and post bond when entering the state. Cincinnati's approximately 3,000 blacks resisted the enforcement of these laws by rioting and making plans for a mass exodus to Canada. Serving as the principal agents of the ultimately rather small group that emigrated to Canada were Israel Lewis and Thomas Cresap, who contracted to purchase 4,000 acres from the Canada Land Company for six thousand dollars. When it became clear, however, that they could not raise that kind of money, they purchased 800 acres for their proposed black community with the help of donations from Quakers in Indiana and Ohio. Lewis then went on a recruitment mission in New York state, and managed to sign up the black abolitionist grocer Austin Steward (1793–1865), Nathaniel Paul, and Paul's brother Benjamin Paul (?-1836), a Baptist minister in New York City. By July 1831 the community had established a Board of Managers, with Steward serving as Chairman, and had approximately 200 participants.[11]

Despite the disillusionment evident in his 1829 speech, it is difficult to say why Paul chose to transplant himself to Canada. Was he renouncing the United States? Though it is true that some blacks emigrated to Canada as an act of renunciation, for many other antebellum blacks a move to Canada signalled a continued commitment to the promises of U.S. nationalism. Their hope was that the development of black communities on the northern borders of the U.S. would provide U.S. whites with images of blacks' ability to rise and economically prosper in a

supposedly nonracist society, images that they thought might help to create opportunities for blacks in the United States. By contrast, the movement to develop
black communities in the southern Americas, spearheaded by Martin Delany and
William Wells Brown during the 1850s, was an effort to develop black nation-states
wherein African Americans would join with other peoples of color (in Nicaragua
and Haiti, for example) and renounce their claims to U.S. citizenship. To be sure,
some black communitarians conceived of their groups as Canadian communities
and felt warmly toward a nation that seemed considerably less racist than the U.S.;
but Wilberforce never developed much of a distinctive identity or an alternative
nationalism. Its principal leaders retained ties with the U.S., and abolitionists such
as Benjamin Lundy and William Garrison regarded Wilberforce as a community
that showed the possibilities of black uplift in the U.S. I would speculate that Paul
initially chose to participate in Wilberforce mainly because he regarded the community as having the potential to improve the lot of blacks in the U.S., and thus of
fulfilling the vision of his 1827 Fifth of July address. His extant writings reveal little
evidence of an attachment to Wilberforce or Canada. In fact, what is striking about
Paul's participation in Wilberforce is how briefly he lived there, and how quickly
he developed new attachments and a new sense of identity and purpose.

That new identity was in some ways forced upon Paul, for just several months
after arriving at Wilberforce, he was charged by the community to return to New
York and board a ship for England on a fundraising mission. Wilberforce had virtually no capital and thus it was decided, as Austin Steward reports in his 1857
memoir, *Twenty-Two Years a Slave, and Forty Years a Freeman*, that the community
should send out "two agents for the purpose of soliciting aid for the erection of
houses for worship, and for the maintenance of schools in the colony."[12] Israel
Lewis was authorized to seek support in the U.S., while Paul was tapped for Great
Britain. What ensued is not a pretty story, as conflicts arose among the three principal leaders that eventually led to the collapse of the community in 1837. But
although Paul's mission to Great Britain was intimately connected to his identity
as a member of the black Wilberforce community, that identity very quickly was
transmuted into what could be termed a transatlantic (or "black Atlantic") identity which, oddly enough, was both highly racialized and deracialized. Like Frederick
Douglass during the mid-1840s, Paul experienced in England a heightened sense
of identity and purpose as a black man, while at the same time discovering enormous possibilities in what he came to regard as an Enlightenment humanist world
of racial egalitarianism in which color potentially meant very little. Embracing
this dualistic (black/postracial) transatlantic identity, Paul did his most significant
and impassioned cultural work.

It is worth pausing here briefly to consider Paul's enthusiastic embrace of
the egalitarian promises of Enlightenment universalism, particularly with respect
to his politics of black nationalism. Paul Gilroy and many others have linked the
Enlightenment to the newly emergent racial "sciences" of the time that worked to
buttress proslavery thinking in the U.S. and elsewhere. For these critics of the Enlightenment, there is no contradiction between, say, Thomas Jefferson's egalitarian

philosophies, on the one hand, and his racist writings and practices as a slaveowner, on the other. Gilroy thus urges historians to address minorities' perspectives on "such central categories of the Enlightenment project as the idea of universality, the fixity of meaning, the coherence of the subject, and, of course, the foundational ethnocentrism in which these have all tended to be anchored."[13] In an excellent recent essay on the politics of Enlightenment humanism, Amanda Anderson notes that "the philosophes' constructions of universal human nature often bore all too markedly the imprint of European culture and history," but she goes on to observe that even a fictive universality can serve useful purposes in allowing "dominated groups to struggle for inclusion under the rubric of the Rights of Man."[14] Whether or not Paul regarded universality as "fictive," while in England he found the concept useful (and liberating) for articulating a politics of black nationalism that departed from his prior Fifth of July politics by placing considerably less emphasis on the role of the nation-state in fulfilling his antiracist project of black uplift and black community-formation. That said, during his British tour he found it difficult to speak from universalist perspective, as he was regularly presented by British and U.S. abolitionists as an African American whose very blackness and ethnicity gave an added authenticity to his pronouncements. To his credit, Paul worked strategically with these multiple identities to challenge the American Colonization Society, champion blacks' social and political rights, and even accomplish some modest fundraising for Wilberforce.

Though the documentary record is relatively sparse, consisting only of a small number of newspaper accounts, we can nevertheless do a reasonably good job of reconstructing the shape and significance of Paul's British tour. As described in the 17 September 1831 *Liberator*, Paul's mission to England was initially related very specifically to the goal of raising funds for the Wilberforce colony. In an article titled "Colony in Upper Canada," the anonymous writer notes that the "Rev. Nathaniel Paul, agent of the Wilberforce Settlement in Canada, and formerly pastor of the African Baptist Church in this city, arrived here [Albany] on Wednesday, the 10th August, bringing with him letters of introduction, and other credentials authorizing him to visit Great Britain, to solicit such aid as may be conducive to the prosperity and future welfare of that infant settlement." But by the time Paul set sail for England on 31 December 1831, the reportage in the *Liberator* suggests that something more was at stake in his transatlantic voyage than simply soliciting funds for Wilberforce. In a front page article in the 14 January 1832 *Liberator*, the author "R." (most likely the black abolitionist Charles Remond) now refers to Paul's goal of obtaining "funds in aid of this little Colony [Wilberforce]" as his "ostensible purpose" of going to England, and concludes with a poem pointing to a significantly larger purpose. In a key stanza, R. writes:

And when you arrive on Albion's shores,
May you with holy fervor trace
The unjust treatment of our foes,
Who spurn, exile, our helpless race.[15]

Clearly, R. regards Paul as undertaking the mission of representing the "race" and specifically of describing blacks' sufferings in the U.S. The evidence makes it clear that Paul very quickly subordinated his Wilberforce mission to what he regarded as his larger role of working for the emancipation of U.S. blacks. As Paul himself reports in a letter of 3 July 1832 to William Lloyd Garrison, which was reprinted in an August 1832 article in the *Liberator* titled "Rev. Nathaniel Paul," he has taken the measure of his British audiences and seen that "the people of this country are alive to the cause of abolition." Paul excitedly reports on the first material result of his speaking efforts: "What would you think, sir, of seeing a petition *a half mile long*, and containing more than ONE HUNDRED THOUSAND NAMES, sent to the Congress of the United States? Surely you would think that, ere long, slavery must be abolished in this country."[16]

Central to Paul's abolitionist campaign was a concerted effort to expose the mendacity of the American Colonization Society. For right around the time Paul arrived in England, the ACS leader Elliott Cresson arrived in England to begin a speaking tour on behalf of his group, entreating concerned Britons to help the cause of African Americans by donating funds to ship them to Liberia. During 1832 Paul met with the British abolitionists Captain Charles Stuart and James Cropper in an increasingly successful campaign to undermine Cresson's arguments; and in 1833 Paul was joined on the antislavery lecture circuit by William Lloyd Garrison, whose forceful attack on the ACS, *Thoughts on African Colonization* (1832), had had a significant impact in England. Together, Paul and Garrison identified the ACS as one of the principal enemies of blacks in the U.S. As Garrison's recent biographer Henry Mayer reports, Paul developed two large arguments that he would sound again and again in his speeches of 1832 and 1833: "He would tell meetings . . . of the overwhelming opposition to colonization among American blacks, and he would defend his fellow citizen Garrison from Cresson's smears that he was a mere pamphleteer who lacked standing in the United States because he had served a jail term on a libel charge."[17]

By all available accounts, Paul was enormously successful as a speaker, and it was precisely his success that made him such an influential figure in his own time and beyond, paving the way for Charles Remond, Frederick Douglass, and many other black abolitionists who made successful tours of the British antislavery circuit. Over the course of Paul's tour, white British and U.S. abolitionists discovered that antislavery arguments were particularly compelling when made by a black, someone who could speak from first-hand experience about the ravages of racism and slavery, and someone whose intelligence and moral authority made a mockery of proslavery assertions of black inferiority and dependency. As the secretary of a local antislavery society in Edinburgh wrote to the British abolitionist George Thompson on Paul's triumphal speaking engagement: "I never saw one more kindly treated by all parties. The color of his skin was an excellent introduction to him, something surely that will surprise brother Jonathan. I never saw the feeling of sympathy for the manner in which the free blacks in America are treated, so powerfully brought forth. Here there is no prejudice about the color of a man's skin.

The darker it is, the more likely is he to receive kind attention and support."[18] Aware that Paul had a special relationship with British abolitionist audiences, Thompson, Garrison, and many other abolitionists sought to share the stage with the dark-skinned Paul, who inevitably found himself addressing colonization and abolition at the expense of Wilberforce.

In his attacks on the American Colonization Society, Paul challenged racialist notions that blacks "naturally" belonged in Africa, and perhaps more important, regularly sounded the black nationalist themes of his Fifth of July address, insisting again and again on African Americans' rights to citizenship in the United States. Thus Wilberforce had to be presented, in effect, as a means to an end: as a voluntary black community near the borders of the U.S. (wholly unlike the comparatively involuntary colony of Liberia) that would demonstrate blacks' capabilities of becoming productive citizens in the U.S. Writing to Garrison in April 1833, he describes the speeches he has been delivering of late: "I have been engaged, for several months past, in traveling through the country and delivering lectures upon the system of slavery as it exists in the United States, the condition of the free people of color in that country, and the importance of promoting the cause of education and religion generally among the colored people. My lectures have been numerously attended by from two to three thousand people, the Halls and Chapels have been overflown, and hundreds have not been able to obtain admittance." He goes on to describe his meeting with Thomas Clarkson and his breakfasting "with the venerable WILBERFORCE." As for the Wilberforce mission itself: "I do not hold out the delusive idea that the whole of the colored people are going to Canada; but have invariably said, that in spite of all that will ever remove there, or to any other part of the world they will continue to increase in America."[19]

Two major extant speeches by Paul give a powerful sense of the ways in which he made the argument for blacks' rights to U.S. citizenship by invoking the nation's ideological commitment to the principles of 1776. In these speeches, ironically, he also makes transnational appeals to his auditors' assumed egalitarian sentiments to argue in nationalistic terms for African Americans' rights to U.S. citizenship. At a meeting of over 2,000 abolitionists at London's Exeter Hall, Paul, who shared the stage with Garrison, George Thompson, Daniel O'Connell, and many other prominent abolitionists, began his speech by defending Garrison from the smears of Cresson and other colonizationists, pointing out that Garrison had been jailed for libel for having had the temerity to insult a merchant whose ships were used for the slave trade. At the heart of Paul's speech, however, which mostly concerned itself with ridiculing the politics and methods of the ACS, were scathing remarks on the contradictory practice of slavery in the new republic, attacks that were no doubt greatly enjoyed by his British auditors. Paul sarcastically proclaims: "Perhaps it is not generally known that in the United States of America—the land of freedom and equality—the laws are so exceedingly liberal that they give to man the liberty of purchasing as many negroes as he can find means to pay for. . . and also the liberty to sell them again." And in his resounding attack on the American Colonization Society, he repeatedly invokes "American" ideals of "freedom and equality" to challenge the ACS's conviction that Africa was the "natural" place for blacks. According to Paul, the ACS has closed its eyes to blacks' crucial place in the founding and development of the U.S., and "undertakes to expel from their native country hundreds of thousands of unoffending and inoffensive individuals, who, in time of war, have gone forth into the field of battle, and have contended for the liberties of that country." In this respect, the ACS, like the southern slave power, works "to rob the colored men in that country of every right, civil, political or religious, to which they are entitled by the American Declaration of Independence."[20]

Soon after delivering his successful Exeter Hall speech, Paul again pressed his argument against the American Colonization Society in a forceful article titled "Compensation for Slaves," which was printed in the 31 August 1833 *Liberator* and was probably first delivered as a speech to British abolitionist audiences. "Compensation for Slaves" is one of Paul's most powerful pieces of writing and deserves to be better known. In the article, Paul, working with a common trope of eighteenth-century antislavery writings, attacks an ACS proposal to compensate southern slaveholders for freeing their slaves, arguing that such a compensation plan would be akin to paying a thief for the return of stolen property, and would inevitably promote various forms of corruption and deceit, such as slaveowners attempting to sell off to the ACS their infirm and elderly slaves. In the manner of his Fifth of July address, he also invokes the *Declaration* to expose the moral shortcomings of the ACS project. As with his many other references to the Declaration, he points to the contradictions inherent in a plan in which a nation committed to the principles of human equality treats some people as if they were merely property.

But there is a significant difference in his invocation of the *Declaration* in this essay, for he presents the *Declaration* less as a founding document of the United States than as a powerful expression of ideas about human rights shared by enlightened men and women throughout the world. In short, he presents the Declaration as but one of many late-eighteenth-century statements on human equality, with the implication that Jefferson's document needs to be reconceived in an international Enlightenment context as a contribution to emerging universalist notions of the evils of the despotic, uncivilized, and antiquated practice of slavery. Inspired by Britain's momentous West Indian Emancipation Act of 1833, he refers to "the immediate and universal emancipation of the slaves, in all the British Islands in the Gulf of Mexico" as "one of the most cheering and important events for the happiness of mankind, which has happened since the Declaration of Independence." Linking the *Declaration* to world revolutionary movements, to the general improvement of "mankind," and not just specifically to the ideological origins of the U.S., Paul builds his speech to a climactic mandate that, as was the case with many of Thomas Paine's writings, can be regarded in simultaneously national and transnational (and even postnational) terms: "BE FREE!"[21]

Paul's liberatory mandate can also be regarded in transracial (or postracial) terms in relation to his emerging commitment to a cosmopolitan universalism that had important sources in the Enlightenment. Though he rhetorically foregrounded what could be termed a politics of color authenticity in his Exeter Hall speech—"the complexion that I wear . . . shall speak in my behalf"—during his four years in Great Britain he became increasingly attracted to a transnational notion of a humanist community that could see beyond color. Thus he identifies as one of the great evils of the ACS that its leaders and members think only in terms of color, desiring to ship the free blacks from the U.S. simply "[b]ecause the God of heaven has given them a different complexion from themselves." Opposed to African colonization, which arguably also had ideological sources in the discourses of what Gilroy terms "the Enlightenment Project," Paul, as in other of his post-1827 writings, takes care to downplay any genealogical, racial, or cultural attraction he might feel to Africa, speaking only of his pity for what he terms "the sad condition which that country [sic] is in," and championing the importance of an enlightened leadership that will lead Africa from "vilest superstition" to "civilization and Christianity."[22] That vision of an enlightened, nonracist group of leaders, as conveyed in Paul's speeches and letters of the period, was clearly inspired by his amazement at what he regarded as an absence of color prejudice in England. In his April 1833 letter to Garrison, for example, he states, "Here, if I go to church, I am not pointed to the 'negro seat' in the gallery; but any gentleman opens his pew door for my reception."[23] Paul's response to a perceived lack of prejudice was not to embrace British nationalism but rather to celebrate a transnational community of enlightened, educated, humane "gentlemen," as represented by such international reformers as Clarkson, Wilberforce, Garrison, Thompson, and O'Connell. Paul's own ability on a personal level to see beyond the nation-state and race was demonstrated sometime in 1833, when he married a white English woman (about whom, unfortunately, we know very little).

For Steward and the Wilberforce Board, however, Paul's move towards what could be termed a cosmopolitan abolitionism, particularly as emblematized by his marriage to a white woman, pointed to the limits of Paul's color-blind transnationalism. From their perspective, Paul had had his black nationalism co-opted by whites who had little sympathy for the project that had sent Paul to England in the first place. But to understand the full context of Steward's disillusionment with Paul, we need to return to 1831, for it was at that time that Steward and the Wilberforce Board of Managers, shortly after authorizing Israel Lewis to solicit funds in the U.S., came to regard their U.S. agent as a thief. Convinced that Lewis was taking funds intended for Wilberforce for his own personal gain, the Board dismissed him in late 1831. In response, Lewis, who retained the support of Paul's brother Benjamin, threatened to sue the Board for defamation of character, and he continued collecting money for what he now called his own Wilberforce Colonization Company. Beginning in 1833, the *Liberator* began to print regular notices, signed by Wilberforce's Board and the prominent white abolitionist Arthur Tappan, warning subscribers against giving their Wilberforce donations to Lewis, whom they presented as a con man attempting "to gull the public out of money for individual purposes."[24] The *Liberator's* warnings led to Lewis's disgrace, and he soon vanished from sight. As far as fundraising was concerned, then, the community's hopes lay with Nathaniel Paul. These hopes were expressed in a declaration from the Wilberforce Board of Managers printed in the 16 July 1836 *Liberator*: "That although we have not received One Hundred Dollars from said LEWIS, yet when we shall have received the funds collected by our Agent, REV. NATH'L. PAUL, in England, for us, we will refund, as far as our abilities will allow, and our friends may require, the money contributed for our *supposed benefit*, by them in the States."[25]

Increasingly impatient for Paul's return, Steward and the Wilberforce Board sent the Canadian Henry Nell to England with the mission of bringing Paul back to Wilberforce; but Nell himself became enamored of England (perhaps for the very reasons Paul had been enamored) and decided to remain there. In *Twenty-Two Years a Slave*, Steward attacks Nell as "less worthy of confidence than the agent [Paul]," and states (incorrectly) that Paul returned to New York in the fall of 1834 and was unwilling to come to Wilberforce until the spring of 1835. In fact, as the 1836 notice of the Board's desire for Paul's return suggests, Paul continued his successful British tour through 1835 and early 1836. The 19 December 1835 *Liberator* printed a resoundingly positive assessment of Paul's accomplishments while overseas: "Mr. Paul's statements contributed most materially to accomplish the glorious measure of slave emancipation in the British dominions in the opinion of every friend to the abolition party in England. . . . The name of the American Paul is rendered dear to every friend of humanity in Great Britain, and his memory is enshrined in the grateful remembrance of the emancipated race whose fetters he has assisted to unloose."[26] Significantly, this anonymous writer says nothing about Paul's Wilberforce connection, assessing his value in relation to Great Britain but more importantly in relation to a universalist notion of "every friend of humanity."

In *Twenty-Two Years a Slave*, Steward presents Paul as a veritable money-making machine who "was making money too easily, to like to be interrupted."[27] But Paul eventually did return to Wilberforce, arriving sometime in the spring of 1836, most likely in response to the news that his brother Benjamin had recently died; and when he did return, Paul, to Steward's considerable outrage, claimed that the Board owed *him* money and not the other way around. As he explained to the Board, while abroad he had collected over eight thousand dollars for Wilberforce, but his expenses during this same period were over seven thousand dollars, and because the salary he and the Board had agreed on was fifty dollars a month, the Board owed him approximately one thousand dollars. Steward concedes that, according to their contractual agreement, the group indeed did owe Paul money, though he states that as a man of honor, and as someone concerned about Wilberforce, Paul at the very least should have repaid the initial $700 he was loaned to make the British trip. Also, Steward is clearly skeptical of Paul's claim, which he made to the Board, that he loaned Garrison $200 for his return trip to the United States and that the Wilberforce Board should assume this expense. (In an appendix to *Twenty-Two Years a Slave*, Steward prints a June 1856 letter from Garrison denying that the loan ever took place, but Garrison's memory was faulty; two decades earlier, in a letter of 17 December 1835 to Lewis Tappan, Garrison stated that Paul lent him the money "so that I could return home without begging."[28])

Having demonstrated that "as far as the monied interest of the colony was concerned, [Paul's] mission was an entire failure," Steward nevertheless allows that Paul may have accomplished some good on his British tour: "It is said that he continually addressed crowded and deeply interested audiences, and that many after hearing him, firmly resolved to exert themselves, until every chain was broken and every bondman freed beneath the waving banner of the British Lion. Perhaps his arduous labors assisted in freeing the West Indian islands of the hateful curse of Slavery; if so, we shall not so much regret the losses and severe trials, it was ours to bear at that time." Nevertheless, despite some of the relatively positive things he has to say about Paul, Steward conveys his sense of the overall failure of Paul's mission by focusing on—indeed scapegoating—Paul's white British wife as the reason for Paul's neglect of Wilberforce. For Steward immediately follows his description of Paul's financial accountings by asking how he managed to take care of an aristocratic white wife, implying that he must have done so with funds he collected for Wilberforce: "his expenses had been considerable; besides, he had fallen in love during his stay in England, with a white woman, and I suppose it must have required both time and money to woo and win so fine and fair an English lady."[29]

Though no extant information is available on Paul's wife, one has to assume that this woman, like Frederick Douglass's British companion Julia Griffiths, was a committed abolitionist who, in linking herself to a relatively poor black man, had made considerable financial and social sacrifices. Nonetheless, Steward attempts to make his case against Paul through a highly unflattering description of Paul's wife in all of her supposedly queenly, narcissistic glory: "we were immediately ushered into the presence of Mrs. Nathaniel Paul, whom we found in an inner apartment, made by drawn curtains, carpeted in an expensive style, where she was seated like a queen in state,—with a veil floating from her head to the floor; a gold chain encircling her neck, and attached to a gold watch in her girdle; her fingers and person were sparkling with costly jewelry. Her manners were stiff and formal, nor was she handsome, but a tolerably fair looking woman of about thirty years of age; and this was the wife of our agent for the poor Wilberforce colony!"[30] What makes this description particularly unfair is that Steward is describing her in the process of consoling the recently bereaved wife of Benjamin Paul.

Steward's scapegoating persists into his account of how Nathaniel Paul returned to Albany and died in poverty, illness, and obscurity. Steward blames Paul's wife for this downfall: "I have been told that his domestic life was far from a peaceable or happy one, and that in poverty, sorrow, and affliction, he lingered on a long time, till death at last closed the scene."[31] Paul died in 1839, but hardly in obscurity. When he returned to Albany he became pastor of the Union Street Baptist Church and continued his antislavery preaching. African American newspapers of the period present a picture of a vital abolitionist presence who was highly respected for his antislavery and antiracist politics. In a lecture of February 1838, delivered to the Albany Anti-Slavery Society and reprinted in the 14 March 1838 issue of *The Friend of Man* (Utica), Paul showed that he remained acutely aware of the problem of color prejudice in the U.S., and that rather than abandoning black people, as Steward implicitly suggests, he retained a Fifth of July black nationalist politics that urged blacks and whites alike to live up to the egalitarian ideals of the *Declaration* and Revolution. In this February 1838 lecture, Paul attacks slavery and the slave masters, but focuses on the racism that remains pervasive among abolitionists, warning of "the kind of abolitionist who hated slavery, 'especially that which is 1,000 or 1,500 miles off,' but who hated even more 'a man who wears a colored skin.'" It would seem likely that Paul presented this speech in partial response to the implicit and explicit condemnations of his interracial marriage that he likely received from white abolitionists when he returned to Albany. Viewed from this perspective, his marriage to a white woman would have only contributed to, rather than undercut, his consciousness of himself as a black in a racist nation. Evidence for the persistence of Paul's political activism can also be found in a June 1839 issue of *The Colored American*, the most influential African American newspaper of the time, which announced, in light of Paul's gravely ill condition, "a subscription meeting at Albany which would feature the last public appearance of the popular figure, Nathaniel Paul, pastor of the Union Street Baptist Church."[32] Even as he struggled with the illness that would take his life later that year, Paul was making plans to attend this important gathering of black editors, writers, and readers.

Swayed by Steward's negative assessment of Paul in his autobiography, the historian Robin W. Winks concludes, "If Lewis was a felon, Paul was a fool."[33] Steward presents Paul as particularly foolish in marriage, with the suggestion that such foolishness points to Paul's selfishness, dishonesty, and disloyalty to his race. But in focusing on Paul's wife, Steward ultimately displays his inability to understand the transnational and transracial dimensions of Paul's black nationalism as he redefined it in England. Hardly a fool, Paul realized while in England that there were larger matters to address than Wilberforce, and in developing his identity during that period as a transatlantic abolitionist, he entered a vital political context that brought him into contact with the leading Anglo-American abolitionists and helped to define the role of the black abolitionist in England from the mid-1830s to the time of the Civil War. Though Paul came to embrace an Enlightenment humanist politics of universal emancipation, he never stopped trying to find a way to improve the lot of African Americans and black peoples, and his improvisatory, transatlantic politics of antislavery paved the way for figures as diverse as Charles Remond, William Wells Brown, Martin Delany, and even Frederick Douglass—all of whom crossed borders, considered separatist, transnational, or transracial options, but generally retained an allegiance to a Fifth of July vision of a contradictorily flawed put potentially redeemable United States.[34] Paul's career may therefore be taken as both exemplary and paradigmatic, reminding us of the conceputal fluidity of race and nation in the careers of a number of representative African American male leaders. Not the least significant aspect of Paul's career is that he was also a first-rate speaker and writer; his 1827 Fifth of July speech and his

1833 "Compensation for Slaves" merit an important place in the canon of African American writings. Attending to Paul's writings helps us to see more clearly the complex rhetorical and cultural work integral to the development of the creatively resilient black nationalism of the nineteenth century.

NOTES

My thanks to Vincent Carretta, Leonard Cassuto, Russ Castronovo, and Philip Gould for their helpful comments on earlier drafts of this essay.

1. "Abolition of Slavery," *Freedom's Journal* 20 April 1827, 2. For useful backgrounds on slavery and New York, see Shane White, *Somewhat More Independent: The End of Slavery in New York City* (Athens: University of Georgia Press, 1991).

2. Though relatively obscure, even among historians of black abolitionism, Paul had a major impact on what could be termed Black Atlantic abolitionism. Significantly, a Paul letter and two of his speeches are the opening three selections in the important collection *The Black Abolitionist Papers. Volume I. The British Isles, 1830–1865*, ed. C. Peter Ripley et al. (Chapel Hill: University of North Carolina Press, 1985). The editors provide a brief biographical note on Paul, which helped to initiate my own research.

3. Sterling Stuckey, ed., *The Ideological Origins of Black Nationalism* (Boston: Beacon Press, 1972), 6, 1. See also Wilson Jeremiah Moses, ed., *Classical Black Nationalism: From the American Revolution to Marcus Garvey* (New York: New York University Press, 1998).

4. Paul Gilroy, *The Black Atlantic: Modernity and Double Consciousness* (Cambridge: Harvard University Press, 1993), 4, 35.

5. Nathaniel Paul, *An Address, Delivered on the Celebration of the Abolition of Slavery, in the State of New-York, July 5, 1827* (Albany: John B. Van Steenbergh, 1827), 12, 11, 18–19. On black elevation, see Frederick Cooper, "Elevating the Race: The Social Thought of Black Leaders, 1827–1850," *American Quarterly* 24 (1972): 604–25; and Robert S. Levine, *Martin Delany, Frederick Douglass, and the Politics of Representative Identity* (Chapel Hill: University of North Carolina Press, 1997), chap. 1.

6. Martin Robison Delany, *The Condition, Elevation, Emigration, and Destiny of the Colored People of the United States* (1852; rpt. New York: Arno Press, 1969), 12.

7. Paul, *An Address, Delivered on the Celebration of the Abolition of Slavery*, 3, 12, 8, 13.

8. Paul, *An Address, Delivered on the Celebration of the Abolition of Slavery*, 6, 10, 11, 21, 23, 16. (The original text has "massy fetters" but "mossy fetters" seems the more likely manuscript phrasing.) On the American Colonization Society and U.S. nationalism, see David Waldstreicher, *In the Midst of Perpetual Fetes: The Making of American Nationalism, 1776–1820* (Chapel Hill: University of North Carolina Press, 1997), 302–10. On John Russwurm, see Floyd J. Miller, *The Search for a Black Nationality: Black Emigration and Colonization, 1787–1863* (Urbana: University of Illinois Press, 1975), 84–89.

9. Paul, *An Address Delivered on the Celebration of the Abolition of Slavery*, 16, 15.

10. Nathaniel Paul, *An Address, Delivered at Troy, on the Celebration of the Abolition of Slavery, in the State of New York, July 6, 1829—Second Anniversary* (Albany: John B. Van Steenbergh, 1829), 6–7, 8, 10, 16.

11. On Wilberforce, see William H. Pease and Jane H. Pease, *Black Utopia: Negro Communal Experiments in America* (Madison: The State Historical Society of Wisconsin, 1963), chap. 3; and Robin W. Winks, *The Blacks in Canada: A History* (1971; rpt. Montreal: McGill-Queen's University Press, 1997), 153–62. See also Richard C. Wade, "The Negro in Cincinnati, 1800–1830," *Journal of Negro History* 39 (1954): 43–57.

12. Austin Steward, *Twenty-Two Years a Slave, and Forty Years a Freeman*, ed. Jane H.

Pease and William H. Pease (1857; rpt. Reading, Massachusetts: Addison-Wesley Publishing Company, 1969), 114.

13. Gilroy, *The Black Atlantic*, 55; for a fuller elaboration of his ideas, see the subsection "Slavery and the Enlightenment Project" (46–58). On the Enlightenment and racism, see also Henry Louis Gates, Jr., *Figures in Black: Words, Signs, and the "Racial" Self* (New York: Oxford University Press, 1987), esp. chap. 1; and Thomas F. Gossett, *Race: The History of An Idea in America* (1963; rpt. New York: Oxford University Press, 1997), chap. 3. For an influential reading of connections between Enlightenment thought and antislavery, see David Brion Davis, *The Problem of Slavery in the Age of Revolution* (Ithaca: Cornell University Press, 1975).

14. Amanda Anderson, "Cosmopolitanism, Universalism, and the Divided Legacies of Modernity," *Cosmopolitics: Thinking and Feeling Beyond the Nation*, eds. Pheng Cheah and Bruce Robbins (Minneapolis: University of Minnesota Press, 1998), 272, 282. Anderson's argument on the emancipatory potential of a "fictive" universality draws on Etienne Balibar, "Ambiguous Universality," *differences* 7 (1995): 48–74.

15. "Colony in Upper Canada," *Liberator*, 17 September 1831, 150; R., "Rev. Nathaniel Paul," *Liberator*, 14 January 1832, 5, 6.

16. "Rev. Nathaniel Paul," *Liberator*, 25 August 1832, 135.

17. Henry Mayer, *William Lloyd Garrison and the Abolition of Slavery* (New York: St. Martin's Press, 1998), 162. Mayer patronizingly refers to Paul's speeches as the fulfillment of "assignments" (162) given by British abolitionists. The evidence suggests, however, that Paul was an extremely eloquent and independent speaker who was able to develop arguments on his own or in consultation with his abolitionist colleagues. For an excellent discussion of Paul's work with British abolitionists in attacking Cresson, see R. J. M. Blackett, *Building an Antislavery Wall: Black Americans in the Atlantic Abolitionist Movement, 1830–1860* (Baton Rouge: Louisiana State University Press, 1983), 53–69. In addition to his lectures, Paul published a pamphlet that reprinted anti-ACS resolutions and addresses by African Americans; see Paul, *Reply to Mr. Joseph Phillips' Enquiry, Respecting "The Light in which the Operations of the American Colonization Society Are Viewed by the Free People of Colour in the United States"* (London, 1832).

18. "The Rev. Nathaniel Paul in Scotland," *Liberator*, 7 February 1835, 22.

19. Nathaniel Paul to William Lloyd Garrison, letter of 10 April 1833, in *Liberator* 22 June 1833, rpt. in *Black Abolitionist Papers*, 38, 39. Garrison and Paul would together visit Clarkson in the summer of 1833, and at that meeting, according to Garrison, Paul convinced Clarkson to withdraw his support from the ACS. See Blackett, *Building an Antislavery Wall*, 67.

20. "Speech by Nathaniel Paul, Delivered at Exeter Hall, London, England, 13 July 1833," *The Black Abolitionist Papers*, pp. 45, 46–47. See also *Speeches Delivered at the Anti-Colonization Meeting in Exeter Hall, London* (Boston, 1833), 13–15.

21. Nathaniel Paul, "Compensation for Slaves," *Liberator*, 31 August 1833, 137, 138

22. "Speech by Nathaniel Paul, Delivered at Exeter Hall," *Black Abolitionist Papers*, 44 46, 48; Gilroy, *The Black Atlantic*, 46.

23. Paul to Garrison, letter of 10 April 1833, *Black Abolitionist Papers*, 38.

24. "Wilberforce Colony," *Liberator*, 13 April 1833, 57. See also "Caution to the Public," *Liberator*, 9 March 1833, 40.

25. "Israel Lewis," *Liberator* 16 July 1836, 113.

26. Steward, *Twenty-Two Years a Slave*, 152; Rev. Nathaniel Paul," *Liberator*, 19 December 1835, 204.

27. Steward, *Twenty-Two Years a Slave*, 115.

28. Garrison's letter of 17 December 1835 to Lewis Tappan describing how he bor-

rowed money from Paul is cited in Benjamin Quarles, *Black Abolitionists* (New York: Oxford University Press, 1969), 21, and is available in the Lewis Tappan Papers at the Library of Congress, Washington, D.C. In a letter of June 1856 from William Lloyd Garrison to Austin Steward, Garrison asserts: "I borrowed no money, nor had I any occasion to ask of loan of my friend, Paul" (*Twenty-Two Years a Slave*, 205).

29. Steward, *Twenty-Two Years a Slave*, 159.

30. Steward, *Twenty-Two Years a Slave*, 160–61.

31. Steward, *Twenty-Two Years a Slave*, 161. The story of Paul's putative decline into poverty, illness, and obscurity is also rehearsed by Winks, *The Blacks in Canada*, 161. For brief remarks on Paul as a vital abolitionist in the late 1830s, see Quarles, *Black Abolitionists*, 47, 87.

32. See *The Friend of Man*, 14 March 1838, 3; and *The Colored American*, 27 June 1839, 2.

33. Winks, *The Blacks in Canada*, 160. In *Black Utopia*, Pease and Pease similarly conclude that "Paul was a rascal, but not a criminal" (60).

34. While in England, Remond, Douglass, and Brown, like Paul, were attracted to the promise of a color-blind, transnational humanism. Prior to the Civil War, Delany attempted to develop separatist black communities in Central and South America and in Africa, and lived for several years in Canada; Brown became involved in the Haitian Emigration Movement, and just before the Civil War Douglass himself seriously considered the possibility of Haitian emigration. With the advent of the Civil War, Delany, Douglass, and Brown reembraced their July Fifth visions of a redeemed United States, and all three were passionate U.S. nationalists during the Reconstruction period.

BIBLIOGRAPHY

Anderson, Amanda. "Cosmopolitanism, Universalism, and the Divided Legacies of Modernity." *Cosmopolitics: Thinking and Feeling Beyond the Nation*. Eds. Pheng Cheah and Bruce Robbins. Minneapolis: University of Minnesota Press, 1998. 265–289.

Anon. "Abolition of Slavery." *Freedom's Journal*. 20 April 1827: 2.

———. "Caution to the Public." *Liberator*. 9 March 1833: 40.

———. "Colony in Upper Canada." *Liberator*. 17 September 1831: 150.

———. "Israel Lewis." *Liberator*. 16 July 1836: 113.

———. "Rev. Nathaniel Paul." *Liberator*. 14 January 1832: 5–6.

———. "Rev. Nathaniel Paul." *Liberator*. 25 August 1832: 135.

———. "Rev. Nathaniel Paul." *Liberator*. 19 December 1835: 204.

———. "The Rev. Nathaniel Paul in Scotland." *Liberator*. 7 February 1835: 22.

———. "Speech by Nathaniel Paul, Delivered at Exeter Hall, London, England, 13 July 1833." *The Black Abolitionist Papers*. Ed. C. Peter Ripley et al. 44–52.

———. *Speeches Delivered at the Anti-Colonization Meeting in Exeter Hall, London*. Boston: 1833.

———. "Wilberforce Colony." *Liberator*. 13 April 1833: 57.

Balibar, Etienne. "Ambiguous Universality." *differences* 7 (1995): 48–74.

Blackett, R. J. M. *Building an Antislavery Wall: Black Americans in the Atlantic Abolitionist Movement, 1830–1860*. Baton Rouge: Louisiana State University Press, 1983.

Cooper, Frederick. "Elevating the Race: The Social Thought of Black Leaders, 1827–1850." *American Quarterly* 24 (1972): 604–25.

David, David Brion. *The Problem of Slavery in the Age of Revolution 1770-1823*. Ithaca: Cornell University Press, 1975.

Delany, Martin Robison. *The Condition, Elevation, Emigration, and Destiny of the Colored People of the United States*. 1852. New York: Arno Press, 1969.

Gates, Henry Louis, Jr. *Figures in Black: Words, Signs, and the "Racial" Self*. New York: Oxford University Press, 1987.

Gilroy, Paul. *The Black Atlantic: Modernity and Double Consciousness*. Cambridge: Harvard University Press, 1993.

Gossett, Thomas F. *Race: The History of An Idea in America*. 1963. New York: Oxford University Press, 1997.

Levine, Robert S. *Martin Delany, Frederick Douglass, and the Politics of Representative Identity*. Chapel Hill: University of North Carolina Press, 1997.

Mayer, Henry. *William Lloyd Garrison and the Abolition of Slavery*. New York: St. Martin's Press, 1998.

Miller, Floyd J. *The Search for a Black Nationality: Black Emigration and Colonization, 1787–1863*. Urbana: University of Illinois Press, 1975.

Moses, Wilson Jeremiah, ed. *Classical Black Nationalism: From the American Revolution to Marcus Garvey*. New York: New York University Press, 1998.

Paul, Nathaniel. *An Address, Delivered at Troy, on the Celebration of the Abolition of Slavery, in the State of New York, July 6, 1829—Second Anniversary*. Albany: John B. Van Steenbergh, 1829.

———. *An Address, Delivered on the Celebration of the Abolition of Slavery, in the State of New-York, July 5, 1827*. Albany: John B. Van Steenbergh, 1827.

———. Letter to William Lloyd Garrison, 10 April 1833. *The Black Abolitionist Papers*. Ed. C. Peter Ripley et al. 37–43.

———. *Reply to Mr. Joseph Phillips' Enquiry, Respecting "The Light in which the Operations of the American Colonization Society Are Viewed by the Free People of Colour in the United States."* London: 1832.

———. "Compensation for Slaves." *Liberator*. 31 August 1833: 137–138.

Pease, William H., and Jane H. Pease. *Black Utopia: Negro Communal Experiments in America*. Madison: The State Historical Society of Wisconsin, 1963.

Quarles, Benjamin. *Black Abolitionists*. New York: Oxford University Press, 1969.

Ripley, C. Peter, et al., eds. *The Black Abolitionist Papers. Volume I. The British Isles, 1830–1865*. Chapel Hill: University of North Carolina Press, 1985.

Steward, Austin. *Twenty-Two Years a Slave, and Forty Years a Freeman*. 1857. Ed. Jane H. Pease and William H. Pease. Reading, Massachusetts: Addison-Wesley Publishing Company, 1969.

Stuckey, Sterling, ed. *The Ideological Origins of Black Nationalism*. Boston: Beacon Press, 1972.

Wade, Richard C. "The Negro in Cincinnati, 1800–1830." *Journal of Negro History* 39 (1954): 43–57.

Waldstreicher, David. *In the Midst of Perpetual Fetes: The Making of American Nationalism, 1776–1820*. Chapel Hill: University of North Carolina Press, 1997.

White, Shane. *Somewhat More Independent: The End of Slavery in New York City*. Athens: University of Georgia Press, 1991.

Winks, Robert W. *The Blacks in Canada: A History*. 1971. Montreal: McGill-Queen's University Press, 1997.

INDEX

Declaration of Independence and,
227, 228
Ellicott, George, and, 239*n*21
impact on abolition by, 234
Jefferson, Thomas, and, 218- 224,
226, 231, 232, 239*n*17
liberties of social caste, pushed by,
219
moral reading of the Revolution by,
229, 230
scientific interest expressed by, 218
Barlow, Joel, 235
Bassard, Katherine Clay, 195
Battle of Gibraltar, 59
Beatson, John, 35*n*5
Beattie, James, 20, 28, 37*n*35
Beecher, Lyman, 245
Behn, Apra, 54
Benezet, Anthony, 25, 28, 37*n*34, 179
Belinda
racial stereotypes and, 4, 5
Berlin, Ira, 196*n*7
Bhabha, Homi, 70*n*34
Bible, 29, 30, 31, 47, 246
allusion to, 177
ambiguity of, 5
authority of, 5
culturally emblematic function of, 47
Equiano, Olaudah, and, 139
language of, 190, 191
"linguistic inventiveness" and, 196*n*4
misreadings of, 32
Biblical Beginnings (O'Neale), 196*n*7
Bickerstaff, Isaac, 215*n*53
Birkhead, Edith, 213*n*9
The Black Abolitionist Papers, 257*n*2
Black Abolitionists (Quarles), 259*n*28
*The Black Atlantic: Modernity and Double
Consciousness* (Gilroy), 257*n*4
The Blacks in Canada: A History (Winks),
257*n*11
black elevation, 245
Paul, Nathaniel, on, 246, 247
black nationalism, 242-257
the Bible and, 246
co-optation of, 253, 254
egalitarianism and, 248
market culture effecting, 244, 245
Paul, Nathaniel, on, 243
politics of, 249, 256
postnationalism and, 244
separatism and, 243
themes of, 251

*Black and White: The Negro and English
Society* (Walvin), 212
black religion, 195*n*3
Black Religion and Black Radicalism
(Wilmore), 195*n*3
Black Song: The Forge and the Flame
(Lovell), 196*n*5
*Black Utopia: Negro Communal Experi-
ments in America* (Pease), 257*n*11
Blackburn, Robin, 38*n*41
Blacket, R.J.M., 258*n*17, 258*n*19
Blumenbach, Johann Friedrich, 36*n*10
Boswell, James, 213*n*26
Boulukus, George E., 214*n*36
Bound and Determined (Castilian), 41
Breen, Jennifer, 36*n*15
Brent, Linda, 11
British Anti-Slavery Society, 74
Brown, Christopher L., 35*n*1
Brown, William Wells, 243, 248
Building an Antislavery Wall (Blackest),
258*n*17
Burnaby, Andrew, 22, 36*n*17
Burnham, Michelle, 48
Burr, Sandra, 3
Butterfield, Stephen, 72

Canada Land Company, 247
capitalism
freedom and, 128
slavery in, 127
Capitalism and Antislavery (Drescher), 21
captivity, 39
acculturation in, 48
body effected by, 43
cultural differences in, 47
Indian, 39-40
narratives of, 39, 40
value of slaves in, 39, 40
whites in, 43
captivity narratives
authenticity of, 41, 42
black men writing, 42
Christian faith in, 44, 45, 46, 47, 50
conventions of, 41, 45, 48, 121
displacement in, 49, 50
Indian representation in, 44
literary development of, 42
racial difference in, 48, 49
skin color represented in, 44
Carboy, Hazel, 69*n*8
Caretta, Vincent, 17, 70*n*30, 207
Carretta, Vincent, 3, 17, 70*n*30, 181, 200, 207